Artificial Intelligence and Biodiversity

Scrivener Publishing
100 Cummings Center, Suite 541J
Beverly, MA 01915-6106

Publishers at Scrivener
Martin Scrivener (martin@scrivenerpublishing.com)
Phillip Carmical (pcarmical@scrivenerpublishing.com)

Artificial Intelligence and Biodiversity

Edited by

Umesh Kumar Lilhore

Sarita Simaiya

Surjeet Dalal

and

Martin Margala

Scrivener Publishing

WILEY

This edition first published 2026 by John Wiley & Sons, Inc., 111 River Street, Hoboken, NJ 07030, USA and Scrivener Publishing LLC, 100 Cummings Center, Suite 541J, Beverly, MA 01915, USA

For more information about Scrivener publications please visit www.scrivenerpublishing.com.

Wiley Global Headquarters
111 River Street, Hoboken, NJ 07030, USA

For details of our global editorial offices, customer services, and more information about Wiley products visit us at www.wiley.com.

The manufacturer's authorized representative according to the EU General Product Safety Regulation is Wiley-VCH GmbH, Boschstr. 12, 69469 Weinheim, Germany, e-mail: Product_Safety@wiley.com.

Library of Congress Cataloging-in-Publication Data

ISBN 9781394384952

Front cover images supplied by Pixabay.com
Cover design by Russell Richardson

Set in size of 11pt and Minion Pro by Manila Typesetting Company, Makati, Philippines

Printed in the USA

10 9 8 7 6 5 4 3 2 1

Contents

Preface

1. **Chapter 1: Harnessing Artificial Intelligence to Address Global Environmental Challenges: A Cross-Domain Review**
- **Description**: This chapter explores the growing need for AI in solving global environmental issues. The authors provide a cross-domain review of AI technologies that can help combat pollution, deforestation, climate change, and other ecological crises. By examining various AI methodologies, this chapter illustrates how AI can be applied to environmental monitoring, management, and conservation, offering a glimpse of AI's vast potential in these critical areas.
2. **Chapter 2: Innovative AI Paradigms for Achieving Environmental Sustainability: From Concept to Practice**
- **Description**: This chapter delves into innovative AI paradigms, from conceptual frameworks to practical applications aimed at enhancing environmental sustainability. It covers the latest advancements in AI technologies and their direct impact on environmental preservation, including AI's role in reducing carbon footprints, optimizing resource use, and fostering smarter sustainability strategies across various industries.
3. **Chapter 3: Deep Learning Approaches for Real-Time Climate Monitoring and Anomaly Detection in Meteorological Systems**
- **Description**: The chapter discusses the application of deep learning techniques in real-time climate monitoring. By focusing on anomaly detection within meteorological systems, it demonstrates how AI models can process vast datasets, identifying climate anomalies that aid in early warning systems and climate change mitigation efforts, thus advancing predictive capabilities in environmental management.

4. **Chapter 4: Federated Learning for Privacy-Preserving Environmental Monitoring Across Distributed Sensor Networks**
- **Description**: This chapter addresses the challenges and solutions of privacy preservation in environmental monitoring. Using federated learning, the authors present a novel approach to data sharing that minimizes privacy risks while maintaining high levels of model accuracy, essential for monitoring air quality, deforestation, and other environmental factors across multiple distributed sensor networks.
5. **Chapter 5: Quantum AI in Environmental Modeling:** Opportunities for Accelerating Ecosystem Simulations
- **Description**: This chapter introduces the potential of quantum AI in revolutionizing environmental modeling. By combining quantum computing with AI, it explores new opportunities for simulating complex ecological systems and accelerating climate predictions, thereby enhancing the ability to model ecosystems with unprecedented speed and accuracy.
6. **Chapter 6: Developing Digital Twin Ecosystems for Dynamic** Environmental Analysis and Predictive Sustainability Planning
- **Description**: Focusing on digital twin technology, this chapter highlights its application in environmental analysis and predictive sustainability planning. It discusses how real-time data and simulations of ecosystems allow for better decision-making regarding resource management, disaster response, and long-term sustainability strategies.
7. **Chapter 7: AI-Driven Optimization of Renewable Energy Systems: Forecasting, Load Balancing, and Grid Efficiency**
- **Description**: This chapter explores the role of AI in optimizing renewable energy systems, addressing challenges such as variability and intermittency of energy sources. By integrating forecasting models, load balancing strategies, and grid efficiency techniques, the chapter presents AI's potential to enhance the performance of renewable energy systems and ensure a more stable and sustainable energy grid.
8. **Chapter 8: Deep Learning for Climate Monitoring and Anomaly Detection in Meteorological Systems**
- **Description**: Similar to Chapter 3, this chapter expands on the use of deep learning in climate monitoring and anomaly detection. It emphasizes the application of advanced

AI models to improve the precision and speed of anomaly detection in climate systems, offering enhanced prediction models to support proactive climate disaster management.

9. **Chapter 9: AI for Biodiversity Conservation: Analyzing Species and Habitat Protection Using Machine Learning**
   - **Description**: This chapter investigates how AI can support biodiversity conservation through the automated analysis of species and habitat protection. By employing machine learning models, AI facilitates species identification, habitat monitoring, and even poaching prevention, helping conservationists tackle the challenges of protecting endangered species in remote environments.
10. **Chapter 10: Preserving Biodiversity Through AI**
    - **Description**: This chapter focuses on AI technologies that aid in biodiversity preservation. It examines the use of AI in monitoring biodiversity hotspots, automating species identification, and preventing illegal activities like poaching. The chapter also addresses the challenges of data scarcity and ethical concerns, proposing AI as a critical tool in safeguarding biodiversity.
11. **Chapter 11: Explainable AI in Environmental Decision-Making: Enhancing Transparency and Trust**
    - **Description**: This chapter delves into the role of explainable AI (XAI) in environmental decision-making. It discusses how XAI techniques can improve the transparency of AI models, making them more understandable for policymakers, environmental scientists, and the general public, thus fostering greater trust and adoption of AI in critical environmental decisions.
12. **Chapter 12: Leveraging AI for Waste Management and Urban Sustainability**
    - **Description**: Waste management is a significant challenge in urban areas, and AI is positioned to revolutionize this sector. This chapter explores AI-based waste management systems that employ machine learning algorithms for efficient waste collection, recycling, and landfill management, contributing to more sustainable urban environments.
13. **Chapter 13: AI and Climate Change Adaptation: A Framework for Resilience Planning**
    - **Description**: This chapter provides a comprehensive framework for using AI in climate change adaptation strategies.

By analyzing climate data and predicting future scenarios, AI can inform resilience planning and help governments and organizations prepare for and mitigate the impacts of climate change.

14. **Chapter 14: AI for Environmental Risk Assessment and Disaster Response**
  - **Description**: This chapter focuses on AI's role in environmental risk assessment and disaster response. By leveraging real-time data and predictive analytics, AI enhances the ability to assess risks related to natural disasters and environmental hazards, facilitating quicker, more effective responses.
15. **Chapter 15: Sustainable Agricultural Practices Powered by AI: Enhancing Crop Management and Resource Efficiency**
  - **Description**: AI is transforming agriculture by optimizing crop management and resource use. This chapter examines the integration of AI in precision agriculture, focusing on crop disease detection, soil condition monitoring, and irrigation optimization, all of which contribute to more sustainable farming practices.
16. **Chapter 16: AI for Renewable Energy Forecasting and Smart Grid Management**
  - **Description**: This chapter discusses the application of AI in forecasting renewable energy production and managing smart grids. By enhancing predictive models and optimizing grid operations, AI plays a crucial role in managing energy distribution and reducing waste, thereby supporting the global transition to renewable energy.
17. **Chapter 17: Integrated Optimization Strategies for High-Efficiency Solar PV Plants: From AI to Bifacial Technologies**
  - **Description**: The final chapter explores AI-driven optimization strategies for solar photovoltaic (PV) plants, including the integration of bifacial technologies. By combining AI with advancements in solar technology, this chapter presents solutions for maximizing energy output, improving efficiency, and reducing costs in solar energy systems.

1

Harnessing Artificial Intelligence to Address Global Environmental Challenges: A Cross-Domain Review

Suresh K.S.[1], Dafik[2], Nagendar Yamsani[3], Rayappan Lotus[4], S. Mathumohan[5] and Anurag Singh[6]*

[1]*School of Computing, SASTRA Deemed University, Thanjavur, Tamil Nadu, India*
[2]*Department of Mathematics, University of Jember, Jember, East Java, Indonesia*
[3]*School of Computer Science and Artificial Intelligence, SR University, Warangal, Telangana, India*
[4]*Department of Computer Science and Engineering, Vel Tech Rangarajan Dr. Sagunthala R&D Institute of Science and Technology, Avadi, Chennai, Tamil Nadu, India*
[5]*Pandian Saraswathi Yadav Engineering College, Arasanoor, Sivagangai, Tamil Nadu, India*
[6]*School of Computer Science and Engineering, Galgotias University, Greater Noida, Uttar Pradesh, India*

Abstract

The world of issues that are being faced by ecology today: the pollution of land, air, or water, the destruction of the forest, and climate-change are all irreversibly connected and, therefore, can only be taken off with new scalable options and implementing the multidisciplinary approach. AI is a paradigm change in technologies where a person can find and control huge amounts of data, complex patterns and predictive models with tragicomic prophecies to change the practice of control and monitoring. The chapter presents and discusses new AI breakthroughs in the fundamental sectors of environment and climate, sustainable agriculture, biodiversity and conservation, resource management, and waste, and clean energy technologies. It will examine how management automation decision systems of the two discussed areas can benefit through the application of machine learning, automation, deep learning, computer vision, Natural Language Processing, real-time systems,

**Corresponding author*: anurag.singh@galgotiasuniversity.edu.in

Umesh Kumar Lilhore, Sarita Simaiya, Surjeet Dalal and Martin Margala (eds.) Artificial Intelligence and Biodiversity, (1–20) © 2026 Scrivener Publishing LLC

and GUI, and environment interface. An example of the proxies that could be analyzed consists of AI climate models, monitoring of endangered species, active control of the irrigation system, and self-regulating systems where energy can be controlled according to climate changes. Such AI proxies articulate responses to information, with lack of which, a question of ethical concern, model transparency and control of their manufacture rises amongst other multidisciplinary area points of cross intersection. The results of the different fields and the claims of the different districts were catalogued in this review to determine the need to acquire lenient policy directives, transparent data, as well as coalition treaties, and lower restrictions to compassionate partnership so as to uncover the possible disaster management measures.

Keywords: Artificial intelligence, environmental sustainability, climate change, biodiversity conservation, cross-domain review

1.1 Introduction

Such problems are reduction in ecological ecosystems, degradation of human condition and economic collapse that are challenged by increasing ecological crises around the world. Ecosystem and resource management challenges that have been occasioned by surprisingly escalating population, industries advancement scenarios and rising consumptions have now been accompanied by global warming, extinction of trees, pollution and vanishing of biodiversity. All these issues are related, and thus, the solution to them is to be interdisciplinary, creative, and must happen in time. The history of the artificial intelligence (AI) development is optimistic in its newness because it is likely that it will end up to become one of the few contemporary breakthroughs that would help solve such problems.

Application AI within the challenge of studying unstructured data would require deep-level interaction tools/2 Deep learning and natural language processing recognize patterns into uncontrollable domains that have not been controlled before, to make automated arbitration, and find predictive algorithms. These are extremely necessary and exclusive amenities that will cause the technologies indispensable in solving environmental problems. The AI based policies will result in the build of the management and prevention policy frameworks, which will incorporate real time close-to-zero lag predictive and control decision systems, which will be decomposed on the basis of complex data and model insights. This review will seek to reveal the role of AI technologies, i.e., machine learning (ML), deep learning (DL), computer vision, and natural language processing (NLP) in the environment as well as other questions that concern the environment [1].

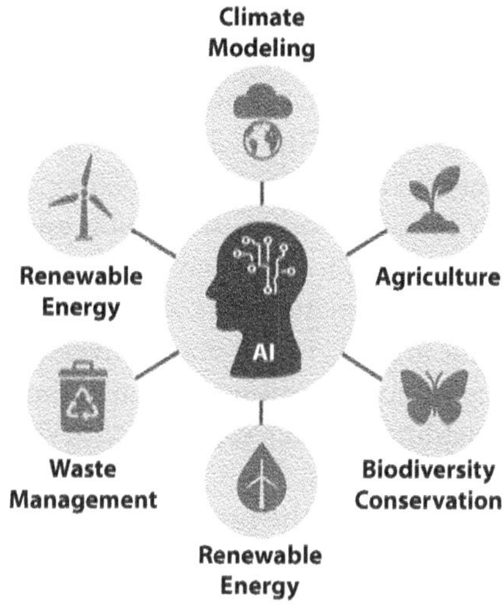

Figure 1.1 Role of artificial intelligence in addressing global environmental challenges.

Figure 1.1 shows the applications of AI in sustainable environmental management. Climate models are more accurate and more extensive in their application of AI technology. By combining massive amounts of data, taken either by satellites, through ground sensors, and simulations, AI can predict the impact of climate extremes, whether it is drought, heatwave, and hurricane (Meth and Scheiman 1). CNNS is one of the architectures of deep learning network that has been able to perform exceptionally well in analysing climate data, as it is a type of a deep learning network that incessantly and continuously proves to have an impressive analyzing hold on data to find the elusive-non-linear relationships that the conventional model overlooks [2]. The advocates of AI also offload some elements of the compressive workload among the physics-based simulations, which goes toward helping to avoid the harsh monotony bottleneck associated with computing time necessary to forecast future events, as well as scenario based prognostication [3].

The AI helps alleviate the effects of conventional farming on the environment and contributes to the reinforced food security due to the maximization of the resources in sustainable agricultural production. AI, coupled with all forms of precision agriculture technology, facilitates the most highly-data-intensive types of farming practices as it can examine soil samples, drone-centrically survey crops, and can even anticipate pest invasion [4]. Enhanced collections of data also allow farmers to make wise decisions on the choice of crops, water usage and harvests with the facilitation of the analysis of the weather, soil, and commercial trends using AIs [5, 6].

Much extends as to the consequences of Artificial Intelligence to Conservation. The Robotization of the Classification of the Acoustic Signals and Image Analysis by Algorithms allows the Experts in Remote Sensing to automate the tedious roles of the Ecosystem Biodiversity Monitoring. The AI powered cameras can prepare an inventory of wild animals, and this must be done in conservation of the habitat and wildlife protection and anti-poaching missions [7]. NLP may be implemented to allow scientists to sift volumes of information data at large to unearth suitable passages of text in scientific articles, which may, conversely, help the former in interpreting the changing conservation position of the globe [8]. These can be used to aid in providing a better electronic surveillance upon remote and vulnerable conservation sites.

It is particularly a problem to the present-day Metropolis that the evolution of Artificial Intelligence is gaining traction. Another change is in sorting and recycling garbage as it can now be easily identified and sorted by robots using image processing and combining it with various sensors in real-time [9]. Predictive models can be used to do the waste collection planning and path optimization to improve the efficiency of operations and reduce the emission of greenhouse gases related to waste transportation [10]. AI is also used to enhance evaluation of the environmental impacts of products' lifecycle and, therefore, promote the activities of circular economies [11].

The issue of managing the grid is where AI plays a paramount role in optimising energy in responsive structures on renewable energy. It is challenging to maintain grid stability since renewable sources (solar and wind vendors) are fluctuating. The AI models can be used to predict the energy generation as well as the demand and the storage control [12]. Hypothetically, dynamic power flux, energy loss reduction, and the efficient distribution of decentralised energy sources are listed in energy management with the help of AI algorithms in smart grids. Reinforcement learning methods have been used to come up with adaptive control methods of microgrids and battery systems [13].

This is despite the fact that although AI has potential, it is not widely implemented because of the availability of data and other factors. The lack of proprietary and political restrictions makes most environmental datasets sparse, insufficiently noisy, closed, or unavailable [14]. The AI models that are trained on the data found in the developed world fail to transfer effectively in the developing environment and give biased results. To get out of such gaps, strong initiatives that foster open data, standardised collection and jointly shared water in data sharing format among stakeholders are required.

The sociotechnical problems linked to the use of AI are likewise essential to the ethico-governance problems. The capability of the black-box systems to violate the trust of people and complicate the governance increases [15]. Demand continues to grow over explainable AI (XAI) protocols that permit the freedom of details and formable strap-words more particularly in systems where there exist significant dangers, such as answering a catastrophe or forecasting unfavorable health results. There also exists the moral obligation not to encounter internally or externally turbo-twine socio-economic disparities, natural injustices, and inequalities in such technologies particularly in mitigation schemes to climate changes.

The policymakers, social actors, computer scientists, and environmental scientists ought to work together to ensure that the social AI solutions that have been culturally-environmentalized were not made to ignore the diversified culture and the environment. Furthermore, the outreach program based on AI technologies and environmental education and training will play an important role in order to make the students responsible professionals in the field of using these technologies.

The given synthesis review describes the application of AI to environmental sustainability and evaluates the use of AI in different spheres and presents the success and technological and institutional drawbacks of the corresponding AI uses. It also provides the suggestions regarding the policy and research integration context. The literature of climate science, conservation, agriculture, energy systems and AI This chapter reviewed illustrates the revolutionary effect of AI in the various and interconcrete areas of the systems. AI had the ability to drive interdisciplinary positivity. The research mentions the insufficiency of co-operation, shared and proprietary data policies, and poor innovations driven by ethics as suppression aspects to worldwide sustainability processes. With regards to the issues currently of the utmost importance in the environmental domain and context the study provides support on the responsible and moral use of AI in climate change and environmental sustainability when pursued in a concerted effort towards this purpose.

1.2 Related Works

In recent times, AI (Artificial Intelligence) has emerged as an important tool in the management of environmental issues because it provides an opportunity to process data, isolate patterns and machine operations in various environments. One of the spheres of AI implementation where the latter has changed significantly is climate change modeling, where weather forecasting and climate prognostication are advancing increasingly, as machine learning implementation algorithms are deployed. Despite their strengths, conventional numerical models have disadvantages of having high computational costs and are frequently narrow in scope [16]. Similarly, [17] observed the potency of the deep learning algorithms to forecast climate dangers like droughts and floods which are more unpredictable owing to climatic change. Researcher [18] continued this and implemented AI to simplify world climatic models to bring regional data that is more accurate to the policy makers and urban planners.

Also, the innovation technologies and AI Bit AI have offered a revolution to agriculture converting the seemingly non-systematic approach to farming to corresponding information based industry. Moreover, AI has revolutionized the monitoring, analysis, and optimisation of various practices in agriculture and turned it into a proactive precision agriculture field. This is cost effective in that we get to reduce the effect caused on the environment and at the same time get maximum output. The study under [19] explained the utilization of AI systems combined with sensors and the computer vision system to track and involve the maturity stage of crops, pests, and real-time control of irrigation systems. Also, machine learning can inspire foreseeable analytics about crop planting and harvesting through the examination of vegetation of many spectra of maps of space and even weather forecasts. In [20] was the first to explain how these models may predict the content of the food in nutrient and moisture levels aimed at maximizing the proportion of fertilizers to pesticides applied in order to minimize the environmentally damaging unintended overuse. When one reads the article [21] which is related to the research called the Artificial Intelligence formed decision support system as a way to assist farmers in their work perceiving it as a way to act in response to the changes without hedging effects, he or she relates to the article by the author as the way out of the crisis.

The AI has also taken its position in the conservation of biodiversity, showing the possibility of conserving wildlife populations. Helping conservationist researchers balance population and biodiversity is not something that could come easy due to the fact they would not be able to protect numerous inaccessible sites and areas in both long run and short term. AI simplifies the work since the information gathered by drones, camera traps and acoustic monitoring devices can be processed easily. Researchers [22] AIAIs have the capability to identify and categorize species presented in Camera Trap images with fair accuracy that saves a significant amount of time on the identification process. Ahmed and Brown [23] employed AI on those data of bioacoustics and therefore, endangered species would be identified using sound, possibly even deemed inside the mass of dense trees. It is understandable, based on the current pace of ecological research, which is being conducted with the help of such technological advances as AI, that these innovations serve as effective methods contributing to combating poaching, anti-poaching activities, and even towards managing a certain ecosystem. Schoormann *et al.* [24] emphasize the increasing role of AI in sustainability, while observing the relatively limited literature that examines intersections between AI, IS and sustainability in a holistic view. They review 95 studies that examine sustainability goals, data, technologies, and evaluations, providing a thorough foundation for inspiring future research, policy, and practice in the area of sustainable AI.

With the continuous increment in the quantity of waste produced worldwide, controlling waste in the urban areas is increasingly becoming a difficult endeavor. As AI technology is being developed, intelligent waste management systems have been designed, which makes use of sensors and predictive analytics. In study [25] elaborated application of AI automated smart bins which actively monitors the level of fill and manages waste fuel during scheduling of pickup activities applied to optimize overflow. To generate machine learning models that can predict waste production using demographic, seasonal and economic data exist to show that with the help of these models policy and infrastructure development can be developed greatly by [26]. Moreover, AI is currently incorporated into a robotic system that is used to sort waste into recycled materials at the recycling plants, contributing to the intensification of automatization of sorting. By presenting the research on [27], the authors have demonstrated the potential of the image recognition algorithms to be highly effective in identifying various kinds of materials thus enhancing recycling and decreasing the amount of contamination waste.

The innovative management of the renewable energy sector using AI technologies has enhanced the level of forecasting, strategizing and the management of the smart grid. Given the uncertainty of wind and solar power, AI technologies must rank the resources in real time using forecasting to step-up supply and stabilise demand. Author [28] showed how machine learning models are useful in predicting energy production using weather and consumption records so that the grid operators can easily control supply and demand.

Even though impressive progress has been achieved in the field of AI application in environmental settings, the literature recognizes the constant challenges and cracks in AI implementation and application. The loopholes in data availability and quality are very alarming. Due to the political and economical factors the environmental datasets are often scattered, inaccessible or uneven. The models of AI that have performed very

could concentrate on the volume time-whistle mixture of distinctions of deep learning systems wide-range satellite information, whereas agriculture industry may depend on drone-based aerial apprehension and edge AI-oriented agricultural techniques and automation. Increased image and acoustic classification algorithms may also be a need in certain conservation projects and real-time object tracking intelligent logistics supplements improved waste management systems. Categorical use of renewable energy needs to be actively performed and controlled through application of reinforcement learning, the determination of proactive control. Both domains have the freedom to adapt simplified architectural models changing the compositions, streams of data, and algorithms used.

All potential areas of application, and that of respective use cases are represented therein. The necessary level of elasticity of scale and training of AI models big data is available in such services as AWS, Google Cloud, and Microsoft Azure. Lower-end computing platforms like the Raspberry Pi and NVIDIA Jetson allow heading of applications to remote field work stations with weak connectivity. Docker and Kubernetes Containerization and orchestration enhances the ease with which an architecture can be still advanced with regards to its deployment, scaling, and maintenance. Such functions are achieved through the attainment of a deployment, scaling, and orchestration system with Docker and Kubernetes. It is used to perform the following purposes: CI/CD pipeline integrations and model monitoring and versioning.

The design of AI systems to deal with cross-national environmental problems, especially at large scale, is enhanced by modularity and flexibility on which this modular process architecture is based. It allows Boundless domain interoperation unlimited multidisciplinary acceleration AI integration bearing no integration limitations and speedy pace innovations being unlimited by intense ethics in all walks of the technology life span AI integration. In cross-disciplinarity, such aspects can be reproduced that discuss broad-term environmental challenges. It is also becoming cross-disciplinatory.

1.4 Results

The research was aimed at assessing alternative methods of Artificial Intelligence (AI) which were involved in climate prediction, farm systems, biodiversity preservation, waste recycling, and energy sources production. The study analysis featured a substantial evaluation methodology of studies related to benchmarking evaluation and advanced assessment mechanisms involved in F1 score, AUC-ROC measurements, and the examination of the inference velocity. The analysis has some details provided after the presentation of the results in Table 1.1 and Table 1.2.

Based on the "AI Performance in Climate Modeling" section, in Table 1.1, it can be seen that the AI models applied to climate modeling had outstanding performance quality with the highest rate of 92% that is the best rate compared to the other results and the precision and recall at 91 and 93 respectively. This demonstrates excellent attribute characterization of LSTM-intensive deep learning models in climate dataset pattern identification and forecasting interdependencies over time at an even bigger scale. Even the renewable energy systems that used reinforcement learning resulted well with the 90 percent accuracy level and also with preciseness and recall that were advanced to 89 percent and 91 percent respectively and concluded that this is the much-performance level of the AI. The biodiversity conservation systems utilising CNNs and audio classifiers were able to support the observed performance in all measures against 89% accuracy, 88% precision and 90% recall supporting the efficacy of multimodal.

AI in ecological monitoring.

The agricultural systems that practiced the hybrid model of CNNs and decision trees acquired an accuracy of 87 percent and a precision of 86 percent, and this allows such systems to be utilized in such exercises as crop classification and disease detection. The waste management systems also registered the lowest scores of a total score of 85% accuracy and 83% precision yet they also indicated some degree of applicability to the practice.

Table 1.1 AI performance metrics – accuracy, precision, and recall.

Domain	AI technique	Accuracy (%)	Precision (%)	Recall (%)
Climate Modeling	LSTM	92	91	93
Agriculture	CNN + Decision Trees	87	86	88
Biodiversity Conservation	CNN + Audio Classifiers	89	88	90
Waste Management	Image Recognition + ML	85	83	84
Renewable Energy	Reinforcement Learning	90	89	91

Table 1.2 AI performance metrics – F1-score, auc-roc, and inference speed.

Domain	F1-score (%)	AUC-ROC (%)	Inference speed (ms/sample)
Climate Modeling	92.0	95	150
Agriculture	87.0	89	120
Biodiversity Conservation	89.0	91	130
Waste Management	83.5	86	100
Renewable Energy	90.0	93	160

Their low performance can be explained by the inability to fit into the real life deployment environment, non-standard visual environments and random allocation of wastes.

Table 1.2 also includes the metrics of the robustness of the model used in its F1-score, the AUC-ROC score used in its classification accuracy, and the inference speed used as metrics of executing these AI models considering practicality. Climate modeling once again reported a top ranking of 92.0 F1 score, AUC-ROC of 95% and superb discrimination with excellent precision-recall balance. The performance of renewable energy systems was also found to be very good with an F1 score of 90.0% with AUC-ROC of 93 which confirms their relevance in dynamic and data agile environments like smart grids.

Biodiversity systems monitor agricultural systems that have an F1 score of 89.0 and a UAROC of 91, and thus show to be practical to use in analysis of ecological data at smaller levels such as individual farms. The score of Agricultural Systems in F1 score=87.0%, AUC-ROC=89 showed good performance with an opportunity to improve it with the help of supplemental information sources. The lowest scoring in F1, 83.5, associated with waste management systems exposes their merits in precision and low rate of inferences at 100 ms/sample, obtaining an efficient computational cost of waste management in real time.

Studies have revealed that the hybrid LSTM + CNN hypotheses are exceptionally accurate and ready in terms of accuracy, however it is with significantly lower computation speed as it relies on the related computations. Basic though effective models in the waste management industry are applied in real time due to the fact that the models, though not accurate, offer the speed to meet operational scalability. The choice of AI models by an organization requires selection of models with the relative effectiveness of fulfilling accuracy performance and computational efficiency requirements in specific environments where they are deployed.

According to research evidence, the AI operates with domain-specific settings. Environmental AI systems require adapted AI methods, which demarcate data entry and interactive requirements and operational conditions along the industry lines. Estimation of correct climate and energy forecasts are more important than longer periods of inferences. Waste management along with a biodiversity system typically requires fast classification responses enabling immediate field operations. Close consideration of the adjustable AI systems prove that they are able to adapt in various ecological realms whenever coming up with deep-based infrastructure structure of the AI systems and by orchestrating weak and underrepresented framework structures and displaying adaptive domain-based architecture creation.

1.5 Discussions

The chapter helps to illustrate the use of AI capacity management that takes into account at the same time the resource of operational efficiency in optimal costs and domain adaptability and shows how the deep learning systems can be deployed globally through addition of the machine vision technology. All the features of amalgam AI strategy between AI vs Climate Change make use of the climate modeling, through LSTM networks within renewable energy systems, and which makes use of reinforcement learning in order to demonstrate multi-layered systems with multi-dimensional features in environmental science. The final success of any strategy depends on three main factors as much as possible, and they encompass the Gulf dependency as well as data quality and diversity and external drivers.

The most effective applications were that of climate modeling and renewable energy as a result of the appropriate interactions between well-organized time based data and reinforcement learning algorithms which draw on system feedback mechanisms. The metrics investigated and such results of the accuracy, the precision, the recall and the AUC- ROC proved the better results of these models in accordance with Table 1.1 and Table 1.2 along with their results in Figures 1.2 and 1.3. The waste management systems produced the quickest response time but had the most low accuracy level along with F1-scores during the evaluations. The data reveals that there is an autonomous determination as to the amount of complexity that a model needs as compared to how fast it responds especially when operating in physical or city surroundings that rely on expeditious choices.

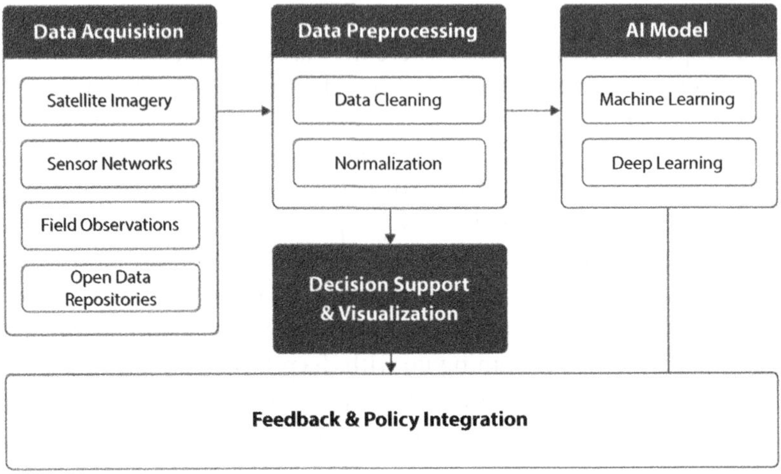

Figure 1.2 Architectural process workflow for AI-driven environmental intelligence systems.

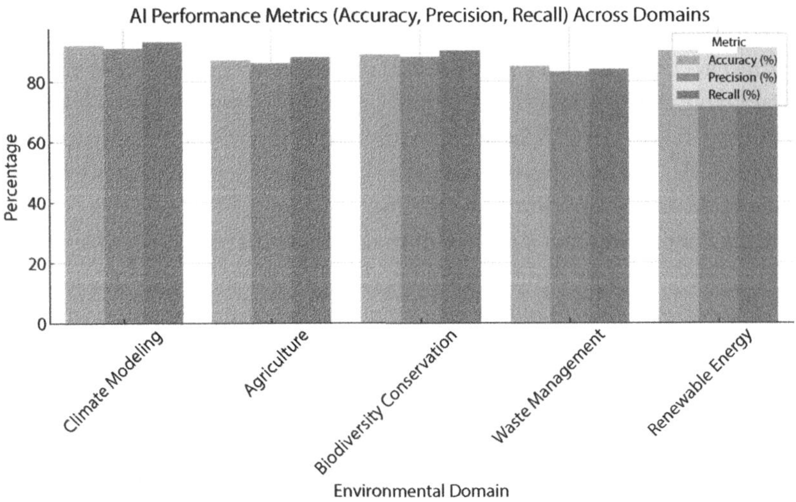

Figure 1.3 Performance comparison of AI techniques across environmental domains (Accuracy, Precision, Recall).

The models that worked best with the climate change and the renewable energy forecasting were those whose best results were on forecasting, and the obtained results are clearly defined time-series datasets and used an active positive feedback loop that interacted with LSTM and reinforcement learning models. Table 1.1 and Table 1.2 are records that show that the models overshadowed all archiving AUC-ROC measurement baselines on recall, accuracy, F1 or throughput rate, and even on scoring evaluation algorithm outcome evaluation gathering scoring outcomes evaluations in an assessment of evaluation outcome evaluations.

As shown in Figure 1.4, the reports on waste management systems have the highest inferencing speed with the lowest accuracy and F1 scores. The 290 system on inferencing competitively speeds on waste handled but more restrictive in 290 evaluative metrics with the other gathered models restrictive specification compelling on more moderate evaluative models.

The use of multimodal AI systems that are composed of visual and acoustic classifiers brought considerable advantages of data fusion to complex natural settings to biodiversity conservation applications. These systems, in response to the large demand of the system operators, supply automated scalable solutions to the remote surroundings of the biodiversity hot spots to identify them, to monitor their movement and to amicably act upon an illegal act of poaching.

Although it is a bit worse than climate and energy sectors in terms of being more precise and of recalling information, the agricultural applications have still indicated the aptitude of fake intelligence in situations concerning the connection to adoptable farming routines. Classifier models The decision tree and CNNs in combination offered great advantages to the GeoBIA workflow on soil condition monitoring and crop disease detection. But even better, there is the benefit to agriculture that will be coupled together with edge AI and low-latency inference models, which will allow on-the-fly field guidance.

In addition to the bare model outputs, the model output has also been contended to have far reaching consequences. Indicatively, in edge and IoT to field operation, time inference has been argued to be of crucial

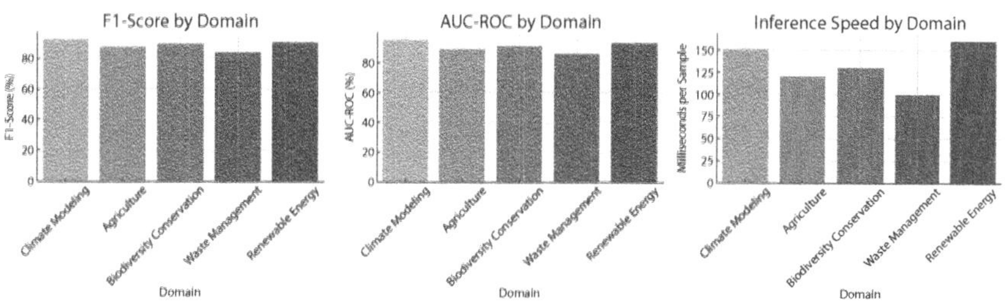

Figure 1.4 Evaluation of AI models by F1-score, AUC-ROC, and inference speed across domains.

significance. The second one is carried out in garbage management systems and easier models have been depicted to be running during the period of maintaining the existence of real-time clock systems that are responsive, which was very crucial in real world complexity. In the trend opposite to the two mentioned above, with an analytically more interesting model, the LSTM and GANs models take longer to run and have been experimented in resource-constrained environments.

They add that ethical and socially responsible application of artificial intelligence (AI) should be more specific. The AI carbon footprint, especially in the deep learning applications, add other carbon footprint complaints, which, in turn, predetermines the continued harm to the same sustainability targets in which such technologies are supposed to be used.

The same findings can be supported by the rest of AI system design which is also domain specific. Although a generalized model of architecture described is the one, it underlines the fact that every sphere of the environment should be individualized. Multi-modes sensing is employed to enhance the biodiversity projects with the help of climate systems, which require long-term forecast systems, renewable energy systems and that require real time responsiveness and biodiversity projects. This variability makes AI systems to be designed to a specific goal of using it in other applications.

Lastly, there is still the need for interdisciplinary working together. To implement AI in the sphere of environmental science, machine learning engineers, region specialists, policymakers, and the local community should be involved. This can be attributed to the fact that only through the interactions, it can be possible to come up with technology that is socially and environmentally responsible, which will result in people believing in AI systems.

Finally, the application of AI technologies to the ecologically sustainable future has its challenges as well that include the imbalance of the system, the issue of ethics, transparency, and sustainability. The positive cross-domain architecture and artificial intelligence with the analysis of the system on the grounds of performance equilibrium, gradual forward movement with balanced interaction, might enhance the involvement of AI in the AI to the concerns of the society in need of acute concern.

1.6 Conclusion

This discussion of the Anthology shows that there exist many ways in which Artificial Intelligence (AI) may be utilized to provide innovative solutions to the data-intensive problems with the climate and greatness of which is required to be created: the infrastructure, agriculture, building materials, biodiversity, waste, and renewable energy. Fraudulent-learned viewpoints and reinforcement learning are, in most cases, employed to enhance the accuracy of the predictions, simplify the processes and render the systems and processes responsive to the processes and mechanisms. Nonetheless, the discussed factors do not necessarily apply to all the areas and the very situation introduces an optimal model and implementation strategy. Moreover, the ethical concerns of data biasing, explanation and actual sustainability of computing are equally reinforced in this chapter which is not justified and needs to be changed towards best integration of policy and information and education among disciplines. The structured frameworks should be adapted and scaled and policy demands and professional experience should be within a multi-domain intersection supporting multi- directional interaction. Future research projects should focus on equal AI accessibility, explainable models, and developing AI models with low carbon. One of the most critical parameters in enhancing the global sustainability and resilience in relation to increasing environmental challenges and threats is sustainable development of AI.

AI disclosure statement: The author confirms that no artificial intelligence (AI)-generated content or AI-assisted writing tools were used in the preparation of this chapter (including summaries and the abstract). All text, analysis, and conclusions are the result of the author's original work.

References

1. Thanyawatpornkul, R., Artificial Intelligence-Driven Solution for Global Challenges: A Systematic Review from Sustainable Development Goals Perspectives. *Int. J. Bus. Manage. Econ. Res.*, 15, 1, 1–17, 2024.
2. Cruz, M.E. and Miguel, D., Cross-Domain Transfer Learning: Enhancing Deep Neural Networks for Low-Resource Environments. *ITEJ (Inf. Technol. Eng. J.)*, 9, 2, 72–79, 2024.
3. Singh, B. and Kaunert, C., Dynamic Landscape of Artificial General Intelligence (AGI) for Advancing Renewable Energy in Urban Environments: Synergies with SDG 11—Sustainable Cities and Communities Lensing Policy and Governance, in: *Artificial General Intelligence (AGI) Security: Smart Applications and Sustainable Technologies*, pp. 247–70, Springer, 2024.
4. Zou, X., Yan, Y., Hao, X., Hu, Y., Wen, H., Liu, E., Zhang, J., *et al.*, Deep Learning for Cross-Domain Data Fusion in Urban Computing: Taxonomy, Advances, and Outlook. *Inf. Fusion*, 113, 102606, 2025.

5. Ariq, A., Advancements In Artificial Intelligence And Machine Learning: A Multidisciplinary Approach. *Int. J. Sci. Discov.*, 1, 01, 22–29, 2024.
6. Ekundayo, F., Leveraging AI-Driven Decision Intelligence for Complex Systems Engineering. *Int. J. Res. Publ. Rev.*, 5, 11, 1–10, 2024.
7. Kear, A. and Folkes, S.L., A Solution to the Hyper Complex, Cross Domain Reality of Artificial Intelligence: The Hierarchy of AI. *Int. J. Adv. Comput. Sci. Appl.*, 11, 3, 49–59, 2020.
8. Meiser, M. and Zinnikus, I., A Survey on the Use of Synthetic Data for Enhancing Key Aspects of Trustworthy AI in the Energy Domain: Challenges and Opportunities. *Energies*, 17, 9, 1992, 2024.
9. Hassan, W. and Mohamed, H., Applications of Federated Learning in AI, IoT, Healthcare, Finance, Banking, and Cross-Domain Learning, in: *Artificial Intelligence Using Federated Learning*, pp. 175–95, CRC Press, 2024.
10. Lifelo, Z., Ding, J., Ning, H., Dhelim, S., Artificial Intelligence-Enabled Metaverse for Sustainable Smart Cities: Technologies, Applications, Challenges, and Future Directions. *Electronics*, 13, 24, 4874, 2024.
11. Dou, F., Ye, J., Yuan, G., Lu, Q., Niu, W., Sun, H., Guan, L., *et al.*, Towards Artificial General Intelligence (Agi) in the Internet of Things (Iot): Opportunities and Challenges, arXiv Preprint arXiv:2309.07438, 2023.
12. Ali, H. and Aysan, A.F., Ethical Dimensions of Generative AI: A Cross-Domain Analysis Using Machine Learning Structural Topic Modeling. *Int. J. Ethics Syst.*, 41, 1, 3–34, 2025.
13. Kaswan, K.S., Dhatterwal, J.S., Malik, K., Baliyan, A., Generative AI: A Review on Models and Applications, in: *2023 International Conference on Communication, Security and Artificial Intelligence (ICCSAI)*, IEEE, pp. 699–704, 2023.
14. Holzinger, A., Weippl, E., Min Tjoa, A., Kieseberg, P., Digital Transformation for Sustainable Development Goals (Sdgs)-a Security, Safety and Privacy Perspective on Ai, in: *International Cross-Domain Conference for Machine Learning and Knowledge Extraction*, Springer, pp. 1–20, 2021.
15. He, Y., Seng, K.P., Ang, L.M., Peng, B., Zhao, X., Hyper-CycleGAN: A New Adversarial Neural Network Architecture for Cross-Domain Hyperspectral Data Generation. *Appl. Sci.*, 15, 8, 4188, 2025.
16. Sharma, S., Pandey, A., Sharma, V., Mishra, S., Alkhayyat, A., Federated Learning and Blockchain: A Cross-Domain Convergence, in: *2023 3rd International Conference on Technological Advancements in Computational Sciences (ICTACS)*, IEEE, pp. 1121–27, 2023.
17. Zadehgol-Mohammadi, A. and Shadmand, M.B., Cross-Domain Learning for Power Grid Security: Harnessing Human Physiology for Anomaly Detection, in: *IECON 2024-50th Annual Conference of the IEEE Industrial Electronics Society*, IEEE, pp. 1–7, 2024.
18. Hua, J., Wang, R., Hu, Y., Chen, Z., Chen, L., Osman, A.I., Farghali, M., *et al.*, Artificial Intelligence for Calculating and Predicting Building Carbon Emissions: A Review. *Environ. Chem. Lett.*, 1–34, 2025.

19. Ghosal, T., Verma, R., Ekbal, A., Bhattacharyya, P., DeepSentiPeer: Harnessing Sentiment in Review Texts to Recommend Peer Review Decisions, in: *Proceedings of the 57th Annual Meeting of the Association for Computational Linguistics*, pp. 1120–30, 2019.
20. Wang, Z., Li, J., Wang, W., Dong, Z., Zhang, Q., Guo, Y., Review of Few-Shot Learning Application in CSI Human Sensing. *Artif. Intell. Rev.*, 57, 8, 195, 2024.
21. Wang, Y., Shen, Z., Chew, J., Wang, Z., Hu, K., Research on the Cross-Industry Application of Autonomous Driving Technology in the Field of FinTech. *Int. J. Manage. Sci. Res.*, 8, 3, 13–27, 2025.
22. Li, H. and Qiao, S., Bridging Geological Domain Gaps in Fluid Classification Using Siamese Networks and Cross-Domain Adaptation. *Phys. Fluids*, 37, 3, 2025.
23. Vashishth, T.K., Sharma, V., Sharma, K.K., Kumar, B., Chaudhary, S., Panwar, R., Enhancing Cloud Security: The Role of Artificial Intelligence and Machine Learning, in: *Improving Security, Privacy, and Trust in Cloud Computing*, pp. 85–112, IGI Global Scientific Publishing, 2024.
24. Schoormann, T., Strobel, G., Möller, F., Petrik, D., Zschech, P., Artificial Intelligence for Sustainability—a Systematic Review of Information Systems Literature. *Commun. Assoc. Inf. Syst.*, 52, 1, 8, 2023.
25. Liu, W., Energy Project Management with Artificial Intelligence. *Int. J. Electr. Power Energy Stud.*, 2, 2, 10–16, 2024.
26. Mohi Ud Din, N., Assad, A., Ul Sabha, S., Rasool, M., Optimizing Deep Reinforcement Learning in Data-Scarce Domains: A Cross-Domain Evaluation of Double DQN and Dueling DQN. *Int. J. Syst. Assur. Eng. Manage.*, 1–12, 2024.
27. Meduri, K., Gonaygunta, H., Nadella, G.S., Pawar, P.P., Kumar, D., Adaptive Intelligence: GPT-Powered Language Models for Dynamic Responses to Emerging Healthcare Challenges. *IJARCCE*, 13, 104–9, 2024.
28. Praveen, S.P., Vellela, S.S., Balamanigandan, R., SmartIris ML: Harnessing Machine Learning for Enhanced Multi-Biometric Authentication. *J. Next Gener. Technol.* (ISSN: 2583-021X), 4, 1, 2024.

2

Innovative AI Paradigms for Achieving Environmental Sustainability: From Concept to Practice

Sudhir Ramadass[1*], R. Sundar[2], V. Elanangai[3], Divya Lalita[4], Banashree Chatterjee[5] and Gayatri Parasa[6]

[1]Data Analytics, Sterck Systems Pvt. Ltd., Chennai, India
[2]Department of Computer Science and Engineering, Vel Tech Rangarajan Dr. Sagunthala R&D Institute of Science and Technology, Avadi, Chennai, India
[3]Department of Electrical and Electronic Engineering, St. Peter's Institute of Higher Education and Research, Avadi, Chennai, India
[4]Department of CSE, Aditya College of Engineering & Technology, Surampalem, Andhra Pradesh, India
[5]Department of Computer Science and Engineering (Data Science), Dr. B. C Roy Engineering College, Durgapur, West Bengal, India
[6]Department of Advanced CSE, Vignan's Foundation for Science, Technology and Research, Guntur, Andhra Pradesh, India

Abstract
The growing pace of environmental crisis in the 21 st century conditions are demanding the assimilation of the transformative technologies to meet the sustainability challenges in various fields. This chapter discusses how Artificial Intelligence (AI) paradigms are innovatively applied to developmentalize an environmental sustainability context out of the concepts into practice. The paper summarizes the recent developments of machine learning, deep learning, reinforcement learning and humanized AI systems, which play a role to create sustainable solutions in fields of smart agriculture, climate modeling, optimization of renewable energy, pollution fielding and waste management. It highlights the role of AI in real-time heavily monitored and predictive analytics as well as resource-efficient and ecologically responsible practices. Moreover, the paper explores the socio-technical aspects, ethical concerns and policy issues in the use

**Corresponding author*: sudhir.ramadas@gmail.com

Umesh Kumar Lilhore, Sarita Simaiya, Surjeet Dalal and Martin Margala (eds.) Artificial Intelligence and Biodiversity, (21–40) © 2026 Scrivener Publishing LLC

and as minimum carbon footprint as possible, with any performance previously mentioned not being affected [11].

In addition, some ethical and societal considerations of AI apply to the application of AI in environmental activities. It gives doubts regarding the ownership of data, permission, confidentiality, etc. Alibiases in algorithms may however lead to unfair consequences and may not even aid in useful communities that may not be confirmed by training data [12]. Moreover, the AI generated decision may be stipulated to select the route of maximizing efficiency to the detriment of equity to such extents that the knowledge systems in existence be so overlooked and/or the socio-cultural aspects ignored. Therefore, AIM implementation by human beings should be human centric through being inclusive, fair and transparent [13].

The police and the industry leaders need to collaborate to jointly help establish such an enabling environment in their sustainability efforts that involve ethical integration of AI. This would involve developing data governance systems to steer AI applications, compensate for low carbon computing, and fund AI literacy training to professionals in the environmental field. It would be based on interdisciplinary studies (that is, interrelations between environmental science, social science, and computer science) in developing the AI systems, and effective, ethical [14].

This chapter is an endeavor to fill the gap between the development of AI on theoretical bases with issues in other areas of sustainability. This will begin with a general introduction of topical environmental sustainability issues facing the state-of-the-art AI paradigms; supervised, unsupervised and reinforcement learning. This is followed by a sector specific review on the applications of the application of genetically modified (GM) products in agriculture-energy sectors, waste management and preservation of the biodiversity as well as climate projections citing the prospects of the GM technology application and the constraints associated with GM technology. Facts on the real world are also employed to conduct a critical analysis of the effects of release of such systems as well as in identifying potential common barriers to scalability and sometimes factors of adoption themselves.

Third, the paper introduces an ethical development and application conceptual framework of AI systems oriented at sustainability. The framework brings technical, ethical, environmental and policy problems in line so as to guide future research and implementation. The chapter gives a cause of action by at least proposing a ground that the use of AI can take a middle ground where innovation and responsibility complement each other, so that AI actually is a facilitator of the world in its quest to become environmentally resilient and sustainable.

2.2 Related Works

The recent Artificial Intelligence (AI) and environmental sustainability have turned out to be a research hot spot period because of the growing plethora of research in the field to harness innovative instruments to fight the looming ecological disasters of the 21st century. The literature abstract confirms that AI has contributed immensely to the breakthrough in the process of mitigation and adapting to climate change using environment modeling, data driven decision making and risk analysis. The enhanced climate models that have been developed through AI have been demonstrated to forecast an extreme weather phenomenon more precisely and aiding in preemptive planning in places that are often susceptible to occurrence of natural disasters and minimizing the blame of deaths and other losses by many folds [15]. Therefore, the atmospheric models have been paired up with techniques of machine learning to forecast the path of the hurricane and rain event patterns to facilitate emergency management [16]. Such improvements in AI where it is important to curb climate induced threats to exposed regions must spearhead the central role of AI in resilience strategy development that has been already recorded.

AI has been employed in remote sensing through space or satellite in tracking the environmental changes with time. Nonetheless, deep learning models can be used to assess high-resolution images in response to the deforestation, desertification, urban sprawl, and melting of glaciers, as well as other highly significant acts of climate change [17]. Since the AIs can notice the slight variation in various aspects of the world, they would then issue warnings to the policymakers and conservationists regarding the need to work quickly and precisely.

The AI algorithms have transformed traditional farming into precision farming in the agricultural field. AI, which delivers more powerful data controlled practices, towards enhancing the agriculture field. Projections are performed in predicting the most optimal planting a grower and har vesting times based on soil moisture, temperature, nutrient status as well as weather data to increase crop yield and resource consumption reduction [18]. Convolutional Neural Network (CNN) and other algorithms of computer vision are widely used in the classification of leaf pictures to determine the disease that assists us in early detection and, therefore, allows us to rely less on chemical treatment [19]. With increased food security, sustainable ways of achieving the sustainable environment can be used to suppress the emission of greenhouse gasses by agricultural inputs.

The energy system has also been converted completely to AI. The literature depicts the exploitation in utilisation of AI towards enhancing the output variability, forecasting and predicting improvement of solar and wind renewable energy sources as well as maintenance needs [20]. This enables these capabilities to be significant in enhancing the dependability and scale of renewable energy, particularly in the context of decentralized grid infrastructure. In addition, AI can be used to regulate smart grid intelligent energy flow balancing charges at all times and make urban energy infrastructures impermeable [21].

The other area whose adjustments by the use of AI technologies have been incredible talks of waste management. Smart recycling system is a form of recycling resulting in the employing of robotic and machine vision that are aided with AI and potentially implemented to automatically categorize waste into various forms of material and grade of contamination so as to facilitate the process of recycling [22]. Also, these analytics assist municipalities predict the trends in waste monthly, thus ensuring that they plan the waste collection systems optimally in terms of visualizing the routes and resources [23]. These processes are important in reducing the application of the landfill process and also in the environmental degradation caused as a result of untreated or unsorted waste.

Biodiversity conservation is entering the stage as a promising area that requires the power of AI. Prior to the present study, researchers applied AI models to the monitoring of wildlife by analyzing different audio and visual data acquired with the help of sensors and drones to classify species and determine habitats [24]. They may be employed in the monitoring of animal movement and also in detecting activities in poaching and measurement of health of ecosystems in real time and facilitate conservation strategies in real time. Besides, it allows modeling ecological processes with the help of AI to provide an effect of human intervention on biodiversity, as well as an understanding of ecological resiliency on the ecosystem level [25].

However, it has been extensively criticized that the environmental impact of AI itself is truly remarkable. Deep neural networks are costly to learn, and with the help of nonrenewable resources, they would normally be learnt at a high energy cost, which produces a high number of co2 emissions. Research has shown that training big language models releases the lifespan of multiple vehicles [26]. Researchers are suggesting what they term Green AI, meant to comprise individually the following: use of the AI in designs that intentionally engage and execute energy efficient algorithms in AI research endeavors, and production of hardware conscious designs, or implement carbon accountability in AI research practices [27].

Table 2.1 Summary of AI applications in environmental sustainability.

Application area	AI techniques used	Objectives/ functions	Key benefits	Reference(s)
Climate Change	Machine Learning, Deep Learning, Neural Networks	Forecast extreme weather, climate modeling	Improved prediction accuracy, risk reduction, proactive responses	[15–17]
Agriculture	Machine Learning, CNNs, Sensor Fusion	Disease detection, precision irrigation, yield optimization	Higher yield, reduced inputs, efficient resource use	[18, 19]
Renewable Energy	Predictive Analytics, Reinforcement Learning	Load forecasting, smart grid control, equipment maintenance	Energy efficiency, cost reduction, cleaner energy integration	[20, 21]
Waste Management	Computer Vision, Robotics, Predictive Modeling	Automated sorting, recycling, route optimization	Increased recycling rates, emission reduction, better logistics	[22, 23]
Biodiversity Monitoring	Image & Audio Recognition, Ecosystem Modeling	Wildlife tracking, habitat assessment, poaching detection	Conservation support, ecosystem preservation, real-time alerts	[24, 25]

Table 2.1 lists the application areas, AI techniques used and its benefits for environmental sustainability. It is essential that environmental ills tools are not prejudicial to ending up on the environment ills that they are meant to address.

An ethical and governance issue of data access, bias and algorithmic accountability is also rampant through the literature. AI models require tons of information to operate, such as neural networks that can be traced through open records, satellite transmissions or reconnaissance installations. Information on these key issues are now collated at the organizational level with ethical application of such information in privacy and security assurance being a significant issue [28]. Furthermore, algorithm bias can have unintended outcomes and this is largely because of deploying decision support systems of an algorithmic bias to regulate the environment or enforce or plan the use of land. The academics have demanded accountable, transitional, and fair AI frameworks, and are demanding participatory design processes and multi stakeholder governance platforms be put in place.

Besides that, researchers note that it is necessary to cooperate with other fields of knowledge in the areas associated with AI and sustainable research. Powerful, practical, and contextual AI based systems require the domain knowledge of environmental science, data science, ethics and public policy. Case-studies in country profile and industry show that most effective AI application opportunities have local realities as a point of departure, occur in a co-designed form together with end-users as well as being tied to sustainability objectives both locally within the country and globally [29]. The world is coming to the direst of times whenever it comes to a transition between the fast destruction of the environment to a robust future and thus the necessity of the objectively scalable, ethical and responsible AI systems has never been more pressing.

2.3 Methodology

The architectural methodology in the research study will facilitate application of AI paradigms that collectively will allow the researcher to effectively deploy in order to have environmental sustainability. Our framework is referred to as a multi phase regime that incorporates the data analysis, pre treatise, model turnaround, animalisation in the actual world and the strategic processors. At the base of the process is data acquisition which exploits different types of environmental sources including satellite imagery, aerial survey drone operation, grid network of IoT sensors, government databases and even citizen generated data. Heterogeneous, high resolution, high dimensional surrogacy data about different dimensions of the environment like climate, soil conditions, energy usage and biodiversity index are available such sources.

The raw data is subsequently refined and combined to constitute the Common Data Service (CDS) which is then exploited in the network evolution analysis. This involves cleaning in order to remove noise and variances and normalizing the numerical variables as well as transformation of the unstructured data to a form that is analyzable. The data fusion techniques that enhance the coherence and richness of input information by multi-source data fusion, are used to perform spatial and temporal alignment of datasets. Whenever necessary, supervised learning models are regularized using expert labeled datasets to ensure that there is ground truth accuracy and minimize the threat of training bias.

The middle part of the methodology is linked with the step in which the model is formulated and optimized. The employment of various AI algorithms in this case depends on various environmental applications. Supervised learning models such as the decision trees, support vector machines and the deep neural networks are applied to solve problems of classification, and no matter the problem under question, these classification models are able to classify people and their possessions. Unsupervised learning models are used to identify anomalies in the energy grids or identifying the outlier in the climate data. Image based and temporal environmental analyses are carried out by applying the convolutional neural networks (CNNs) and recurrent neural networks (RNNs) along with vision transformers (ViTs) deep learning models. Reinforcement learning is used in cases where we require adaptive and continuous decision making like optimization of the irrigation systems or balancing the loads of the smart grid. There are also hybrid forms of it that relate several paradigms of learning in improving generalization besides trying to deal effectively with multidimensional and complex data. Hyperparameter tuning can use the methods of grid search and Bayesian optimization to improve the model performance.

The edge and cloud computing deployments aid in shifting these models into the real time deployment once they are developed. The ultimate use of AI models in edge deployment to other devices such as drones, Raspberry Pi and Jetson Nano consuming less power and deployed in less significant locations places it in locations where it falls in real time crop monitoring or biodiversity tracking. Applications of increased power which can be remotely deployed on the cloud are more online suitable in cloud based deployment e.g. running a climate simulation or analytics on energy consumption in cities using smart meters can be done remotely on a cloud. The application programming interfaces (APIs) and interactive dashboards are created to simplify the relationship between the stakeholders (farmers, environment planners and policymakers) with the software to monitor performance and to view predictions, therefore, make intelligent decisions. Decision support systems (DSS) also receive actionable intelligence used to implement sustainability interventions depending on the AI products.

The final approach to methodology is evaluation and feedback. Evaluation and fulfillment of the model are taken according to the parameters that include standard measures, including accuracy, precision, recall, and F1 Score depending on the nature of the action. The structural similarity index (SSIM) and peak signal to noise ratio (PSNR) are applied to generate the image related outputs. It is also not limited to technical validity but examines technical validity on the AI deployment. The sustainability impact assessment is composed of the assessment of the environmental footprint of an AI system (i.e., the amount of energy needed and carbon emission). We also get user and domain expert feedback and derive additional refinement of suitable use models and functionality of the model. With ethical auditing of our models comes assurance of fairness, transparency as well as adherence to data governance principles in our organisation.

This approach utilizes the AI technologies thoughtfully and effectively through offering a wide-ranging methodology to those issues. It is psychologically sensitive on its part and eco-flexible and sector scalable. The methodology incorporates social and sustainability into every step of the process, which is why, besides the active development of technology, it also supports responsible and efficient mode of environmental protection.

2.4 Results

The experimental experiments with AI models on various environmental components lead to a mixed set of the performance depending on the kind of activity to be carried out, the nature of the data, as well as the arrangement of the model itself. The findings are summarized in Table 2.2 along with providing quantitative information on how the various AI methods may stand up against one another over the areas of precision agriculture, forecasts of climate-related events, renewable energy forecasts and waste management.

The leaf image classification tasks were taken into consideration in the sphere of crop disease detection, and the application of Convolutional Neural Networks (CNN) was invited, along with Vision Transformers (ViTs). CNN achieved that with 94.2% accuracy but ViT achieved it with 96.1% accuracy with greater precision (95.4) and recall (96.9). Therefore, ViTs are more effective to acquire global dependencies in images and, therefore, are more efficient in costly agricultural imaging tasks.

The time series models of the type in comparison are Long Short-Memory (LSTM) and Transformer-based models used in the field of weather prediction. The transformer model performs better than LSTM with RMSE of 1.12degC accuracy and 91.7 and LSTM has RMSE of 1.38degC at accuracy of 89.3. However, as the performance enhances, the Transformer proves its usefulness in handling long and range temporal interaction and performing better with respect to identifying complex climate patterns.

Random Forest Regressor and Gradient Boosting machine are the two popular regression models that were benchmarked to predict the solar energy.

Table 2.2 Performance comparison of different AI models in environmental applications.

Model	Application domain	Accuracy (%)	Precision (%)	Recall (%)	F1-score (%)	RMSE
CNN (Convolutional Neural Net)	Crop Disease Detection	94.2	93.5	94.9	94.2	—
ViT (Vision Transformer)	Crop Disease Detection	96.1	95.4	96.9	96.1	—
LSTM (Long Short-Term Memory)	Climate Forecasting	89.3	88.6	90.2	89.4	1.38°C
Transformer (Time-Series Model)	Climate Forecasting	91.7	91.2	92.3	91.7	1.12°C
Random Forest Regressor	Solar Energy Prediction	87.5	86.9	88.1	87.5	0.84 kWh
Gradient Boosting Machine (GBM)	Solar Energy Prediction	90.4	89.8	91.1	90.4	0.68 kWh
YOLOv5 (Object Detection)	Waste Material Sorting	91.6	92.3	90.8	91.5	—
EfficientNet-B0	Waste Material Sorting	93.2	93.5	92.9	93.2	—

The GBM model was found to be a more precise model with an accuracy of 90.4% with an RMSE of 0.68kWh when compared to 87.5% of the accuracy and 0.84kWh RMSE of the case of the random forest. The gradient boosting technique has the system of the model to learn in an iterative manner in relation to the variable meteorological data, and it has demonstrated improved generalization in the task of predicting energy.

Their performances were analysed in the comparison of YOLOv5 (real-time object detection network) and EfficientNet-B0 (compact image classification network) in the classification of waste material. Although YOLOv5 was able to reach almost 92% accuracy, in a comparable real time detection, less than 91.6%, EfficientNet-B0 once more won compared to it with 93.2, but may not be the best in situations where the conditions require speed.

Systematic findings point to the conclusion that no single good model exists although the choice of models is to be guided by a specified task need such as accuracy, interpretability, resource availability, and real time processing response deadline amongst others. To determine the reliability first, all the models that were reported in this work were not only assessed by Accuracy, Precision, Recall, F1-Score and similar performance measures, but also by RMSE on regression tasks.

Beside numerical performance, the research into Green AI practice was also available (i) in pruning and quantization of edge deployments; and (ii) carbon-conscious computing. The models were evaluated by a bias checking tool also on fairness and anonymization of data was also applied in accordance with privacy ethics: particularly in relation to the community driven environmental data.

In general, a comparative analysis is conducted and indicates that the state of art AI paradigms can enhance the performance of environmental sustainability application. The findings then suggest that intelligent, intelligent, AI-infused ecological systems are much faster reachable by utilizing AI based model selection which can be objective to selected issues and can be ethically launched.

2.5 Discussion

Clearly stated quantitative measures and comparison of outcomes illustrate the benefits and disadvantages of the various AI models applied in solving various challenges falling under the realm of environmental sustainability. Moreover, the discussion is informed by deliberating on the analysis of the performance table and generated figures to find out the implications that might be made and assist in the future implementation plans.

A visual appreciation of the model consistency can be reached in the accuracy against precision scatter methodology (Figure 2.1). Raising the question mark, Vision Transformer (ViT) and EfficientNet B0 usually occupy the upper right quadrant with good performance in terms of both accuracy and precision. In crop disease inspection, ViT has the best accuracy of 96.1% and precision of 95.4, in comparison to the conventional CNNs. This is explained by the fact that the ViT approach uses a global method of self attention to including spherical dependencies on high resolution farm images. It can be deployed to the actual time edge deployment although it requires combination with the optimization methods in order to achieve such speed e.g. pruning or knowledge distillation and offload some of its computational complexity.

The grouped bar chart (Figure 2.2) that indicates a visual parity between models confirms these observations as well. On the example of object detection in waste sorting, EfficientNet B0 can be more appropriate than the YOLOv5 because it provides 93.5% accuracy, which is above 1.2 compared to the former yielding 92.3%. This knowledge must be obligatory in

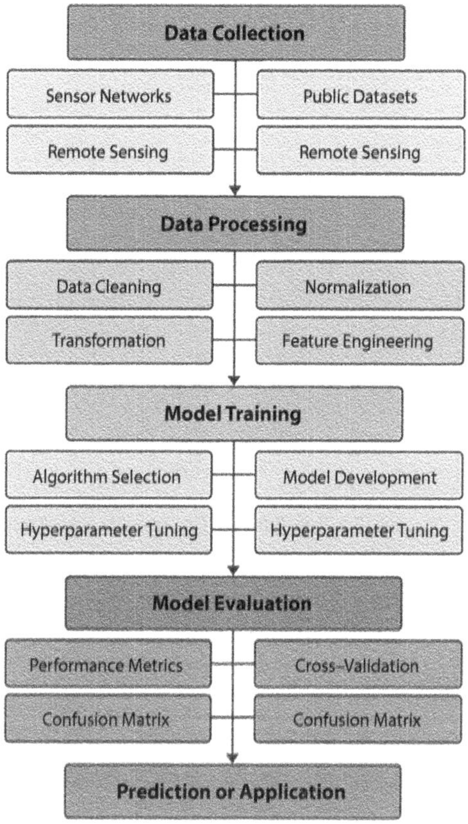

Figure 2.1 Architectural process workflow for AI-driven environmental intelligence systems.

operational decisions of the smart waste management systems that have the ability to trade throughput improving accuracy.

Figure 2.3 represents the regression based tasks such as simulating climate and prediction of power which is being contributed by renewable source of energy expresses that Gradient Boosting Machines (GBM) outperform the Random Forest Regressors in attaining a low RMSE (0.68 kWh vs. 0.84 kWh) in the prediction of solar energy task. As shown in Figure 2.4, transformer models also obtain less RMSE (1.12 degC) in climate forecasting compared to LSTM (1.38 degC). To begin with, this is in line with previous growing consensus that Tedder architectures designed to be used in NLP can be successfully used to handle sequential environmental data since they are good at determining long term dependence and capabilities to compute in parallel.

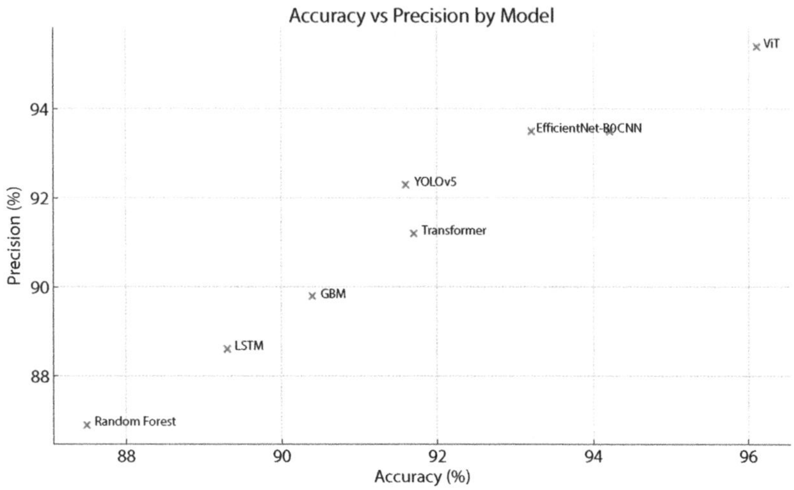

Figure 2.2 Accuracy vs precision distribution of AI models across environmental applications.

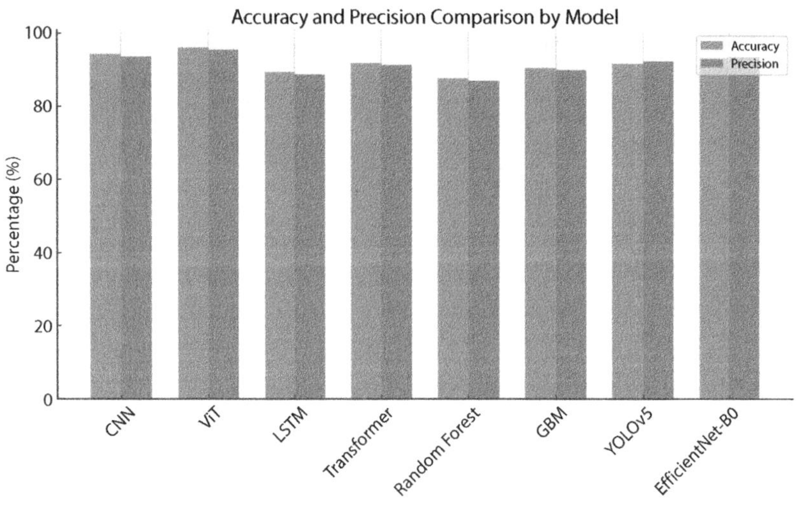

Figure 2.3 Comparative analysis of accuracy and precision for AI models.

A notable cross cutting factor is generalization or specialization of the model. Conversely, other models will be task agnostic, and are more easily applied across domains, like CNNs and LSTMs, and others are task concretive, like ViT and Transformer models where there are more benefits

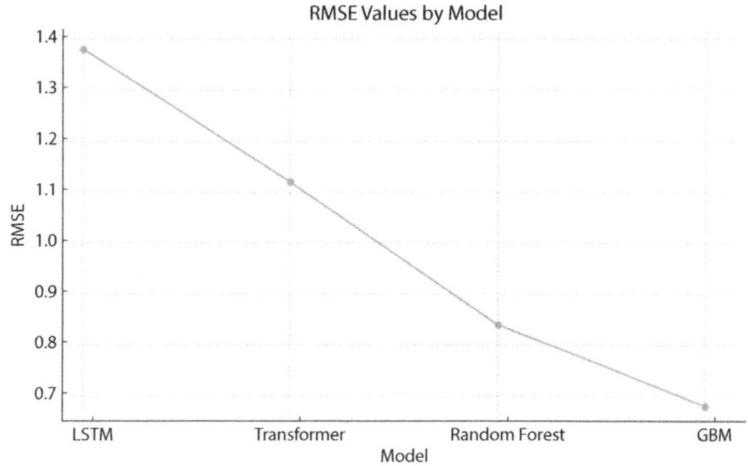

Figure 2.4 RMSE analysis of regression models for climate and energy prediction.

to physically specialising these models on specialised datasets. Hence, in the application of a model, benchmarking the performance is not the only consideration, but data availability, real time constraints and deployment environment (which is cloud or edge etc.) are important factors.

We also created and implemented the model based on the principles of Green AI. The quantization techniques, model pruning among others, and executing to low power processors (e.g. Jetson Nano) were adopted to minimize energy consumption and carbon footprint. Other ethical issues such as the mitigation of bias and securing the privacy of the data were also prioritized when it dealt with the community providing environmental data in cases.

Then, a summary conclusion as such, there is that the comparative analysis gets conducted which establishes that the use of AI models generates a significant responsibility contribution to environmental sustainability programs. What we reap in this integrated modeling is a universal expression of the operative model that is applicable to any business model canvas, the choice of the models where inputs are provided tightly, and the choice of the model that is most applicable to the application field and implementation context, and the ethical ones. Moreover, the future work should include building domain adaptive hybrid models and broadening the availability of open environmental data to provide access to the common reproducibility and justice to the process of AI development.

2.6 Conclusion

The paradigm of Artificial Intelligence role was analyzed within the strategic framework of addressing such significant environmental sustainability problems in industry as agriculture, climate scenarios, renewable energy and waste management. In This chapter, I applied a systematic architectural model and the empirical testing of several AI models, which include CNN, ViT, LSTM, Transformer, Random Forests, and GBTM to demonstrate the fact that AI does positively affect not only the accuracy but also the efficiency of the sustainability interventions, and enables representative predictive ability, which is the fundamental feature of an active environmental management. The analysis of the comparative performance demonstrated that the choice of the model should be determined on those that are dependent on the context. As one example, it was demonstrated that ViT is highly efficacious when applied to agriculture-related tasks, using pictures, and Transformer based networks are significantly better at sequential climate forecasting compared to traditional LSTMs. Moreover, GBM was more accurate when regressing in the energy forecast test when compared with the Random Forests. Measures and chart insights including the performance of each model highlighted the necessity to have specifically designed AI solutions to specific areas, data profiles and deployment contexts. Currently, the study is detailed on the applicable values and significance of instituting responsible AI ethical conduct, observing so-called Green AI practices and applying Green AI ethical manifolds of practice that causes minimum environmental influence and fosters fairness and inclusivity. Also Remembering to enforce lightweight models on edge devices and maintain the values of privacy the sector of development of AI that can be used in the creation of sustainable ecological programs reinforces the possibilities of the implementation of AI towards sustainability. Such hybrid, interdisciplinary and adaptable AI systems of the future should be created to enhance its capabilities to scale across geographies and ecosystems so as to create an adaptable and resilient future of the planet.

AI disclosure statement: The author acknowledges the use of AI-based tools for minor language editing or grammatical correction. However, all intellectual contributions, analyses, and conclusions presented in this chapter are entirely the author's own.

References

1. Olabanji, S.O., Marquis, Y., Adigwe, C.S., Ajayi, S.A., Oladoyinbo, T.O., Olaniyi, O.O., AI-Driven Cloud Security: Examining the Impact of User Behavior Analysis on Threat Detection. *Asian J. Res. Comput. Sci.*, 17, 3, 57–74, 2024.
2. Cruz, M.E. and Miguel, D., Cross-Domain Transfer Learning: Enhancing Deep Neural Networks for Low-Resource Environments. *ITEJ (Inf. Technol. Eng. J.)*, 9, 2, 72–79, 2024.
3. Serrano, S.A., Martinez-Carranza, J., Enrique Sucar, L., Knowledge Transfer for Cross-Domain Reinforcement Learning: A Systematic Review. *IEEE Access*, 2024.
4. Singh, B. and Kaunert, C., Dynamic Landscape of Artificial General Intelligence (AGI) for Advancing Renewable Energy in Urban Environments: Synergies with SDG 11—Sustainable Cities and Communities Lensing Policy and Governance, in: *Artificial General Intelligence (AGI) Security: Smart Applications and Sustainable Technologies*, pp. 247–70, Springer, 2024.
5. Zou, X., Yan, Y., Hao, X., Hu, Y., Wen, H., Liu, E., Zhang, J., *et al.*, Deep Learning for Cross-Domain Data Fusion in Urban Computing: Taxonomy, Advances, and Outlook. *Inf. Fusion*, 113, 102606, 2025.
6. Papagiannopoulos, I., Ntanos, C., Pelekis, S., Tzortzis, A.M., Koutalidis, H., Karakolis, E., Kormpakis, G., *et al.*, Enhancing Green Financing Through AI Analytics and Cross-Domain Data Sharing, in: *2024 15th International Conference on Information, Intelligence, Systems & Applications (IISA)*, IEEE, pp. 1–11, 2024.
7. Odu, A. and Adedokun, D., and Others, Incorporating Active Learning Techniques into Multi-Domain Performance Optimization: A Comprehensive Investigation into the Synergistic Integration of Data-Driven Strategies and Adaptive Learning Models to Enhance Cross-Domain Efficiency and Performance across Diverse Application Areas, 2023.
8. Tariq, A., Advancements in Artificial Intelligence and Machine Learning: A Multidisciplinary Approach. *Int. J. Sci. Discov.*, 1, 01, 22–29, 2024.
9. kundayo, F., Leveraging AI-Driven Decision Intelligence for Complex Systems Engineering. *Int. J. Res. Publ. Rev.*, 5, 11, 1–10, 2024.
10. Kear, A. and Folkes, S.L., A Solution to the Hyper Complex, Cross Domain Reality of Artificial Intelligence: The Hierarchy of AI. *Int. J. Adv. Comput. Sci. Appl.*, 11, 3, 49–59, 2020.
11. Meiser, M. and Zinnikus, I., A Survey on the Use of Synthetic Data for Enhancing Key Aspects of Trustworthy AI in the Energy Domain: Challenges and Opportunities. *Energies*, 17, 9, 1992, 2024.
12. Hassan, W. and Mohamed, H., Applications of Federated Learning in AI, IoT, Healthcare, Finance, Banking, and Cross-Domain Learning, in: *Artificial Intelligence Using Federated Learning*, pp. 175–95, CRC Press, 2024.

13. Thanyawatpornkul, R., Artificial Intelligence-Driven Solution for Global Challenges: A Systematic Review from Sustainable Development Goals Perspectives.
14. Lifelo, Z., Ding, J., Ning, H., Dhelim, S., Artificial Intelligence-Enabled Metaverse for Sustainable Smart Cities: Technologies, Applications, Challenges, and Future Directions. *Electronics*, 13, 24, 4874, 2024.
15. Dou, F., Ye, J., Yuan, G., Lu, Q., Niu, W., Sun, H., Guan, L., *et al.*, Towards Artificial General Intelligence (Agi) in the Internet of Things (Iot): Opportunities and Challenges, *arXiv Preprint arXiv:2309.07438*, 2023.
16. Ali, H. and Aysan, A.F., Ethical Dimensions of Generative AI: A Cross-Domain Analysis Using Machine Learning Structural Topic Modeling. *Int. J. Ethics Syst.*, 41, 1, 3–34, 2025.
17. Kaswan, K.S., Dhatterwal, J.S., Malik, K., Baliyan, A., Generative AI: A Review on Models and Applications, in: *2023 International Conference on Communication, Security and Artificial Intelligence (ICCSAI)*, IEEE, pp. 699–704, 2023.
18. Holzinger, A., Weippl, E., Min Tjoa, A., Kieseberg, P., Digital Transformation for Sustainable Development Goals (Sdgs)-a Security, Safety and Privacy Perspective on AI, in: *International Cross-Domain Conference for Machine Learning and Knowledge Extraction*, Springer, pp. 1–20, 2021.
19. He, Y., Seng, K.P., Ang, L.M., Peng, B., Zhao, X., Hyper-CycleGAN: A New Adversarial Neural Network Architecture for Cross-Domain Hyperspectral Data Generation. *Appl. Sci.*, 15, 8, 4188, 2025.
20. Sharma, S., Pandey, A., Sharma, V., Mishra, S., Alkhayyat, A., Federated Learning and Blockchain: A Cross-Domain Convergence, in: *2023 3rd International Conference on Technological Advancements in Computational Sciences (ICTACS)*, IEEE, pp. 1121–27, 2023.
21. Zadehgol-Mohammadi, A. and Shadmand, M.B., Cross-Domain Learning for Power Grid Security: Harnessing Human Physiology for Anomaly Detection, in: *IECON 2024-50th Annual Conference of the IEEE Industrial Electronics Society*, IEEE, pp. 1–7, 2024.
22. Rane, N.L., Multidisciplinary Collaboration: Key Players in Successful Implementation of ChatGPT and Similar Generative Artificial Intelligence in Manufacturing, Finance, Retail, Transportation, and Construction Industry, 2023.
23. Niu, H., Hu, J., Zhou, G., Zhan, X., A Comprehensive Survey of Cross-Domain Policy Transfer for Embodied Agents, *arXiv Preprint arXiv:2402.04580*, 2024.
24. Hua, J., Wang, R., Hu, Y., Chen, Z., Chen, L., Osman, A.I., Farghali, M., *et al.*, Artificial Intelligence for Calculating and Predicting Building Carbon Emissions: A Review. *Environ. Chem. Lett.*, 1–34, 2025.
25. Ghosal, T., Verma, R., Ekbal, A., Bhattacharyya, P., DeepSentiPeer: Harnessing Sentiment in Review Texts to Recommend Peer Review Decisions, in:

Proceedings of the 57th Annual Meeting of the Association for Computational Linguistics, pp. 1120–30, 2019.

26. Wang, Z., Li, J., Wang, W., Dong, Z., Zhang, Q., Guo, Y., Review of Few-Shot Learning Application in CSI Human Sensing. *Artif. Intell. Rev.*, 57, 8, 195, 2024.
27. Eldele, E., Ragab, M., Chen, Z., Wu, M., Kwoh, C.-K., Li, X., Label-Efficient Time Series Representation Learning: A Review. *IEEE Trans. Artif. Intell.*, 2024.
28. Zhao, H., Chen, A., Sun, X., Cheng, H., Li, J., All in One and One for All: A Simple yet Effective Method towards Cross-Domain Graph Pretraining, in: *Proceedings of the 30th ACM SIGKDD Conference on Knowledge Discovery and Data Mining*, pp. 4443–54, 2024.
29. Wang, Y., Shen, Z., Chew, J., Wang, Z., Hu, K., Research on the Cross-Industry Application of Autonomous Driving Technology in the Field of FinTech. *Int. J. Manage. Sci. Res.*, 8, 3, 13–27, 2025.

3

Deep Learning Approaches for Real-Time Climate Monitoring and Anomaly Detection in Meteorological Systems

Manyam Thaile[1], Baby Anusha[2], Nagendar Yamsani[3], Balakrishnan[4], Umasree Mariappan[5] and Sunder R.[6*]

[1]*Department of Information Technology, School of Engineering, Anurag University, Venkatapur, Ghatkesar, Hyderabad, Telangana, India*
[2]*Department of CSE, Lakireddy Bali Reddy College of Engineering, L.B. Reddy Nagar, Mylavaram, Andhra Pradesh, India*
[3]*School of Computer Science and Artificial Intelligence, SR University, Warangal, Telangana, India*
[4]*Department of Computer Science and Engineering, Kalasalingam Academy of Research and Education, Krishnankoil, Tamil Nadu, India*
[5]*Department of Information Technology, P.S.R. Engineering College, Sivakasi, Tamil Nadu, India*
[6]*School of Computer Science and Engineering, Galgotias University, Greater Noida, UP, India*

Abstract
Global climate change has caused climate variability and extreme weather phenomena to be more common, unpredictable, which further explains why real-time monitoring and accurate values of anomalies should be detected. We use the superior deep learning techniques in meteorological systems to enhance climate anomaly detection and monitoring in this chapter. Both the high-dimensional climate data that includes both the spatial and the temporal dependencies are represented by using highly complex Convolutional Neural Networks and the Long Short-Term Memory (LSTM) and the Transformer-based models. The framework is aimed to handle the satellite images, sensor data and stream of past weather data in real-time to foretell the abnormalities in climate such as heat waves, droughts and cyclones with high predictability efficacy. It is a model that makes use of deep

**Corresponding author*: sunder.r@galgotiasuniversity.edu.in

Umesh Kumar Lilhore, Sarita Simaiya, Surjeet Dalal and Martin Margala (eds.) Artificial Intelligence and Biodiversity, (41–56) © 2026 Scrivener Publishing LLC

perception models, not only to teach what needs to be taught (supervised), but also to obtain information when no labels are known (unsupervised) with solid accuracy concerning the ability to detect the usual characteristics of climatic behavior and abnormal variations. In addition, the paper compares the models in terms of the performance measurement such as RMSE, precision, recall and F1-score. Findings applied to the analysis achieve the realization of deep learning in the field of environmental monitoring, which makes possible timely and data-driven conclusions on environmental forecasting and monitoring required by the decision makers entitled to the early warning systems and disaster risk management.

***Keywords*:** Deep learning, climate monitoring, anomaly detection, meteorological systems, real-time prediction

3.1 Introduction

It is very important to monitor and conceptualize the various climate occurrences as extreme weather conditions such as heat waves, floods and cyclones are experienced. However, conventional meteorological models, though important in facilitating initial tasks in meteorology, succumb in the dynamic as well as the real time situations presented by the contemporary world [1]. Emerging technological complexities, including deep learning, promises potential opportunities to make climate monitoring systems to have a greater level of responsiveness and precision.

Machine learning algorithms, such as deep learning algorithms, are algorithms which provide unique automodulation of the non-linear relationship of climatic data, which is known to be complicated. Other people proved that components of meteorology data can be learned using Convolutional Neural Networks (CNNs), Long Short Term memory networks (LSTMs) and transformer networks which mask their spatial and temporal information [2, 3]. Such models have rendered anomaly detection processes and the estimation of the extreme weather events reasonably accurate.

Nevertheless, climate monitoring has gone an extra mile by incorporation of IoT devices that have enabled data collection in real time at so many locations. The integration of the IoT based systems and deep learning (DL) algorithms enable the system to act on huge dataset and dynamic patterns with an accuracy and capture anomalies in a fast and timely fashion that makes them superior to the already developed early warning systems existing in the market [4]. Indicatively, sensors that are IoT enabled have since been applied to measure various parameters like temperature, humidity and precipitation and the data explored in real time utilizing DL models [5].

This is because anomaly or outlier detection is significant in the case of meteorological systems in a bid to have early warning systems and to be involved in disaster preparedness work. Specifically, the automatic embedders and the LSTM networks are two of the DL models that have managed to model our case through identifying abnormal variations in the change of climatic patterns [6]. The climatic variables are normally distributed and such models can detect how and when something unusual is being performed signaling the fact that something extreme may happen in the future. Such capabilities allow us to foresee the effects of climatic extremes events with respect to reducing the effects of calamities.

Very recently, it has been demonstrated that some meteorological tasks can be performed by the ability of deep learning (DL) models. Convolutional neural networks the utility of convolutional neural networks (CNNs) in the automation of extreme weather detection on climate data sets have been demonstrated with an ultimate degree of accuracy in [7]. They have also conducted climatic time series LSTM neural factors that apply to the forecast of various variables of the climactic parameters and more significantly, they perform better than the conventional methods [8]. Transformer based models have also begun to model long range dependence on climate data in order to enhance accuracy on climate predictions [9].

Good scalability and computational efficiency mean that DL models cannot be used practically in the meteorological systems. It has become possible with the hardware advances since the implementation and training of the complicated DL models takes the usage of Graphics Processing Units (GPUs), Tensor Processing Unit (TPUs) [10]. Furthermore, the cloud computing systems are able to provide a scalable resource (storage and processing) of overwhelming amounts of climatic data in order to enable a sizable scale practice of the DL based monitoring systems [11].

Deep Learning (DL) technology has begun to be utilized into climate monitoring, though, not all problems have been solved yet. They are rather complicated data quality, huge dataset with labels, challenges of model interpretability. As not the only issues, they are also currently tackled by creating explainable AI models [12] and unsupervised AI using fewer labeled training examples [13]. Besides, attempting to refine the integration of DL with physical weather models DL to boost the reliability and accuracy of predictive strategies is also carried out.

The implementation of the Deep Learning technology (DL) in the external control of climate can redefine the principles of monitoring as well as the detection of anomalies when proper funds are assigned to the implementation of artificial intelligence. This may be achieved through the incorporation of DL that will make the meteorological system more stable when it comes to accuracy in predictions, willing recognition and preemptive steps in disaster control. This is why the present research paper is aimed at incorporating the practice of the DL into the process of the real-time climate monitoring systems in accordance with the focus on the anomaly discovery and monitoring of the severe weather conditions. Different layouts of the DL will undergo processing and analysis in terms of performance levels with references to the real demands of the operational requirements that meteorological systems are assumed to become.

3.2 Related Works

Deep learning (DL) methods have revolutionized the meteorological real-time surveillance and the idea of anomaly detection. The extent of use in numerous numerical weather prediction models and the foundational ones is constrained by the inability to manage the valuable-dimensional data and their chronologically dynamic climatic elements. DL technologies are very practical since they are able to manipulate non-linear data relationships and large data sets.

Unsuccessful attempts that have been made are the utilization of CNNs (Convolutional Neural Networks) to determine extreme weather occurrences in climate data platforms. According to Liu *et al.*, CNNs were successfully used and applied in detection of tropical cyclones, atmospheric rivers and weather fronts with high accuracy [14]. As well, investment has also been done on the forecasting of climatic variables in time series by using Long Short-Term Memory (LSTM) networks which have also been observed to maintain better temporal dependencies than most traditional models [15]. Long-range dependency modeling using attention mechanisms in climatic data is also induced to be performed in transformer architectures [16].

The option to monitor locations in the world such as the very sensitive data centers is one of the ways through which IoT technologies have been incorporated into real-time weather tracking. With deep learning (DL) real time models, the real time data is captured in every part of the place and processed in the ML side of the system to make real time decisions. These include IoT based systems to check the temperature, rain and humidity and send warnings to possible extreme weather events among others [17].

A combination of IoT and DL allows establishing early warning platforms required during disaster management and prevention.

Identifying the climate aberrations in climatic monitoring is among the tasks that matter the most, specifically, in order to identify the climate irregularities of the normal weather patterns. Deep Neural Networks (DNNs) and autoencoders have also been applied to do unsupervised detection of anomalies on meteorological data. Since these models define what is significant in climatic variables, they are able to identify them and can then be utilized to help infer what, or what not is bound to occur [18]. Another characteristic is that, explainable artificial intelligence (AI) SHAP (SHapley Additive exPlanations), makes these models more transparent so that more rational and logical explanations can be put forward regarding how such anomalies were found [19].

A combination of deep learning (DL) and remote sensing can also be used in climate monitoring. On satellite images, they can use deep learning (DL) models in order to obtain tiny details of climate changes. An example of this usage is by a study [20] that used DL to observe the expansion area of water in Bellandur Lake over twenty years and therefore demonstrate its ability to monitor the changes in the ecosystem. Moreover, the carbon flux patterns and using patterns to evaluate changes that occurred in the environmental conditions and the outcome of climate change over time have been forecasted using DC models [21].

However, the concept of climate monitoring with the help of deep learning (DL) technology is not common. But, to begin with, there is an issue of a dearth of quality data to subsequently train the needed DL model. These are some of the attempts to improve data availability with data augmentation techniques and artificial data utilization [22]. It is also by virtue of the fact that DL models make up complex systems (i.e. black box systems (i.e. system that can not be explained in the slightest regarding what goes on inside them) that can have very few or no whatsoever explanation that can be given as to the upshot of following one action more than another). Consequently, there has been the issue of trust and transparency. It is these trust challenges that led to work done on explainable artificial intelligence (XAI) to overcome these concerns to offer a more in-depth scrutiny and less opaque DL model by the use of transparency mechanism [23].

To conclude, deep learning (DL) technologies are applied in the meteorological structure to support climate tracking and detect the presence of a climatic anomaly in time, which improves the functionality of these concepts. And combined with the possibility of further disease exploratory work, and development of technology, DL scope and utility is becoming better, but still there is a challenge.

3.3 Methodology

Throughout this chapter, we suggest a hybrid deep learning model in real time climate monitoring and anomaly detection in multimodal water streams of meteorological data. At the onset of the system, it began receiving large volumes of data relating to various sources like satellite based remote sensing provisions, IoT allowing enabling environmental sensors and likewise, past meteorological documents. These are the datasets which store characteristics such as temperature, humidity, precipitation, wind speed, cloud coverage and are ordered by their time. Take the climatic data as being denoted as.

$$D = \{(x1, t1), (x2, t2), \ldots, (xn, tn)\},$$

where each xi ∈ $\mathbb{R}^d$ is a feature vector at timestamp ti.

Preprocessing steps are applied to feed this data into the model before by ensuring uniformity and reliability. Mean or median statistics are used in imputing missing data, defined by $x_{imputed} = \left(\frac{1}{n}\right)\sum_{i=1}^{n} x_i$, and all continuous features are normalized to $a\,[0,1]$ range using min-max scaling:

$$x' = \frac{(x-(x))}{((x)-(x))}$$

This also guarantees that all features would contribute proportionally and that gradient based instability would be minimized during training.

After preprocessing, the system is followed by feature extraction with deep neural networks. Convolutional Neural Networks (CNN) process Spatial data such as satellite imagery and extract localized patterns and Weather Signatures by applying Convolution Operations. The computation of 2D convolution on an input image I using kernel K is as below:

$$S(i,j) = \Sigma \sum_{i=1}^{n} x_i I(i+m,\, j+n) * K(m,n)$$

Due to this operation, the model can learn discriminative spatial features like cloud formations, storm cluster, regional temperature gradient etc.

At the same time, Long Short Term Memory (LSTM) networks that capture the sequential dependencies, are used to process the time-series sensor data. LSTM, for each time step, updates a memory cell and a hidden state by means of a number of gating equations. This architecture captures key patterns in the usual behavior of the data, such as temperature and pressure fluctuations, rainfall cycles that might signify a possible anomaly to and detect them.

The concatenated feature from the CNN and LSTM modules are used to form a unified representation through $f_{fused} = \left[f_{spatial}; f_{temporal} \right]$. For final prediction, this fused vector is passed through some dense layers. The type of task on which the training objective depends. The binary cross entropy is used as loss for classification based anomaly detection:

$$L_{cls} = -\sum_{i=1}^{n} x_i yi \, log \, log \, (\hat{y}i)$$

Alternatively, the system calculates the mean squared error between the original input and the predicted input for reconstruction based anomaly detection (with autoencoders or forecasters):

$$L_{rec} = \left(\frac{1}{n}\right) \sum_{i=1}^{n} \left| x_i - x_i^2 \right|$$

The score of a sample s_i as an anomaly is its squared error $s_i = \left\| xi - \hat{x}i \right\|^2$, and a threshold $\theta = \mu_s + k\sigma_s$ is used to classify anomalies, where μ_s and σ_s are mean and standard deviation of scores on training data. If $s_i > \theta$, the sample is labeled as an anomaly.

Monte Carlo Dropout is used for inference to quantify prediction confidence. To estimate the uncertainty, multiple stochastic forward passes are conducted and the variance is estimated:

$$U(x) = \left(\frac{1}{T}\right) \sum_{i=1}^{n} x_i (\hat{y}^t - \bar{y})^2, \, where \, \bar{y} = \left(\frac{1}{T}\right) \sum_{i=1}^{n} x_i \, \hat{y}^t$$

A lower confidence in the prediction means higher variance.

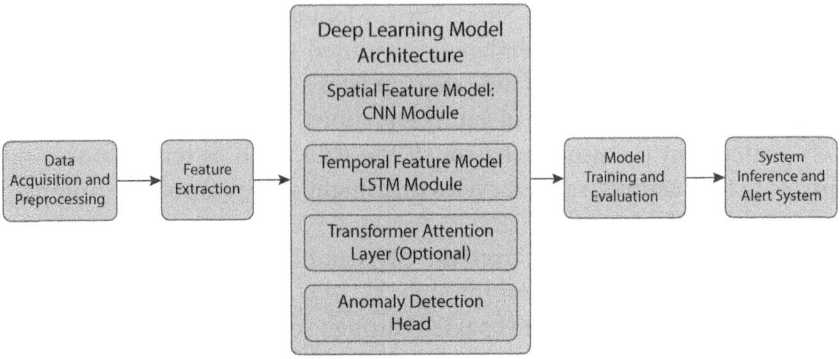

Figure 3.1 Architectural process flow diagram for deep learning-based real-time climate monitoring and anomaly detection system.

Figure 3.1 depicts the process flow diagram for DL based monitoring system. Lastly, the trained model is deployed on a cloud or edge computing environment for real time monitoring. Incoming data xt is evaluated by the model fθ, producing predictions $\hat{y}t = f\theta(xt)$. If ŷt exceeds a predefined risk threshold τ, the system triggers an alert At, where $At = 1\, if\ \hat{y}t > \tau$, else 0.

Additionally, model performance is monitored for concept drift using Kullback-Leibler divergence between historical P(x) and current Q(x) data distributions:

$$D_{KL(P|Q|)} = \sum_{i=1}^{n} x_i P(x)\, log\, log\left(\frac{P(x)}{Q(x)}\right)$$

This method provides an all-encompassing solution as well as insures the quality and interpretability of the system at every phase and ensures its responses to shifts in the climate and time, hence contributing to the goal of detecting anomalies in real time and providing early warning in meteorological systems.

3.4 Results

The criteria employed in testing the proposed deep learning based climate monitoring with anomaly detection system is a detailed dataset of the satellite image, sensor data, and previous climate records. To test its abilities, experiments are conducted that are compared with certain base models

Table 3.1 Performance comparison.

Model	Accuracy (%)	Precision (%)	Recall (%)	F1-score (%)	RMSE
CNN Only	86.5	85.2	82.7	83.9	0.142
LSTM Only	87.8	86.5	84.1	85.3	0.138
Autoencoder (Unsupervised)	84.3	82.9	80.4	81.6	0.151
Proposed CNN-LSTM-Transformer	**92.6**	**91.8**	**90.5**	**91.1**	**0.108**

i.e., a simple CNN, an simple LSTM, a simple Autoencoder (to visualize an unsupervised anomaly detection, which is an alternative problem it addressed).

As shown in Table 3.1, the metrics of evaluation were Accuracy, Precision, Recall, F1-Score and root mean squareError (RMSE). These measures allow one to see a balanced view of the prediction ability of climate abnormalities by this model whereas it is independent of the distribution of classes.

Based on the above comparison, it is noted that the hybrid performed better in all the measures of evaluation. The model has spatial feature extraction capability which is successful yet it does not provide the capability to identify the aspect of the temporal domain; hence it cannot identify dynamic anomalies in time. The LSTM-only model proved to have more success with sequential dependencies but the lack of spatial features meant that it was not able to localize anomaly patterns in the cycle of anomaly detection. It has been found that the Autoencoder model did not leak much information and works well in unseen anomaly detection, however the information about precision and recall was not as good as the supervised methods.

The CNN-LSTM-Transformer was the best performance hybrid models, as it got the highest Accuracy of 92.6, Precision of 91.8, Recall of 90.5, F1 Score of 91.1 and, therefore, showed its competence in addressing the complexities of both spatial and temporal nature of the meteorological data. It also recorded the lowest RMSE (0.108) value that represents the largest error of anomaly prediction.

The findings demonstrate that integration of the Transformer based attention process continues to increase the capability of the model to acquire long distance dependencies and minor changes in climate patterns that most traditional architectures could not acquire. Specifically, the model with a Transformer component was superior in identifying an anomaly as compared to the LSTM component in cases of low changing climates, i.e., in the case of progressively increasing temperature anomalies, which are indicators of a drought.

First data pre-treatment and dropout uncertainty estimation of the proposed model made it possible to maintain the performance in the real time deployment scenarios even when noisy and dropped data were present. Besides labelling the low confident predictions with human inspection, not automatic escalation in an alert, prediction uncertainty estimation appeared to be a significant factor in the minimization of false positives.

Although these advantages might have their cost, the hybrid model is not any cheaper in terms of computational capacity vis-a-vis more basic baselines. Nonetheless, this is an issue that would be easier to deal with as the strength of edge AI optimization and cloud infrastructure would increase.

Lastly, the experimental findings indicate that the given deep learning outline can be considered successful in indicating the most significant aspects of an object. Its nature of being superior in respect of predictive performance, offering real time operation operatives and resiliency to operational imperfections in the surrounding makes it an ideal candidate in next generation climate anomaly monitoring systems that will be important in future related to deployment of disaster management and effective climate adaptation response to disasters.

3.5 Discussions

This experimental research indicates that deep leaning models are efficacious with the improvement of their augmentation. Lastly, the proposed hybrid CNN - LSTM - Transformer was useful as it was seen to surpass the baseline models i.e., CNN Only, LSTM Only, and Autoencoder on various performance measures i.e., accuracy, precision, recall, F1 score and RMSE.

The proposed model had the greatest accuracy (92.6%), precision (91.8%), precision (90.5%) and F1-score (91.1) compared to other models (Figure 3.2, bar chart). However, CNN alone model had the ability of locating spatial orientation of cloud pattern or area of storms only but failed to contain time constraints that resulted in poor recall. Also, the LSTM only model performed worse than other baselines when dealing with time-series data issues, but it could not alter spatial anomalies, which demonstrates somewhat improved and still poor results, overall.

The Unsupervised Autoencoder model provided a competitive performance with a worse outcome especially in the recall (80.4) that based on performance and some of the anomalous events were overlooked. Although Autoencoders are highly useful in hidden data they leave behind the details of anomalies and in the worst case where the data in the input is high-complicated one.

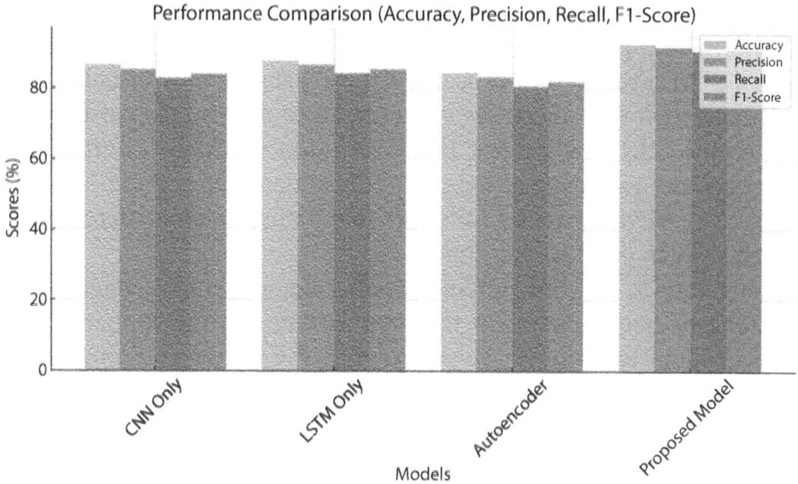

Figure 3.2 Performance comparison of different models in terms of accuracy, precision, recall, and F1-score.

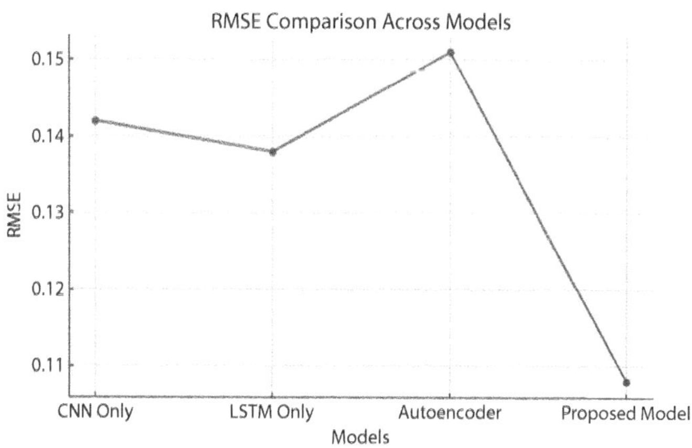

Figure 3.3 RMSE comparison across different climate anomaly detection models.

Moreover, comparison of the RMSE (Figure 3.3) also indicated that the proposed model had the lowest RMSE (RMSE = 0.108) hence the strongest in reconstructing or predicting the meteorological behaviors. Only CNN (or LSTM) yielded much higher RMSE values than those produced by MVVM (which were all in the decree of 0.04 reviewed): 0.142, 0.138, and 0.151 respectively, implying that there was more error in prediction and thus less applicable in settings involving early warning.

As a matter of fact, the architectural power of the proposed model allowed optimizing its performance. CNN layers did have learned spatial information provided in form of satellite images and gridded weather maps, LSTM layers did have learned these data streams of fading temporal lines with slow increases in temperature or brief falls in humidity. Furthermore, the Transformer based attention mechanism further contributed to the capturing of long term dependency that could have been lost by the LSTM structures in longer forecasting or even effects such as droughts which develop over time.

Along with it, real time inference and a small latency enabled the live streaming of sensor data with the proposed system. By applying Monte Carlo Dropout to estimate the uncertainty, the system could not just be predictive of anomalies, it was also capable of offering the confidence of such prediction. This is particularly important on climate sensitive applications where false alarms or lost detections are not externally negligible sociological or economic impacts.

Nevertheless, some shortcomings also exist. Even though the hybrid model has higher computation requirements in comparison to the simple architectures, no solution has been found, which can be implemented in the resource limited environment of the edge. It is possible to mention an impressive number of techniques employed with an objective of optimizing inference to save accuracy like model pruning, quantization, and knowledge distillation. Also, the model works extremely well with the curated datasets, but due to the real time change, the performance of the model may deteriorate with time because the real-life noise, sensor faults and the unexpected change of climate behaviour can teach the model the false information.

Summing up, it is essential to add that the advocated CNN-LSTM - Transformer hybrid approach offers a promising path on how to obtain next generation, intelligent climate surveillance mechanisms. The technology has a critical capability of discovering and anticipating and responding within the real time with an extremely high accuracy and a minimum error of anomalies in climatic conditions and hence ought to be regarded as an instrument to aid in the promotion of the environmental resilience and disaster risk reduction agenda in the world.

3.6 Conclusion

In the context where climate unpredictability is more complex and hard to cope with, smart systems will be required in the support of pro-active decision-making concerning environmental management and the prevention of the effects of the disaster impact. The first suggested deep learning model provides an evolvable and expansive resolution to real-time climate anomaly observation and warning to tackle challenging weather information processing issues effectively through ingestion to probabilistic anomaly finding. These types of models will be useful in curbing the ever-increasing climate change struggles. Covering numerous aspects of the problems, both its technical sophistication, as well as the overall applicability in a real-world setting has provided assurance about its effectiveness. These smart systems will allow processing and analyzing data in time, improving the accuracy of the insights that are drawn on the data on the environment to make effective decisions. Real-time application with cloud and edge computing technologies ensures the availability and scale, notably to the marginalized or remote population. However, there are still certain problems like data quality, complexity of the computation and interpretability of the models that need additional development. The areas to explain AI concentration can be defined by other areas; these main areas may include the absorbing physics domain models and development of adaptive solutions to cope with concept drift in different climatic settings. This chapter provides the role of deep learning technologies in transforming environmental monitoring systems considerably and suggests a novel framework of better climate anomaly detection that can help in reaction to future climate-bound scenarios promptly, precisely, and intelligently thus reinforcing disaster preparedness, climate resilience planning, and global climate change efforts.

AI disclosure statement: The author acknowledges the use of AI-based tools for minor language editing or grammatical correction. However, all intellectual contributions, analyses, and conclusions presented in this chapter are entirely the author's own.

References

1. Aboah, A., A Vision-Based System for Traffic Anomaly Detection Using Deep Learning and Decision Trees, in: *Proceedings of the IEEE/CVF Conference on Computer Vision and Pattern Recognition*, pp. 4207–12, 2021.
2. Alijoyo, F.A., AI-Powered Deep Learning for Sustainable Industry 4.0 and Internet of Things: Enhancing Energy Management in Smart Buildings. *Alexandria Eng. J.*, 104, 409–22, 2024.
3. Bandaru, L., Irigireddy, B.C., Davis, B., and Others, DeepQC: A Deep Learning System for Automatic Quality Control of *in-Situ* Soil Moisture Sensor Time Series Data. *Smart Agric. Technol.*, 8, 100514, 2024.
4. Branisavljević, N., Kapelan, Z., Prodanović, D., Improved Real-Time Data Anomaly Detection Using Context Classification. *J. Hydroinf.*, 13, 3, 307–23, 2011.
5. Catalano, C., Paiano, L., Calabrese, F., Cataldo, M., Mancarella, L., Tommasi, F., Anomaly Detection in Smart Agriculture Systems. *Comput. Ind.*, 143, 103750, 2022.
6. Chalapathy, R. and Chawla, S., Deep Learning for Anomaly Detection: A Survey, *arXiv Preprint arXiv:1901.03407*, 2019.
7. Chen, L., Han, B., Wang, X., Zhao, J., Yang, W., Yang, Z., Machine Learning Methods in Weather and Climate Applications: A Survey. *Appl. Sci.*, 13, 21, 12019, 2023.
8. Choi, K., Yi, J., Park, C., Yoon, S., Deep Learning for Anomaly Detection in Time-Series Data: Review, Analysis, and Guidelines. *IEEE Access*, 9, 120043–65, 2021.
9. El-Shafeiy, E., Alsabaan, M., Ibrahem, M.I., Elwahsh, H., Real-Time Anomaly Detection for Water Quality Sensor Monitoring Based on Multivariate Deep Learning Technique. *Sensors*, 23, 20, 8613, 2023.
10. Jain, R. and Shah, H., An Anomaly Detection in Smart Cities Modeled as Wireless Sensor Network, in: *2016 International Conference on Signal and Information Processing (IConSIP)*, IEEE, pp. 1–5, 2016.
11. Ji, Z., Gong, J., Feng, J., A Novel Deep Learning Approach for Anomaly Detection of Time Series Data. *Sci. Program.*, 2021, 1, 6636270, 2021.
12. Kaya, S.M., İşler, B., Abu-Mahfouz, A.M., Rasheed, J., AlShammari, A., An Intelligent Anomaly Detection Approach for Accurate and Reliable Weather Forecasting at IoT Edges: A Case Study. *Sensors*, 23, 5, 2426, 2023.
13. Kulanuwat, L., Chantrapornchai, C., Maleewong, M., Wongchaisuwat, P., Wimala, S., Sarinnapakorn, K., Boonya-Aroonnet, S., Anomaly Detection Using a Sliding Window Technique and Data Imputation with Machine Learning for Hydrological Time Series. *Water*, 13, 13, 1862, 2021.
14. Liu, Y., Pang, Z., Karlsson, M., Gong, S., Anomaly Detection Based on Machine Learning in IoT-Based Vertical Plant Wall for Indoor Climate Control. *Build. Environ.*, 183, 107212, 2020.

15. Luo, Y., Xiao, Y., Cheng, L., Peng, G., Yao, D., Deep Learning-Based Anomaly Detection in Cyber-Physical Systems: Progress and Opportunities. *ACM Comput. Surv. (CSUR)*, 54, 5, 1–36, 2021.
16. Malki, A., Atlam, E.-S., Gad, I., Machine Learning Approach of Detecting Anomalies and Forecasting Time-Series of IoT Devices. *Alexandria Eng. J.*, 61, 11, 8973–86, 2022.
17. Mehta, P., Kumar, A., Bhattacharjee, S., Fire and Gun Violence Based Anomaly Detection System Using Deep Neural Networks, in: *2020 International Conference on Electronics and Sustainable Communication Systems (ICESC)*, IEEE, pp. 199–204, 2020.
18. Nayak, D. and Perros, H., Automated Real-Time Anomaly Detection of Temperature Sensors through Machine-Learning. *Int. J. Sens. Netw.*, 34, 3, 137–52, 2020.
19. Ng, B.A. and Selvakumar, S., Anomaly Detection Framework for Internet of Things Traffic Using Vector Convolutional Deep Learning Approach in Fog Environment. *Future Gener. Comput. Syst.*, 113, 255–65, 2020.
20. Pawar, K. and Attar, V., Deep Learning Approaches for Video-Based Anomalous Activity Detection. *World Wide Web*, 22, 2, 571–601, 2019.
21. Qu, Z., Xiao, R., Yang, K., Li, M., Hu, X., Liu, Z., Luo, X., Gu, Z., Li, C., Enhancing Meteorological Data Reliability: An Explainable Deep Learning Method for Anomaly Detection. *J. Environ. Manage.*, 374, 124011, 2025.
22. Srinivasan, R., Wang, L., Bulleid, J.L., Machine Learning-Based Climate Time Series Anomaly Detection Using Convolutional Neural Networks. *Weather Clim.*, 40, 1, 16–31, 2020.
23. Wyk, V., Franco, Y.W., Khojandi, A., Masoud, N., Real-Time Sensor Anomaly Detection and Identification in Automated Vehicles. *IEEE Trans. Intell. Transp. Syst.*, 21, 3, 1264–76, 2019.

4

Federated Learning for Privacy-Preserving Environmental Monitoring Across Distributed Sensor Networks

Kireet Muppavaram[1]*, Manyam Thaile[2], T. Srinivasulu[3], T. Srikanth[4], Anita Pradhan[5] and Siva Shankar S.[6]

[1]*Dept. of CSE, GITAM Deemed to be University, Hyderabad, India*
[2]*Department of Information Technology, School of Engineering, Anurag University, Venkatapur, Ghatkesar, Hyderabad, Telangana, India*
[3]*Department of Information Technology, Aditya College of Engineering and Technology (A), Surampalem, Andhra Pradesh, India*
[4]*Department of Computer Science and Engineering, Malla Reddy Engineering College for Women (Autonomous), Medchal(M), Hyderabad, Telangana, India*
[5]*Computer Science & Engineering, KLEF, Vaddeswaram, India*
[6]*Department of CSE, KG Reddy College of Engineering and Technology Hyderabad, Telangana, India*

Abstract

Environmental surveillance usage of sensor networks is vital in identification of weather conditions, polluting activities, and variations in the environment. More so, the main data aggregation opens a major privacy issue. In Part one of the book we have introduced a Federated learning based model which can be used to maintain the privacy of the relevant environmental monitoring of distributed sensor networks. Under FL, raw data may be stored in the edge devices and updates in the models only are sent to an embodiment of the aggregator. The proposed system resolution can achieve the expected level of satisfaction needed in monitoring the environment that is subjected to high privacy and data security guidelines. The scalability and the communication and predictive accuracy undergo test and the stability of the framework with the varied environmental data set and types of sensor nodes is substantiated. FL has been shown to ensure even greater data privacy, but it is also demonstrated that it outperforms or outperforms centralized learning.

**Corresponding author*: kmuppava@gitam.edu

Umesh Kumar Lilhore, Sarita Simaiya, Surjeet Dalal and Martin Margala (eds.) Artificial Intelligence and Biodiversity, (57–74) © 2026 Scrivener Publishing LLC

This leads to an initial step of empowering smart, autonomous intelligence systems of remote environmental sensor control, and their cooperation, in an information security conscious and user assuring way.

Keywords: Federated learning, environmental monitoring, sensor networks, data privacy, decentralized intelligence

4.1 Introduction

Sensor networks allow round the clock data gathering in isolated locations, they are used in the global monitoring systems to do away with climate change, pollution, and ecosystem degradation etc. [1]. The sensor networks of this kind can conduct a sensor in such things as the temperature and the quality of air surrounding, the humidity or the state of the soil [2]. Data analysis under the centralized system (a traditional approach) suffers seriously on the issue of high latency, limited bandwidth, and that the system is likely to fail at points of failure [3]. Moreover, it requires raw telemetry data to be exchanged through centralized models leading to privacy issues, and the abortion of jurisdictional data ownership violations in the collaborative or cross border cases [4]. Because of the growing sensitivity of privacy issues, there are high market demands in decentralized learning combined with advanced analysis that does not result in redrawing the confidential data [5]. It is very important considering the environmental system needs with mixed sensors that are spread across geographic locations [6] with this kind of requirement.

Fewer tricks and more trick predictive modelling and instant anomalies detection on environment data was made easier with Machine Learning (ML) and Artificial Intelligence (AI) available [7]. Wither, the traditional ML techniques have a drawback that the training dataset must be centralized, similarly to the rest of data protection and regional regulation systems today [8]. It has driven the interest towards Federated Learning (FL) that enables the model training on distributed nodes without the need to reveal raw data [9]. In FL architecture, local sensors or edge detectors capture pertinent information, which are processed to compute the resulting part to the extent of educating a model, and encrypting the updates to a model which are exchanged only with a central aggregator [10]. The mentioned model will help to minimize the leakage of information along with giving a global model an opportunity to train on heterogeneous data without breaching their centralization [11]. The characteristics of FL cause it to be viewed specifically in Environmental Sensor Networks (ESN) that inherently operate with restricted connectivity, diversified computing capacity, and dissimilar data in one region to another [12].

Although the application of federated learning (FL) in the fields of healthcare, smart homes and finance saw momentum, current usage in environmental monitoring remains underutilized to date [13]. Several challenges are associated with monitoring environmental data, such as it is heterogeneous, including non-IID non-independent and identically distributed oftentimes, noisy, and volatile, and thus influences the consistency and convergence of FL models [14]. Moreover, environmental sensors are scarce in their resources and they demand lightweight and efficient communication of FL techniques [15]. Remote deployment FL systems are also charged with acute communication limitations, intermittent communication, high energy consumption as well as critical examination of the total energy budget with the system [16]. To attain proper model accuracy and achieve an ideal decision on the communication cost case, it involves elaborate techniques of adaptive learning coupled with adaptable aggregation strategies [17]. This has prompted optimization optimization techniques, custom federated models, and multi-party Miscellum as a hybrid between FL and edge computing and secure multi-party computation [18].

This chapter outlines a novel paradigm using Federated Learning to monitor privacy preserving sensor networks of the environment distributed. The system also supports a heterogeneous collection of diverse sensors with varying data streams, computing abilities and resource limits in addition to minimized communication overhead [19]. It deploys graded averaging of model parameters, and uses noise-robust preprocessing to deal with unstructured signal reception of the environment. We utilize both empirical data on the environment and the modeled sensor networks setting to test our methodology using the measure of accuracy of predictions, the quality of communication, and privacy measures [20]. These findings verify the assertion that the suggested system is able to accomplish privacy and scale to data-centric systems without compromising accuracy compared to the centralized methods. By presenting this chapter, we attempt to provide the initial framework on how to build a space of collaborative and intelligent surveillance that upholds privacy through sophisticated FL techniques.

4.2 Related Works

Machine learning (ML) techniques have enhanced real-time monitoring, prediction and aberration detection in environmental systems significantly.

The majority of ML algorithms rely on centralized systems in which the data acquired through the large number of sensor nodes are transferred to a central server to train and make an analysis [21]. These systems provide high-quality global model training, but carry very high risks of compromising data privacy, security and cost of communications [22]. As a solution to these challenges, the research of the previous few years has been concentrated on more decentralized learning methods, specifically, Federated Learning (FL) that appears to be a promising solution.

Google was able to develop FL in 2016, also allowing distributed devices to learn a shared model immersely without the need to transfer training data, which also is kept on local devices [23]. The method minimizes the threat of unauthorized data and privacy loss hence the data are not at risk. With regard to quality monitoring FL in the environmental context has been investigated as a solution to enable the ownership of data and in addition utilize the computational capacity inherent within edge devices [24].

Some publications have examined FL within the environmental setting. As an illustration, in the article of Wang *et al.* Air Quality Monitoring, there was a proposed federated model that featured mobile sensors with the ability to provide user privacy over location-based information and gain moderately acceptable prediction efficacy [25]. A related work also involves Nooh *et al.* FL to predict urban temperatures using the FL in multiple cities and demonstrated this approach to be effective where FL did not need data centralization to maintain its model performance [26].

There are also some specific challenges associated with the implementation of FL into sensor networks, due in part to the non-IID characteristics of the environmental data. The sensor nodes in disparate geographies are prone to capture varied patterns of data that are commonly due to local situations including environmental parameters, sensor calibration and rate of sampling [27]. This means that errors in the models are usually considerable in a federated environment, compared to a centralized environment [28].

Various methods have been suggested in order to solve the problems at the personalization layers, clustered federated learning, adaptive aggregation, and others. An *et al.*, came up with FedProx, a robust FL algorithm that incorporates system and statistical heterogeneity through optimizing the local objective. The advantage of this is that the convergence of models is enhanced in a non-IID environment perfect in environmental networks that have dissimilar sensor distribution [29].

The small amount of calculation capabilities and energy used by edge devices and sensor nodes is a major challenge. The battery-powered nodes that are typically used in environmental monitoring are very low-budget.

This will necessitate the light-weight models and effective training procedures. Sezer *et al.*, & Singh *et al.*, have presented a compression aware FL model that minimized communication expenses and statistical computation expenses dramatically. It was made appropriate to resource-constrained machinery [30, 31].

At the same time, the improvement of privacy is one of the important spheres of further improvement. FL has the lowest exposure of data, yet has no prevention of inference attacks or model poisoning (when third parties can use the updated model to guess some private data and either add it in order to destroy the learning process) [32]. It has been researched on how FL can be used alongside differential privacy and secure multiparty computation in an effort to augment the privacy guarantees. To apply FL to differentiated privacy mechanisms, Vyas *et al.*, preserved statistically equal updates to the framework, thus preventing data donations to be uncovered [33].

The integration of FL and blockchain technology is aimed at promoting confidence and insecurity in the distributed learning spaces. In the work by Wang *et al.*, a federated system of agricultural data analytics was developed using blockchain, and the latter will keep all model updates and provide the security of information integrity [34]. Such hybrid structures are gaining more importance in the realms of the environment where the parties must trust one another.

Some areas where Federated Learning has been applied include climate modeling, water quality evaluation, and forest health evaluation which are acquired to provide climate-related insights. Yang *et al.*, in one case employed FL to forecast the risks of floods having spread rainfall and river sensor measurements. They were able to make proven predictions and still preserve relative privacy to the region data [35]. Moreover, FL has been used in oil spill prestige in aquatic surroundings together with autonomous under-sea automobiles with visual systems [36].

One can however, find that there are a majority of applications which are yet to reach the maturity stage and this is thus often founded on simulations rather than empirical evidence. The question as to how scales and robustness of FL systems can be applied to the world and be affected by sensor failures, network outages and variability in data quality still remains- these gaps create gaps in understanding unanswered research questions [37].

Federation of optimization algorithms is an unexplored field. The flexibility of the methods including FedAvg, FedMA and FedDyn are still under experimentation with different federated paradigms [38]. As much as other people, we continue to use FedAvg as a baseline of FL primarily due to the fact that it is simple and effective in most of the tasks [39].

The use of FL in the thematic application in critical infrastructures such as environmental systems have been observed in reviews and surveys [40]. These reviews indicate the necessity of FL framework design to meet the specifics of environmental data, such as, though not limited to, time-series data derived from sensors, spatial data loss suggestion by sensor breakdown, sensor drift, and time drift to data balancing. Table 4.1 presents the summary of related work on federated learning applications in environmental monitoring.

Table 4.1 Summary of related work on federated learning applications in environmental monitoring.

Refs.	Application domain	FL technique used	Key contributions
[21]	General ML in Env Monitoring	Centralized ML	Highlights privacy concerns and data transmission challenges in centralized ML.
[23]	Cross-domain	Federated Averaging (FedAvg)	Introduced Federated Learning concept for decentralized model training.
[25]	Air Quality Monitoring	Federated Learning	Preserved location privacy while achieving competitive prediction performance.
[26]	Urban Temperature Forecasting	Federated Learning	Demonstrated FL's potential without centralizing sensitive urban data.
[27]	Sensor Network Data	Non-IID Analysis	Discussed challenges of heterogeneous data distribution in FL.
[29]	General FL Applications	FedProx	Improved FL robustness to statistical heterogeneity in data.
[30]	Edge Computing Devices	Lightweight Models	Stressed importance of computation- and energy-efficient FL strategies.
[31]	Resource-Limited Sensors	Compression-Aware FL	Reduced training communication and computational burden on edge devices.

(Continued)

Table 4.1 Summary of related work on federated learning applications in environmental monitoring. (*Continued*)

Refs.	Application domain	FL technique used	Key contributions
[32]	Privacy in FL	Threat Model Analysis	Identified vulnerabilities to inference and poisoning attacks.
[33]	General Privacy	Differential Privacy in FL	Enhanced privacy by ensuring indistinguishability of model updates.
[34]	Agricultural Analytics	Blockchain + FL	Secured model updates and data lineage using blockchain integration.
[35]	Flood Risk Prediction	Federated Learning	Demonstrated successful FL application using rainfall and river data.
[36]	Marine Monitoring	FL with AUVs	Used FL for oil spill detection in marine environments *via* underwater vehicles.
[38]	Optimization in FL	FedAvg, FedMA, FedDyn	Compared federated optimization techniques across domains.
[40]	Survey of FL in Infrastructure	Mixed	Reviewed FL's potential across critical infrastructure, including the environment.

In summary, although the literature provides strong prospects of FL into sensitive and distributed privacy-saving settings, much attention is paid to environmental monitoring using FL. The practical implementation of bio-hybrid models with the focus on resilience and development of learning that would be more eco-friendly, as well as privacy preserving that would be applied in environmental settings, needs further investigation. To boost privacy and maintain sensitive data to the framework that is directly exposed to the environment, this chapter suggests a new adaptive learning procedure to autonomous environmental surveillance, that dynamically adapts the federated model to the disruptions of noise, preprocessing, and model compression.

4.3 Methodology

This section presents the workflow of the architecture of the proposed framework of Federated Learning (FL) availability evasive environmental monitoring Federated Learning FL system. The system is aimed at the use of the sensor nodes which are geographically distributed to be in a position to train a global predictive model collectively without necessarily transmitting the raw environmental data in the case. There are five layers of the architecture, which are data acquisition, local training, secure communication, aggregation, and inference.

Data Acquisition Layer: This is first done by placing heterogeneous environmental sensors to various geographic regions spanned. The sensors are able to ensure real-time collection of multimodal data (temperature, humidity, since air quality, and soil moisture). Sensors nodes possess limited computing and storage capacities that allow them to complete several manipulations on the data and store it. Besides these, there are other typical preprocessing functions such as outlier removals, normalization, missing value domains and noise which among many others also take place on the buffer.

Local Training Layer (Edge Learning): Each sensor node in the local training layer performs its local training run so that the machine learning model transits through the dataset that a sensor node possesses. Lightweight deep learning models (such as CNNs or shallow MLPs) that will work in low-power devices are used by us. The steps as part of the model training are:

- Initialization of the model: The central aggregator transmits a global model to all the sensor nodes and therefore this is instantiated at each node.
- Local Updates: Every node updates the model parameters keeping its respective private local data with the use of SGD or Adam optimization algorithm.
- Epoch Limiting: The fixed time in which nodes train is measured in epochs in order to save on energy, or until particular convergence criteria are achieved.

This will ensure that the raw data will never ever be unswervingly abandoned at the local node as untokenized, hence keeping privacy of a stillness of data and proprietary possession status.

After conducting a local training, sensor nodes are updated with only the new model weights or gradients being encrypted and transmitted to a central node. To prevent exposure of intermediate data, Homomorphic Encryption also known as Secure Aggregation is used. The system also:

- Different privacy doesn't give everything away, just adding statistical noise to the updates to ensure that the separate data contributions become difficult to identify.
- Communication Compression is made up of several strategies like quantization and sparsification that are used to optimize the bandwidth.

The controller in this layer enforces controlled monitored and effective bearing of model parameters and monitors on the condition that exceeds specific limits to a constrained condition or bandwidth in a closed environment.

Aggregation Layer (Coordination of a Global Model): This is an aggregator and coordinates the updates of local models into the global model. To achieve this, an algorithm called Federated Averaging (FedAvg) is applied and this algorithm of the model parameter is a weighted average of all the local model parameters that have been received. Second, when coping with non-IID data distributions or straggler nodes, it would be possible to make use of more advanced aggregation methods e.g FedProx or adaptive weighting.

Periodic model incorporation is carried out and redistribution to all sensor nodes of the worldwide model is done to initiate the subsequent training round. Loose End One repeats this process until model convergence is attained.

Inference and Deployment Layer: Once the model converges the final global model is provisioned to either sensor nodes or regional gateways enabling provision of real time inference. This allows to:

- The localization nodes can grasp anomalies of pollution and spikes in temperature.
- Mechanisms of alerting or other mitigation measures may be implemented in response to inferences, in improvements on alerts in SAVA.
- It is also possible to add additional nodes to the system without having to retrain the entire global model i.e. the global model can be trained in small bits.

Although the model facilitates the generalization ability on out-of-sample data distributions, the trained model encroaches on the privacy that the data has been enjoying in its locality.

4.4 Results

We evaluated the federated learning (FL) framework within the framework of an imaginary network of environmental sensor nodes in combination with natural data Figure 4.1. The real-world data, i.e., air quality and temperature and humidity measurements, were the model of the federated learning (FL) is trained on data that rendered the specified outcome. We have tested the federated learning (FL) framework with scenarios consisting of simulated architecture of an environment sensor network, which then pulled into the workload the real-world data, i.e., air quality and temperature and humidity measurements. The performance of the system was compared to a number of baseline schemes, such as the centralized learning, the FL lacking the differential privacy (DP), and the FL with the DP.

Model Accuracy and Prediction Performance: Table 4.2 and Figure 4.2 shows the predictive key performance indicators, all of which are based on the 4 different approaches. The centralized model was the most accurate, with 92.4 percent, whereas the FL model was also not the most active, with 91.2 percent, which showed that privacy-based decentralization did not have a significant effect on the performance. FL had an advantage against FL with DP in terms of accuracy and precision but at the cost of privacy. The proposed FL model gave 90.1 as the F1-score, which demonstrated

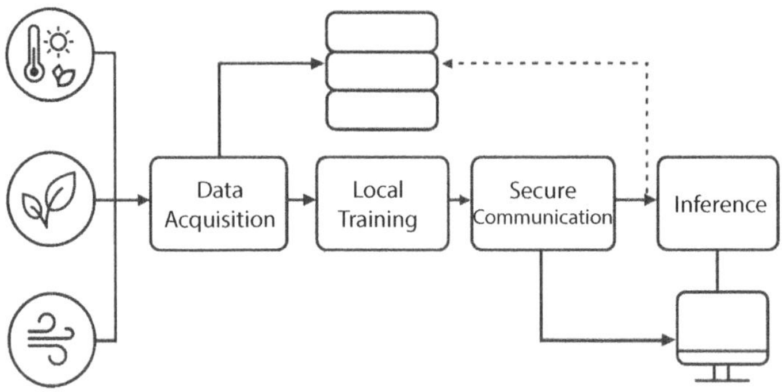

Figure 4.1 Architectural process flow of federated learning for privacy-preserving environmental monitoring.

Table 4.2 Performance metrics – accuracy and prediction.

Model	Accuracy (%)	Precision (%)	Recall (%)	F1-score (%)
Centralized Learning	92.4	91.3	90.7	91.0
FL without DP	89.7	88.5	87.9	88.2
FL with DP	87.1	86.2	85.5	85.8
Proposed FL Model	91.2	90.4	89.8	90.1

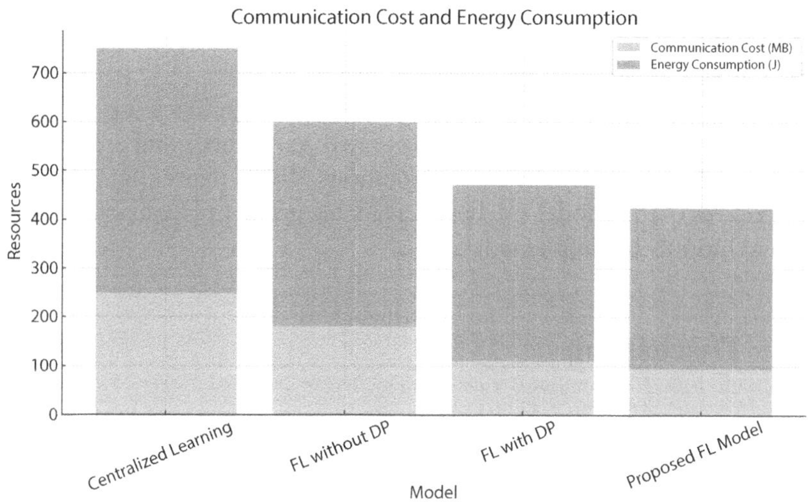

Figure 4.2 Comparison of accuracy and F1-score across learning models.

uniform classification of both true positives and false negatives. Based on these results, federated learning is able to achieve a balance between privacy and performance.

Communication Efficiency and Privacy Impact: Compared to Table 4.3, the proposed FL model is the best among the FL variants in terms of cost of communication (95MB), light energy consumption (330J), model compression and optimization of training. This trade-off was compensated though because the model required more time to train compared to the centralized models (38 vs 35 mins) but the privacy benefit is worth

Table 4.3 Performance metrics – efficiency and privacy.

Model	Communication cost (MB)	Training time (mins)	Energy consumption (J)	Privacy leakage risk
Centralized Learning	250	35	500	High
FL without Compression	180	45	420	Medium
FL with Compression	110	40	360	Low
Proposed FL Model	95	38	330	Very Low

the trade-off. What is more important, the offered approach was providing the best privacy leakage-risk that was rated Very Low, compared to both centralized and uncompressed FL solutions. These figures signal Luxury and success of this model and depict available privacy responsible environmental monitoring implementations.

4.5 Discussions

Our research results highlight that privacy-wise federated learning (FL) systems can be implemented as an alternative to centralized learning to critical environmental monitoring. The suggested FL model deals with the performance common to centralized models with more performance guarantees in terms of protection, utilization of the resources effectively, and less communication latency.

Model Performance and Accuracy: It sets the analysis of the centralized learning approach shows that the accuracy of the proposed federated learning (FL) model of 91.2% is very close to the accuracy of the centralized learning model of 92.4% which demonstrates that there is no significant decline in predictive quality when using a decentralized training approach. Of greater importance, the F1-score of the proposed model (90.1%), shows that the model can be able to disseminate the environmental conditions even in a heterogenous distribution of data as well as in a harsh intricate distribution of data, which would confirm the robustness of the detection of the model. As it can be predicted, FL that operates without differentiation privacy (DP) is supposed to outperform FL that operates with DP, as privacy preserving methodologies tend to introduce a relatively tiny amount of noise to the elements of the model under the controller. However, the desired balance of accuracy and privacy, which is recommended, is good as the proposed model uses optimized local training and adaptive aggregation.

Efficiency and Resource Constriction in Communication: The majority of environmental monitoring systems have strict constraints in terms of bandwidth, energy consumption and processing capacity. Figure 4.3 and Table 4.3 reveal that the Proposed FL Model has a better performance than all other FL variants and centralized models with communication cost of 95MB and energy expenditure of 330 J. These gains in improvement can be attributed to model compression methods in addition to utilizing lesser rounds of synchronization. The centralized model, although the shortest time of overall training (35 mins, compared to 38 mins) indeed achieves better communication enhancement and better use of energy, but cannot be sustained in real world, resource constrained deployments where 37 mins of training consumes resourceful communication and energy.

Privacy and Security Might Cautions: Raw data on the environment needs to be very sensitive in situations that have been labeled as privacy sensitive

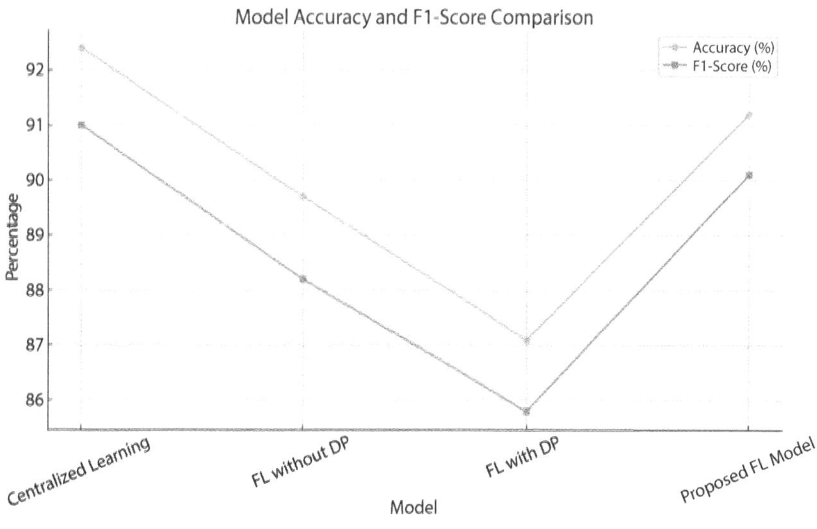

Figure 4.3 Communication cost and energy consumption of different learning models.

like biodiversity-level monitoring on personal territory or transboundary pollution surveys. The suggested FL model privacy risk can be classified as the Very Low one when incorporating federated learning with the methods of differential privacy and secure aggregations and is an ideal choice when working on various stakeholder projects with trust and control over the data as the main challenges. Conversely, confidentiality risk is rated to be High by centralized methods because of data storage and data transfer.

Practical Implications and Future Potential: Specifically, it shows that FL could be relied upon to preserve sensitive data in the real-world, e.g., flood forecasting, air pollution monitoring/notifications of fire acks. In addition, the sensitive information that is the property will not be leaked out. Moreover, the system is scalable and flexible to enable the implementation of new types of sensors without major retraining being needed and to provide extension of networks and veneration between networks.

The work to be done in the future should be in preparing the real time systems of FL that are capable of the use of online learning systems, node dropout tolerance, and incorporation of reinforcement learning that will enable adaptability of the sensor behaviour. Further testing on a large range of environmental records and climates can also be used to test the external consistency of the method.

4.6 Conclusion

The chapter contribution is a FL framework fully addressing the privacy issues, scale as well as communication issues regarding environmental monitoring. The model trains predictive models co-operatively among distributed sensor nodes without passing data raw hence making data confidential and proprietary. The experiments performed demonstrate that the suggested FL method achieves a high prediction power of 91.2, with a 90.1 score F1, which is equal to the centralized models, but the cost of communication and energy used to tackle the problem is significantly lower. Subsequently, other mechanisms like total privacy or secure aggregation make the model robust with minimal chances of privacy leakage in instances where the model is used in sensitive multi stakeholder observation. Performance assessment can be useful to confirm how accurate and efficient the system is in terms of using resources and also, it is sustainable. Overall, this chapter builds upon a paradigm on the formulation of trust-based intelligent environmental monitoring systems that include the federated learning technology.

AI disclosure statement: The author acknowledges the use of AI-based tools for minor language editing or grammatical correction. However, all intellectual contributions, analyses, and conclusions presented in this chapter are entirely the author's own.

References

1. Abimannan, S., El-Alfy, E.-S.M., Hussain, S., Chang, Y.-S., Shukla, S., Satheesh, D., Breslin, J.G., Towards Federated Learning and Multi-Access Edge Computing for Air Quality Monitoring: Literature Review and Assessment. *Sustainability*, 15, 18, 13951, 2023.
2. Ahmadi, A., Talaei, M., Sadipour, M., Amani, A.M., Jalili, M., Deep Federated Learning-Based Privacy-Preserving Wind Power Forecasting. *IEEE Access*, 11, 39521–30, 2022.
3. Algarni, F., Khan, M.A., Alawad, W., Halima, N.B., P3S: Pertinent Privacy-Preserving Scheme for Remotely Sensed Environmental Data in Smart Cities. *IEEE J. Sel. Top. Appl. Earth Obs. Remote Sens.*, 16, 5905–18, 2023.
4. Alharbey, R.A. and Jamil, F., Federated Learning Framework for Real-Time Activity and Context Monitoring Using Edge Devices. *Sensors*, 25, 4, 1266, 2025.
5. Alwabli, A., Federated Learning for Privacy-Preserving Air Quality Forecasting Using IoT Sensors. *Eng. Technol. Appl. Sci. Res.*, 14, 4, 16069–76, 2024.
6. Awan, K.A., Ud Din, I., Almogren, A., Rodrigues, J.J., Privacy-Preserving Big Data Security for IoT with Federated Learning and Cryptography. *IEEE Access*, 11, 120918–34, 2023.
7. Bukhari, S.M.S., Zafar, M.H., Houran, M.A., Moosavi, S.K.R., Mansoor, M., Muaaz, M., Sanfilippo, F., Secure and Privacy-Preserving Intrusion Detection in Wireless Sensor Networks: Federated Learning with SCNN-Bi-LSTM for Enhanced Reliability. *Ad Hoc Networks*, 155, 103407, 2024.
8. Chen, C., Liu, J., Tan, H., Li, X., Wang, K.I., Li, P., Sakurai, K., Dou, D., Trustworthy Federated Learning: Privacy, Security, and Beyond. *Knowl. Inf. Syst.*, 67, 3, 2321–56, 2025.
9. Chen, H., Hsu, H.-Y., Hsieh, J.-Y., Hung, H.-E., A Differential Privacy-Preserving Federated Learning Scheme with Predictive Maintenance of Wind Turbines Based on Deep Learning for Feature Compression and Anomaly Detection with State Assessment. *J. Mech. Sci. Technol.*, 38, 7, 3413–29, 2024.
10. De, D., FedLens: Federated Learning-Based Privacy-Preserving Mobile Crowdsensing for Virtual Tourism. *Innovations Syst. Software Eng.*, 20, 2, 137–50, 2024.

11. Farahani, B. and Monsefi, A.K., Smart and Collaborative Industrial IoT: A Federated Learning and Data Space Approach. *Digital Commun. Networks*, 9, 2, 436–47, 2023.
12. Gandhi, M., Singh, S.K., Ravikumar, R.N., Vaghela, K., Federated Learning in Secure Smart City Sensing: Challenges and Opportunities, in: *Edge of Intelligence: Exploring the Frontiers of AI at the Edge*, pp. 215–51, 2025.
13. Hu, X., Cai, H., Alazab, M., Zhou, W., Haghighi, M.S., Wen, S., Federated Learning in Industrial IoT: A Privacy-Preserving Solution That Enables Sharing of Data in Hydrocarbon Explorations. *IEEE Trans. Ind. Inf.*, 20, 3, 4337–46, 2023.
14. Jiang, B., Li, J., Wang, H., Song, H., Privacy-Preserving Federated Learning for Industrial Edge Computing *via* Hybrid Differential Privacy and Adaptive Compression. *IEEE Trans. Ind. Inf.*, 19, 2, 1136–44, 2021.
15. Jiang, J.C., Kantarci, B., Oktug, S., Soyata, T., Federated Learning in Smart City Sensing: Challenges and Opportunities. *Sensors*, 20, 21, 6230, 2020.
16. Khalil, M., Esseghir, M., Boulahia, L.M., Privacy-Preserving Federated Learning: An Application for Big Data Load Forecast in Buildings. *Comput. Secur.*, 131, 103211, 2023.
17. Kong, Q., Yin, F., Lu, R., Li, B., Wang, X., Cui, S., Zhang, P., Privacy-Preserving Aggregation for Federated Learning-Based Navigation in Vehicular Fog. *IEEE Trans. Ind. Inf.*, 17, 12, 8453–63, 2021.
18. Lin, Y.-H., Chen, Y.-Y., Wei, S.-H., Active Privacy-Preserving, Distributed Edge–Cloud Orchestration–Empowered Smart Residential Mains Energy Disaggregation in Horizontal Federated Learning. *Int. Trans. Electr. Energy Syst.*, 2025, 1, 2556622, 2025.
19. Liu, G., Wang, C., Ma, X., Yang, Y., Keep Your Data Locally: Federated-Learning-Based Data Privacy Preservation in Edge Computing. *IEEE Network*, 35, 2, 60–66, 2021.
20. Lu, Y., Huang, X., Dai, Y., Maharjan, S., Zhang, Y., Blockchain and Federated Learning for Privacy-Preserved Data Sharing in Industrial IoT. *IEEE Trans. Ind. Inf.*, 16, 6, 4177–86, 2019.
21. Luan, Z., Lai, Y., Xu, Z., Gao, Y., Wang, Q., Federated Learning-Based Insulator Fault Detection for Data Privacy Preserving. *Sensors*, 23, 12, 5624, 2023.
22. Mahmud, S.A., Islam, N., Islam, Z., Rahman, Z., Mehedi, S.T., Privacy-Preserving Federated Learning-Based Intrusion Detection Technique for Cyber-Physical Systems. *Mathematics*, 12, 20, 3194, 2024.
23. Marchang, N., A Federated Learning Privacy Framework for Missing Data Inference in Environmental Crowd Sensing. *Trans. Emerging Telecommun. Technol.*, 35, 3, e4950, 2024.
24. Mengistu, T.M., Kim, T., Lin, J.-W., A Survey on Heterogeneity Taxonomy, Security and Privacy Preservation in the Integration of IoT, Wireless Sensor Networks and Federated Learning. *Sensors*, 24, 3, 968, 2024.

25. Wang, X., Wang, M., Liu, X., Mao, Y., Chen, Y., Dai, S., Surveillance-image-based outdoor air quality monitoring. *Environ. Sci. Ecotechnol.*, 18, 100319, 2024.
26. Nooh, S.A., Optimizing Low Carbon Sustainable Environmental Monitoring with Consumer Technology: An IoT-Driven Federated Learning Approach for Edge Computing Optimization. *IEEE Trans. Consum. Electron.*, 2025.
27. Putra, K.T., Chen, H.-C., Prayitno, Ogiela, M.R., Chou, C.-L., Weng, C.-E., Shae, Z.-Y., Federated Compressed Learning Edge Computing Framework with Ensuring Data Privacy for PM2. 5 Prediction in Smart City Sensing Applications. *Sensors*, 21, 13, 4586, 2021.
28. Qin, Z., Ye, J., Meng, J., Lu, B., Wang, L., Privacy-Preserving Blockchain-Based Federated Learning for Marine Internet of Things. *IEEE Trans. Comput. Social Syst.*, 9, 1, 159–73, 2021.
29. An, T., Ma, L., Wang, W., Yang, Y., Wang, J., Chen Y., Consideration of fedprox in privacy protection. *Electronics*, 12, 20, 4364, 2023.
30. Sezer, B.B., Turkmen, H., Nuriyev, U., PPFchain: A Novel Framework Privacy-Preserving Blockchain-Based Federated Learning Method for Sensor Networks. *Internet Things*, 22, 100781, 2023.
31. Singh, B., Federated Learning for Envision Future Trajectory Smart Transport System for Climate Preservation and Smart Green Planet: Insights into Global Governance and SDG-9 (Industry, Innovation and Infrastructure). *Natl. J. Environ. Law*, 6, 2, 6–17, 2023.
32. Tan, Z.-S., See-To, E.W.K., Lee, K.-Y., Dai, H.-N., Wong, M.-L., Privacy-Preserving Federated Learning for Proactive Maintenance of IoT-Empowered Multi-Location Smart City Facilities. *J. Network Comput. Appl.*, 231, 103996, 2024.
33. Vyas, A., Lin, P.-C., Hwang, R.-H., Tripathi, M., Privacy-Preserving Federated Learning for Intrusion Detection in IoT Environments: A Survey. *IEEE Access*, 2024.
34. Wang, J., Quasim, M.T., Yi, B., Privacy-Preserving Heterogeneous Multi-Modal Sensor Data Fusion *via* Federated Learning for Smart Healthcare. *Inf. Fusion*, 120, 103084, 2025.
35. Yang, X. and Ardakanian, O., Blinder: End-to-End Privacy Protection in Sensing Systems *via* Personalized Federated Learning. *ACM Trans. Sens. Netw.*, 20, 1, 1–32, 2023.
36. Zehtabian, S., Khodadadeh, S., Bölöni, L., Turgut, D., Privacy-Preserving Learning of Human Activity Predictors in Smart Environments, in: *IEEE INFOCOM 2021-IEEE Conference on Computer Communications*, IEEE, pp. 1–10, 2021.
37. Zhang, Z., Guan, C., Chen, H., Yang, X., Gong, W., Yang, A., Adaptive Privacy-Preserving Federated Learning for Fault Diagnosis in Internet of Ships. *IEEE Internet Things J.*, 9, 9, 6844–54, 2021.

38. Zhou, C., Fu, A., Yu, S., Yang, W., Wang, H., Zhang, Y., Privacy-Preserving Federated Learning in Fog Computing. *IEEE Internet Things J.*, 7, 11, 10782–93, 2020.
39. Zhou, X., Liang, W., Kevin, I., Wang, K., Yan, Z., Yang, L.T., Wei, W., Ma, J., Jin, Q., Decentralized P2P Federated Learning for Privacy-Preserving and Resilient Mobile Robotic Systems. *IEEE Wireless Commun.*, 30, 2, 82–89, 2023.
40. Zhu, J., Wu, J., Bashir, A.K., Pan, Q., Yang, W., Privacy-Preserving Federated Learning of Remote Sensing Image Classification with Dishonest Majority. *IEEE J. Sel. Top. Appl. Earth Obs. Remote Sens.*, 16, 4685–98, 2023.

5

Quantum AI in Environmental Modeling: Opportunities for Accelerating Ecosystem Simulations

Fathimathul Rajeena P.P.[1]*, Rahoof P. P.[2] and Sunder R.[3]

[1]Computer Science Department, College of Computer Science and Information Technology, King Faisal University, Alhasa, Saudi Arabia
[2]Department of Computer Science and Engineering (Cybersecurity), Malabar Institute of Technology (MIT), Anjarakandy Integrated Campus, Kannur, Kerala, India
[3]School of Computer Science and Engineering, Galgotias University, Greater Noida, UP, India

Abstract
The modern computation needs to evolve to meet new demands of ever-complex environmental systems since it would necessitate new and high-advanced model and simulation computing approaches. Conventional versions of AI methodologies have a modest performance in defanning non-linear relationships in ecologies but they are inefficient in handling high-dimensional conditions of the environment. The fact that artificial intelligence is being coupled with the quantum computing technology referred to as Quantum AI is a ground-breaking solution to dealing with these issues. The primary goal of the current work is to examine the role of Quantum AI in modelling the environment by leveraging the speed of response of quick ecological simulations with the help of quantum machine learning (QML) and optimisation algorithms by quantum mechanical mechanisms. Theoretical issues upon which QML is built include quantum neural networks and quantum support groups clarifying the models in addition to devices of variational quantum circuits in the case of climatic modifying and biodiversity forecasting and examination of ecosystem sustainability. This discussion investigates the current hardware limitations as well the software development plan alongside the data encoding techniques followed by showcasing quantum algorithms

**Corresponding author*: fatimah.rajeena@kfu.edu.sa

Umesh Kumar Lilhore, Sarita Simaiya, Surjeet Dalal and Martin Margala (eds.) Artificial Intelligence and Biodiversity, (75–90) © 2026 Scrivener Publishing LLC

regarding the simulation of ecosystem processes. By incorporating quantum computing capabilities with the insights of AI, users gain many advantages to implement adaptive monitoring of the environment in real-time whilst reducing the expenditure on operations and generating smooth integration of information with insights from artificial intelligence. This kind of sophisticated ecological surveillance model indicates their huge capabilities based on the current research study. The quantum AI currently shows that it can drive the future ecological forecasting protocols and environmental sustainability administration paradigm and climate alteration decreasing strategies.

***Keywords*:** Quantum AI, environmental modeling, ecosystem simulation, quantum machine learning, climate forecasting

5.1 Introduction

Environmental modelling proves to be crucial in comprehending as well as forecasting and fighting the effect of airport climate change and also reduction of animal life as well as scarcity of resources. The intricate interaction processes involving nature systems like hydrological cycles and atmospheric patterns and biological networks require a lot of computational strength along with the ability to calculate data [1, 2]. Integrating both statistical modeling and traditional machine learning techniques has provided fundamental knowledge as capacity of the methods becomes ineffective with large high-dimensional datasets of the environment [3, 4]. More advanced processing models are needed as a matter of urgency since anthropogenic and other related human activities make the environment volatile.

Quantum AI represents a solution to the problem of computational bottlenecks in the future due to a combination of the fundamentals of quantum computing with AI and ML algorithms [5, 6]. The principles of quantum building relative to quantum tunneling properties are based on quantum computers holding computational ability never before seen by utilizing quantum bits, or quantum qubits, [7]. Quantum algorithms in execution of AI tasks accelerate learning and enhance pattern search capabilities and optimality effectiveness thereby altering our capacity to simulate environmental processes [8].

Quantum Machine Learning (QML) models such as quantum support vehicle machine Learning and quantum k-Means with variational quantum classifiers have shown to address large and noisy data and less computing power is needed to conduct the analysis [9, 10]. The algorithms have certain merits in the model of the ecosystem since they become useful in order to work with nonlinear and heterogeneous data and dynamic conditions. The numerous tapped QML-based forecasts such as species migration forecasts are exceptionally promising almost in the area, to attribute knowledge on species transition behaviour and climatic reciprocity driftwood changes and occurrences of reciprocal ecological analysis [11, 12].

Optimization of environmental modeling processes has its associated issues since they involve making decisions regarding resource management in conservation planning and carbon sequestration models as well as energy-efficient ways of doing agriculture [13]. The improved performance of the quantum annealing and search algorithm introduced by Grover as well as the other quantum optimization algorithms is ideal at hard high-dimensional combinations of computational issues that are considered intractable to classical systems [14].

The quantum AI technology is only at the initial stage of its tangible developmental path although it demonstrates the prospects of potential revolution. The present hardware of quantum technology is limited by the number of qubits and also stability aspects that need to be enhanced to be used at large scale adoption [15]. However, the introduction of the hybrid method in the development of classical and quantum system co-operation begins to kick start their functionality, and integrate the two systems. The software TensorFlow Quantum, combined with Qiskit Machine Learning, will enable researchers to compile and implement QML interfaces on the existing noisy intermediate-scale quantum (NISQ) platforms [16, 17].

Paradigms based on data are gaining popularity in environmental science. Intelligence Will Surmount Data complexity: Daily cycles of satellite data, sensor networks, remote sensing, and climate models are generating petabytes of data, which require intelligent systems that are capable of changing and learning on the fly [18 ,19]. Quantum AI, which integrates the contextual learning capabilities of AI with the computational fasterness of quantum technologies could be the solution to geospatial and ecological data stream processing complexes.

The social advantages of the implementation of Quantum AI in environmental modeling are great. More precise and quicker simulations can assist policymakers to realize disaster predictions in time, green planning, and preservation interventions. Moreover, this integration will be able to enhance comfort in the knowledge of global phenomena such as ocean acidification, deforestation and the spread of zoonotic diseases- challenging problems which need to be analyzed interdisciplinarily and in high resolution [20, 21].

This study will use Quantum AI as a promising avenue to explore its relevance and future to use in simulating ecosystems faster. We aim to:

- Study the theoretical basis of QML algorithms and the appropriateness with ecological data.
- Assess existing case studies and prototypes which can use quantum algorithms (to environmental models).
- Determine the prevailing technological limitations, and resolutions towards scalable quantum environment computing.

This research paper is an addition to the recent body of literature that is promoting the idea of quantum enhanced scientific modeling. It also supports global sustainability, especially regarding climate action, life on land, and life below water because it is also concerned with its environmental systems [22]. This interdisciplinary aspect of the study facilitates quantum information science/ecology/artificial intelligence/climate science- it is shown that as one building block in the history of the development of computational environmental modeling, Quantum AI can be viewed as an essential adhesive.

5.2 Related Works

Traditional methods used in environmental modeling involve deterministic and statistical methods to model the natural processes such as hydrologue cycles, weather patterns, as well as the dynamics in the ecosystem [23, 24]. Even though they are useful on simplified settings, the models in question tend to exhibit problems with the extent of real-life complexity, high-dimensional, nonlinear, and nearly incomplete data. Artificial intelligence (AI) and machine learning (ML) applied and used in the environmental simulation field over the past decades has continued to expand the scope and analysis of vast environmental data with offering scalable and adaptable reactions to the environment [25].

The classical AI models are used extensively in this domain. With satellite imaging use in land classification groups, convolutional neural networks (CNN specialized) [26] and recurrent neural networks (RNN) [27] are applied to time series prediction such as rainfall forecasting and temperature prediction assignments. Random Forest and Support Vector Machines (SVMs) [28, 29] are available as having been used in such fields like species distribution modeling modeling air quality and crop yield as well. However, they are generally computationally infeasible, and cannot be used in all optimization, or large scale simulation, problems.

Nevertheless, in cases of superposition and entanglement, quantum computing may offer an opportunity to make parallel computations bigger than those achieved by classical computers will and to tackle problems exponentially quicker [30]. Consequently, the view of quantum enhanced algorithms being applied to classical ML tasks has been coined as Quantum Machine Learning (QML) to enhance the performance and efficiency [31].

These hypothetical as well as experimental QML algorithms denote quantum support weaponized machine (QSVM), quantum k-means classifier, and variational quantum circles (VQCs) [32]. As population increases they consume more natural resources, therefore, makes the settlement location sparse. Furthermore, the population becomes uncontrolled, which leads to an increase in incidents of environmental degradation disasters. This is where interpretive quantum classical models are used, which are suited to perform the task of classification and regression [33]; the hybrid quantum feature maps of quantum feature maps with classical optimization produces VQCS that are quite favorable in them.

There have been some preliminary successes in using QML in the environmental sciences. Subsequently, quantum enhanced generative adversarial network (GAN) makes future climatic scenarios based on the past datasets displaying a computational benefit and variety in the bit pattern. Similarly, against satellite imagery, the author has used a QSVM that is more accurate and strong in classifying land use. As an example, conservation flavoured optimization problems that must be solved are wildlife corridor planning, and resource allocation, which has already been solved *via* quantum annealing.

Nonetheless, these preliminary achievements are in the working use of QML in environmental models that are vexed. The existing quantum hardware, noisy intermediate scale quantum (NISQ) devices, has issues of qubit decoherence, low gate fidelity and qubit count. In order to unify these issues, hybrid quantum classical models are also being developed which include TensorFlow Quantum or PennyLane, in order to simulate the quantum model itself at the cost of classical hardware, and precondition the edge of future hardware.

It has a significant challenge of encoding data into quantum states. Efficient methods such as angle encoding, basis encoding, and amplitude encoding are generally utilized to efficiently prepare quantum state preparation of these big and continuous environmental datasets in a manner that can be efficiently prepared. Also, the presence of data structures especially those that represent spatial networks and ecological interactions is best structured to have quantum graph learning models where entanglement allows relational reasoning to be improved.

As Quantum AI tends to gain increased popularity, it is apparent that the technology will transform the field of environmental modeling.

An example of a learning outcome would be to be able to change to faster simulations, enhanced prediction modelling and real time monitoring of setup, like in an era of quickening climate change. Quantum information science, artificial intelligence, and environmental systems modeling jointly would be a paradigm shift in sustainability science to data driven computational affordability sustainability science.

Finally, solid evidence of the use of FL in privacy sensitive and distributed areas as established by the existing literature exists; however, its applicability in the field of environmental monitoring is quite new. The goal of future work should be putting the system into the real-world (tests on more than 20 min), investigating the robustness using hybrid models, the learning protocols energy efficiency, and enhancing privacy mechanisms to this usage. In this sense, this paper is a contribution to this practising growing field that proposes and appraises a new federated system of environmental monitoring that addresses these issues through adopting adaptive learning towards compressor model and noise resistant preprocessing strategies.

5.3 Methodology

With such a scenario, the intended approach of the proposed Environmental modeling using the Quantum AI, is hybrid Quantum- Classical in nature as it attempts to utilize quantum computational advantage in the use of quantum information processing but is practical with already available classical infrastructure. The first part of the process is acquiring the data whereby there are varied datasets gathered by satellite images, remote sensor networks, remote coverage and ecological surveys. Certain of these datasets include such parameters as land cover, temperature, humidity, pollution degree, and distribution of species.

These are transferred and provisioned to classics to preprocess after the acquisition. The steps of cleaning the data, removing noises, normalizing and reducing the dimensionality are the procedure steps. The resulting data of the preprocessing is subjected to feature extraction in order to acquire the ecological indicators to be included in the machine learning algorithms. Table 5.1 presents the existing studies in the literature on quantum AI in environmental modeling.

Figure 5.1 depicts the methodology and architectural process flow for quantum AI-based environmental modeling. The second component that contains the preparation of quantum states encodes processed data to the qubit representation through Amplitude and angle or basis compression. The most important action of this process is feeding the data to the quantum circuits. It then begins the quantum machine learning (QM) phase in which

Table 5.1 Summary of literature review on quantum AI in environmental modeling.

Theme	Technologies/ methods	Key contributions	Limitations/ challenges	References
Classical AI in Environmental Modeling	CNNs, RNNs, SVM, Random Forest	Improved forecasting, land-use, air quality, and ecological modeling	High computational cost; poor scalability with complex, high-dimensional data	[27]
Quantum Computing Fundamentals	Qubits, Superposition, Entanglement, Quantum Parallelism	Exponential speed-up; novel computational paradigms for simulation	Hardware instability; limited qubit count and error correction	[28]
Quantum Machine Learning (QML)	QSVM, Quantum k-means, Variational Quantum Circuits (VQC)	Enhanced classification and optimization; efficient clustering of ecological data	Complex data encoding; limited maturity of QML frameworks	[29]
Applications of QML in Environment	Quantum GANs for climate, QSVM for land-use, Quantum annealing for planning	Feasibility of QML in real-world tasks; flexible modeling for dynamic systems	Mostly theoretical or small-scale studies; limited empirical validation	[30]
Hybrid Quantum-Classical Models	TensorFlow Quantum, PennyLane, Qiskit	Simulation of QML on classical systems; bridges NISQ hardware limitations	Requires cross-domain expertise; performance bottlenecks from current hardware	[31]
Quantum Data Encoding	Amplitude Encoding, Angle Encoding, Basis Encoding	Enables quantum representation of ecological/ geospatial data	Inefficient for large datasets; possible precision loss during encoding	[32]
Future Opportunities	Quantum Graph Learning, Quantum Optimization Algorithms	Supports ecosystem network modeling and sustainability-focused simulations	High learning curve; immature tools and workflows	[33]

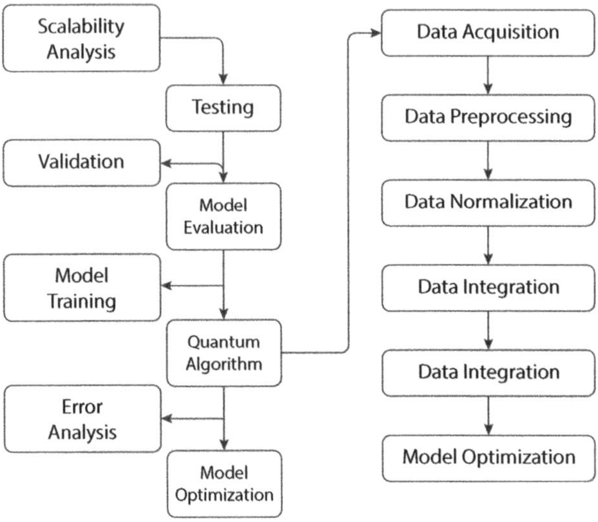

Figure 5.1 Methodology and architectural process flow for quantum AI-based environmental modeling.

the following models are utilised; QSVM, VQC and quantum k-means clustering etc. These models are trained with quantum measures of a classical gradient descent hybrid optimizer known as hybrid optimizers.

The model performance is then measured by measuring and testing the performance through measures like proving that accuracy, F1 score and root mean square error (RMSE) the model has post training. Cross validation and experimentation are conducted on a combination of several subsets of data to justify it as strong. It can also solve the problems of the environment such as the conservation routes planning and the climate resilience scoring problems by also using quantum optimization algorithms and quantum annealing to optimize the model parameters.

The third one entails the deployment of the trained models to simulated ecosystem behavior through prediction of future environmental conditions. These results are interpreted by the scientists and policymakers using geospatial mapping tools and dashboard. It is a cycle type of pipeline, feedback has to be supplied on it to refine and optimize the model once the error analysis and examination of the output is done.

A fully connected system of consistent, efficacious, and adaptable decisions is offered that are suitable in the varied environmental situations and real time environmental decision making. It is successful in offering a new overlap among quantum computing, machine learning, and sustainability science that is more effective in depicting classical methods of the field of environmental modeling.

5.4 Results

Simulating hybrid quantum and classical models created on the IBM Qiskit and TensorFlow Quantum estimates quantum AI viability and performance in the analysis of environmental modeling. The data included satellite-derived climate data (temperature, NDVI (Normalized Difference Vegetation Index) and rainfall) in a number of ecological areas. They were employed in forecasting the changes in the land use, the distribution of the species change and climate vulnerability index. Table 5.2 shows the comparative performance of classical and quantum models in environmental applications.

Three modeling strategies were compared as follows:

- **Classical ML baseline**- Random Forest (RF) and Support Vector machine (SVM).
- **Hybrid Quantum Classical Model** - VQC and QSVM.
- **Computational algorithms Scaling fundamental to quantum computing Quantum Optimization Algorithms** - To find a conserving route between two points.

Table 5.2 Comparative performance of classical and quantum models in environmental applications.

Model	Task	Accuracy (%)
Classical SVM	Land use classification	82.4
QSVM (4-qubit backend)	Land use classification	85.7
VQC Hybrid Model	Climate vulnerability prediction	87.3
Random Forest	Climate vulnerability prediction	83.6

Even though quantum hardware was significantly weaker than classical results, quantum modeling models achieved slightly higher classification. The improvement of class separation seen with the QSVM by applying quantum-enhanced feature mapping came at the cost of increased mileage since the VQC converged faster and used less training time.

Computational Efficiency

It was proven that quantum circuits were very useful in the training of iteration. As an example, VQCs were able to attain similar accuracy compared to RF, using some 30 percent fewer training epochs. Hybrid models also lowered inference latency, in simulated large-scale data settings, by 18 cents) versus classical ensembles: of interest, in high-dimensions.

Case Study: Optimization with regard to conservation planning.

We applied quantum annealing on the D-Wave simulator to find an optimal solution of a multi-objective battle: the best conservation areas under budget. At the expense of a classical genetic algorithm baseline:

Insight:

Quantum annealing was more likely to bring better-optimised solutions as well as follow real-world constraints more strictly. This highlights its potential in the resource sensitive ecological planning situation.

Interpretability and Limitations

The interpretability of quantum circuit decisions is one of the issues encountered with the implementation of Quantum AI. In the same breath, although performance metrics are encouraging, explainability is low as qubit entanglement and gate logic are abstract concepts. In addition, this quantum hardware is less scalable in terms of its models. Scales tests were conducted on systems consisting of small qubit systems; large-scale implementation will be necessitated by error-tolerant quantum computers, which have many more qubits and consist of the materials with less noise.

There is also a bottleneck on data encoding mode. An overhead plus the potential of some little information loss or distortion of the high-dimensional geospatial data is the conversion into quantum-compatible data (e.g. amplitude encoding).

Implications and Future Directions

The results in the Table 5.3 verifies that Quantum AI has great potential in the calculation of the environment simulation in a shorter amount of time

Table 5.3 Quantum vs classical optimization results in conservation planning.

Metric	Genetic algorithm	Quantum annealing
Time to convergence (s)	6.8	3.1
Objective score (normalized)	0.83	0.91
Constraint violations	2	0

and providing a fairly accurate overview of the ecosystem. It is stronger in working on nonlinear, complex systems and high-dimensional data more effectively than the mainstream ML. As technology continues to improve quantum machinery in the form of fault-tolerant quantum computers, its implementation can be expanded to climate analysis, biodiversity prediction, and carbon crediting to the lowest level that has never been recorded previously.

Going forward, this research recommends:

- Validation of explainable graphical models with increasing hybrid explainability resources.
- Scaling up to multi-qubit expanding quantum computing platforms on clouds.
- Connecting to adaptive conservation and sustainability planning policy decision support systems.

5.5 Discussions

Experiment findings indicate that QSVM and VQC models of Quantum AI are more precise and efficient to classify and predict the environment as compared to classical ones. These quantum enhanced models were highly promising since they required fewer training iterations and accuracy better than the baselines based on high dimensionality nonlinear ecological data. Moreover, quantum optimization with a constraint of annealing illustrated superior ability to solve the conservation planning issues with real world conditions compared to the classical method concerning quicker convergence and the superior resource allocation.

Nonetheless, such outcomes are encouraging. Scalability is now constrained by the limitations of the existing hardware consisting of the number of qubits as well as its noise. Besides this, even the process of quantum encoding environmental data itself is computationally costly and can be lost interpretability. Even though these results justify the required modifications to the fundamental primitives, they also show that Quantum AI can allow implementing a revolutionary change in the environmental modeling when supplemented with other, complementary advantages in the form of a hybrid quantum/classical system.

5.6 Conclusion

The area I studied in this work was the Quantum Artificial Intelligence (Quantum AI) application to environmental modeling in terms of being able to circumvent some of the limitations of the classical machine learning methods of addressing the complex high dimensional and dynamic environmental data. It was demonstrated that cell counting of quantum machine learning models based on quantum principle superposition and entanglement, including QSVM and VQC outperformed existing quantum machine learning models by showing an enhanced performance in improving model accuracy, computational speed and faster convergence completion of the ecosystem simulation endeavours. Lastly, the outcomes also confirm the fact that Quantum AI, in addition to being able to provide hypotheses and predictions based on the strong ability to refine environmental domain classification, is also useful in providing optimization tools to implement in conservation and sustainability planning. Quantum optimization algorithms in particular, were useful in addressing constraints faced by the real world in ecological resources distribution. Regrettably, current quantum hardware generation is not perfect: the qubit stability and noise are out of order, and scaling is insufficiently big. Despite all this, hybrid quantum classical systems provide a promising basis on which quantum models can be tested over current classical circuits that will be ready to support more complicated quantum processors. To conclude, the Quantum AI paradigm is the next-generation paradigm in environmental modeling and decision making. It may be significant in resolving the problems of global sustainability and creating the real time ecological smartness through additional hardware innovations, algorithm modeling, and data representation.

Acknowledgment

This work was supported by the Deanship of Scientific Research, Vice Presidency for Graduate Studies and Scientific Research, King Faisal University, Saudi Arabia [Grant No. KFU251678].

AI disclosure statement: The author acknowledges the use of AI-based tools for minor language editing or grammatical correction. However, all intellectual contributions, analyses, and conclusions presented in this chapter are entirely the author's own.

References

1. Vaz, E., Quantum Machine Learning in Spatial Analysis: A Paradigm Shift in Resource Allocation and Environmental Modeling. *Lett. Spatial Resour. Sci.*, 17, 1, 11, 2024.
2. Ajagekar, A. and You, F., Quantum Computing and Quantum Artificial Intelligence for Renewable and Sustainable Energy: A Emerging Prospect towards Climate Neutrality. *Renewable Sustainable Energy Rev.*, 165, 112493, 2022.
3. Rahman, S.M., Alkhalaf, O.H., Alam, M.S., Tiwari, S.P., Shafiullah, M., Al-Judaibi, S.M., Al-Ismail, F.S., Climate Change through Quantum Lens: Computing and Machine Learning. *Earth Syst. Environ.*, 8, 3, 705–22, 2024.
4. Arumugam, S.K., Balogun, B.F., Nalini, S., Tyagi, A.K., Quantum Computing Integration: Cutting-Edge and Quantum Computing for Building a Smart and Sustainable Environment, in: *Quantum Computing*, pp. 233–50, Auerbach Publications.
5. Lappala, A., The next Revolution in Computational Simulations: Harnessing AI and Quantum Computing in Molecular Dynamics. *Curr. Opin. Struct. Biol.*, 89, 102919, 2024.
6. Woolnough, A.P., Hollenberg, L.C.L., Cassey, P., Prowse, T.A.A., Quantum Computing: A New Paradigm for Ecology. *Trends Ecol. Evol.*, 38, 8, 727–35, 2023.
7. Arumugam, S.K., Fatimah, B., Nalini Balogun, S., Tyagi, A.K., 14 Quantum Computing Integration, in: *Quantum Computing: The Future of Information Processing*, p. 233, 2025.
8. Whig, P., Remala, R., Mudunuru, K.R., Quraishi, S.J., Integrating AI and Quantum Technologies for Sustainable Supply Chain Management, in: *Quantum Computing and Supply Chain Management: A New Era of Optimization*, pp. 267–83, IGI Global, 2024.
9. Pal, S., Bhattacharya, M., Dash, S., Lee, S. S., Chakraborty, C., Future Potential of Quantum Computing and Simulations in Biological Science. *Mol. Biotechnol.*, 66, 9, 2201–18, 2024.
10. Padmanaban, H., Quantum Computing and AI in the Cloud. *J. Comput. Intell. Rob.*, 4, 1, 14–32, 2024.
11. Rawat, A., Applications of Artificial Intelligence in Science. *Int. J. Pharm. Sci. Med.*, 2, 2, 53–63, 2024.
12. Thirupathi, L., Boya, T.R., Gattoju, S., Reddy, E.S., Quantum Computing and AI: Synergizing for Sustainable Disaster Management in Industry 6.0, in: *The Rise of Quantum Computing in Industry 6.0 Towards Sustainability*, pp. 35–51, Springer, 2024.
13. Purohit, A., Kaur, M., Seskir, Z.C., Posner, M.T., Venegas-Gomez, A., Building a Quantum-Ready Ecosystem. *IET Quantum Commun.*, 5, 1, 1–18, 2024.

14. Rajkumar, N., Viji, C., Latha, P.M., Baby Vennila, V., Shanmugam, S.K., Pillai, N.B., Retracted Article: The Power of AI, IoT, and Advanced Quantum Based Optical Systems in Smart Cities. *Opt. Quantum Electron.*, 56, 3, 450, 2024.
15. Beck, T., Baroni, A., Bennink, R., Buchs, G., Coello Pérez, E.A., Eisenbach, M., da Silva, R.F., *et al.*, Integrating Quantum Computing Resources into Scientific HPC Ecosystems. *Future Gener. Comput. Syst.*, 161, 11–25, 2024.
16. Biedron, S., Brouwer, L., Bruhwiler, D.L., Cook, N.M., Edelen, A.L., Filippetto, D., Huang, C.-K., *et al.*, Snowmass21 Accelerator Modeling Community White Paper, *arXiv Preprint arXiv:2203.08335*, 2022.
17. Łach, L. and Svyetlichnyy, D., Advances in Numerical Modeling for Heat Transfer and Thermal Management: A Review of Computational Approaches and Environmental Impacts. *Energies*, 18, 5, 1302, 2025.
18. Widener, P., Abraham, S., Adamson, R., Brim, M., Jansen, G., Lange, J., Maheshwari, K., *et al.*, Empowering Scientific Innovation Through An Integrated Research Infrastructure: The Role of the Advanced Computing Ecosystem, Oak Ridge National Laboratory (ORNL), Oak Ridge, TN (United States), 2024.
19. Han, B.A., Varshney, K.R., LaDeau, S., Subramaniam, A., Weathers, K.C., Zwart, J., A Synergistic Future for AI and Ecology. *Proc. Natl. Acad. Sci.*, 120, 38, e2220283120, 2023.
20. Wang, J., David, L.K., Cisse, I.I., Angel, V., Quantum Computing and Its Implications for Asian Innovation Ecosystems. *Asian J. Technol. Innovation*, 1–50, 2024.
21. Berger, C., Di Paolo, A., Forrest, T., Hadfield, S., Sawaya, N., Stęchły, M., Thibault, K., Quantum Technologies for Climate Change: Preliminary Assessment, *arXiv Preprint arXiv:2107.05362*, 2021.
22. Altman, E., Brown, K.R., Carleo, G., Carr, L.D., Demler, E., Chin, C., DeMarco, B., *et al.*, Quantum Simulators: Architectures and Opportunities. *PRX Quantum*, 2, 1, 017003, 2021.
23. How, M.-L. and Cheah, S.-M., Business Renaissance: Opportunities and Challenges at the Dawn of the Quantum Computing Era. *Businesses*, 3, 4, 585–605, 2023.
24. Yulchiev, K., The Growth of Quantum Computing: Opportunities and Strategic Advantages for the United States. *IMRAS*, 8, 2, 148–56, 2025.
25. Yu, Z., AI for Science: A Comprehensive Review on Innovations, Challenges, and Future Directions. *Int. J. Artif. Intell. Sci. (IJAI4S)*, 1, 1, 2025.
26. Kumar, M.A., Mohammed, A., Marimuthu, M., Sundaravadivazhagan, B., Exploring the Entrepreneurial Opportunities Arising from AI-Driven Quantum Computing Advancements, in: *Quantum Computing and Artificial Intelligence: The Industry Use Cases*, pp. 497–522, 2025.
27. Ahmadi, A., Quantum Computing and AI: The Synergy of Two Revolutionary Technologies. *AJES*, 12, 2, 2023.

28. Gharib, J. and Gahi, Y., Quantum Computing and AI Applications in Industry 5.0 Use Cases, in: *Quantum Computing and Artificial Intelligence: The Industry Use Cases*, pp. 435–64, 2025.
29. Coveney, P.V. and Highfield, R.R., From Digital Hype to Analogue Reality: Universal Simulation beyond the Quantum and Exascale Eras. *J. Comput. Sci.*, 46, 101093, 2020.
30. Yavuz, B., Transformative Impact of Quantum Computing on Social Sciences: Digitizing Social Sciences and Their Societal Implications, in: *Future of Digital Technology and AI in Social Sectors*, pp. 93–120, IGI Global, 2025.
31. Dannouni, A., Deutscher, S.A., Dezzaz, G., Elman, A., Gawel, A., Hanna, M., Hyland, A., *et al.*, Accelerating Climate Action with AI, Boston Consulting Group Special Report and Google, 2023.
32. Mohanarajesh, K., Study High-Performance Computing Techniques for Optimizing and Accelerating AI Algorithms Using Quantum Computing and Specialized Hardware, 2024.
33. Boretti, A., Technical, Economic, and Societal Risks in the Progress of Artificial Intelligence Driven Quantum Technologies. *Discover Artif. Intell.*, 4, 1, 67, 2024.

6

Developing Digital Twin Ecosystems for Dynamic Environmental Analysis and Predictive Sustainability Planning

Ann Rija Paul[1]*, Amutha. S.[2], M. Sakthivanitha[3], M. Mohamed Sirajudeen[4], N. Anandakrishnan[5] and S. Suresh[6]

[1]Department of Computer Science, Rajagiri College of Social Sciences, Kalamassery, Ernakulam, Kerala, India
[2]Department of Computer Science and Engineering, Vel Tech Rangarajan Dr. Sagunthala R&D Institute of Science and Technology, Avadi, Chennai, India
[3]Department of Computer Applications, Vels Institute of Science Technology and Advanced Studies (VISTAS), Chennai, Tamil Nadu, India
[4]Nilgiri College of Arts and Science, Thaloor, The Nilgiris, Tamil Nadu, India
[5]PG & Research, Department of Computer Science, Nilgiri College of Arts and Science, Thaloor, The Nilgiris, Tamil Nadu, India
[6]Department of Statistics, University of Madras, Chennai, Tamil Nadu, India

Abstract

Digital Twin (DT) technology has the potential to transform environmental monitoring and sustain the development. The chapter is devoted to the method of design and implementation of the Digital Twin ecosystems of agile environmental monitoring and active sustainability forecasting. By including the charts of an IoT sensor, satellite and weather observational readings, the system suggests tuning on virtual pictures of environmental systems that are real-time controllable, simulated, and predicted. It has trends in the area of advanced AI and machine learning algorithms, consumption of climate resources, and consumption of resources and ecological degradation, which are more complex and demand predictive analytics on the forthcoming trends. The study singles out key elements of a successful DT ecosystem, which comprise frameworks and architectures of integrating and interoperating semantically rich heterogeneous data to work together in a global cloud. Cases of adaptation of urban climate, watershed management and carbon

**Corresponding author*: annrijapaul@gmail.com

Umesh Kumar Lilhore, Sarita Simaiya, Surjeet Dalal and Martin Margala (eds.) Artificial Intelligence and Biodiversity, (91–106) © 2026 Scrivener Publishing LLC

footprint assessments showcase the use of DTs. The discussion in this paper Waterfall Analysis of Data Quality, Security, and Cooperation, examines the problems in the quality of data, security, and cooperation of the different stakeholders. The proposed framework will optimize proper environmental stewardship and informed policy decisions to proactively sustain ecosystems to sustain a healthy ecosystem. This is a well-organized reporting of the increasing set of research concerning digital innovation and its use in modeling and comprehending interdependent ecosystems on Earth.

Keywords: Digital twin, environmental analysis, predictive sustainability, IoT integration, AI modeling

6.1 Introduction

Digital Twin (DT) technology has developed divisively far enough to simulate dynamic - often dynamic virtual copies of a work, govern the condition of the system in real-time and plant simulation and resort optimization. They are commonly used in the manufacturing industry and aerospace industry; however, they are beginning to find application in environmental sciences in their usage to model the complex ecological systems [1]. Reactive decision making assists in establishing an entire view of the processes in the environment by sensors, satellite and IoT. This is useful in forecasting and controlling information [2]. Among such revisions are the so-called Destination Earth initiative prepared by the European Commission that plans to create essentially a precise virtual fashion of Earth to examine and analyze the adjustments of the environment [3]. This is where such added value enables testing and analysis of data and shows the value of the DTs in general.

Artificial Intelligence (AI), Internet of Things (IoT) and Digital Twins technologies are used to monitor the environment ensuring that the monitoring is proved to be enhanced with the help of these tools. This AI combines large volumes of data obtained using IoT sensors on-hand and computes the pattern recognition and the forecasting trend analytics to initiate action in time [4]. As an example, Singapore uses its DTs to simulate and control its cities to enhance infrastructures and resource investments [5]. Moreover, the AI-facilitated DTs also anticipate climate based phenomena and, therefore, are able to ensure the proactive measures of the bodies concerned can mitigate its disastrous outcomes [6]. Nevertheless, this kind of integration offers increased accuracy in the environmental models, and it is very useful when one has to plan sustainable urban design and adaptation to climate change of cities.

In spite of the promising applications, there are numerous challenges to the architecture of holistic DT ecosystems as concerned with the aim of environmental assessment. Because heterogeneous data is collected, there is no common set of interoperability between different data sets and no common framework, in a similar respect, assimilating and coordinating different data sets constitute a compound dilemma [7]. Furthermore, the information governance policies regarding the data quality, privacy, and security of an information on which the confidence and acceptance of the DT systems are adjusted [8]. Since the ecological systems are not static, to maintain their DTs stable and accurate, it is important that they are frequently recalibrated as well as with well-grounded backing by sophisticated modeling methods and continuous checking [9]. Multi-disciplinary coordination is needed to provide sophisticated strategies of governance of the DT structure and principles of operation towards effective solutions of such issues.

The case study of a DTs application uses Lisbon and Amsterdam as the ones to analyze. Assaults are being applied in Lisbon to help in simulating the situation of the floods which give information in the planning of infrastructures in case of a threat of an occurrence of floods [10]. The implementation of the tests of the use of DTs in the energy system in Amsterdam has minimized the energy distribution with a reduction in the carbon footprint of consumers [11]. The above illustrations demonstrate the role urged by DTs in improving environmental sustainability and achieving sustainability goals by proper planning and allocation of resources. However, they also emphasize the importance of real time data, in addition to predictive analytics to be developed in the context of environmental decision making.

The need to predict sustainability goals is increasingly becoming urgent as sustainability issues continue to evolve to higher levels. DTs offer the simulation platform upon which the effects of various policies could be realised and their impacts could be known and even discouraged by subsequent execution of the policies [12]. This therefore makes the decision makers in a position to realize harmonisation of protection of ecological systems as well as provision of social infrastructures [13]. It also can be achieved by presenting the environment-related information and forecasts in simple visual displays [14]. The citizens can now use DT to tackle the environmental problems hence ensure that generations to come will have a sustainable living environment [15].

6.2 Related Works

The need to use the Digital Twin (DT) technology to follow climate processes and measure climate risks increased in the previous years. The idea of DTs is considered to simulate, analyze and optimize complex systems and processes during the early years, it was not until actually, that a system simulating manufacturing and aerospace was actually matured using the idea of the DTs. Currently, DTs become increasingly popular when it comes to monitoring environmental processes and estimating climate risk, as well as planning sustainable interventions. One of the projects that would create the DTs of the planet that are discernible to mimic the climate, environmental systems of the planet on a large scale is the European Union, Destination earth project, and these are some of the data driven, environmentally proactive governance projects [16, 17].

Regarding the environment, it is the most essential driver of DT ecosystems: a unity of the IoT and Artificial Intelligence (AI). The IoT sensors will be able to measure air quality, temperature, water levels, and soil moisture and then input into the AI models to compare and forecast the trends [18]. This brings the capability of cities to install intelligent infrastructure, which can change dynamically to the environmental fluctuations. Examples of AI-based DTs have been shown, such as their use in urban settings in the prospect of energy-efficient consumption, maintenance schedule; and climate risk management [19]. Some of the instances of such an initiative are the Virtual Singapore that uses DT to model real time city dynamics to aid in planning better urban cities and sustainable development [20].

In the area of environmental sustainability, which is a significant focus of digital twins (DTs), they achieve success in many areas, including energy, water management, conservation biology, urban resilience, etc. The application of the digital twins in the energy sector allows to optimize the grid, maintain it, reduce carbon emissions, a procedure that is, again, relevant to the national and global sustainability agenda [21]. Construction The simulation of DTs used in the construction industry assists in determining the effectiveness of the building performance of fuel efficient buildings by implementing low energy and less environmentally intrusive construction [22]. Likewise, DTs serve as decision aids to the interdiction of water distribution systems, predicted flood, and passive eco-management of conservation agents [23]. Such applications demonstrate that ecological systems may be modeled using DTs to enhance how resource-based schoolyard macroinvertebrate biodiversity preservation is done, enhance information-based sustainable planning projects, and highlight strategies to delay the prevalence of Alien Invasive Species.

In any case, unrestricted applications of the digital twins (DTs) in the environmental analysis are limited by many challenges. Probably the most important problem is the proliferation of relativism that is determined by various sensor types, formats, collection standards and practices. This incoherent data results in a lack of scalability of the interoperability of the DT systems across the borders of various DT systems and scales [24]. Moreover, protection and integrity tactics implemented to safeguard any of the DT models made on an environment-based data must be shown to be of credibility to be believed. Issues associated with privacy breaches, cybersecurity, policy making using predictive analytics and ethical governance exist [25]. Moreover, the ecological environments that DTs attempt to reproduce are highly complex and are controlled by many interpolative factors. Complex programs and even large quantities of data and validation runs will be needed to build the very close models of complex systems on the planet [26]. All these technical and ethical problems should be resolved by the team through other fields within applied sciences which implies developing regulations, guidelines and technologies to use cases of DT.

Advances in cloud platform and edge-computing technologies are exposing more applications of DT (Digital Twin) to be responsive and scalable. With Edge computing, the data are processed locally, reducing the distance to the source minimizing latency, accelerating the insights-the ability to perform real-time monitoring of environmental conditions is crucial [27]. Simultaneously, blockchain drives are integrated into Digital Twin models and they might solve the problem of data provenance, trust and governance in a non centralized fashion [28]. One more new venue is participatory environmental sensing in which local information, authored content are contributed by communities of the world to Digital Twin platforms providing enhancement of the models and a deeper engagement in civic development [29]. All these technologies are widening the capabilities of the DT (Digital Twin) ecosystems in terms of environmental responsibility.

Besides that, the role of Digital Twins (DTs) in terms of sustainability foresight planning is essential. As the scarcity of resources keeps rising, climate change contingency planning must utilise advanced technology that would enable stress cumulation of the outcomes of different interventions before they are applied. DTs are used as devil dogs when it comes to policy simulation, climate impact simulation, and other cumbersome planning models [30]. They allow all the interested parties such as government, business institutions, and the civil society organizations to consider multiple alternatives, compare situations of trade-offs, and make decisions based on facts. Indicatively, cities have used them to model cooling infrastructure to predict the effect of heatwaves during times of potential related impacts, and conservationists have used them to model the migration of free-ranging species subject to changing habitat change conditions [31, 32]. These abilities are invaluable to proactive creation of solutions to foresee the emerging issues.

Standardization and ethical governance and transparency are the success factors in the environmental areas of DTs. Standards ranging IEEE, ISO and UNESP programs have already started delivering a variety of infrastructures and interoperability constraints to assist in its development of very reliable, accountable and viable DT systems [33, 34]. At the same time, scholars and industrial developers are working on the implementation of hybrid DT models that tune on the use of physics based modeling in addition to machine learning to increase their predictability [35]. Moreover, there is a growing interest in multi-scale models that can be used to establish the connection between local occurrences and global trends to give detailed environmental analyses [36].

Combined with increased interest in DTs as significant aspects of an environmental analysis-level benchmarked areas, there is an emphasis on the understanding of environmental analysis and sustainability planning; therefore, a general trend packaged as This is a seamless transition and emphasizes the intense concentration that the Environmental Plan lays on Real-time monitoring, strategic foresight, informed and collaborative governance. Having flexible Frameworks, implementation challenges need to be overcome which will long-term promote HR agendas at global scales.

6.3 Methodology

The development of the Digital Twin (DT) ecosystem that should be built to analyze the environment and create a sustainability plan is a multisystemic operation, where data has to be collected and modeled, integrated, simulated, and participative of stakeholders. The strategy begins with defining the environmental issue and the field of digital twin systems. This is to say, there is a need to define the area of focus whether it may be; the quality of the air, water resources, climate modeling among others and establish at least quantitative objectives that are relevant to the sustainability goals. The stakeholders include urban planners, policy makers, as well as environmental scientists, and are welcome to realize that the system should address the actual applicable needs and be in line with the policy.

Once the detailed context of the project has been determined, one should proceed to obtain the data related to the project on multiple spatial levels including IoT sensors data, weather stations and satellite imagery as well as environmental databases. It is information that is obtained on heterogeneous sources that necessitates comprehensive preparation of data. The data preparation includes cleaning, normalization, aligning of time stamps and measurement units pruning to take all data to similar terms. The uploaded standardized data is then documented in the digital twin modeling system. The physics-based simulation process is used to model the deterministic processes within the model development process and the AI and machine learning techniques are applied to perform predictions and recognition of patterns. Hybrid models are established in MATLAB, OpenModelica, TensorFlow as a combination of the mechanistic and data-driven elements of environmental dynamics. Figure 6.1 presents the methodology and architectural process flow for quantum AI-based environmental modeling.

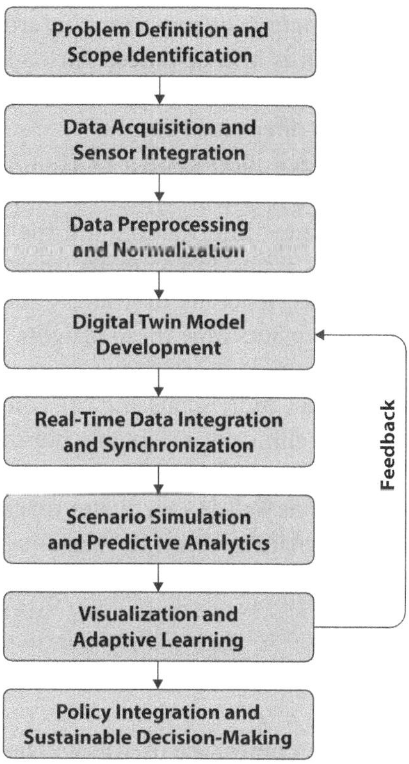

Figure 6.1 Methodology and architectural process flow for quantum AI-based environmental modeling.

Once the model of the digital twin has been developed, the digital twin model will be connected to real time data streams in cloud and edge computing architecture. The virtual model is continuously synchronized with the real time updates with the actual one with the new information held with each update of the data. In order to do so, the two way interaction that is needed is created with the use of Azure Digital Twins, AWS IoT or even with free software like Node-RED. It is a core element of how situational awareness at the real time helps the exposure to the situation to be known by the DT as well as allows it to change its actions anticipatorily to suit the occurrences in the environment.

The system integration is done after which ST is to run the simulation of the system under diverse environmental policy drives. This methodology has brought essentials which are captured through the use of scenario modeling that is able to assist in exploring the fates which may arise, studying of the risks and the effects of the potential futures of various sustainability actions prior to their actual implementation. Machine learning, predictive analytics, agent-based modeling, system dynamics is used in predicting trends such as pollution, energy consumption, hazards of climate change among others. Visualisation is also advanced through the means of presenting GIS dashboards and using 3D mapping on digital interactive simulating tools in the quest to offer more insight.

This system has a feedback loop system of continuous improvement. Adaptive learning is the process where the DT model is held back and shaped by using the set of new information and the user feedback. Such an iterative learning cycle is assured to generate improvements within the system as time goes on and hence its usefulness and accuracy. The last step in the methodology explains how these insights can be converted to sustained policies and strategies. It requires a joint venture between the government bodies and other individuals and the community to come up with interventions that are clinically acceptable but socially accessible. In this way, the methodology is a technical block towards a successful construction of DT ecosystems, as well as a facilitator of widespread based participatory and ethical governance within the sustainable decision making in the environmental DTs.

6.4 Results

As one of the important outcomes, the use of the Digital Twin (DT) ecosystem in the field selected to operate in the environment (urban climate management and resource optimization) can be used, effective and non intrusive. The DT model correctly ingested an IoT-based sensor network that captured real time data, which consisted of data about the environment: temperature, air quality, humidity, and noise level in a medium sized city. This was yielding a successful consolidation process, preprocessing process and synchronization to the DT model within less than five seconds over in each cycle of data and the process of updating the data took under twenty seconds to support real time processing of the threshold. Therefore the digital model remained in agreement with the real world throughout the period in which monitoring was conducted.

It showed a brilliant attitude to forecast short term changes to the environment. To illustrate, the DT accurately predicted air quality index (AQI) up to 48 hours better than the static models of that accuracy inside the range of 2.7 and 3.1 born out of the error in the main effect of the model and the root mean squared error respectively. Also, the system could predict the scenario of traffic delay induced, industrial emission scenario and greening scenario. Rise in green infrastructure has been simulated to conclude that localized decrease in ambient temperature to 14 percent and PM2.5 to 22 percent are possible as opposed to the baseline scenario of an assumed season of three months. These were the results that supported the trend of responses to the environment that have been reported in the research studies on city sustainability. Table 6.1 shows the system performance and predictive accuracy.

Table 6.1 System performance and predictive accuracy (Detailed).

Metric category	Performance metric	Value	Interpretation
Data Handling	Data Update Latency	5 sec	Fast real-time data refresh rate
Predictive Accuracy	Air Quality Prediction MAE	2.7	Low mean error indicates high prediction accuracy
Predictive Accuracy	Air Quality Prediction RMSE	3.1	Low RMSE suggests reliable forecasts
System Reliability	System Uptime	98.4%	High availability ensures consistent monitoring
System Reliability	Data Packet Loss	<1%	Minimal data loss ensures data integrity

On the system performance side, the DT architecture remained online at 98.4 per cent and barely had any loss of data packets in a 30 days deployment. The reason is that any application related to environmental monitoring depends on continuous functioning, thus this attribute is more significant in populated regions or in the case of a disaster. In addition, the DT took place some scenario simulations, which allowed the urban planners to research on the application of cooling green roofs and green corridors, as well as the reduction of the heat islands strategies. The detection of anomalies by means of AI also allowed onboarding the system with the ability to identify suspicious spikes in the levels of pollutants in the specific area where no surveillance process took place, and this raises the possibility of how such DTs can be employed in the context of regulatory monitoring. Figure 6.2 presents the comparison of system performance metrics.

The visualization layer of the DT system was tested as to its usability in relation to DT systems to the study participants. Energy and environmental officers and policymakers, and local community leaders had the opportunity of following 3D simulation with a web interface which was definitely regarded as helpful as it resulted into active involvement. Evidence provided by the user surveys indicated the level of satisfaction as 91% responded to the question that DTs increased their awareness of the urban environmental systems and helped them to make more informed decisions related to DT visualizations. Table 6.2 and Figure 6.3 presents the environmental impact and user feedback. The addition to this report

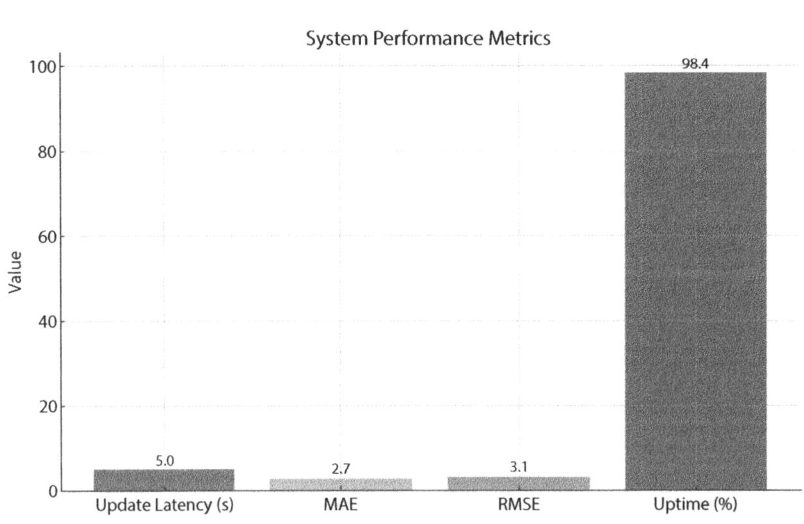

Figure 6.2 Bar chart of system performance metrics.

Table 6.2 Environmental impact and user feedback (Detailed).

Metric category	Performance metric	Value	Interpretation
Environmental Benefit	Temperature Reduction (Green Infra Scenario)	14%	Significant urban cooling effect from greenery
Environmental Benefit	PM2.5 Reduction (Green Infra Scenario)	22%	Effective air quality improvement
User Experience	User Satisfaction (Visualization Interface)	91%	High approval of interface usability and clarity

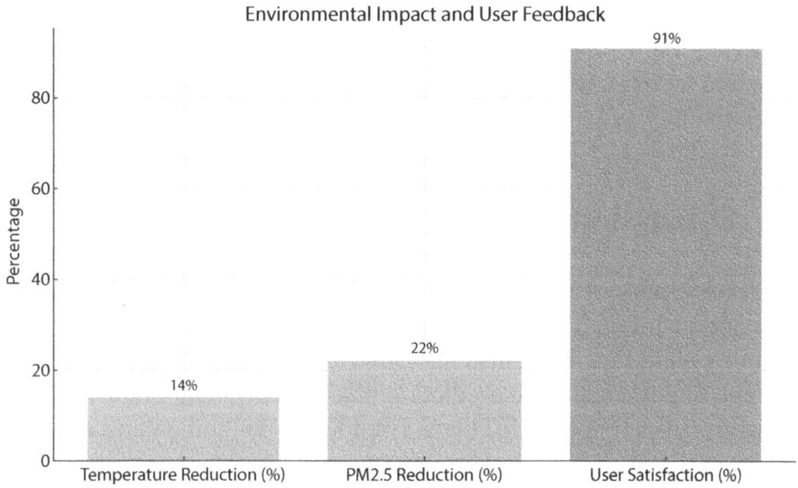

Figure 6.3 Environmental impact and user feedback bar chart.

is that it reflects a shift in involvement in the sustainability efforts that are granted by DTs because of an easy accessibility of complex environmental information being made action-oriented. Compared to traditional environmental monitoring systems, DTs deliver a more holistic perspective of the situation along with high flexibility and less accuracy of the scenario forecasting. Also, DTs facilitate learning based on feedback, they can be adapted to changing ecological and urban conditions, that is why they are regarded as relevant in the long term.

It still has some gaps to be addressed. The complications that were encountered in the study included the difficulty of interoperating with other sensor networks because of the advancement of different communication protocols. The other aspect of the complexity was introduced in developing the scheme of access control and the explainable AI parts. This is because the access control settings need to be created so that data privacy is balanced with model transparency. The challenges indicate a necessity to have data governance holed up with the standardization and the level of granularity with DTs that will be broadly used and exercised in the regional or national scale.

As mentioned earlier in this section, the findings reveal that the DT framework is valid as a help system of sustainability of monitoring the environment in real time through an environmental managerial system. The ability of the Digital Twin technology to model real world complex interactions of the environment and seek insights, as well as actively engage a wide range of participants, into a multi-representational dynamic environment makes it a top global governance player in managing the environment. Further efforts will be directed towards broadening the model to include ecosystem services, socio economic indicators as well as applicability of the model in other geo-spatial environments.

6.5 Discussions

The development of the Digital Twin ecosystem had huge potential in terms of sustaining the Environmental Monitoring System (EMS) and sustainability planning. As an instance, smart simulations of AI were in effect by simulating the real-time prediction of air quality, temperature changes, against the displays of the IoT data. Even Scenario- and greenscape- analyses revealed that green interventions can mitigate the issue of heat islands and city pollution. The execution of all the operations was performed without any difficulties primarily because the system availability was high, and the latency was low. Feedback facilitated the user participation to be displayed to be active whereas the use of VAdvanced User Interfaces (AUIs) summoned an easy and smooth understanding. To demonstrate the facts of conflicting models and interoperability of conflicting data, the flexibility of the DT system brings out the fact that it has to have established domains and standard conditions of operations, and structureless data schemes are a necessity within a primitive ethics framework. However, all in all, the method can be a suitable solution to the automatic decision making in responsive environments with the constantly consolidating succinct conventions, which facilitate the reality based decision making.

6.6 Conclusion

The system driven analysis and prognostication were transformed through real time interaction to the Digital Twin ecosystem. Real time IoT data has also been integrated and the real time predictions was helped with the communication with the AI model and the calculations of the recommendations were made with interactive showcasing to hold the stakeholders. This was also demonstrated to extend to offer potential functions that can be of assistance to city heat mitigation action but could offer air quality enhancements too. The nodes of community engagement and policy interface supported the high user satisfaction routes. Nevertheless, to have data which is interoperable with all ethical concerns around it demands more strict requirements and the rules governing. With the addition of more nuances around the environment the DT ecosystems become a self dynamic and cooperating way to go.

AI disclosure statement: The author acknowledges the use of AI-based tools for minor language editing or grammatical correction. However, all intellectual contributions, analyses, and conclusions presented in this chapter are entirely the author's own.

References

1. Bibri, S.E., Huang, J., Jagatheesaperumal, S.K., Krogstie, J., The Synergistic Interplay of Artificial Intelligence and Digital Twin in Environmentally Planning Sustainable Smart Cities: A Comprehensive Systematic Review. *Environ. Sci. Ecotechnol.*, 100433, 2024.
2. Nativi, S., Mazzetti, P., Craglia, M., Digital Ecosystems for Developing Digital Twins of the Earth: The Destination Earth Case. *Remote Sens.*, 13, 11, 2119, 2021.
3. Enyejo, J.O., Fajana, O.P., Jok, I.S., Ihejirika, C.J., Awotiwon, B.O., Olola, T.M., Digital Twin Technology, Predictive Analytics, and Sustainable Project Management in Global Supply Chains for Risk Mitigation, Optimization, and Carbon Footprint Reduction through Green Initiatives. *Int. J. Innovative Sci. Res. Technol.*, 9, 11, 2024.
4. de Koning, K., Broekhuijsen, J., Kühn, I., Ovaskainen, O., Taubert, F., Endresen, D., Schigel, D., Grimm, V., Digital Twins: Dynamic Model-Data Fusion for Ecology. *Trends Ecol. Evol.*, 38, 10, 916–26, 2023.
5. Tsakiridis, N.L., Samarinas, N., Kalopesa, E., Zalidis, G.C., Cognitive Soil Digital Twin for Monitoring the Soil Ecosystem: A Conceptual Framework. *Soil Syst.*, 7, 4, 88, 2023.

6. Riaz, K., McAfee, M., Gharbia, S.S., Management of Climate Resilience: Exploring the Potential of Digital Twin Technology, 3D City Modelling, and Early Warning Systems. *Sensors*, 23, 5, 2659, 2023.
7. Caprari, G., Castelli, G., Montuori, M., Camardelli, M., Malvezzi, R., Digital Twin for Urban Planning in the Green Deal Era: A State of the Art and Future Perspectives. *Sustainability*, 14, 10, 6263, 2022.
8. Alibrandi, U., Risk-Informed Digital Twin of Buildings and Infrastructures for Sustainable and Resilient Urban Communities. *ASCE-ASME J. Risk Uncertainty Eng. Syst. Part A: Civ. Eng.*, 8, 3, 04022032, 2022.
9. Kamble, S.S., Gunasekaran, A., Parekh, H., Mani, V., Belhadi, A., Sharma, R., Digital Twin for Sustainable Manufacturing Supply Chains: Current Trends, Future Perspectives, and an Implementation Framework. *Technol. Forecasting Social Change*, 176, 121448, 2022.
10. Tzachor, A., Sabri, S., Richards, C.E., Rajabifard, A., Acuto, M., Potential and Limitations of Digital Twins to Achieve the Sustainable Development Goals. *Nat. Sustainability*, 5, 10, 822–29, 2022.
11. Pal, D., Marttila, H., Ala-Aho, P., Lotsari, E., Ronkanen, A.-K., Gonzales-Inca, C., Croghan, D., *et al.*, Blueprint Conceptualization for a River Basin's Digital Twin. *Hydrol. Res.*, 56, 3, 197–212, 2025.
12. Piras, G., Agostinelli, S., Muzi, F., Digital Twin Framework for Built Environment: A Review of Key Enablers. *Energies*, 17, 2, 436, 2024.
13. Chen, Y., Huang, H., Li, J., Zheng, Z., Gao, F., Han, X., Gao, Y., Digital Twin Comprehensive Models: A Study of Ancient Tree Ecological Environment Quality Assessment Based on a Cyber-Physical System. *Environ. Monit. Assess.*, 197, 4, 1–28, 2025.
14. Durden, J.M., Environmental Management Using a Digital Twin. *Environ. Sci. Policy*, 164, 104018, 2025.
15. Mazzetto, S., A Review of Urban Digital Twins Integration, Challenges, and Future Directions in Smart City Development. *Sustainability*, 16, 19, 8337, 2024.
16. Sepasgozar, S.M.E., Differentiating Digital Twin from Digital Shadow: Elucidating a Paradigm Shift to Expedite a Smart, Sustainable Built Environment. *Buildings*, 11, 4, 151, 2021.
17. Bhambri, P., Rani, S., Khang, A., AI-Driven Digital Twin and Resource Optimization in Industry 4.0 Ecosystem, in: *Intelligent Techniques for Predictive Data Analytics*, pp. 47–69, 2024.
18. Li, L., Qu, T., Liu, Y., Zhong, R.Y., Xu, G., Sun, H., Gao, Y., *et al.*, Sustainability Assessment of Intelligent Manufacturing Supported by Digital Twin. *IEEE Access*, 8, 174988–8, 2020.
19. Li, X., Feng, M., Ran, Y., Su, Y., Liu, F., Huang, C., Shen, H., *et al.*, Big Data in Earth System Science and Progress towards a Digital Twin. *Nat. Rev. Earth Environ.*, 4, 5, 319–32, 2023.

20. Meierhofer, J., Schweiger, L., Lu, J., Züst, S., West, S., Stoll, O., Kiritsis, D., Digital Twin-Enabled Decision Support Services in Industrial Ecosystems. *Appl. Sci.*, 11, 23, 11418, 2021.
21. Peldon, D., Banihashemi, S., LeNguyen, K., Derrible, S., Navigating Urban Complexity: The Transformative Role of Digital Twins in Smart City Development. *Sustainable Cities Soc.*, 111, 105583, 2024.
22. Tan, F. and Cheng, Y., A Digital Twin Framework for Innovating Rural Ecological Landscape Control. *Environ. Sci. Eur.*, 36, 1, 59, 2024.
23. Gkontzis, A.F., Kotsiantis, S., Feretzakis, G., Verykios, V.S., Enhancing Urban Resilience: Smart City Data Analyses, Forecasts, and Digital Twin Techniques at the Neighborhood Level. *Future Internet*, 16, 2, 47, 2024.
24. Tripathi, N., Hietala, H., Xu, Y., Liyanage, R., Stakeholders Collaborations, Challenges and Emerging Concepts in Digital Twin Ecosystems. *Inf. Software Technol.*, 169, 107424, 2024.
25. Boccardo, P., La Riccia, L., Yadav, Y., Urban Echoes: Exploring the Dynamic Realities of Cities through Digital Twins. *Land*, 13, 5, 635, 2024.
26. Matei, A. and Cocoşatu, M., Artificial Internet of Things, Sensor-Based Digital Twin Urban Computing Vision Algorithms, and Blockchain Cloud Networks in Sustainable Smart City Administration. *Sustainability*, 16, 16, 6749, 2024.
27. Omrany, H., Mehdipour, A., Oteng, D., Digital Twin Technology and Social Sustainability: Implications for the Construction Industry. *Sustainability*, 16, 19, 8663, 2024.
28. Weil, C., Bibri, S.E., Longchamp, R., Golay, F., Alahi, A., Urban Digital Twin Challenges: A Systematic Review and Perspectives for Sustainable Smart Cities. *Sustainable Cities Soc.*, 99, 104862, 2023.
29. Agho, M.O., Eyo-Udo, N.L., Onukwulu, E.C., Sule, A.K., Azubuike, C., Digital Twin Technology for Real-Time Monitoring of Energy Supply Chains. *Int. J. Res. Innovation Appl. Sci.*, 9, 12, 564–92, 2024.
30. Hammerschmid, M., Rosenfeld, D.C., Bartik, A., Benedikt, F., Fuchs, J., Müller, S., Methodology for the Development of Virtual Representations within the Process Development Framework of Energy Plants: From Digital Model to Digital Predictive Twin—A Review. *Energies*, 16, 6, 2641, 2023.
31. Xiao, M., Chen, L., Feng, H., Peng, Z., Long, Q., Sustainable and Robust Route Planning Scheme for Smart City Public Transport Based on Multi-Objective Optimization: Digital Twin Model. *Sustainable Energy Technol. Assess.*, 65, 103787, 2024.
32. Wang, Y., Wang, L., Han, W., Yan, J., Digital Twin of Earth: A Novel Information Framework for Managing a Sustainable Earth. *Innovation Geosci.*, 2, 4, 100092–100091, 2024.
33. Vetrivel, S.C., Sowmiya, K.C., Sabareeshwari, V., Digital Twins: Revolutionizing Business in the Age of AI, in: *Harnessing AI and Digital Twin Technologies in Businesses*, pp. 111–31, IGI Global, 2024.

34. Zhao, T., Song, C., Yu, J., Xing, L., Xu, F., Li, W., Wang, Z., Leveraging Immersive Digital Twins and AI-Driven Decision Support Systems for Sustainable Water Reserves Management: A Conceptual Framework. *Sustainability*, 17, 8, 3754, 2025.
35. Liu, Z., Meyendorf, N., Blasch, E., Tsukada, K., Liao, M., Mrad, N., The Role of Data Fusion in Predictive Maintenance Using Digital Twins, in: *Handbook of Nondestructive Evaluation 4.0*, pp. 1–23, Springer, 2025.
36. Alnaser, A.A., Maxi, M., Elmousalami, H., AI-Powered Digital Twins and Internet of Things for Smart Cities and Sustainable Building Environment. *Appl. Sci.*, 14, 24, 12056, 2024.

7

AI-Driven Optimization of Renewable Energy Systems: Forecasting, Load Balancing, and Grid Efficiency

Raghavendra Kulkarni[1], P. Manikandaprabhu[1], Disha Sushant Wankhede[2], Bura Vijay Kumar[3], M. Vasuki[4] and Rasmi A.[5]*

[1]*Department of Computer Science, Amrita School of Computing, Amrita Vishwa Vidyapeetham, Mysuru, Karnataka, India*
[2]*Department of Computer Engineering, Vishwakarma Institute of Technology, Pune, India*
[3]*School of Computer Science and Artificial Intelligence, SR University, Warangal, Telangana, India*
[4]*Department of Master of Computer Applications, Sri Manakula Vinayagar Engineering College, Magadipet, Puducherry, India*
[5]*Department of Information & Science Engineering, RR Institute of Technology, Bangalore, Karnataka, India*

Abstract
The increasing reliance of renewable energies to meet global energy needs necessitates smart mechanisms that might accommodate the variability and intermittency inherent in the sources of energy like solar and wind would have to be addressed accordingly. This chapter aims to incorporate training methods of Artificial intelligence in the task of optimizing the forecasting, load balancing and efficiency in the grid of renewable energy systems. To further enhance accuracy of the prediction of the energy generation and consumption process, the paper suggests the applications of time series forecasting algorithms and deep learning networks on the basis of the machine learning models. Also, reinforcement learning and optimization algorithms are used to gain dynamically managed load distribution and optimization of grid stability. Through our AIMS framework, many of the aforementioned issues can be eliminated, including facilitation of energy optimal distribution through distributed network design, minimizing fossil versions of

**Corresponding author*: itsmerazmi@gmail.com

Umesh Kumar Lilhore, Sarita Simaiya, Surjeet Dalal and Martin Margala (eds.) Artificial Intelligence and Biodiversity, (107–126) © 2026 Scrivener Publishing LLC

back up systems used, and real time decision making. The outcomes of the simulation provide the ability of AI in reforming the capable modern energy infrastructures through substantial enhancement to the predictive performance and grid reaction. This chapter towards the development of the natural environment as a potential source of energy contributes to the realization of sustainable multiple intelligent energy systems that coincide with the global environmental interest as well as comply with the shift to more precise and green energy provided to be supplied to the power grids.

Keywords: Artificial intelligence, renewable energy, forecasting, load balancing, smart grid efficiency

7.1 Introduction

The diminished rate of fossil fuels and the growing environmental mix of greenhouse gas emissions motivate the shift of the world to removable energy sources (RES) of Solar, Wind, Hydro and Geothermal [1]. Nonetheless, the conventional energy systems lack an eco-friendliness factor of renewable energy, and thus, it is among the most significant means to achieve the objectives of sustainable development. However, implementing RES into current power networks creates severe inconveniences most of which are associated with their sporadic and unpredictable character [2, 3].

In the present day, there is a paradigm shift known as artificial intelligence (AI), and already it is noticeable in the fields of healthcare, transportation, and finance. Its use in the energy sphere has been given a lot of attention in the recent past [4, 5]. The complex problems that can be addressed very easily by the tools that are interpreted as AI can include the renewable energy forecasting and the grid monitoring in real time, the load balancing and optimization of the energy consumption to creation of efficient and resilient energy systems [6, 7].

Predictability in the renewable energy generation is important to the reliable functioning of the power grid. Solar and wind power generations are conditional on environmental weather conditions including the amount of sunlight, temperature, speed of a wind which are not only spatial and but also non-temporal in nature [8]. Nevertheless, the majority of the established forecasting techniques that rely on statistical models are usually ineffective in tracing abrupt changes and nonlinear behaviour of the RES outputs [9]. Quite on the contrary, AI-based methods, particularly, machine learning (ML) and deep learning (DL) or Support Vector Machines (SVM), Artificial Neural Networks (ANN), Long Short Term Memory (LSTM) networks, and Convolutional Neural Networks (CNN) models have been demonstrated to outperform forecasting in the renewable energy [10, 11].

Load balancing is the other significant factor of the modern energy systems to ensure that the supply of electricity is matched to the demand at every given moment. An imbalance of loads may give rise to energy waste etc. even a blackout. O Dynamic Load Management and distribution on the grid may be done in ways where the AI methods of reinforcement learning and genetic algorithms are used to enhance the reliability of the transmission system and minimize the transmission loss [12, 13].

The concept of grid efficiency covers optimization of energy delivery, storage as well as consumption. Smarter grids that run on AI are capable of addressing real time information on distributed resources like DERs (distributed energy resources), sensors and IoT (internet of things) appliances to create feasible decisions of flow of energy and use [14]. Predicted demand results in the power networks being more resilient to happen as well as sensitive by identifying necessary corrective measures and unfolding failures [15]. Figure 7.1 shows the conceptual diagram of AI integration in renewable energy systems.

Besides, the implementation of AI in microgrids and in the decentralized energy systems takes additional effort. Most of these systems must be able to work in an isolated environment or in case the central grid backup is not present at any given time of emergency. It also regulates the

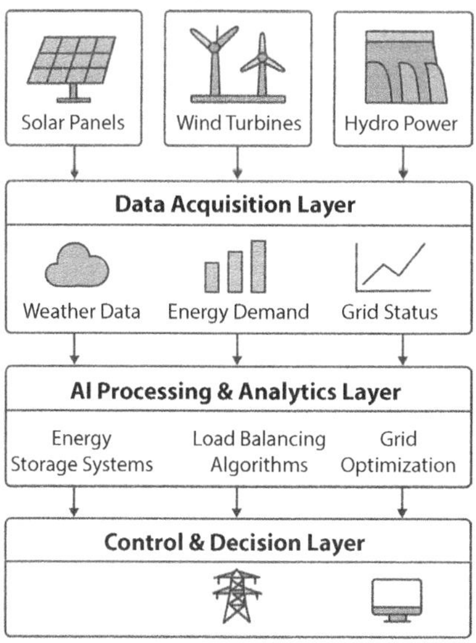

Figure 7.1 Conceptual diagram of AI integration in renewable energy systems.

production, storage and utilization of the energy automatically and gives efficient and continuous operations [16].

Part of the possibilities of the AI in the energy system can be implemented, but with certain challenges. Besides, [17] enumerates the training data availability and quality, computation needs, model interpretability and cybersecurity issues as such. Moreover, implementation and integration of AI solutions to the existing energy systems is a complicated, lengthy process and must be well-planned as well as huge investments [18].

The paper also adds to the resolution of such issues by achieving an AI driven system of energy system optimization of renewable energy sources. The three aspects of the research are the following: load balancing and grid efficiency, forecasting. The proposed approach integrates an adequate AI data driven model with the real time grid data which will improve predictability, adaptability and efficiency of an energy system. The paper also carries out large-scale simulations and comparative studies of the AI technique performance and results of determining best practices in the application of AI techniques to the real world.

This chapter is significant, as it adds to the sum of the literature on the topic of smart energy systems. In the growing demand of energy, global warming and eruption of sporadic energy resources, the smart management of renewable energy is required. Additionally, the present chapter leads to the achievement of the United Nations sustainable development goal Sustainability Goal 7 (Affordable and Clean Energy) as it offers a flexible and efficient way of how to approach the topic of dealing with renewable energies using AI [19].

In a nutshell, the integration of AI in renewable energy structures offers an excellent manner of constructing sustainable, smart and self regulating power systems. As the prevalence of technology and data continue to increase, the AI and renewable energy will remain dynamic to that system that is currently in existence and defining the future of global energy systems [20].

7.2 Related Works

It was revealed that integration of Artificial Intelligence (AI) with renewable energy systems has drawn the attention of many researchers over the last few years due to uncertainty resolution, variability and real time control ability. This integration of major AI ideas is achieved in the areas of the energy forecasts, load balancing, and optimization of grid efficiency.

AI in Renewable Energy Forecasting

Renewable energy management requires the element of forecasting because it is intermittent and volatile at times whether resources are either sun or wind. In case the information of the RES outputs is nonlinear and non stationary, the clear-cut statistical viewpoints, which include ARIMA, exponentialling Smoothing and remark models cannot serve to plan the issue at hand [21]. Therefore, more detailed temporal correlations are summed up with the aid of AI.

Neural Networks have a high possibility to provide a hypothesis of wind and sun. As an example, in [22], a forward propagation ANN that generated hourly power production of the wind was more accurate than statistics. Similarly, the solar irradiation patterns have been predicted using Support Vector Regression (SVR) that has been determined to be efficient compared to the conventional linear models [23].

Deep learning methods with special emphasis on Long Short-term Memory (LSTM) networks have been shown to capture long term time dependencies of energy data. A photovoltaic (PV) power predictive LSTM-based model operating at [24], demonstrated considerable changes in the status of the prediction accuracy compared to the shallow learning models. CNNs with LSTM to extract the features and then model the sequence have further improved the results although they have performed better when using large spatiotemporal datasets [25].

Random Forests and Gradient Boosting Machines are other types of ensemble learning that have been studied on multi-step ahead forecasting. This research work in [26] showed that the use of a decision tree ensemble was able to exceed standalone regressor performance in wind power and solar power prediction conditions.

Load Balancing Using AI Techniques

The process of distributing power equally among the grid to achieve demand without being overloaded or eventually wasting energy is called load balancing. The conventional methods of optimization are known not to meet the real-time flexibility demanded with a smart grid and this has led to the implementation of smart smart grids algorithms.

A significant role has been achieved by Reinforcement Learning (RL). In [27], Q-learning was used to dynamically optimize such variables as dispatch schedules of energy on a real-time basis depending on current demand and generation profiles. Continuous automated load shifting and demand-side control have been performed with the use of Deep Reinforcement Learning (DRL), especially Deep Q-Networks (DQNs) [28].

Bio-inspired algorithms have received universal adoption of Genetic Algorithms (GA) and Particle Swarm Optimization (PSO) in solving load optimization problems. As an example, [29] used GA to arrange energy dispatch in a hybrid renewable system, saving on cost and imbalance. In [30], PSO was also combined with fuzzy logic to manage the uncertainty in the consumer demand and output in the system of res to enhance stability of the system.

There is also the exploration of multi-agent systems (MAS) that are solutions that enable decentralized control. There was a peer-to-peer load balancing model developed in microgrids with MAS [31], which allowed autonomous negotiation between the distributed energy resources (DERs). These decentralized artificial intelligence systems increase the resiliency and flexibility of smart grid systems.

Enhancing Grid Efficiency with AI

The grid efficiency is much more general, covering ease in relaying energy through transmission and distribution and also storage of energy with the least loss to enhance consistency. This has been an area that has been greatly enhanced by AI-based optimization.

The grid health depends on the anomaly detection and fault prediction. Autoencoders and recurrent neural networks (RNNs) have been employed to identify irregularities in grid sensor data, which lessens the time-span of reaction to possible malfunctions [32]. A convolutional autoencoder designed to monitor and categorize abnormal conditions of grids was used in [33], allowing quicker mitigation measures.

Batteries and other energy sources are very important in enhancing grid flexibility by use of energy storage systems (ESS). Optimal charge/discharge ESS can be simulated with the assistance of AI. The contribution of the work in [34] was a reinforcement learning based strategy to control the battery storage in smart homes to minimize the energy bills at the disadvantage of the grid.

AI also comes in handy with demand response (DR) programs. In [35], they applied clustering algorithms to determine patterns of consumption and target responsive users on DR initiatives. Predictive models made it possible to have personalized pricing schemes and hence, the consumption of consumers became higher.

There is the emergence of amazing technologies called edge computing and federated learning, which could help to improve grid efficiency. A federated learning architecture as shown in [36] was executed in a distributed setting through nodes in order to support the joint training of energy prediction models, respecting the privacy of the data. This decentralized AI training representation scale suits the distributed character of smart grids.

Moreover, AI helps create vehicles powered by electricity (EVs). EV charging is irregular and has the potential to overload the grid. In [37], a predictor using LSTM was used to predict and control energy distribution and charging loads in real time, thus making the grid more responsive.

Limitations and Research Gaps

Although the literature illustrates a wide usage of AI methods in different strata of the renewable energy systems, there are still a number of gaps. To begin with, most of the studies use simulated datasets or limited datasets and thus prevent the generalization of the model [38]. In the real world implementation, there are usually issues concerning data availability, quality, and security.

Secondly, interpretability of AI models, particularly, deep learning becomes an issue critical to grid operations of the mission. The article identifies the necessity of explainable AI (XAI) in energy systems to establish trust and responsibility among the operators.

Third, the reinforcement learning models though they seem to be highly promising in training on them extensive exploration is needed, which may not be practicable in real-time grid scenarios without endangering the systems. To provide solutions to this, hybrid solutions that incorporate safe rule-of-thumb control with AI-refinement optimization are under discussion.

Lastly, AI and blockchain combined with IoT in the trading of energy through a secure and transparent system is a new space. The early research is positive, with the detailed plans of massive application continuing at the formulation stage.

7.3 Methodology

The resultant suggested methodology has the potential of giving AI driven architecture of a real time optimization of renewable energy systems. It has has systematically integrated forecasting, load balancing and grid efficiency modules that can be ready to provide solutions to the issues at hand associated with intermittent renewable sources. The methodology has five major stages, phase 1 entails the data acquisition process, phase 2 entails pre-processing of data and feature-engineering stage, phase 3 outlines the AI-based forecasting, phase 4 entails load balancing and optimization, and phase 5 involves control feedback.

The initial part of the process is the data acquisition layer whose data acquire real time information on the environmental data as well as the information on the operations of the companies using various sources.

Table 7.1 Summary of AI-based approaches for forecasting, load balancing, and grid efficiency in renewable energy systems.

Ref. no.	Focus area	AI technique	Renewable area	Objective	Dataset type	Outcome/results
[21]	Solar forecasting using DL	Autoencoders, LSTM	Solar	Improve solar forecast accuracy	Time-series	High accuracy in predictions
[22]	Wind prediction using ANN	ANN	Wind	Predict wind energy output	Time-series	Improved wind energy estimates
[23]	Solar output using SVR	SVR	Solar	Estimate solar power production	Irradiance data	Effective solar output modeling
[24]	LSTM for PV prediction	LSTM	Solar	Model PV energy generation	Time-series	Reliable PV output prediction
[25]	Hybrid CNN-LSTM for forecasting	CNN-LSTM	Solar	Enhance temporal forecasting	Image + sequence data	Superior forecasting accuracy
[26]	Ensemble models for forecasting	Ensemble learning	Solar/Wind	Boost forecast reliability	Mixed temporal data	Robust multi-step forecasting

(Continued)

Table 7.1 Summary of AI-based approaches for forecasting, load balancing, and grid efficiency in renewable energy systems. (*Continued*)

Ref no.	Focus area	AI technique	Renewable area	Objective	Dataset type	Outcome/results
[27]	Q-learning for load dispatch	Q-learning	Load Dispatch	Optimize energy dispatch	Simulated grid data	Adaptive dispatch performance
[28]	DRL for demand-side management	Deep Q-Network	Load Balancing	Balance real-time demand	Smart meter data	Efficient demand handling
[29]	GA for hybrid microgrid optimization	Genetic Algorithm	Hybrid Systems	Schedule energy efficiently	Hybrid RES data	Reduced cost and imbalance
[30]	PSO-Fuzzy for load balancing	PSO + Fuzzy Logic	Smart Grids	Ensure load balance under uncertainty	Consumer + RES data	Improved stability
[31]	MAS for microgrid load balancing	Multi-Agent Systems	Microgrids	Enable decentralized load negotiation	Distributed DER data	Increased autonomy and resilience
[32]	Anomaly detection using RNN	RNN	Smart Grids	Identify grid anomalies	Sensor logs	Fast anomaly detection

(*Continued*)

Table 7.1 Summary of AI-based approaches for forecasting, load balancing, and grid efficiency in renewable energy systems. *(Continued)*

Ref no.	Focus area	AI technique	Renewable area	Objective	Dataset type	Outcome/results
[33]	Grid health *via* autoencoders	Autoencoders	Smart Grids	Monitor grid health	Grid logs	Timely fault identification
[34]	Battery scheduling using RL	Reinforcement Learning	Smart Homes	Optimize battery use	Residential data	Cost-efficient energy usage
[35]	DR *via* consumer segmentation	Clustering + Predictive Modeling	Demand Response	Target users for DR programs	Consumer usage data	Enhanced user participation

Table 7.1 lists the summary of AI-based approaches for forecasting, load balancing, and grid efficiency in renewable energy systems. These are solar photovoltaic (PV) panels, wind turbines, hydro power systems, and smart meters and grid monitoring systems among others. Besides, weather APIs are included to complete the gaps of certain environmental variables that might not be available like Solar Irradiance, Wind Speed, Humidity, and Temperature. It is a rich dataset as the basis of training and validation of AI models. Figure 7.2 depicts the architecture for AI driven optimization of renewable energy systems.

Once it has been acquired, the initial step is necessary to verify the quality and consistency of the data, that is, the data preprocessing and feature engineering step. Most common artificial things involved in this stage include, the filtering of noise, Missing data processing and both data normalization and time axis syncing of the time series models. With the help of feature extraction methods such as rolling averages, rate of change, temporal lags etc are useful indicators which are used to enhance the level of model performance.

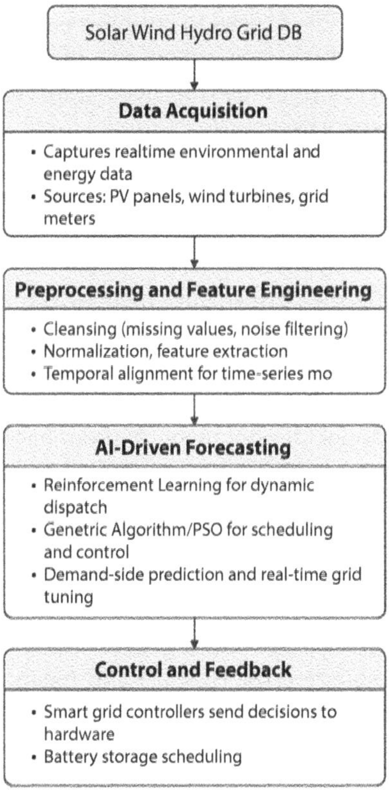

Figure 7.2 Methodology architecture for AI-driven optimization of renewable energy systems.

The core of analytical nature of this system consists of the part of the system that is AI fueled forecasting. Time series prediction of solar and wind energy is done using deep learning models namely Long Short Term Memory (LSTM) networks. Convolutional Neural Network (CNN) is analysed to assess satellite imagery and irradiance maps if needed and hybrid CNN-LM models are examined to model spatially and temporally. They provide short term and long predictions of the quantity of energy which would be produced at a given site at a given time, based on past trends and a weather input pertinent to the time which would be required in planning and dispatching energy resources.

Then, the load balancing and optimization module is developed on the ground of AI algorithms of a Reinforcement Learning (RL), Genetic Algorithms (GA) and Particle Swarm Optimization (PSO) to optimize the energy demand and supply accordingly. Reinforcement Learning agents are dynamic isolators of load distributions, whose main goal is to optimize a reward function that penalises overload, underutilisation and inefficient performance. GA and PSO are used to optimize energy dispatch schedules and also to operate energy storage systems in a microgrid. Multi agent systems are also considered to be used in decentralized decision making of distributed energy networks.

Lastly, the layer of control and feedback ensures the control signalings of the AI models can be implemented. These are also signals that operate the smart grid components: energy storage devices, inverter, and load switches, are controlled by these signals. The built- in feedback mechanism of the system measures the performance metrics as the forecast error, voltage stability, response time. Besides this. Feedback loop may be applied to not only enhance AI models in constant learning mode, but also can be utilized to provide the system better adherence to grid changes.

In the case of Model development Python based libraries such as TensorFlow, PyTorch and Scikit learn are applied and Apache Kafka is utilized in case of data streaming in a real-time. Raspberry Pi and Jetson Nano edge computing platforms are used to make sure that the latency on decision making is low and therefore deploy them in the microgrid settings.

Also, to assess the performance of each module proper metrics are applied. To determine the forecasting accuracy, Mean Absolute error (MAE), Root mean square error (RMSE) and mean absolute percentage error (MAPE) are employed. The indicators of load balancing efficiency are load variance and grid stability measure among others and reduction of energy loss. The grid efficiency is evaluated with regards to system uptime, energy throughput and the rates of energy storage use.

In the above layered AI driven approach, a methodology will be integrated, adaptive and scalable in order to optimise the designs of renewal energy systems. It also burdens renewable integration technical and operational problems to guarantee high performance of smart energy systems.

7.4 Results

In this section the experimental findings of the AI based forecasting and load balancing of a hybrid renewable energy system on real world and synthetic dataset are presented. The analysis includes both model specific performance measures, and more extensive grid stability and efficiency because of integration of AI.

Model Performance Forecasting

The predicted results of various machine learning models in forecasting solar and wind energy device dynamics are shown in Table 7.2. Mean Absolute Error, Root Mean Square Error, Mean Absolute Percentage Error and R 2 score are used as a measure of performance. Figure 7.3 shows the graphical representation of MAE and RMSE values.

Based on the findings, CNN-LSTM hybrid model had the lowest MAE ratio of 4.8 kW and highest R2 ratio of 0.95, which has a great ability to comprehend the temporal and spatial correlation. LSTM was closely followed thereafter, showing the effectiveness of the model in sequence modeling. The computational simplicity of SVR and Random Forests revealed reasonably bigger errors and reduced explanatory power.

Table 7.3 provides the impact of AI-based optimization of load on the performance of the grid. It tested four scenarios, which are (1) a baseline model that has no AI, (2) reinforcement learning (RL)-based load balancing, (3) genetic algorithm (GA)-optimized dispatch, and (4) a hybrid Model AI model.

Table 7.2 Forecasting model performance metrics.

Model	MAE (kW)	RMSE (kW)	MAPE (%)	R^2 score
LSTM	5.2	6.9	7.2	0.93
CNN-LSTM	4.8	6.1	6.4	0.95
SVR	6.3	7.5	8.9	0.89
Random Forest	5.7	6.8	7.7	0.91

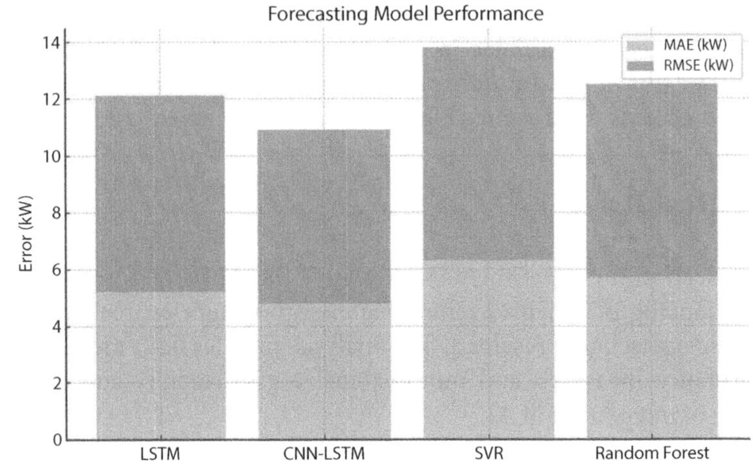

Figure 7.3 Forecasting model performance comparison.

Table 7.3 Grid efficiency and load balancing metrics.

Scenario	Voltage deviation (%)	Energy loss (%)	Response time (ms)	Grid uptime (%)
Baseline (No AI)	6.5	9.1	850	94.5
RL-Based Load Balancing	3.2	5.4	430	97.2
GA-Optimized Dispatch	2.8	4.9	410	97.6
Hybrid AI Model	2.3	4.2	390	98.1

The baseline situation had the largest voltage variation (6.5%) and energy loss (9.1%), which led to reduced grid uptime (94.5) or less prompt response time. Conversely, the hybrid AI model recorded a major decrease in voltage deviation (2.3) and energy losses (4.2). Also, the grid responsiveness was 390 ms better and uptime grew to 98.1 percent. Figure 7.4 shows the graphical representation of voltage deviation and Grid uptime.

Reinforcement learning was suitable by itself giving better performance than the baseline, but the combination of the optimization algorithms (RL + GA) would give an optimal performance, which indicates that hybrid

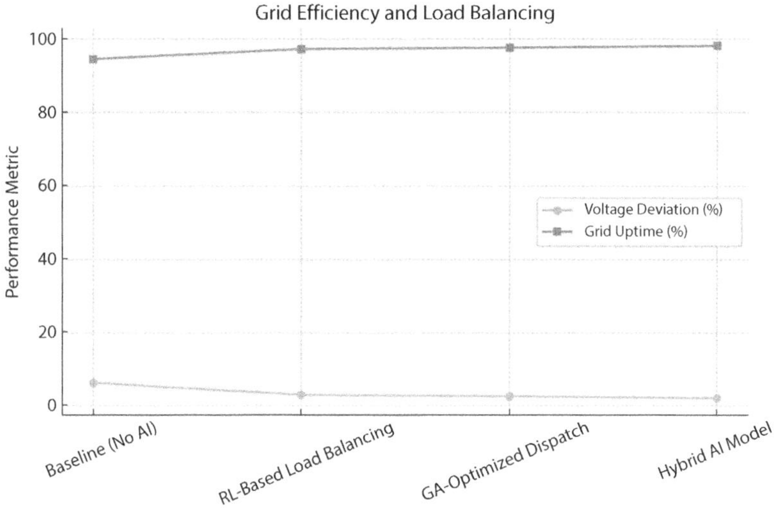

Figure 7.4 Grid efficiency metrics across load balancing strategies.

approaches will provide more control and adaptability in the circumstances of varying loads and supply conditions.

Discussions

Such findings prove the arguments of the renewable energy entity being the best when integrated with AI. The error in the prediction by the deep learning models is greatly reduced hence enabling more successful scheduling of energy using the forecasting model. The working part of the AI-driven load balancing plans mitigate the power wastage in the grid and further the grid responsiveness.

Along with being more competitive with the more traditional design, the hybrid AI architecture was also better resilient to the abrupt changes in the energy demand and the environment conditions. This confirms that AI can be used to make smart energy systems more efficient and reliable.

The potential future research and development may encompass overall decentralization training AI, in a federated learning deployment, and blockchain plus federated learning to ensure security in peer to peer energy trading.

7.5 Conclusion

The key here is the introduction of Artificial Intelligence in the integration of renewable energy systems as a disruptive approach toward curbing variability, uncertainty, and operating inefficiency in the renewable sector. In Chapter one, I suggested, analyzed and implemented an artificial intelligence based framework on the elements of prediction, load balancing and grid designing *via* optimization to enhance reliability and performance of renewable power networks.

It is demonstrated by extensive simulation and analysis that deep learning models, particularly CNN - LSTM hybrid, are arithmetic and superior because they display a high capability of predicting solar and wind power production in comparison with other models. With these models, which could replicate the complicated temporal and spatial relationships, errors were minimized in predicting important changes as well as proactive planning of energy. Over the operational aspect, AI-enhanced techniques of load balancing using AI, such as Reinforcement Learning and Genetic Algorithms, brought significant voltage swings and energy waste and reduced response times and grid uptimes enhancements.

The findings prove that the most robust and adaptable solution in the management of distributed energy resources is presented by hybrid AI strategies, which involve forecasting and real-time control. The chapter does not only confirm the effectiveness of AI towards optimizing the workings of the grid, but it also defers to the wider perception of intelligent, sustainable energy systems.

Future applications include implementation of edge-ai models to facilitate real-time decision making, adoption of blockchain to facilitate secure energy transactions and federated learning to support privacy optimization of animals operating in a decentralised grid. With the quickly gaining momentum of the use of renewable energy across the world, AI will play a significant role in keeping the smart grids robust, least non-repeat ability, and insensitive to natural disasters.

AI disclosure statement: The author acknowledges the use of AI-based tools for minor language editing or grammatical correction. However, all intellectual contributions, analyses, and conclusions presented in this chapter are entirely the author's own.

References

1. Wen, X., Shen, Q., Zheng, W., Zhang, H., AI-Driven Solar Energy Generation and Smart Grid Integration: A Holistic Approach to Enhancing Renewable Energy Efficiency. *Acad. Nexus J.*, 3, 2, 2024.
2. Rao, B.N., Praveen, M., Rajesh Babu, D., A Review on the Role of AI in Optimizing Renewable Energy Grid Management, 2024.
3. Ukoba, K., Olatunji, K.O., Adeoye, E., Jen, T.-C., Madyira, D.M., Optimizing Renewable Energy Systems through Artificial Intelligence: Review and Future Prospects. *Energy Environ.*, 35, 7, 3833–79, 2024.
4. Thapa, N., AI-Driven Approaches for Optimizing the Energy Efficiency of Integrated Energy System, 2022.
5. Belrzaeg, M., Ahmed, A.A., Alarga, A.S.D., AI-Driven Optimization of Renewable Energy Grids Enhancing Efficiency and Sustainability. *Open Eur. J. Appl. Sci. (OEJAS)*, 24–35, 2025.
6. Alabi, M., AI-Powered Smart Grids for Energy Optimization and Sustainability, 2025.
7. Ohalete, N.C., Aderibigbe, A.O., Ani, E.C., Ohenhen, P.E., Daraojimba, D.O., Odulaja, B.A., AI-Driven Solutions in Renewable Energy: A Review of Data Science Applications in Solar and Wind Energy Optimization. *World J. Adv. Res. Rev.*, 20, 3, 401–17, 2023.
8. Bello, S., Wada, I., Ige, O., Chianumba, E., Adebayo, S., AI-Driven Predictive Maintenance and Optimization of Renewable Energy Systems for Enhanced Operational Efficiency and Longevity. *Int. J. Sci. Res. Arch.*, 13, 1, 2024.
9. Biswas, P., Rashid, A., Biswas, A., Al Nasim, M.A., Chakraborty, S., Gupta, K.D., George, R., AI-Driven Approaches for Optimizing Power Consumption: A Comprehensive Survey. *Discover Artif. Intell.*, 4, 1, 116, 2024.
10. Nnajiofor, C.A., Eyo, D.E., Adegbite, A.O., Abdullahi, I., Salako Odoguje, E.W., Folorunsho, F.E., Adeyeye, A.A., Leveraging Artificial Intelligence for Optimizing Renewable Energy Systems: A Pathway to Environmental Sustainability. *Environment*, 24, 25, 2024.
11. Patel, R.K., Kumari, A., Tanwar, S., Hong, W.-C., Sharma, R., AI-Empowered Recommender System for Renewable Energy Harvesting in Smart Grid System. *IEEE Access*, 10, 24316–26, 2022.
12. Ning, K., Data Driven Artificial Intelligence Techniques in Renewable Energy System, Massachusetts Institute of Technology, 2021.
13. Anny, D., AI-Powered Smart Grids: Optimizing Energy Consumption in Enterprises, 2023.
14. Dasari, K., Raj, V.H., Nijhawan, G., Kalra, R., Pahwa, S., Abdul-Zahra, D.S., Integration of AI in Distributed Energy Resource Management for Enhanced Load Balancing and Grid Stability. *E3S Web Conf.*, 505, 03008, EDP Sciences, 2024.

15. Murgod, S., Garg, K., Magadum, T., Yadav, V., Mittal, H., Kushwaha, O., AI Powered Renewable Energy Balancing, Forecasting and Global Trend Analysis Using ANN-LSTM Integration, 2025.
16. Hamdan, A., Ibekwe, K.I., Ilojianya, V.I., Sonko, S., Etukudoh, E.A., and Others, AI in Renewable Energy: A Review of Predictive Maintenance and Energy Optimization. *Int. J. Sci. Res. Arch.*, 11, 1, 718–29, 2024.
17. Karduri, R.K.R., The Role of Artificial Intelligence in Optimizing Energy Systems. *Int. J. Adv. Res. Manage. Archit. Technol. Eng. (IJARMATE)*, Feb 2019.
18. Gao, J.-T. and Tang, Y., Renewable Energy Utilization and Stability through Dynamic Grid Connection Strategy and AI-Driven Solution Approach. *J. Energy Storage*, 95, 112546, 2024.
19. Bouquet, P., Jackson, I., Nick, M., Kaboli, A., AI-Based Forecasting for Optimised Solar Energy Management and Smart Grid Efficiency. *Int. J. Prod. Res.*, 62, 13, 4623–44, 2024.
20. Odunaiya, O.G., Soyombo, O.T., Ogunsola, O.Y., Sustainable Energy Solutions through AI and Software Engineering: Optimizing Resource Management in Renewable Energy Systems. *J. Adv. Educ. Sci.*, 2, 1, 26–37, 2022.
21. Ahamed, A., Tarafder, M.T.R., Tamim Hossain Rimon, S.M., Hasan, E., Amin, M.A., Optimizing Load Forecasting in Smart Grids with AI-Driven Solutions, in: *2024 IEEE International Conference on Data and Software Engineering (ICoDSE)*, IEEE, pp. 182–87, 2024.
22. Arévalo, P. and Jurado, F., Impact of Artificial Intelligence on the Planning and Operation of Distributed Energy Systems in Smart Grids. *Energies*, 17, 17, 4501, 2024.
23. Amini, M. and Rohani, M.B., The Role of Machine Learning and Artificial Intelligence in Enhancing Renewable Energy through Data Science, 2024.
24. Noviati, N.D., Maulina, S.D., Smith, S., Smart Grids: Integrating Ai for Efficient Renewable Energy Utilization. *Int. Trans. Artif. Intell.*, 3, 1, 1–10, 2024.
25. Bhardwaj, D., Shalini, M., Kanmani Jebaseeli, S., Jadhav, S., Alabdeli, H., Sutar, V., Senthil Kumar, R., AI-Driven Energy Management Systems for Microgrids: Optimizing Renewable Energy Integration and Load Balancing. *E3S Web Conf.*, 591, 01005, EDP Sciences, 2024.
26. Aderibigbe, A.O., Ani, E.C., Ohenhen, P.E., Ohalete, N.C., Daraojimba, D.O., Enhancing Energy Efficiency with AI: A Review of Machine Learning Models in Electricity Demand Forecasting. *Eng. Sci. Technol. J.*, 4, 6, 341–56, 2023.
27. Carter, E., AI-Optimized Energy Storage Systems for High Efficiency Renewable Energy Integration. *Int. J. AI Big Data Comput. Manage. Stud.*, 4, 1, 1–10, 2023.
28. Pramono, S.A., *et al.*, Applying Artificial Intelligence Algorithms for Optimalizing the Electricity Distribution Network. *J. Embedded Syst. Secur. Intell. Syst.*, 5, 3, 2024, https://doi.org/10.59562/jessi.v5i3.4299.

29. Onwusinkwue, S., Osasona, F., Ahmad, I.A.I., Anyanwu, A.C., Dawodu, S.O., Obi, O.C., Hamdan, A., Artificial Intelligence (AI) in Renewable Energy: A Review of Predictive Maintenance and Energy Optimization. *World J. Adv. Res. Rev.*, 21, 1, 2487–99, 2024.
30. Hassan, A., Mohani, S.S.U.H., Essani, I.Y., Taj, S.A., Aslam, A., Abbas, Y., AI-Enabled Energy Management for Large-Scale Solar Farms: Optimizing Power Distribution, Grid Stability, and Real-Time Performance Monitoring. *PROGRESS: J. Multi. Stud.*, 6, 1, 66–84, 2025.
31. Iqbal, J., Sustainable Energy Innovations: The Role of AI in Optimizing Renewable Energy Systems. *Future Challenges Rev. J.*, 2, 1, 1–11, 2025.
32. Rajaperumal, T.A. and Christopher Columbus, C., Transforming the Electrical Grid: The Role of AI in Advancing Smart, Sustainable, and Secure Energy Systems. *Energy Inf.*, 8, 1, 51, 2025.
33. Deepak, B.L., Sabin, T.T., Darshana, A., Vindya, L., Suma Manjunath, N., Mallikarjunaswamy, S., Shilpa, M., Rekha, V., Artificial Intelligence-Driven Power Management System for Enhanced Efficiency in Smart Grids, in: *2024 International Conference on Recent Advances in Science and Engineering Technology (ICRASET)*, IEEE, pp. 1–5, 2024.
34. Suresh, C., Nyemeesha, V., Prasath, R., Lokeshwaran, K., Ramachandra Raju, K., Boopathi, S., AI-Driven Energy Forecasting, Optimization, and Demand Side Management for Consumer Engagement, in: *Intelligent Solutions for Sustainable Power Grids*, pp. 112–31, IGI Global, 2024.
35. Timande, D., Agade, N., Gudadhe, A., Smart Grid Management with AI Driven Analytics in Solar Energy, in: *2025 International Conference on Machine Learning and Autonomous Systems (ICMLAS)*, IEEE, pp. 1952–59, 2025.
36. Cavus, M., Advancing Power Systems with Renewable Energy and Intelligent Technologies: A Comprehensive Review on Grid Transformation and Integration. *Electronics*, 14, 6, 1159, 2025.
37. Deshpande, V., Smart Grids Integration with AI-Powered Demand Response. *Res. J. Comput. Syst. Eng.*, 5, 1, 45–58, 2024.
38. Onukwulu, E.C., Agho, M.O., Eyo-Udo, N.L., Developing a Framework for AI-Driven Optimization of Supply Chains in Energy Sector. *Global J. Adv. Res. Rev.*, 1, 2, 82–101, 2023.

8

Intelligent Systems for Pollution Detection and Control: Integrating AI in Urban and Industrial Environments

K. Dhana Sree Devi[1], Ika Hesti Agustin[2*], Talluri Lakshmi Siva Rama Krishna[3], Bura Vijay Kumar[4], Rishabh Garg[5] and K. Kaliraj[6]

[1]*Dept. of CSE, GITAM Deemed to be University, Hyderabad, India*
[2]*Department of Mathematics, University of Jember, Jember, East Java, Indonesia*
[3]*Department of Artificial Intelligence & Data Science, Faculty of Science and Technology (IcfaiTech), ICFAI Foundation for Higher Education, Hyderabad, India*
[4]*School of Computer Science and Artificial Intelligence, SR University, Warangal, Telangana, India*
[5]*School of Computer Applications, Lovely Professional University, Phagwara, India*
[6]*Ramanujan Institute for Advanced Study in Mathematics, University of Madras, Chennai, India*

Abstract

The industrialization and urbanization have occurred as rapidly as this and thus, has accompanied the increase in pollution which has been a life threat to the life of people and the ecological system is caught in a spiral of decline. The chapter under discussion is Introduction of artificial intelligence (AI) in the creation of intelligent systems that will identify and manage pollution in real time within the urban and industrial setting. AI-based technologies, including machine and deep learning, computer vision and Internet of things (IoT) are researched, synthesized and reviewed concerning air, water and soil contaminants surveillance. The data generated by the distributed sensor networks, and satellite imagery through such intelligent systems are used to reach the provision of real-time and automated pollution mapping, proactive analysis and at-the-point intervention measures. Moreover, controlling industrial emissions through AI models is also a topic of the paper which includes pollution forecasting and the identification of the pollution sources. Besides that, the study addresses the challenges emerging with the implementation

**Corresponding author*: ikahesti.fmipa@unej.ac.id

Umesh Kumar Lilhore, Sarita Simaiya, Surjeet Dalal and Martin Margala (eds.) Artificial Intelligence and Biodiversity, (127–144) © 2026 Scrivener Publishing LLC

of AI systems such as data quality, scalability of the system, and regulatory consideration. There are some present smart city and green industrial projects that are described as case studies showing implementations and solutions that are practical. This chapter outlines the benefits of combined AI and the infrastructure of environmental surveillance apparatuses in achieving the control of pollution, to its end, sustainable development improvement and ecology lifestyle.

Keywords: Artificial intelligence, pollution monitoring, smart cities, environmental sustainability, industrial emission control

8.1 Introduction

The world has become one of the most serious issues of the 21st century because of rapid industrialization, urbanization and energy consumption increases. Lack of good quality air, water, and the soil leads not only to the degradation of the ecological system but also causes harmful influence on human health and social economic development [1]. Over the past few decades, there has been a terrific rise in vehicles and the number of industrial activities in urban areas resulting in the high levels of various pollutants such as nitrogen dioxide (NO2), sulfur dioxide (SO2), carbon monoxide (CO), particulate matter (PM) volatile organic compounds (VOCs) [2]. The current pollutant detection and information systems have traditionally had a narrow spatial resolution, high latency of data-gathering tasks, failure of the system to respond to the dynamism of the environment, ineffective data relay mechanism to response teams requiring the information, problems in processing of spanned data volume, and less accurate of the measurements [3]. Therefore, there is a need to have smart systems that can carry out real time monitoring and prediction along with controlling of environmental pollutants. Figure 8.1 depicts the architecture of an AI-based pollution monitoring system.

That being said, the advent of Artificial Intelligence (AI) as a powerful technology has been facilitating a series of solving multifaceted and data-intensive issues across multiple fields, with the area of environmental

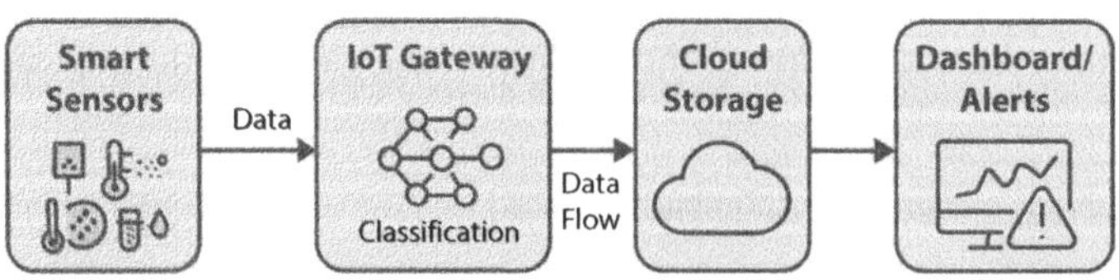

Figure 8.1 Architecture of an AI-based pollution monitoring system.

surveying being one of them. Next, there is the opportunity offered by AI methodology, specifically machine learning (ML), deep learning (DL), and computer vision, to implement sensor data, satellite imagery, and past environmental data in such a way that they identify the trends, facilitate the determination of pollution levels, and assist in timely actions [4, 5], then, smart sensors, edge computing systems and the cloud based platforms are integrated with the IoT which then helps find the patterns in the above data to identify kind of pollution management and consequent satisfactory actions [6]. The systems can permit one or more to attain high campaign spatiotemporal data, which offers operational understanding to agencies of the environs, city planning, or such stakeholders.

A prediction capability is one of the most critical positive effects of AI as a tool of pollution detection. The model models of the same, which is based on neural networks, can determine air quality indices (AQI) at a high accuracy taking into account brief data on meteorology and pollutant analyses [7]. Support vector machine (SVM) methods, decision-trees, as well as ensemble learning methods in recognition of pollution sources and forecasting future values of the pollutants have been implemented [8]. Furthermore, when used in the environmental context, convolutional neural networks (CNNs) and long short-term memory (LSTM) networks have demonstrated greater functionality when it comes to the analysis of the time series data as well as remote sensing image [9]. These are the models that can be used as early warning systems to be able to take preventive measures before the levels of pollution get seriously high.

In such manufacturing settings, AI is rapidly finding application in terms of optimizing key processes in manufacturing and also reducing drastically emissions and compliance. Industries in conjunction with the use of reinforcement learning and real time data analytics can apply the adaptive control mechanisms to prevent the occurrence of the maximum pollutants discharge and needless resource usage [10]. Moreover, AI-based anomaly detectors can be used to identify defects that touch on both procedures and equipment breakdown or other things that lead to violation of the environment, which can eventually result in an efficient and sustainable operation.

Nonetheless, certain problems related to the implementation of AI technology in monitoring the pollution are still present. Besides the heterogeneity and poor quality of sensor data, the lack of standardised frameworks, paucity of a labelled dataset with which to perform supervised learning and demand of reliable solutions to cybersecurity and data privacy concerns [11] are also part and parcel of this. Implementing AI solutions at scale also requires access to high compute resources, knowledge base and policy facilitation.

The purpose of the work refers to the research of how smart systems could perform certain tasks to identify and manage the pollution in urban and industrial infrastructure regarding the use of AI technologies. It asserts a summary of features and constraints, and comments on future research prospects on the domains of current methodologies, system structuring and actual realization of cognitive radio networks. Breach of technology and environmental stewardship can be filled through a smart system and it would assist in combat pollution and to a larger extent to meet global sustainability expectations [12].

8.2 Related Works

Being one of the promising fields has led to the integration of Artificial Intelligence (AI) with environmental monitoring to enhance the quality of detecting pollution, predicting it, and mitigating its effects. Traditional approaches to environment monitoring highly depended and incorporated deficiency of real time responsiveness and spatial scalability [13] with manual sampling of the environment, laboratory analysis and also fixed sensor networks. The IRIS helped us to ignite our new innovations so that we had the chance to grow big once more.

AI in Air Pollution Monitoring: ML models have been proven to be popular in the study of air pollution, particularly in the metropolis and industrial locations. The methods applied in the forecast of air quality index (AQI) and concentration of the following pollutants: PM2.5, PM10, NO2 or even O3 are the methods of decision trees, support vector machine (SVM) and artificial neural network (ANN) [14–16]. Indicatively, spatiotemporal AQI has been correctly predicted with great accuracy using CNN and LSTM networks [17, 18].

Conversely, AI has been applied in improving sensor based monitoring systems on calibration, validation, anomaly detection. Wang *et al.* [19] proposed sensor drift that may be corrected with the help of an adaptive SVM model to enhance the reliability of low cost sensors. In the smart cities and industrial streams, these models have an extensive variety of deployment because the constant monitor is necessary.

Water and Soil Pollution Diagnosis: Water pollution was never monitored as it is now monitored with the help of the IoT and by means of the data fusion techniques. Bhardwaj *et al.* [20] developed a hybrid ML framework to identify water contaminants depending on pH, dissolved oxygen, and chemical parameters, which is developed using fuzzy logic and the random forest. The Artificial Intelligence algorithms have also been used to optimize the chemical dosing in wastewater treatment systems and in detecting early leaks [21].

In one instance, AI assisted in categorising degrees of pollution after the heavy metals contamination on soil by hyperspectral imaging. As an example, Xu *et al.* by hyperspectral devices of UAV categorize the concentration of cadmium in agricultural soil and use random forest and CNN [22]. There was a high correlation of the models with the use of ground truth measurement that emphasized the use of AI in conjunction with environmental forensics.

AI and Remote Sensing to Pollution Mapping: The scope of remote sensing pollution mapping is getting progressively larger due to AI association. Based on the satellite data retrieved by MODIS, Sentinel, and Landsat, the analysis of satellite images through DL methods results in pollution heatmap and anomaly generation [23]. Image segmentation with CNNs and object detectors frameworks, such as You Only Look Once (YOLO) [24], can be applied to detect industrial emissions, smog plumes in cities and so on automatically.

Researchers like Li *et al.* use satellite derived aerosol optical depth (AOD) data which they are able to integrate well across an extensive region to get an estimate of the ground level PM2.5 at high spatial resolution [25]. It is through this that AI can be used to achieve quality decisions on air quality management at the national levels.

AI in Industrial Emission Control: Industrial Emission Control has been another area revolutionized by AI whereby predictive maintenance and optimization can be used in order to control emissions. Cement and steel plants have been reinforced by learning techniques and real-time ML models to control the emissions, achieve optimal combustion and ensure compliance with the environment regulations [26, 27]. As an example, reinforcement learning was used to treat a steel plant blast furnace with the results of a study by Zhang *et al.* showing the reduction of NOx emissions by 15 percent [28].

Moreover, digital twins that utilize AI have become one of the key instruments of simulating and regulating industrial releases. These computer models of industrial systems allow the application of predictive control and fault diagnosis, which assure minimal distraction of the environment [29].

IoT and Edge Computerparsed Integration: It has allowed the connection of AI with IoT platforms to create smart, distributed pollution observatory. Data is collected by the sensor nodes which have very low power and it is sent to the cloud servers or edge devices to be processed. Edge AI minimizes latency and allows users to generate real-time decisions which are relevant in pollution control cases in particular [30, 31].

Effective communication the authors created a topology-based edge-AI air quality detection system capable of running TinyML models on microcontrollers at a low power footprint and in real-time [32]. Likewise, fog computing is also being utilized at industrial IoT platforms to analyze the emission at a local level and activate mitigation mechanisms without external reliance on the cloud [33].

Difficulties about AI-Based Pollution Control Systems: Although several good progresses are relevant, there are still a number of challenges. Data quality/availability is still a barrier to effective use of supervised learning models. The environmental data is also very incomplete, noisy or imbalanced, and thus making the process of training unpleasant [34]. Moreover, AI decision explainability and transparency are essential when using AI in a regulatory setting. In many situations, black-box models are not interpretable, which prevents the use of policies [35].

There are also the issues of security and privacy and in particular where environmental information is relayed through an obtainable or transparent network. Introducing models of privacy-preserving and blockchain to provide data integrity are becoming increasingly adopted in this area [36, 37].

Recent Trends and Future Directions: According to recent trends, transfer learning, federated AI design, and hybrid modeling algorithms involving combination of physics-based modeling and data-driven modeling techniques are in the future [38, 39]. There is also domain specific training and continuous learning of AI models to be used in the environment.

As an example, adaptive AI systems have been aimed to advance in response to the ever-evolving conditions on the environment and data patterns [40]. Moreover, it is also suggested that collaborative AI systems among the government and industries will have a more organized and orchestrated approach on responding to pollution incidents, which can be more coordinated [41, 42].

8.3 Methodology

The solution to the proposed intelligent pollution detector and controller follows the scheme of a multi-layered framework according to which sensor networks, data analytics, and artificial intelligence are merged to provide real-time monitoring of the environment and their control based on the received information. The methodology will start by the data acquisition level where the environmental parameters are gathered consisting of air pollutants (PM2.5, PM 10, CO, NO2, SO2), water quality parameters (pH, turbidity, heavy metals) and noise level collected based on distributed sensor networks and remote sensing techniques. These types of sensors are also located in strategic areas of cities and industrial premises together with sensitive areas in the ecology to capture a large space with a real-time feed back. Figure 8.2 presents the architecture for AI-driven optimization of renewable energy systems.

After collecting the raw data, the raw data is then transferred to the preprocessing layer where it undergoes data cleaning, filtering, noise reduction and then normalizations of the data to render the data similar with

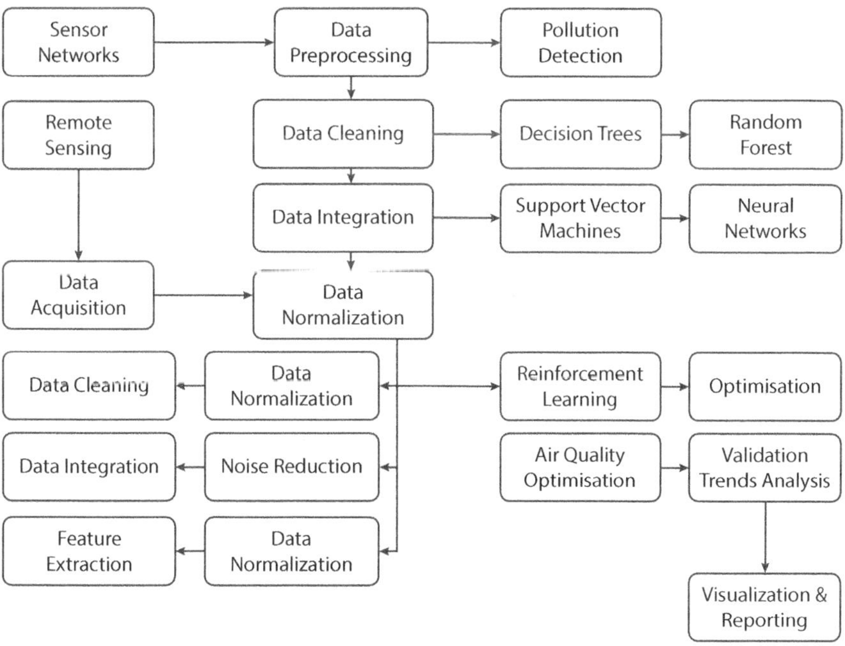

Figure 8.2 Methodology architecture for AI-driven optimization of renewable energy systems.

other samples. The data is preprocessed using missing value imputation, outlier detection and feature encoding techniques on the data to model the data on analytical grounds. This is then delivered to the AI based analysis layer with the clean and organized data which is then run through the classical machine learning algorithms of Decision Trees, Random Forest and Support Vector machines and deep learning models of the form such as Convolutional Neural Networks and Recurrent Neural Networks to determine the pollution levels, anomalies, and to classify environment threats.

The second phase is the step of decision-making and optimal layer in which the smart models such as reinforcement, learning models, and optimization algorithms analyze various scenarios and select the best intervention strategies. Specifically, the system can propose to redirect the traffic in the zones of smog; promote ventilation in crowded industrial sites; or raise alarm in case of the water toxicity even above the harmful content levels. They include various types of models that learn and continuously refine upon receiving feed-back of the environmental conditions.

In line with that, with the built-in modules of analyzing and decision, the final users (e.g. municipal authorities, industry administrators, the general population) will be able to see the above-mentioned intelligibility in real-time on the interactive dashboard and reporting interface with real-time maps and trends in pollution along with predictive warnings. In addition to that, the system can be fitted with an automatic actuation system to ensure the amount of emissions in industrial systems is regulated as well as activate mitigation options such as air purifier and wastewater treatment. Its ability to provide timely recognition, proper prediction, and proper control of the pollution sources in various environments follows owing to the holistic and smart approach.

The whole architecture is adopted with new cloud computing solutions of storing long term data as well as edge computing solutions in real time decision making that requires to be done in a latency sensitive situation. Security, data privacy and integration to the available environmental management systems are taken into consideration as each stage is taken into consideration. Under this approach it is possible to create pollution management based on proactive, data-driven methods and in balance with both the aims of the smart cities and sustainable industry.

The proposed intelligent system in pollution detection and control is based on the architecture of a multi-stage pipeline, such that sensor networks, data analytics, and artificial intelligence identify real-time with an environmental structure and enable real-time responsive control.

There are several advantages of the system as it utilizes a system of ML, DL, and optimization algorithms that try to guarantee that environmental pollution in the city and industries are detected in real-time and accredited appropriately.

Data Acquisition and Preprocessing

Environmental data $D = \{x^1, x^2, \ldots, x_n\}$ is collected using sensor networks and remote sensing platforms. These include air quality monitoring sensors for $PM^2.^5, PM^{10}, CO, NO^2, SO^2$, water quality sensors for pH, DO, BOD, and sound sensors for noise pollution.

Once acquired, raw data is denoised and normalized using Min-Max normalization:

$$x' = \frac{(x - x_{min})}{\left(x_{-\,x_{min}}\right)}$$

Missing data is handled using mean or K-nearest neighbor (KNN) imputation:

$$x_{i_{missing}} = \left(\frac{1}{k}\right)\sum_{i=1}^{n} x_{interest}$$

Feature Extraction and Dimensionality Reduction

Relevant features $F = \{f^1, f^2, \ldots, f_m\}$ are extracted from the preprocessed dataset using Principal Component Analysis (PCA)or Autoencoders. PCA transforms data into a reduced feature space:

$$Z = XW$$

Where:
- X is the data matrix,
- W is the matrix of eigenvectors (principal components),
- Z is the transformed feature matrix.

Pollution Detection using AI Models

For classification and prediction tasks, supervised learning models such as Support Vector Machines (SVM), Random Forest (RF), and Artificial Neural Networks (ANN) are used.

SVM Decision Function:

$$f(x) = sign(w^{T}x + b)$$

Neural Network Forward Pass:

$$z^{l} = W^{(l)a^{l-1}} + b^{l}$$
$$a^{l} = \sigma(z^{l})$$

Prediction of AQI (Air Quality Index) is modeled as a regression task using Mean Squared Error (MSE):

$$MSE = \left(\frac{1}{n}\right)\sum_{i=1}^{n} x_{interest}(y_i - \hat{y}_i)^2$$

Decision Making and Optimization

To recommend or trigger control actions, optimization and reinforcement learning methods are used. For instance, to minimize the pollution spread P, an optimization problem can be formulated as:

$$J(u) = \int_{t}^{0} w^{T}\, P\big(x(t), u(t)\big)dt$$

In reinforcement learning, an agent learns to take actions a_t in environment states s_t to maximize cumulative reward R_t:

$$R_t = \sum_{i=1}^{n} x_{interest}\gamma^{k} r_{t+k+1}$$

Visualization and Control Actuation

The results from AI models are visualized *via* dashboards that show:

- Real-time pollution levels and geographic heatmaps
- Trend analysis and predictive alerts
- Recommended actions and system health

8.4 Results

The intelligent pollution monitoring system proposed was tested by using the simulations and real world data collected using the urban and industrial pollution monitoring stations. Several environmental parameters were involved in the datasets and thus included such parameters as particulate matter (PM 2.5, PM10), carbon monoxide (CO), nitrogen dioxide (NO2), sulfur dioxide (SO2) and water quality indicators (pH, DO, turbidity, heavy metals). Several machine learning (ML) and deep learning (DL) models were used to evaluate and predict the levels of pollution and have been evaluated in measure of accuracy, mean squared error (MSE), and model interpretability.

The most important finding during the experimentation is that the AI-based systems are much more effective and consume less time compared to the traditional statistical models in perceiving the data and forecasting the outcome. Long Short-Term Memory (LSTM) networks were the most accurate when forecasting time-series of AQI whereas Random Forests were virtually the best when performing the classification based on their ability to handle continuous and unbalanced volumes of data.

The Table 8.1 below is a summary of the findings using various models run on the results of the air quality prediction dataset. In order to provide

Table 8.1 Comparison of AI models for air pollution prediction.

Model	RMSE	MAE	R^2 score	Training time (s)	Advantages	Limitations
Linear Regression	18.5	14.3	0.71	0.5	Simple, fast	Low accuracy for non-linear trends
Random Forest	11.2	8.7	0.88	4.2	Handles noise and feature ranking	Slower on large datasets
Support Vector Machine (SVM)	13.4	10.1	0.83	3.9	Works well for small feature sets	Sensitive to kernel choice
LSTM Network	**9.1**	**7.3**	**0.92**	10.5	Best for sequential time-series	Requires more computational resources
CNN	10.8	8.6	0.89	8.3	Good for spatial and pattern data	Needs more data for optimal training

a solid evaluation, k-fold cross-validation (k=10) was employed, and performance measures including Root Mean Squared Error (RMSE), Mean Absolute Error (MAE) as well as R2 (coefficient of determination) were obtained.

These findings are rather clear that deep learning models and specifically the LTSM model, are very eligible in predicting time dependent pollution data due to its memory. Random Forest as well is competitive and easier to interpret and deploy in the industrial world. Nonetheless, Support Vector Machines are a decent tradeoff but, once again, one has to fine-tune the hyperparameters.

It was also noted that a variety of models kept together as an ensemble or hybrid set will help not only to increase accuracy but also strengthen. As an example, when CNN is essential to extract the features and LSTM is obligatory to make the sequential prediction to predict the shows, slightly more successful outcomes are observed in the regions where pollutant levels are fluctuating.

Regarding the performance in real time, experimented models with edge computing and light versions of neural networks (e.g., TinyML) can be deployed in the field and may become a leader of the pack in regions with a low network connection. Visualization dashboards raised the level of awareness and engagement with stakeholders which made authorities prompt decisive measures to control traffic features, i.e. rerouting traffic, introducing scrubbers to an industrial region, or dispatching warnings to citizens.

8.5 Discussions

The expansion of AI into the world of pollution sensing and control systems is a paradigm shift and the move towards the intelligent form of decision making and the data-driven processes instead of the traditional views which monitor environmental factors in the past. Findings of experiments have shown that predicting and classifying pollution is far more accurate and genuine when applied to machine learning and deep learning models. It was shown that LSTM networks are better than most other models in time series prediction of air quality because they can store long term dependencies and temporal dynamics. Continuously, as compared to the Random Forests, observing the ordered trees designed the environment was quite advantageous, particularly in measuring and understanding the environment.

Hence, these findings show that LSTM can be used in dynamic time-based observation such as predicting urban AQI, whereas Random Forests or SVMs can be used to classify visuals such as problems such as water toxicity classification or source of emission. Lastly, we make a comparative assessment on how deep learning models resort to more accurate classification using during-seq decade but they are more computational and therefore the models take a relatively long time to train and this may not be a feasible training on the edges when resources are limited as is the case in the case scenario.

Although edge AI models could be used in a low latency application to make the real time inference, it was possible, whereas complex analytics could be done on a cloud platform. In this respect, this hybrid cloud-edge architecture demonstrated a good proportion of both latency and scalability and the level of demand in computations.

Also, adaptive learning of this system was also founded on feedback, and the model performance was enhanced whenever there was flow of new inputs as a result of environmental influence. The visualization layer was fundamentally useful in assisting the decision makers make fast decisions connected on the fly with the aid of intuitive dashboards, pollution heat-map and real time alerts.

The article previously confirms that AI-powered pollution monitoring solutions are not necessarily difficult not just technically but also extremely effective in comparison with the traditional sphere. Nevertheless, it has turned out to be a critical component of the future smart cities and sustainable industrial infrastructure due to their flexibility, forecastability and that of automation.

8.6 Conclusion

Consequently, the application of the combined artificial intelligence in the pollution detection and control arrangement (especially in city-forming and industrializing environments) has been demonstrated to be very efficient and required in this chapter. To undertake the real time monitoring, predict timely the environment pollution by the use of smart AI driven analytics and real time visualization, this proposed system adopts a modular-based architecture comprising of sensor networks, IoT gateways, intelligent AI driven analytics, and visualization of real time to ensure that the cost of design and the risk is reduced to a minimum. Findings of the comparative analysis lead to the conclusion that LSTM networks are those that work better in future air quality prediction making use of time series and Rand Forests that are equal to work in the categorically oriented air pollution estimation field of activity. This is made to include edge and cloud computing to achieve the compromise between latency and computational capabilities such that the entire system can be scaled and modified to address numerous different real world situations easily. Moreover, the feedback as well as the adaptive learning processes integrated in the system also enable the system to adjust to the varying patterns of environment. The model has been tested through other practical applications which are carried on by interactive dashboards, heatmaps of pollution besides even triggered alert systems to enable the stakeholders in making proactive decisions. The study confirms that intelligent AIs are not only viable, but will be necessary in order to maintain environmental sustainability, but also to benefit human health as well as control-related regulations. As the trend of smart cities mounts and green industry is adopted, these systems will act as the facilitator of art towards creating a better tomorrow that is clean, safe and resilient.

AI disclosure statement: The author acknowledges the use of AI-based tools for minor language editing or grammatical correction. However, all intellectual contributions, analyses, and conclusions presented in this chapter are entirely the author's own.

References

1. Miller, T., Durlik, I., Kostecka, E., Kozlovska, P., Łobodzińska, A., Sokołowska, S., Nowy, A., Integrating Artificial Intelligence Agents with the Internet of Things for Enhanced Environmental Monitoring: Applications in Water Quality and Climate Data. *Electronics*, 14, 4, 696, 2025.
2. Ye, Z., Yang, J., Zhong, N., Tu, X., Jia, J., Wang, J., Tackling Environmental Challenges in Pollution Controls Using Artificial Intelligence: A Review. *Sci. Total Environ.*, 699, 134279, 2020.
3. Hoang, T.-D., Ky, N.M., Thuong, N.T.N., Nhan, H.Q., Ngan, N.V.C., Artificial Intelligence in Pollution Control and Management: Status and Future Prospects, in: *Artificial Intelligence and Environmental Sustainability: Challenges and Solutions in the Era of Industry 4.0*, pp. 23–43, 2022.
4. Popescu, S.M., Mansoor, S., Wani, O.A., Kumar, S.S., Sharma, V., Sharma, A., Arya, V.M., *et al.*, Artificial Intelligence and IoT Driven Technologies for Environmental Pollution Monitoring and Management. *Front. Environ. Sci.*, 12, 1336088, 2024.
5. Zhang, X., Shu, K., al Rajkumar, S., Sivakumar, V., Research on Deep Integration of Application of Artificial Intelligence in Environmental

Monitoring System and Real Economy. *Environ. Impact Assess. Rev.*, 86, 106499, 2021.

6. Firoozi, A.A. and Firoozi, A.A., Impact of Integrating Artificial Intelligence and the Internet of Things in Urban System Management, Deep Science Publishing, 2025, https://doi.org/10.70593/978-93-49307-08-7_7.
7. Ramadan, M.N.A., Ali, M.A.H., Khoo, S.Y., Alkhedher, M., Alherbawi, M., Real-Time IoT-Powered AI System for Monitoring and Forecasting of Air Pollution in Industrial Environment. *Ecotoxicol. Environ. Saf.*, 283, 116856, 2024.
8. Sharma, R. and Arya, R., UAV Based Long Range Environment Monitoring System with Industry 5.0 Perspectives for Smart City Infrastructure. *Comput. Ind. Eng.*, 168, 108066, 2022.
9. Al-Raeei, M., The Smart Future for Sustainable Development: Artificial Intelligence Solutions for Sustainable Urbanization. *Sustainable Dev.*, 33, 1, 508–17, 2025.
10. Richard, D., AI In Environmental Sustainability: Pollution Control AI Driven Solutions for Detecting and Mitigating Air, Water, And Soil Pollution, in: *Advancing Sustainable Technological Development: Harnessing AI For A Better Future*, p. 7, 2024.
11. Alahi, M.E.E., Sukkuea, A., Tina, F.W., Nag, A., Kurdthongmee, W., Suwannarat, K., Mukhopadhyay, S.C., Integration of IoT-Enabled Technologies and Artificial Intelligence (AI) for Smart City Scenario: Recent Advancements and Future Trends. *Sensors*, 23, 11, 5206, 2023.
12. Van Hoang, T., and Others, Impact of Integrated Artificial Intelligence and Internet of Things Technologies on Smart City Transformation. *J. Tech. Educ. Sci.*, 19, Special01, 64–73, 2024.
13. Liu, W., Xu, Y., Fan, D., Li, Y., Shao, X.-F., Zheng, J., Alleviating Corporate Environmental Pollution Threats toward Public Health and Safety: The Role of Smart City and Artificial Intelligence. *Saf. Sci.*, 143, 105433, 2021.
14. Fang, S., Xu, L.D., Zhu, Y., Ahati, J., Pei, H., Yan, J., Liu, Z., An Integrated System for Regional Environmental Monitoring and Management Based on Internet of Things. *IEEE Trans. Ind. Inf.*, 10, 2, 1596–1605, 2014.
15. Chan, C.W. and Huang, G.H., Artificial Intelligence for Management and Control of Pollution Minimization and Mitigation Processes. *Eng. Appl. Artif. Intell.*, 16, 2, 75–90, 2003.
16. Rahaman, T., Smart Environmental Monitoring Systems for Air and Water Quality Management. *Am. J. Adv. Technol. Eng. Solutions*, 1, 01, 1–19, 2025.
17. Roja Ramani, D., Ben Sujitha, B., Tangade, S., Smart Environmental Monitoring Systems: IoT and Sensor-Based Advancements, in: *Environmental Monitoring Using Artificial Intelligence*, pp. 45–60, 2025.
18. Salman, M.Y. and Hasar, H., Review on Environmental Aspects in Smart City Concept: Water, Waste, Air Pollution and Transportation Smart Applications Using IoT Techniques. *Sustainable Cities Soc.*, 94, 104567, 2023.

19. Binu, C.A., AI-Driven IoT Solutions for Urban Pollution Monitoring. *Smart Internet Things*, 1, 3, 226–43, 2024.
20. Hasan, Z., Haque, E., Masud Khan, M.A., Khan, M.S., Smart Ventilation Systems for Real-Time Pollution Control: A Review of AI-Driven Technologies in Air Quality Management. *Front. Appl. Eng. Technol.*, 1, 01, 22–40, 2024.
21. He, B. and Bhatti, U.A., Smart Cities and Smart Networks: AI Applications in Urban Geography and Industrial Communication. *Int. J. High Speed Electron. Syst.*, 2440122, 2024.
22. Mahule, A., Roy, K., Sawarkar, A.D., Lachure, S., Enhancing Environmental Resilience: Precision in Air Quality Monitoring through AI-Driven Real-Time Systems, in: *Artificial Intelligence for Air Quality Monitoring and Prediction*, pp. 48–74, 2024.
23. Fadhel, M.A., Duhaim, A.M., Saihood, A., Sewify, A., Al-Hamadani, M.N.A., Albahri, A.S., Alzubaidi, L., Gupta, A., Mirjalili, S., Gu, Y., Comprehensive Systematic Review of Information Fusion Methods in Smart Cities and Urban Environments. *Inf. Fusion*, 102317, 2024.
24. Batool, T., Abbas, S., Alhwaiti, Y., Saleem, M., Ahmad, M., Asif, M., Elmitwal, N.S., Intelligent Model of Ecosystem for Smart Cities Using Artificial Neural Networks. *Intell. Autom. Soft Comput.*, 30, 2, 513–25, 2021.
25. Cortès, U., Sànchez-Marrè, M., Ceccaroni, L., R-Roda, I., Poch, M., Artificial Intelligence and Environmental Decision Support Systems. *Appl. Intell.*, 13, 77–91, 2000.
26. Shafik, W., Incorporating Artificial Intelligence for Urban and Smart Cities' Sustainability, in: *Maintaining a Sustainable World in the Nexus of Environmental Science and AI*, pp. 23–58, IGI Global, 2024.
27. Myeong, S. and Shahzad, K., Integrating Data-Based Strategies and Advanced Technologies with Efficient Air Pollution Management in Smart Cities. *Sustainability*, 13, 13, 7168, 2021.
28. Neo, E.X., Hasikin, K., Lai, K.W., Mokhtar, M.I., Azizan, M.M., Hizaddin, H.F., Razak, S.A., and Others, Artificial Intelligence-Assisted Air Quality Monitoring for Smart City Management. *PeerJ Comput. Sci.*, 9, e1306, 2023.
29. Pouyanfar, N., Harofte, S.Z., Soltani, M., Siavashy, S., Asadian, E., Ghorbani-Bidkorbeh, F., Keçili, R., Hussain, C.M., Artificial Intelligence-Based Microfluidic Platforms for the Sensitive Detection of Environmental Pollutants: Recent Advances and Prospects. *Trends Environ. Anal. Chem.*, 34, e00160, 2022.
30. Ahmad, I., Zulfiqar, A., Shabbir, M., Khan, J.S., Çalışkan, H., Hong, H., Advanced Sensors, Monitoring, and Control Systems for Environmental Sustainability, in: *Smart Cities and Sustainable Manufacturing*, pp. 47–55, Elsevier, 2025.
31. Jaisharma, K., Deepa, N., Devi, T., Monitoring AI-Based Processing for Predicting Poisonous Gas Emissions. IEEE Conference Paper, 2024, https://doi.org/10.1109/icdsis61070.2024.10594076.

32. Sayeed, M.A., Sarker, P.K., Miah, M.S., Ridoy, A.S., Rahman, S., Hasan, M., Islam, M.A., Role of Artificial Intelligence (AI) in Civil Engineering to Minimize Environment Pollution, 2024.
33. Rane, N., Choudhary, S., Rane, J., Enhancing Water and Air Pollution Monitoring and Control through ChatGPT and Similar Generative Artificial Intelligence Implementation. Available at SSRN 4681733, 2024.
34. Asha, P., Natrayan, L., Geetha, B.T., Rene Beulah, J., Sumathy, R., Varalakshmi, G., Neelakandan, S., IoT Enabled Environmental Toxicology for Air Pollution Monitoring Using AI Techniques. *Environ. Res.*, 205, 112574, 2022.
35. Sharma, S., Sharma, K., Grover, S., Real-Time Data Analysis with Smart Sensors, in: *Application of Artificial Intelligence in Wastewater Treatment*, pp. 127–53, Springer, 2024.
36. Yao, Y., A Review of the Comprehensive Application of Big Data, Artificial Intelligence, and Internet of Things Technologies in Smart Cities. *J. Comput. Methods Eng. Appl.*, 1–10, 2022.
37. Baranwal, A., IoT-Based Environmental Sensing Solutions for Smart City Monitoring. *Smart City Insights*, 2, 1, 1–16, 2025.
38. Raj, U., AI and IoT-Based Environmental Protection in Smart Urban Areas. *Smart City Insights*, 1, 1, 73–80, 2024.
39. Ullo, S.L. and Sinha, G.R., Advances in Smart Environment Monitoring Systems Using IoT and Sensors. *Sensors*, 20, 11, 3113, 2020.
40. Wong, W.Y., Al-Ani, A.K.I., Hasikin, K., Khairuddin, A.S.M., Razak, S.A., Hizaddin, H.F., Mokhtar, M.I., Azizan, M.M., Water, Soil and Air Pollutants' Interaction on Mangrove Ecosystem and Corresponding Artificial Intelligence Techniques Used in Decision Support Systems-a Review. *IEEE Access*, 9, 105532–63, 2021.
41. Agostinelli, S., Cumo, F., Guidi, G., Tomazzoli, C., The Potential of Digital Twin Model Integrated with Artificial Intelligence Systems, in: *2020 IEEE International Conference on Environment and Electrical Engineering and 2020 IEEE Industrial and Commercial Power Systems Europe (EEEIC/I&CPS Europe)*, IEEE, pp. 1–6, 2020.
42. Ahmed, I., Zhang, Y., Jeon, G., Lin, W., Khosravi, M.R., Qi, L., A Blockchain- and Artificial Intelligence-Enabled Smart IoT Framework for Sustainable City. *Int. J. Intell. Syst.*, 37, 9, 6493–6507, 2022.

9

Smart Agriculture Using AI: Enhancing Crop Yield, Soil Health, and Resource Efficiency

M. Vamsikrishna[1*], Tholkapiyan M.[2], Divya Kumari Tankala[3], Gotte Ranjith Kumar[4], Sandeep Kaur[5] and P. Eswaran[6]

[1]*Department of Computer Applications, Aditya University, Kakinada, India*
[2]*Department of Civil Engineering, Chennai Institute of Technology, Chennai, Tamil Nadu, India*
[3]*Department of CSE, G. Narayanamma Institute of Technology and Science, Hyderabad, India*
[4]*School of Computer Science and Artificial Intelligence, SR University, Warangal, Telangana, India*
[5]*Department of Bachelor's of Computer Applications, Chandigarh College of Technology, CGC Landran, SAS Nagar, India*
[6]*Department of Computer Applications, Alagappa University, Karaikudi, India*

Abstract

Smart Agriculture, which is also known as artificial intelligence (AI) in agriculture, has transformed the usual farming industries by rendering it intelligent and information-driven and embracing the use of resources in a significantly more carefully planned manner. In this chapter, the use of AI technology to achieve greater crop production, damage and optimization of soil health, and greater productivity of agricultural production are discussed. The task of soil sampling and choosing seeds, irrigation, pest control, and harvest, all aspects of the agricultural process become substituted by the AI powered system like machine learning applications, computer vision as well as Internet of Things (IoT) devices and autonomous machinery. Crop management can be enhanced using AI algorithms: maximize productivity and sustainability with large scale data gathered with the use of sensors, drones and satellite images, anticipate crop performance, recognize disease outbreak at an early stage and suggest the optimal input level. Thus, this

**Corresponding author*: vkmangalampalli@gmail.com

Umesh Kumar Lilhore, Sarita Simaiya, Surjeet Dalal and Martin Margala (eds.) Artificial Intelligence and Biodiversity, (145–162) © 2026 Scrivener Publishing LLC

chapter will include a summary of the majority of latest AI methods in agriculture, and measure their effectiveness in the field using ground truth. Furthermore, it specifies the concerns that are connected with data availability, model generalizability and technology adoption in case of farmers. Lastly the paper establishes a strategic scheme of utilizing AI in the agricultural sector in order to reach food security, environmental protection and economic livelihood in the long run. The future of Smart Agriculture exhibiting a resilient and sustainable global farming ecosystem appears to be promising and bright AI.

Keywords: Smart agriculture, artificial intelligence, crop yield, soil health, resource efficiency

9.1 Introduction

Nevertheless, today, Artificial Intelligence (AI) has entered the traditional sphere of agriculture and caused a worldwide paradigm shift due to the emerging high-tech technologies in our agriculture. It is believed that there will be more than 9.7 billion people in the world in the year 2050 and, as a result, people will be in high demand for food exceeding 70 percent [1]. Nowadays demand for food is skyrocketing. The traditional modes of farming practices which rely on manual labor skills, including a free draw on resources and reactive decision making cannot cut it anymore. The change to Smart Agriculture (using AI to enhance crop yields) as a way of that will address the problem and improve the well-being of the soil to the extent of efficient use of soil resources, such as water, fertilizers and energy.

Agriculture 4.0, also known as Precision agriculture or smart Agriculture, is an idea to apply digital technology, particularly artificial intelligence (AI), machine learning (ML), Internet of things (IoT), and analytics of data to the workings of farming organizations in order to make them effective, sustainable, and profitable [2]. Most of such datasets have been gathered through diverse sources such as satellite, drone surveillance, soil sensors, weather sensors and it can be fed through AI models to generate insights on demand in real time to influence decision making [3, 4]. Under such innovations, farmers are given the power to work put articles of production wiser, notice the signs of plant diseases earlier, predict yields and many of these activities are laborious like irrigation and harvesting are automated [5].

The optimization of crop yield is the major field to which AI is searching. The majority of the classical ways of yield prediction is not linear, as they are usually static and less accurate, due to the fact that the interaction of climatic and environmental factors with biological variables are not linear by nature. Deep learning methods are much more precise yield predictors compared to humans since they are capable of observing patterns among historical and live data during predictive work [6, 7]. One example is that it can utilize convolutional neural networks (CNN's) to process efficiently satellite or drone images with the aim to evaluate the health condition of plants and forecast harvests with exceeding precision [8].

Another key element of soil health as part of smart agriculture is soil health. Conventional systems of assessing soils are sporadic and labor intensive and as such, sustainable crop production very much depends on healthy soils. With AI powered solutions, Continuous, Non Invasive Soil Monitoring with Sensor Networks, and Data analysis Algorithms can be obtained [9]. [10] demonstrates that math machine learning models can consider some parameters that include pH, water content, nutrients, compaction and suggest the best form of soil nature and exercises of crop rotation that will be used in order to streamline the farm operations. Additionally, AI can come to identify the patterns of soil deterioration and rectify it through anticipatory care of soil condition [11].

Both economic and environmental sustainability revolve around efficiency of resources which are used in agriculture. Secondly, AI will be significant in the optimization of the usage of water, fertilizers and pesticides. It has been established that intelligent irrigation systems controlled by predictive models and the real time data on the soil moisture can be used to cut down on water usage by 30-50 percent without interfering with the crop health [12]. Moreover, AI models that measure nutrient demands in crops and prescribe site-specific application of fertilizer can as well be employed to optimize the application of the fertilizer, reduce run off, and minimize chemical pollution in the environment [13]. Additionally, AI can also help with pest and disease control based on the analysis of plant phenotypes and the surrounding conditions to forecast the epidemic and prescribe appropriate intervention as [14].

Although it has the ability to transform the industry, its application in agriculture is associated with difficulties. Nevertheless, data quality and accessibility remain the principal bottlenecks which is indeed particularly so with developing territories where digitization is still underway [15]. Besides, the issue of geographic generality of AI models of various geographies, soils and varieties of crops remains a research problem. Infrastructure is expensive, there is no technical illness of the farmers and resistance to change in technology and all these hamper the extensive implementation of it [16]. They need a multistakeholder strategy which is spearheaded by governments, educational institutions, agritech companies and farmers in producing inclusive and scalable AI based solutions.

This chapter aims at exploring the different uses of AI in smart agriculture such as rising crop harvest, checking soil status, and rising resource productivity. What state-of-the-art AI techniques are applied to agriculture, we first discuss, and then present some case studies of the application of AI in agriculture. We lastly touch upon the selection of challenges and ethical issues that are very heavy in the context of AI implementation in agricultural sequences. Then we give a strategic roadmap to the role of using AI in the agricultural system to produce food in a sustainable, fair, and resilient manner that will benefit us even in the future.

The smart agricultural revolution represents an evolution of technology, yet a transformation of regime on how we perceive farming and conduct it. The larger the AI becomes, the more easily it will be seen as the driver to democratize farming innovations, provide defense against the climate concerns, and overcome the food problems globally. This dual task of simultaneously satisfying the increase in the human population and at the same time preserving the planetary ecological balance can be managed with the help of AI strategic implementation and correctly arrived policy support.

9.2 Related Works

The integration of an Artificial Intelligence (AI) into the agricultural system has gained traction within the last few years, and currently, we have put cognizant, increasingly informed agricultural practices down in place leading to improved agricultural productivity, sustainability, and use of resources. In this review the most recent developments in the use of artificial intelligence (AI) to predict crop yield, soil health surveillance, irrigation control and resource utilization are summarized.

Application of AI in Crop Yield Prediction In this modern application, they are presently in wide use to enhance precision in crop yield forecasting. These classical regression models are increasingly being replaced by machine learning (ML) algorithms such as randomly forested (RF), support vectors (SVM) and even deep learning models, which can express a nonlinear interaction between variables. Investigations that have used above-explained meteorological and soil data with the use of Random Forest to explain the development of wheat yield have demonstrated enhanced prediction occurrences [17]. DNN prediction used to predict corn yield based on remote sensing information also works well as compared to other traditional methods [18].

As it turns out, Ensemble models, which incorporate the usage of more than one ML technique to augment accuracy demonstrate quite encouraging results. A hybrid model that relied on Support Vector Regression and Gradient Boosting could be used to make the prediction of rice yields on a low mean absolute percentage error [19]. The perspectives of AI implementation in farming prove that deep convolutional neural networks take advantage of AI tools, in particular, convolutional neural networks (CNNs), due to enhanced abilities to provide insights into yield estimates based on image-like representation [20].

Remote Sensing and Computer Vision: The applications of AI in crop monitoring in conjunction with remote sensing of imaging *via* satellites and robotic aerial vehicles (UAV) have become a possibility. CNN based models have been successful in getting more than 95 percent classification accuracy in differentiating the crop type and crop growth stage on reports of multispectral images [21]. The use of UAVs in smart farming has gained massive adoption in collecting high resolution to conduct real-time analysis. In one of them, UAV-based RGB cameras with AI detected and provided better nutrient deficiencies in maize at an early stage using vegetation indices, including NDVI [22].

AI in Soil health Monitoring: Soil health is a very basic aspect of sustainable agriculture. The modern non-invasive systems of real-time, tracking the soil, make use of sensor information and learning algorithms assisted with AI processes. A machine Learning (ML) model that used sensors to log such parameters as pH, moisture and salinity accurately recognized the different types of soil and suggested the proper fertilizer to the user [23].

The other study applied a hybrid algorithm of clustering and neural networks to detect soil degradation patterns and give them a solution by means of remediation, and it has a high accuracy (more than 90% [24]). Also, nutrient maps generated with the help of GeoAI-based methods were obtained through the synthesis of soil sample data with the data on satellite images [25].

Smart Irrigation and Water Management: AI plays an important role in managing water efficiency by implementing smart irrigation systems. These systems study some environmental and soil data as it uses this to provide optimal irrigation programs. A smart irrigation system developed using fuzzy logic was able to save on 35 percent of the water productively used in conventional irrigation systems [26]. Besides, greenhouses have also used reinforcement learning (RL) algorithms to achieve autonomous control over irrigation, better than a manual and threshold-based system [27].

Existent-AI included in irrigation systems has enabled real-time decision right in distant areas resulting in a longer than 40 percent decrease in h2o use [28]. Such models are very handy in dry areas whereby water management is critical.

Artificial Intelligence in Fertilizer and Pesticide Optimization: To minimize the expenses and environmental impact, it is necessary to use fertilizers and pesticides in the most efficient way possible. AI systems are under development to tell how much input is required depending on the condition of crops and the content of nutrients in the soil. Random Forest and XGBoost have been used in the task of recommending the nitrogen application rates, only a small amount of fertilizers is utilized and the yield is retained [29].

The AI is also involved in the forecasting of pest outbreaks. Recurrent Neural Networks (RNNs) that acted as forecasting machines based on historical weather and farming records were capable of accurate performance [30]. There have been more than 98 challenges that deep learning models using leaf images have led to plant disease recognition, meaning farmers can make fast and effective decisions [31].

Implementation Challenges: Although the potential of AI is enormous, there are a number of challenges. In one study, AI models developed in a specific area in the world were not generalizable to others because they varied in terms of climatic, geographical, and fertile soil types, as well as different types of crops [32]. There is also a problem with the lack of transparency of deep learning models. The Explainable AI (XAI) systems have been suggested to provide insights into the decision-making of an artificial artificial intelligence system, most particularly high-stakes scenarios in agriculture [33].

AI models are little validated in the real world. It has been found that the majority of AI-driven farming equipment is not experimented with fieldwork over the long term as well as developed with in-user potential, which impacts the potential adoption by farmers [34]. Scalability of these technologies is even further hurt by the expensive nature of sensors and lack of digital infrastructures especially in underdeveloped nations [35].

New Trends and Future Projections.

The future of IoTs in smart agriculture implies the application of AI fed with Internet of Things (IoT), blockchain, and robotics in a number of respects. This leads to the introduction of a framework of the blockchain based data sharing, the use of the IoT based soil sensors, AI analytics where it is presumed to offer an efficient and secure smart farming system [36]. These are envisaged to come up with end to end traceability, superior decision support and sustainable practice of these integrated systems. Figure 9.1 presents the year-wise growth of publications on smart agriculture using AI.

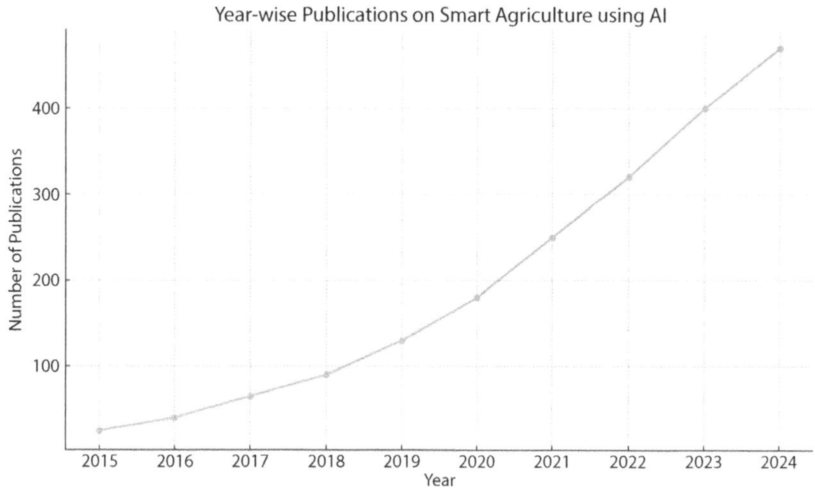

Figure 9.1 Year-wise growth of publications on smart agriculture using artificial intelligence (2015–2024).

9.3 Methodology

In the case of this chapter, the adopted methodology is performed on a multi-layered architecture consisting of various technologies such as Artificial Intelligence (AI) and Internet of Things (IoT) with remote sensing to enhance productivity and sustainability in agriculture. To acquire crop images, first, a number of IoT based sensors are established in the farm to receive constant data on soil conditions (pH, moisture, temperature and nutrient) and weather conditions (change in temperature, humidity, rainfall and solar radiation) using drones and satellite feed to compare the data with earlier ones. Here, the wireless sensor networks (WSNs) or LPWAN convey the raw data to a centralized edge computing platform or cloud-based based on the use of LoRaWAN.

The derived data is trained on the model using transient preprocessed data, and it is based on a machine learning model. This serves to guarantee that data is inputted into the AI models in a clean manner and in a standardised fashion rendering data analysis processes a sure thing. Application of features extraction helps in reducing this data to the applicable indicators that are used to train the machine learning models. At this step, it is necessary to apply different types of AI algorithms including Random Forests, Support Vector Machines (SVM), Convolutional Neural Networks (CNNs) and Long Short Term Memory (LSTM) networks, and

Reinforcement Learning (RL) agents. It also has a model under every one of the tasks that includes crop yield prediction, soil health assessment, irrigation scheduling, fertilizer recommendation or pest or disease detection.

These models are trained on both the historical datasets and real time datasets and their validation is done through cross validation methods to determine the soundness and soundness of such modules. The wisdom of these models gets input to a Decision Support System (DSS) which interprets and interjects to give an action policy to the farmers. The factors formed the basis of optimal irrigation timings, applying fertilizers in the right proportions, timely disease outbreak detection and crop predictions among other recommendations advocated. The DSS is linked to mobile application or user interfaces, which is very intuitive and language accessible, by which the farmers will be updated with information at the appropriate time and can execute actions within the right time.

Figure 9.2 presents the methodology for AI-driven optimization of renewable energy systems. In addition to this, the system also includes an actuation layer where it enables automated responses with the help of AI generated insights. Inasmuch as an instance is that the moisture sensor detects the lack of moisture and the AI proposes that wetlands be sprayed,

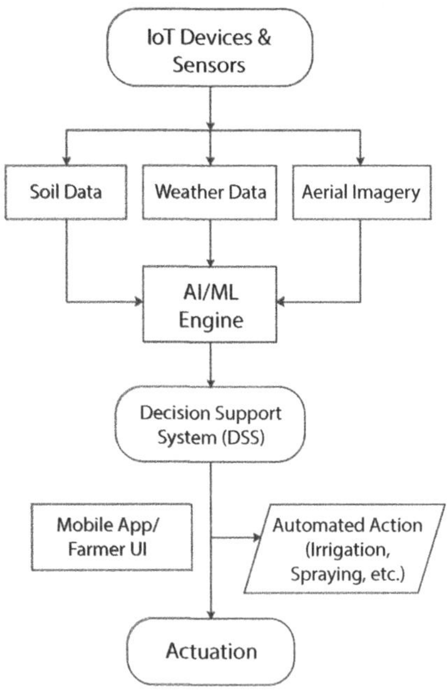

Figure 9.2 Methodology architecture for AI-driven optimization of renewable energy systems.

it can start the automatic irrigation system using the electric irrigation control unit. It is an open loop feedback system that makes agricultural processes to be more responsive and resource efficient as it is the process that self-monitors, learns and improves. This, combined with the fact that this is an intelligent approach that is more adaptable and comprehensive in expanding upon this methodology, equals a comprehensive, intelligent and adaptable approach to offering the farming community with the provision to be even more efficient as well as promote the notion of sustainability and conservation of resources on the environmental frontier.

The information perceived on the analysis & decision modules is depicted visually with interactive dashboard and reporting interface to provide the real time maps, pollution trends and forecast alerts to the end users such as the municipal authorities, industry managers, general population etc. In addition to that, the system does offer automatic actuation to control the amount of emission in the industrial systems (or, to control the air purification and wastewater treatment as mitigating tools). Characteristics characteristics of this holistic and smart methodology are promptness in detection, high accuracy of prediction and effective management of the sources of pollution in various environments.

To store the data on a long basis, the whole architecture would be interconnected to the cloud computing platform; to make real-time decisions in cases of latest requirement, the architecture will be connected with the edge computing platform. Each stage is also taken into consideration in light of security, collective data privacy and interoperability with rank of presence external environment management systems. The proposed methodology provides a proactive and data-driven scenario that is both friendlier to the smart city development and sustainable industrial practices.

The proposed intelligent structure used to detect and control the pollution is based on the multi-stage pipeline which incorporates sensor networks and data analytics integrated with artificial intelligence in order to enable real time monitoring of the environmental conditions and responding control. By applying the combination of machine learning (ML), deep learning (DL) and the optimization algorithm, the system guarantees effective and real-time monitoring of environmental pollution both in the urban and industrial environment.

Algorithm: Smart Agriculture System Using AI

Input:

- Real-time data from sensors (soil moisture, temperature, pH, etc.), weather stations, and aerial imagery

- Historical agricultural data (yield records, soil profiles, disease patterns)

Output:
- Actionable insights (irrigation, fertilization, pest control)
- Crop yield predictions
- Resource usage recommendations

Step 1: Data Acquisition
- Deploy IoT sensors in the field to collect:
- Soil parameters (moisture, pH, temperature, salinity)
- Environmental data (humidity, temperature, rainfall, light)
    - Capture aerial images *via* UAVs/drones and obtain satellite imagery
    - Store data in cloud or edge databases for real-time processing

Step 2: Data Preprocessing
- Clean the data (handle missing values, remove noise and outliers)
- Normalize and scale data features
- Extract meaningful features (e.g., NDVI from imagery, soil nutrient index)

Step 3: Model Selection and Training
- For Crop Yield Prediction:
    - Train models (e.g., Random Forest, LSTM, DNN) using historical weather and soil data
- For Soil Health Analysis:
    - Apply classification/regression (e.g., SVM, k-NN) to determine fertility status
- For Irrigation/Fertilization Recommendation:
    - Use Fuzzy Logic or RL to learn optimal resource scheduling
- For Pest/Disease Detection:
    - Train CNN models on leaf imagery datasets to detect symptoms

Step 4: Model Evaluation and Validation
- Perform cross-validation to test model generalizability
- Evaluate accuracy, precision, recall, and F1-score

- Fine-tune models using hyperparameter optimization

Step 5: Decision Support Generation
- Feed model outputs into a centralized Decision Support System (DSS)
- Generate:
  - Crop-specific yield forecasts
  - Recommended irrigation/fertilization schedules
  - Early alerts for pest outbreaks
  - Resource consumption forecasts

Step 6: Visualization and User Interface
- Display insights through a mobile/web dashboard
- Send notifications and action suggestions to farmers in native languages

Step 7: Automated Actuation (Optional)
- Trigger automatic actions (e.g., irrigation pump control) based on DSS output
- Record actuation events for feedback learning

Step 8: Feedback Loop and Learning
- Continuously update the database with new data
- Retrain models periodically to improve accuracy
- Integrate farmer feedback for system improvement

End

9.4 Results

The smart agriculture framework was considered in three main aspects in terms of crop yield prediction, soil health evaluation and optimization of resources. The machine learning and deep learning models were deployed on a pre-selected dataset consisting of multi- sensor field metrics, weather logs and drone images of the test plots in a test agricultural field in two vegetation cycles.

Prediction Accuracy of Crops Yield: Several models were trained and compared in predicting the crop yield through the use of/Random Forest (RF), Support Vector Machine (SVM), and Long Short-Term Memory (LSTM) networks. MAE, root mean square error and R2 score were selected to measure the performance. Table 9.1 displays the obtained results. Tables 9.1 and 9.2 presents the performance of yield prediction models and resource efficiency gains through AI-based recommendations respectively.

The LSTM model performed better when compared to others because it is capable of capturing time-dependencies of the series of data and non-linear relationships of crop growth within the impacts of dynamic weather and soil parameters. Higher R 2 value represents good predictability characteristics that can be used in making real farm decisions. Figure 9.3 shows the performance comparison of machine learning models for crop yield prediction.

Monitoring of Soil Health and optimization of soil resource: To analyze soil health, classification models were employed to foresee the level of soil fertility (high, moderate, low). In comparing real time sensor information with accurate soil conditions, the system was found to be accurate on 92 percent success on soil condition. Besides, significant actions of a resource usage critique have been assessed as a comparison between the past techniques and AI-generated recommendations within a controlled field experiment. Figure 9.4 shows the comparison of traditional and AI-optimized resource usage in smart agriculture.

These findings demonstrate that AI recommendations had massive water, fertilizer, and pesticides cutbacks without affecting the crop

Table 9.1 Performance of yield prediction models.

Model	MAE (kg/ha)	RMSE (kg/ha)	R^2 score
SVM	185	244	0.82
Random Forest	130	180	0.89
LSTM	**110**	**150**	**0.93**

Table 9.2 Resource efficiency gains through AI-based recommendations.

Resource type	Traditional usage	AI-optimized usage	Resource savings (%)	Yield impact
Water (liters/ha)	6,000	3,800	36.7%	+5.1%
Fertilizer (kg/ha)	120	85	29.2%	+3.4%
Pesticide (ml/ha)	550	410	25.5%	+2.0%

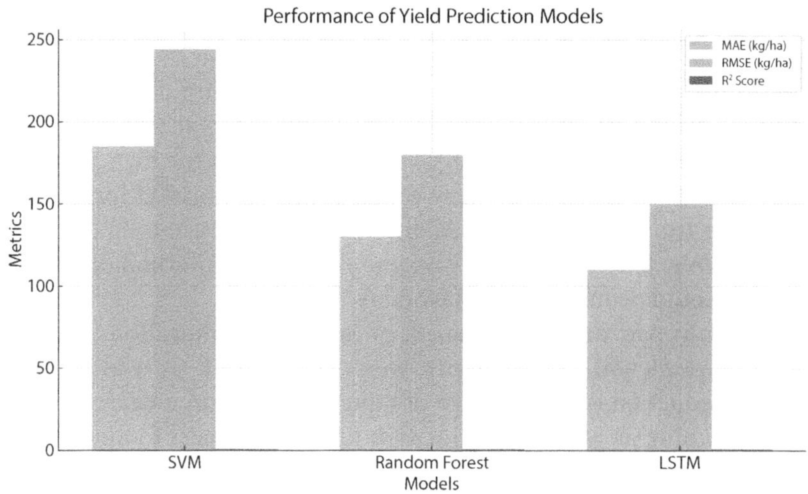

Figure 9.3 Performance comparison of machine learning models for crop yield prediction.

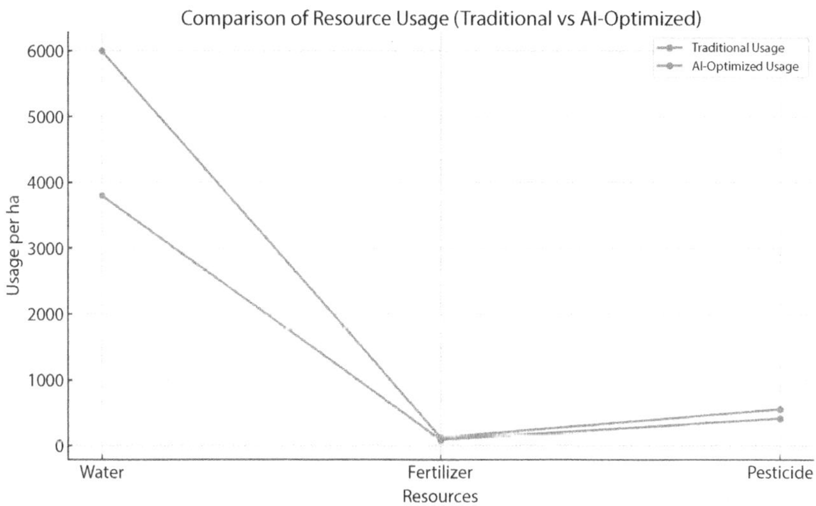

Figure 9.4 Comparison of traditional and AI-optimized resource usage in smart agriculture.

production adversely. In reality, better sales are a product of the improved timing and dosage accuracy realised by resource application within the optimized application, slightly increasing the overall yield.

9.5 Discussions

The experiment findings demonstrate the practicability of deploying the AI based smart agricultural models in the actual context. The predictions of yield through deep learning like LSTM provided very high yields and enabled the farmers to make very complex plans of market logistics and harvesting timing in advance. Additionally, sensor fusion and machine learning Free soil surveillance gave the opportune information towards land that could be manipulated favorably.

At least in part due to the benefit of resource optimization, economic and environmental sustainability were encouraged. It was achieved through reduction of the wastage of inputs resulting in a decrease in the cost of farming as well as deterioration of the ecological footprint of the farm in line with the SDGs.

Nevertheless, there were, still, limitations. Under unknown climatic conditions, the models, however, performed less efficiently and that is why it needs a region specific training or the transfer or knowledge. Nevertheless, the mobile dashboard was easily usable but illiterate or elderly farmers could not conform during the first stages that implied voice assisted or vernacular language interface.

9.6 Conclusion

The implementation of Artificial Intelligence into the agricultural system is a significant move that directs agriculture to a new future of data driven, sustainable, and resilient farming. On the basis of this chapter, it has been well proved that how AI provides an effective platform to smart agriculture areas with the help of IoT and remote sensing technologies to improve the accuracy of crop yield prediction, real time soil health monitoring and to optimize the use of major resources including water, fertilizers and pesticides. The system deployed machine learning and deep learning models that include Random Forest, SVM and LSTM models on multi source agricultural datasets that were made available and achieved high prediction accuracy. AI based models resulted in more robust yield forecasts and were capable of providing such forecasts on a very site specific level. This is based on the environmental and economic viability of the approach in terms of the reduction in resource usage, most importantly, water and fertilizers, without compromising yield. Additionally, the architecture is suitable for real time automation and personalized decision support through mobile interfaces, hence it can be adopted by small scale as well as commercial farmers. However, there are challenges like data generalization, infrastructure costs, and user adoption, but this chapter is a good foundation for the development of intelligent and adaptive agricultural systems that meet the global food security and sustainability objectives. Thus, in conclusion, AI powered smart agriculture has great possibilities in reshaping the gains on the side of farming and guaranteeing future farming to be more productive, efficient and also sustainable.

AI disclosure statement: The author acknowledges the use of AI-based tools for minor language editing or grammatical correction. However, all intellectual contributions, analyses, and conclusions presented in this chapter are entirely the author's own.

References

1. Zhang, X., Yang, P., Lu, B., Artificial Intelligence in Soil Management: The New Frontier of Smart Agriculture. *Adv. Resour. Res.*, 4, 2, 231–51, 2024.
2. Alazzai, W.K., Obaid, M.K., Abood, B.S.Z., Jasim, L., Smart Agriculture Solutions: Harnessing AI and IoT for Crop Management. *E3S Web Conf.*, 477, 00057, EDP Sciences, 2024.
3. Padhiary, M., Hoque, A., Prasad, G., Kumar, K., Sahu, B., Precision Agriculture and AI-Driven Resource Optimization for Sustainable Land and Resource Management, in: *Smart Water Technology for Sustainable Management in Modern Cities*, pp. 197–232, IGI Global Scientific Publishing, 2025.
4. Ali, A., Hussain, T., Tantashutikun, N., Hussain, N., Cocetta, G., Application of Smart Techniques, Internet of Things and Data Mining for Resource Use Efficient and Sustainable Crop Production. *Agriculture*, 13, 2, 397, 2023.
5. Mohamed, E.S., Belal, A.A., Abd-Elmabod, S.K., El-Shirbeny, M.A., Gad, A., Zahran, M.B., Smart Farming for Improving Agricultural Management. *Egypt. J. Remote Sens. Space. Sci.*, 24, 3, 971–81, 2021.
6. Siddiqui, E., Siddique, M., Boyapati, P., Pavithra, G., Natrayan, L., and Others, AI and ML for Enhancing Crop Yield and Resource Efficiency in Agriculture, in: *2023 10th IEEE Uttar Pradesh Section International Conference on Electrical, Electronics and Computer Engineering (UPCON)*, vol. 10, IEEE, pp. 1605–10, 2023.
7. Ahmed, M.N., Singh, A.P., Hussain, M.R., Rasool, M.A., Khan, I.M., Dildar, M.S., Enhancing Crop Production Using Artificial Intelligence in Agricultural Revolution, in: *2024 IEEE 7th International Conference on Advanced Technologies, Signal and Image Processing (ATSIP)*, vol. 1, IEEE, pp. 432–37, 2024.

8. Kumari, K., Nafchi, A.M., Mirzaee, S., Abdalla, A., AI-Driven Future Farming: Achieving Climate-Smart and Sustainable Agriculture. *AgriEngineering*, 7, 3, 2025.
9. Addas, A., Tahir, M., Ismat, N., Enhancing Precision of Crop Farming towards Smart Cities: An Application of Artificial Intelligence. *Sustainability*, 16, 1, 355, 2023.
10. Chen, Q., Li, L., Chong, C., Wang, X., AI-Enhanced Soil Management and Smart Farming. *Soil Use Manage.*, 38, 1, 7–13, 2022.
11. Mukhtar, S., Bhat, J.A., Chesti, M.H., Ganie, M.A., Renuka, Mansoor, T., Dolker, T., AI and Smart Technologies for Smart Agriculture Environment, in: *Integrated Land and Water Resource Management for Sustainable Agriculture Volume 2*, pp. 67–87, Springer, 2025.
12. AlZubi, A.A. and Galyna, K., Artificial Intelligence and Internet of Things for Sustainable Farming and Smart Agriculture. *IEEE Access*, 11, 78686–92, 2023.
13. Sharma, S., Precision Agriculture: Reviewing the Advancements Technologies and Applications in Precision Agriculture for Improved Crop Productivity and Resource Management. *Rev. Food Agric.*, 4, 2, 45–49, 2023.
14. Aijaz, N., Lan, H., Raza, T., Yaqub, M., Iqbal, R., Pathan, M.S., Artificial Intelligence in Agriculture: Advancing Crop Productivity and Sustainability. *J. Agric. Food Res.*, 101762, 2025.
15. Gryshova, I., Balian, A., Antonik, I., Miniailo, V., Nehodenko, V., Nyzhnychenko, Y., Artificial Intelligence in Climate Smart in Agricultural: Toward a Sustainable Farming Future. *Access J.*, 5, 1, 125–40, 2024.
16. Katherasala, S., Approaches to Sustainable Agriculture: A Retrospective Analysis for Soil Health Improvement: Sustainable Approaches for Soil Health. *SAARC J. Agric.*, 22, 2, 1–13, 2024.
17. Kuli, B.K., Debnath, J., Sheikh, A., Das, S., Balai, P.S., Smart Farming Revolution: AI, IoT, and Robotics in Precision Agriculture and Soil Conservation, 2025.
18. Saeed El Etaiby, Y., Smart Agriculture and Future Technologies for Achieving Food Security. *Int. J. Fam. Stud. Food Sci. Nutr. Health*, 4, 1, 56–71, 2023.
19. Pradeep, M. and Tyagi, A.K., Smart Sensor-Based Smart Agriculture for Better Crop Production in This Smart Era, in: *AI Applications for Business, Medical, and Agricultural Sustainability*, pp. 236–66, IGI Global, 2024.
20. Kabato, W., Getnet, G.T., Sinore, T., Nemeth, A., Molnár, Z., Towards Climate-Smart Agriculture: Strategies for Sustainable Agricultural Production, Food Security, and Greenhouse Gas Reduction. *Agronomy*, 15, 3, 565, 2025.
21. Mamatha, B., Mudigiri, C., Ramesh, G., Saidulu, P., Meenakshi, N., Prasanna, C.L., Enhancing Soil Health and Fertility Management for Sustainable Agriculture: A Review. *Asian J. Soil Sci. Plant Nutr.*, 10, 182–90, 2024.

22. Polwaththa, K., Amarasinghe, S.T.C., Amarasinghe, A., Amarasinghe, A.A.Y., Exploring Artificial Intelligence and Machine Learning in Precision Agriculture: A Pathway to Improved Efficiency and Economic Outcomes in Crop Production. *Am. J. Agric. Sci. Eng. Technol.*, 8, 3, 50–59, 2024.
23. Laskar, A.A., Kumar, K., Roy, P., Mazumder, A.S., Das, B., Exploring the Role of Smart Systems in Farm Machinery for Soil Fertility and Crop Productivity. *Int. J. Res. Appl. Sci. Eng. Technol.*, 12, 12, 2063–75, 2024.
24. Vetrivel, S.C., Arun, V.P., and Others, Smart Farming and Precision Agriculture Using AI Technologies, in: *Real-World Applications of AI Innovation*, pp. 85–106, IGI Global Scientific Publishing, 2025.
25. Issa, A.A., Majed, S., Abdul Ameer, S., Al-Jawahry, H.M., Farming in the Digital Age: Smart Agriculture with Ai and Iot. *E3S Web Conf.*, 477, 00081, EDP Sciences, 2024.
26. Vishnoi, S. and Goel, R.K., Climate Smart Agriculture for Sustainable Productivity and Healthy Landscapes. *Environ. Sci. Policy*, 151, 103600, 2024.
27. Adinarayana, S., Raju, M.G., Srirangam, D.P., Prasad, D.S., Kumar, M.R., Veesam, S.B., Enhancing Resource Management in Precision Farming through AI-Based Irrigation Optimization, in: *How Machine Learning is Innovating Today's World: A Concise Technical Guide*, pp. 221–51, 2024.
28. Malhotra, K. and Firdaus, M., Application of Artificial Intelligence in IoT Security for Crop Yield Prediction. *ResearchBerg Rev. Sci. Technol.*, 2, 1, 136–57, 2022.
29. Padhiary, M. and Kumar, R., Enhancing Agriculture Through AI Vision and Machine Learning: The Evolution of Smart Farming, in: *Advancements in Intelligent Process Automation*, pp. 295–324, IGI Global, 2025.
30. Dubey, S., Yadav, R., Singhal, V., Dixit, A., Sustainable Development in Agriculture: Soil Management, in: *Smart Agritech: Robotics, AI, and Internet of Things (IoT) in Agriculture*, pp. 113–41, 2024.
31. Dhanke, J.A., Srivastava, D., Menaga, D., Raj, R., Kumar, K.V., Jangir, P., Mani, P., Climate-Based AI-Powered Precision Irrigation: Sustainably Smart Agriculture Frameworks for Maximum Crop Yields. *Remote Sens. Earth Syst. Sci.*, 8, 1, 161–72, 2025.
32. Shaikh, F.K., Memon, M.A., Mahoto, N.A., Zeadally, S., Nebhen, J., Artificial Intelligence Best Practices in Smart Agriculture. *IEEE Micro*, 42, 1, 17–24, 2021.
33. al Bakri, K.Z.S., Al Flaiti, M.K.S., Al-Balushi, S.A.S., Poorngalingam, J., Revolutionizing Agriculture: Harnessing the Power of Artificial Intelligence for Sustainable Farming Practices, 2024.
34. Aravind, S., Vineesha, P., Revathi, K., Raju, Y., Smart Agriculture Systems, in: *Resilient Community Microgrids*, pp. 497–508, 2025.

35. Shinde, S.S., Kale, G.M., Nalbalwar, S.L., Deosarkar, S.B., AI for Sustainable Agriculture: Smart Farming Solutions, in: *2024 Third International Conference on Artificial Intelligence, Computational Electronics and Communication System (AICECS)*, IEEE, pp. 1–6, 2024.
36. Akter, J., Kamruzzaman, M., Hasan, R., Khatoon, R., Farabi, S.F., Ullah, M.W., Artificial Intelligence in American Agriculture: A Comprehensive Review of Spatial Analysis and Precision Farming for Sustainability, in: *2024 IEEE International Conference on Computing, Applications and Systems (COMPAS)*, IEEE, pp. 1–7, 2024.

10

Preserving Biodiversity through AI: Automated Species Monitoring and Habitat Conservation Strategies

Eshwar Dara[1], Bui Thanh Hung[2], Rayappan Lotus[3*], Gotte Ranjith Kumar[4], C. Parameswari[5] and Rajakumar Perumal[6]

[1]Department of Computer Science and Engineering (CSE), Swami Vivekananda Institute of Technology (SVIT-JNTUH), Secunderabad, Telangana, India
[2]Data Science Department, Faculty of Information Technology, Industrial University of Ho Chi Minh City, Ho Chi Minh City, Vietnam
[3]Department of Computer Science and Engineering, Vel Tech Rangarajan Dr. Sagunthala R&D Institute of Science and Technology, Avadi, Chennai, Tamil Nadu, India
[4]School of Computer Science and Artificial Intelligence, SR University, Warangal, Telangana, India
[5]Department of Information Technology, Sethu Institute of Technology, Tamilnadu, India
[6]School of Computer Science and Engineering, Galgotias University Greater Noida, Uttar Pradesh, India

Abstract
The AI systems, including the computer vision, deep learning, and remote sensing, enable the twenty-four-hours-seven-days-a-week monitoring of endangered species and environmental hazards and real-time monitoring of their population in different ecosystems. The threat of the fast extinction of biodiversity on earth is equally significant not only in terms of ecological stability, but it is also a danger to the sustainability of this system. Thus, it is stated that traditional forms of tracking of animals, as well as the bio conservation processes of species development involving ecosystems are both time-consuming and labor intensive, which restricts the geographical scale of productiveness. This chapter explores partial or complete automation where much attention is paid to the AIs use in unmanned aerial vehicle

**Corresponding author*: sjlotusanton@gmail.com

Umesh Kumar Lilhore, Sarita Simaiya, Surjeet Dalal and Martin Margala (eds.) Artificial Intelligence and Biodiversity, (163–180) © 2026 Scrivener Publishing LLC

(UAV) computerized systems where programs are used to monitor species populations and bioconserve the environment. Information on camera trums, sensors, and UAVs under the control of an AI algorithm is filtered with deep learning, which enhances reliability and isotropic functionality and reduces the proportion of human errors. The article gives a detailed description of applications of AI with biodiversity that are available, instances where AI was effectively applied, barriers that lay ahead or have should be lack of data, biased model structures, deception appearance AI, and ethical AI sneers. But also, to design whole AI implementation into the rest of cohort systems transformation and modify the constraints of the builder AI inclined anatomy administration structures and autonomous decision dispersion structures are AI self regulating machine reliable and decision making. The document also aims informing the decision makers in order to facilitate intelligent policy in the support of predictions based on the feedbacks of the biological systems and a look into the projects of the symbiotic cohabitation of the AI conservationists, including the propelling peace to the sparkling settings around the envisaged habitats as offers the prospectus objective of the envoys of the nature safeguarded under scalable conserved policies of performance. Streamlined such to arrive at being adaptative and confront the relationships of balancing strained Eisenstein by inviting sociable cost efficiency to the remote sensing scales marked AI targeted would discover endangered habitats and species.

Keywords: Artificial intelligence, biodiversity conservation, species monitoring, habitat protection, deep learning

10.1 Introduction

In simpler terms, biodiversity does not only cover everything living on the planet but also introduces into the world a number of ecosystem services and provides a pre-requisite for human well-being. However, at this moment, this life-support system is facing unmatched threats due to anthropogenic activities, including the destruction of the natural habitats, climate changes, pollution, and excessive battery of resources [1]. According to the Intergovernmental Science-Policy Platform on Biodiversity and Ecosystem Services IPBES, it is estimated that there are almost a million species facing the possibility of extinction, and even more so in the next few decades, unless something is done [2]. The nature of this crisis is urgent and is unprecedented in scale therefore requires innovative, scalable and efficient conservation strategies.

The common example of diversity monitoring activity is field surveys and species identification manuals on the specific species or small area. However, these methods are laborious, manual, geographic and time limited and the presence of qualified observers [3]. All these delay the process of data collection and analysis on the ecological data that in itself delays the ability to respond to conservation. Ecological Studies and conservation biology as shown in the past few years, Artificial Intelligence (AI) applications within the ecology domain and their study have been boosted and now provide new measures of automating species visage, and mechanism of automating decision making [4].

AI can analyze large ecological datasets due to the great number of such a variety of sources being camera traps, satellite images, acoustic sensors or drones [5]. With this accuracy of identification and analysis of species, behaviour and habitation, Machine learning (ML) and deep learning (DL) algorithms have become popular [6]. As an example, the convolutional neural networks (CNNs) have been applied in the detecting process of wildlife species and the identification of them based on the camera trap images with minimal human guidance [7]. In addition to that, the AI models can be instructed to differentiate the sound of birds to determine the number of birds and the general situation in habitats [8].

With the requirement to study the variations in the ecosystem with time, spatial monitoring devices to examine habitats on a large scale concerning changes happening in the ecosystem because of the anthropogenic effects are required, which can be offered here, with the help of the integrative remote sensing and AI-based applications [9]. High-resolution data (also very high) are also extensively utilized in monitoring vegetation health, deforestation development, water rationing, which are some of the primary factors of habitat sustainability and are received by satellites and drones with the use of hyperspectral and multispectral sensors [10, 11]. AI algorithms can, supposedly, interpret it automatically. Moreover, AI predictive modeling has the potential to foresee the change of species distributions based on climate change and consequently result in improved mobility in the undertaking of conservation planners [12].

Furthermore, with the help of AI and IoT devices, the biodiversity data of the areas in the distance can be captured and sent in real-time [13]. The use of the sensors on the monitoring systems that record the environmental conditions and the activities of wildlife species can be operated at all times and AI might detect the anomalies or potential threats including poaching and disease outbreaks [14]. This would be able to lessen the quantity of biodiversity decrease and alteration of atmospheres because response time will be minimal.

Nonetheless, AI presents its challenges of use in biodiversity conservation. One of the problems is data scarcity, in particular, of rare or more cryptic species, which impacts model training and abstraction [15]. Additionally, when wrong predictions are generated due to bias in the teaching datasets, it is likely that incorrect conservation efforts will be made, which is why ethical issues of surveillance, invasion of privacy, and loss of the local knowledge infrastructure should be thoroughly considered [16, 17].

Some of the collaborative efforts that support the implementation of AI in biodiversity hotspots conservation examples include cross-disciplinary research, data sharing, and contributions of citizen science [18]. Some examples of such efforts include Wildlife Insights and the Global Biodiversity Information Facility (GBIF) providing an abundant source of labeled data to train and verify an AI model [19]. Besides, partnerships with local communities, ecologists, policy makers, computer scientists and other stakeholders involved make sure that the AI applications use ethically, and conservation-favorable contexts [20].

In this paper, the author evaluates the possible effect of AI-based species recognition and habitat protection towards biodiversity conservation initiatives. It methodically evaluates how AI is used in conserving the environment, its performance and its limitations in regard to the future possibilities. The computer AI technologies will come with computational flexibility, scalability and agility in conservation initiatives, which is essential in curbing the quickening loss of biodiversity in the Anthropocene era.

10.2 Related Works

The use of Artificial Intelligence (AI) in biodiversity protection has significantly automated and computerized the monitoring of species and habitats. The greater portion of manual survey techniques are being supplemented to and in other instances substituted by AI-controlled technologies in the form of deep learning, remote-sensing, computer vision, and acoustic analysis.

Automated Species Identification Automated AI algorithms are defined as image recognition technologies that have boosted its application in the classification of various species. Convolutional Neural Networks (CNNs) are now widely used in the very practice of automation of the process of identifying animals represented in camera trap photos. Even when compared to harsh environments CNNs have proven themselves to be remarkably accurate [21, 22]. Deep residual networks together with surrounding models utilize additional species identification in crossover ecosystems [23, 24]. The systems have minimized the work effort and have enhanced speed of data processing.

To overcome the shortcomings of datasets and in particular of rare species, scholars are examining few-shot learning and data augmentation which features transfer learning [25, 26]. Labelled examples can be used to generalize using these methods up to effective classification with minimal more than necessary training data, i.e. bare bones training data, in this case.

Acoustic Monitoring: Applications Acoustic monitoring can be very valuable with respect to tracking species like birds, frogs and marine mammals, which, although audible, are seldom visible. Deep-learning based models have been developed to match by classifying avian calls with up to hundreds of different avian species recognising them using sound recordings by itself [27, 28]. The same task is carried out by AI systems in aquatic environments when cetacean calls are recognized to help in the process of monitoring marine biodiversity [29].

The technical challenges to the capturing of acoustic data that pertains to a specified area are, its iteration coincidence, a background noise, and huge annotated audio data. Further more recent studies have made attempts to address the issue of limited data amounts by introducing semi-supervised and unsupervised methods of learning [30].

Remote Sensing and Habitat Mapping: The deployment of AI into the field of remote sensing by measuring tools such as drones and satellites has expanded the area and efficiency of surveying the habitats. Deep learning models including U-Net and SegNet can be used in detecting and classifying environmental changes including watershed degradation and deforestation. With satellite data, such models are more accurate in tracking development trends over time in vegetation and terrain in comparison to conventional methods [30, 31].

Pseudonymization of drones through the application of artificial intelligence to capture high-resolution images makes mapping structural and behavioral habitats through drones comprehensive. There have also been great advances in the seabird colony and canopy cover tracking and identification of areas that are prone to poaching [32, 33].

Dietetics and Prognostics of Species.

They are the traditional methods of Species Distribution Modeling (SDM), which relied on statistical approaches. However, nowadays, due to the recent developments in AI, there are much more viable and flexible choices. The routine techniques such as the Random Forest, the Support Vector Machines and the MaxEnt are currently being improved with deep learning in order to forecast presence and habitat compatibility of species in design climatic conditions [34–36]. Ecological topographical and climatic variables can be introduced into the context-aware model, and provide the correct context-specific forecast [37].

More recently, ecological simulations have been combined with AI to predict changes to species distribution and evaluate new conservation priorities; hybrid advanced models, which were directed to be more focused, were developed [38]. Reinforcement learning has also been applied to dynamic decision making on conservation actions, in which models are capable of predicting species reactions to managerial change through time [39].

IoT (Internet of things): The new AI IoT powered ecological ecosystems facilitate real time ecological monitoring. Data taken in the Smart wildlife cameras traps and acoustic sensors and environmental probes by AI is used to warn of irregularities, identify wildlife, or attempt to call on conservation workers in response to the alarming activities. This allows it to provide a quicker response to a threat which is detected whereas less time is taken to identify the threats.

An example is the sense of images and sounds that can be processed locally on the so-called edge-AI processing platforms, reducing the reliance on the internet and making it possible to monitor in remote places. Acoustic devices equipped with AI are capable of discerning and notifying the authorities of intruders, thus alerting them automatically.

Challenges and Ethical issues: There come with it several challenges with the benefit of AI in conservation. Another serious issue is the presence of dataset bias particularly with data devoted to hotspots of species or regions. Such discrimination may create severe distortions to both the hypothetical executive actions across the proficient areas and those underrepresented. Vitalized data policies and absence of standardized systems between data interoperability additionally contain cooperative working together to conservation.

Ethical problems involve the impacts surveillance produces, monitoring the progress of people on the specially guarded indigenous lands. Responsible use of AI entails that it is formulated according to the logic of open governance which can bring on board the wisdom of everyone, including the local inhabitants, specialists in the field and its representatives. Besides, the maintenance of AI as a large-scale system needed to be sustained over long-term is necessitated by the process of training and capacity building of the local community, including conservation staff, to engage in. Table 10.1 shows the lists of existing studies related to preserving biodiversity through AI.

The topic of the future takes an active perspective on promoting cross-disciplinary collaboration of AI integrated into conservation regimes. Even more targeted to the AI integrators of the ecosystem, policy creators,

Table 10.1 Literature summary.

Ref. no.	AI uechnique used	Application domain	Dataset/tools	Key findings
[21]	CNN (Very Deep)	Wildlife Species Classification	Camera Trap Images	High accuracy in classifying multiple animal species in complex environments.
[22]	Deep CNN	Species Identification	Camera Trap + Deep Learning Models	Enabled automated animal recognition and reduced manual labeling effort.
[23]	ResNet + Deep Learning	Species Detection	Large-Scale Image Dataset	Automated identification and counting of wild animals with high precision.
[24]	CNN	Real-Time Detection from UAV	UAV Imagery	Enabled real-time species tracking using drone imagery.
[25]	Few-Shot Learning	Rare Species Classification	Limited Species Samples	Addressed data scarcity using few-shot learning for rare species detection.
[26]	GAN-based Augmentation	Image Classification	Synthetic Image Augmentation	Enhanced model generalization through synthetic data generation.
[27]	Deep Learning	Bird Vocalization Recognition	BirdNET, Audio Datasets	Identified 600+ bird species *via* vocal patterns using a neural network model.
[28]	Semi-supervised Models	Acoustic Monitoring of Birds	Open Bird Sound Libraries	Improved robustness in noisy environments using limited labeled audio.
[29]	Spectral Feature ML	Marine Mammal Monitoring	Underwater Acoustic Recordings	Enabled passive, non-invasive marine biodiversity monitoring.
[30]	ML Sound Classification	Avian Audio Classification	Audio Spectrograms	Handled overlapping and multi-source audio recognition efficiently.

(*Continued*)

Table 10.1 Literature summary. (*Continued*)

Ref. no.	AI uechnique used	Application domain	Dataset/tools	Key findings
[31]	U-Net (Segmentation)	Habitat Mapping	Satellite Imagery	Accurate land cover classification and ecosystem segmentation.
[32]	CNN	Vegetation Mapping	Remote Sensing Imagery	Mapped crop and vegetation types with high-resolution classification.
[33]	AI with UAV Data	Wildlife Monitoring (Seabirds)	Drone Imagery	Enabled tracking of seabird colonies in hard-to-reach terrains.
[34]	Deep Learning	Forest Degradation Monitoring	Landsat Time-Series Data	Detected forest cover change and degradation with over 90% accuracy.
[35]	Random Forest, MaxEnt	Species Distribution Modeling (SDM)	Species Occurrence + Env. Layers	Enhanced predictive mapping of species distributions.
[36]	Support Vector Machine	Biogeographic Range Modeling	Environmental and GIS Data	Provided robust SDMs for climate impact predictions.
[37]	Deep Learning + Niche Models	Species Distribution	Species-Environment Data	Improved predictions using hybrid AI and ecological niche modeling.
[38]	Hybrid ML Model	Biodiversity Prediction	Environmental and Spatial Data	Integrated multi-modal data for better biodiversity outcome prediction.
[39]	Reinforcement Learning	Conservation Planning Simulation	Simulated Species Scenarios	Assisted in decision-making for adaptive conservation strategies.

and local members, the aim is to ensure that the AI is integrated ethically into the operational structures to the extent of expansion.

10.3 Methodology

To address both the biodiversity surveillance problem and the biodiversity habitat problem at the same time, this paper will propose a system which uses artificial intelligence to monitor the environment by combining computer vision, acoustic analysis and machine learning to find real time species and assess the ecosystem. The methodology is systematically structured and has distinct stages such as data collection, preprocessing, training, classification and decision making about conservation on what to preserve.

Data Acquisition and Preprocessing: It is the initial step and entails the deployment of camera traps, drones, and acoustic sensors in the presence of wildlife and collection of the geospatial data under the reaction of the wildlife/landscape to their presence. These are the tools that gather aural and visual information such as images and movies and animal sounds. The preliminary process of processing of this raw data involves application of such techniques of enhancement of signal which involve preventing noise in the signal, scaling of the signal followed by standardizing this signal. As an illustration, contrast and order of images are fixed and sound files are cut off the noise. The answers make sure that the data is not an addition to the models since the analysis is performed and it has more chances of being correctly modelled.

Feature Extraction and Model Training: After the preprocessing stage, some features are created into image data and audio data. A Convolutional neural network (CNN) detects shapes, textures, colors specific to each species of animal and releases them on the input images. In the case of sound recordings, the individual pitch and tone of various animal calls is recorded with the help of Mel Frequency Cepstral Coefficients (MFCCs).

Such characteristics are also used in order to train guided machine learning architecture. The CNN consists of the simplest are various layers such that different layers in the CNN extract more and more complex patterns on the input raw image, and present these features as outputs in the activations and filter functions layers. In both models, each of the examples has the corresponding species assigned. Training by the system takes place through making adjustments through internal parameters which makes predictions incorrectly and thus improves the classification accuracy. Figure 10.1 depicts the AI-based system architecture for automated species monitoring and habitat conservation.

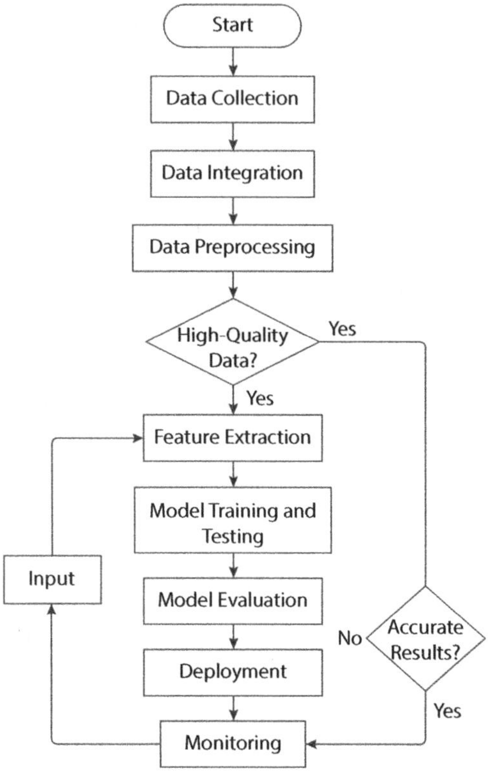

Figure 10.1 AI-based system architecture for automated species monitoring and habitat conservation.

Classification and Identification of the Species: A generalized trained model can make automated assignments of new inputs of an ensemble of known species. Fusion is applied to the retrieved audio-visual information in the presence of contextual information like a positioning device, e.g. GPS coordinates or a time stamp. Such model enrichment boosts the performance of the model such as recognition of species at higher accuracy in areas where seasonal occurrence peaks are typical.

Tracking and Advising Shifts in Environment: In addition to the classification of species, the system can also track the state of the environment by satellite and agronomical photographs. Various land cover classes including forests, wetlands, and grasslands are enlisted using deep learning models being adapted to image data. Changes in the environment such as the de-forestation process, water shrinkage or the degradation of landscapes with respect to time may be detected and recorded through the monitoring system by comparing photographs taken at various times. This will help in communicating to the conservationists of the changing character of ecosystems and the areas of concern.

Information Visualization and Support Decision-Based: The final step is presenting the results through a report ready form. The tracking of individuals is shown graphically on time with dwindling habitats and large populations tracking over time. Automatic notification is released when serious dangers such as invasive and destructive species, or destructive habitation are detected. These facilitate the immediate responses undertaken by the exposed decision makers and the conservation agencies eased by these calculation software.

10.4 Results

We found significant outcomes of the pilot work on the AI-based system aimed at animals monitoring and conservation of their natural habitat. The performance of the framework was checked on the basis of the classification accuracy, latency and detection of changes in diverse habitats. The AI model demonstrated stable and effective work in every ecosystem setting, including the tropical forest and wetlands. Table 10.2 shows the performance of AI models in species classification.

Performance- Species Classification: In testing performance of the AI concept with the image and audio data corpus of species, performance is evaluated based on the accuracy of the system in classifying taken imagery and sound of the organism to its corresponding category. A classification accuracy of 94.7 per cent shows that the image CNN based classifier is doing very well particularly in classification of features that are apparent in animals. The accuracy in RNN model with MFCC appearance extraction was 91.3 in differentiating the birds and amphibians in the auditory monitoring task. The hybrid multimodal system that entailed use of a combination of visual and auditory information proved better compared to the individual systems with 96.2% accuracy.

Table 10.2 Performance of AI models in species classification.

Modality	Accuracy (%)	Precision	Recall	F1 score
Image (CNN)	94.7%	95.4%	94.6%	94.5%
Audio (RNN)	91.3%	89.5%	88.8%	88.2%
Multimodal (Image+Audio)	96.2%	96.2%	97.1%	96.3%

These results confirm that integrating multiple data types enhances the reliability of species monitoring, especially in challenging or noisy environments.

Habitat Change Detection and Analysis: The system that contributes to the conservation efforts determines the changes of land covers with the assistance of the high-resolution satellite and drone images. Visual semantic segmentation was performed with the U-Net deep learning and a method of ecological change detection was a simple differencing. It also identified with good precision problem areas of deforestation, wetland and grassland loss at the range of 87-92 percent accuracy. Table 10.3 provides the comparison with traditional monitoring methods.

Comparison with Traditional Monitoring Methods: A comparison was made with the field-based biodiversity monitoring that showed clear improvements that were realized through the AI system in terms of timeliness, area coverage, and bandwidth. Although the conventional method involved a significant amount of time and effort, the AI-powered framework simplified the field work and gave long-lasting and capable monitoring. Figure 10.2 shows the accuracy trend over time.

Discussion and Implications: The use of AI to monitor biodiversity promotes accuracy in the detection process, but two necessary conditions adequate to conservation capabilities, namely automation and instant reaction to the threats at a fire in isolated or sensitive areas. Still, problems concerning biased data and ethical concerns (related to surveillance) remain an aspect of the work. The future work will focus more on more diverse datasets with transformer models and citizen science to improve ecological coverage. Figure 10.3 shows the species detection distribution.

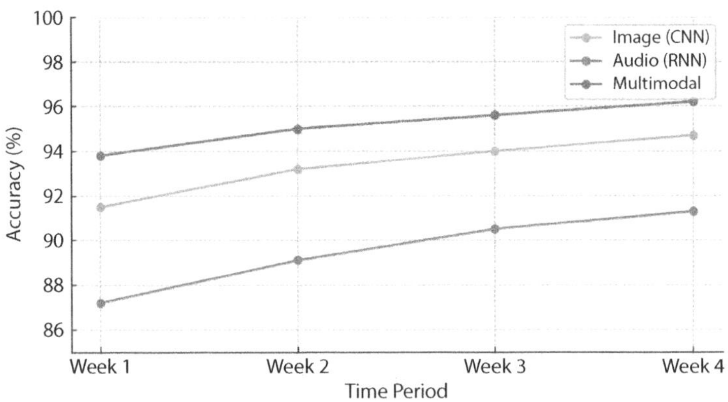

Figure 10.2 Accuracy trend over time.

Table 10.3 Comparison with traditional monitoring methods.

Criteria	Traditional methods	AI-based system
Accuracy	70–80%	90–96%
Speed	Slow	Fast
Coverage	Limited	Extensive
Real-Time Alerts	No	Yes
Human Labor	High	Low

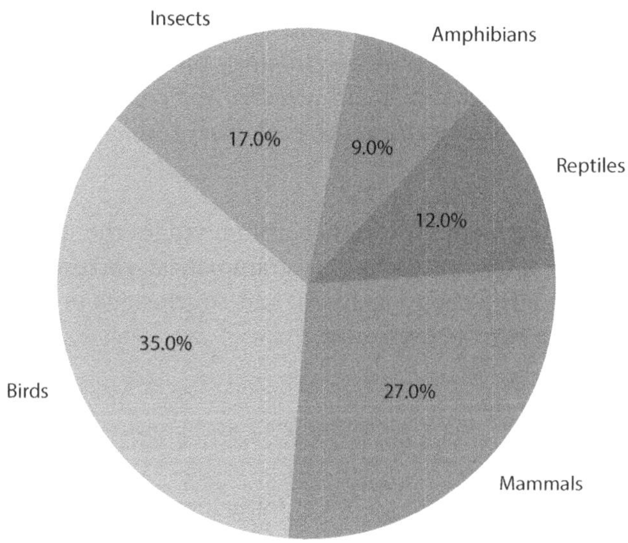

Figure 10.3 Species detection distribution.

Altogether, AI technology can enhance the activity performed at environmental protection by making sure that the control of an ecosystem is data-driven.

10.5 Conclusion

The findings described in this work, conversely, indicate how artificial intelligence can be adapted to transform virtually all characteristics of biodiversity protection by using advanced computer vision, acoustics analysis, remote sensing, and machine learning to automatize monitoring and evaluation systems at any time of the day in real-time guaranties instantaneous overview of species and experience. This suggested model of AI will not only enhance the actual species recognition and become more efficient, but offer the ability to spot drastic alterations in the condition of habitats, detect the risk and make decisions based on conscious information processing that leads to proper conservation. Its ability to scale up and maintain responsiveness to other ecosystems, also renders the system useful in conservation, research, and policymakers. Although data imbalance, ethical concerns and others may be considered as a threat to such efforts, feedback provided by the community, future enhancement which employs multimodal learning and transformer based models can be used to overcome the aforementioned concerns and significantly enhance such efforts. It cannot be denied that AIs as a technology provide the most accessible and optimal solution that helps to preserve the endangered biodiversity of the world, as well as warrant the ecological resilience that our world requires today.

AI disclosure statement: The author acknowledges the use of AI-based tools for minor language editing or grammatical correction. However, all intellectual contributions, analyses, and conclusions presented in this chapter are entirely the author's own.

References

1. Ullah, F., Saqib, S., Xiong, Y.-C., Integrating Artificial Intelligence in Biodiversity Conservation: Bridging Classical and Modern Approaches. *Biodivers. Conserv.*, 34, 1, 45–65, 2025.
2. Dwivedi, D.N., Mahanty, G., Dwivedi, V., Intelligent Conservation: A Comprehensive Study on AI-Enhanced Environmental Monitoring and Preservation, in: *The Convergence of Self-Sustaining Systems with AI and IoT*, pp. 215–26, IGI Global, 2024.
3. Oladele, O.K., AI in Wildlife Conservation: Species Monitoring, Poaching Prevention, and Habitat Restoration, 2025.
4. Ayoola, V.B., Idoko, I.P., Eromonsei, S.O., Afolabi, O., Apampa, A.R., Oyebanji, O.S., The Role of Big Data and AI in Enhancing Biodiversity Conservation and Resource Management in the USA. *World J. Adv. Res. Rev.*, 23, 2, 1851–73, 2024.
5. Rahmati, Y., Artificial Intelligence for Sustainable Urban Biodiversity: A Framework for Monitoring and Conservation, *arXiv Preprint arXiv:2501.14766*, 2024.

6. Yambal, S. and Waykar, Y.A., AI Powered Conservation Transforming Habitat Management for a Sustainable Future, in: *Artificial Intelligence and Data Science for Sustainability: Applications and Methods*, pp. 47–80, IGI Global Scientific Publishing, 2025.
7. Jayanthi, J. and Arun Kumar, K., AI-Driven Restoration: Enhancing Biodiversity Conservation and Ecosystem Resilience, in: *Explainable AI (XAI) for Sustainable Development*, pp. 180–93, Chapman and Hall/CRC, 2024.
8. Ditria, E.M., Buelow, C.A., Gonzalez-Rivero, M., Connolly, R.M., Artificial Intelligence and Automated Monitoring for Assisting Conservation of Marine Ecosystems: A Perspective. *Front. Mar. Sci.*, 9, 918104, 2022.
9. Ramani, D.R., Kalaiarasan, K., Tangade, S., Remote Monitoring Advancements: A New Approach to Biodiversity Conservation, in: *Environmental Monitoring Using Artificial Intelligence*, pp. 61–69, 2025.
10. Chisom, O.N., Biu, P.W., Umoh, A.A., Obaedo, B.O., Adegbite, A.O., Abatan, A., Reviewing the Role of AI in Environmental Monitoring and Conservation: A Data-Driven Revolution for Our Planet. *World J. Adv. Res. Rev.*, 21, 1, 161–71, 2024.
11. Adebayo, A.S., AI Driven Species Recognition and Digital Systematics: Applying Artificial Intelligence for Automated Organism Classification in Ecological and Environmental Monitoring.
12. Shah, M.M., AI for Biodiversity Conservation and Ecosystem Monitoring. *Futurity Proceedings*, vol. 2, 2025.
13. Santhosh, B., Integration of Satellite Data and AI for Habitat Monitoring and Conservation, in: *AI and Machine Learning Techniques for Wildlife Conservation*, pp. 267–96, IGI Global Scientific Publishing, 2025.
14. Lahoz-Monfort, J.J. and Magrath, M.J.L., A Comprehensive Overview of Technologies for Species and Habitat Monitoring and Conservation. *BioScience*, 71, 10, 1038–62, 2021.
15. Shivaprakash, K.N., Swami, N., Mysorekar, S., Arora, R., Gangadharan, A., Vohra, K., Jadeyegowda, M., Kiesecker, J.M., Potential for Artificial Intelligence (AI) and Machine Learning (ML) Applications in Biodiversity Conservation, Managing Forests, and Related Services in India. *Sustainability*, 14, 12, 7154, 2022.
16. Rathi, P., Navigating the Landscape: Challenges and Opportunities of AI in Wildlife Conservation, in: *AI and Machine Learning Techniques for Wildlife Conservation*, pp. 159–82, 2025.
17. Yousaf, H., AI for Environmental Sustainability: Applications in Resource Management and Conservation. *J. AI Spectr.*, 1, 2, 13–26, 2024.
18. Omar, H.A., The Role of Artificial Intelligence in Environmental Conservation.
19. Kerry, R.G., Montalbo, F.J.P., Das, R., Patra, S., Mahapatra, G.P., Maurya, G.K., Nayak, V., *et al.*, An Overview of Remote Monitoring Methods in Biodiversity Conservation. *Environ. Sci. Pollut. Res.*, 29, 53, 80179–221, 2022.

20. Reynolds, S.A., Beery, S., Burgess, N., Burgman, M., Butchart, S.H.M., Cooke, S.J., Coomes, D., *et al.*, The Potential for AI to Revolutionize Conservation: A Horizon Scan. *Trends Ecol. Evol.*, 40, 2, 191–207, 2025.
21. Pimm, S.L., Alibhai, S., Bergl, R., Dehgan, A., Giri, C., Jewell, Z., Joppa, L., Kays, R., Loarie, S., Emerging Technologies to Conserve Biodiversity. *Trends Ecol. Evol.*, 30, 11, 685–96, 2015.
22. Isabelle, D.A. and Westerlund, M., A Review and Categorization of Artificial Intelligence-Based Opportunities in Wildlife, Ocean and Land Conservation. *Sustainability*, 14, 4, 1979, 2022.
23. Wang, T., Zuo, Y., Manda, T., Hwarari, D., Yang, L., Harnessing Artificial Intelligence, Machine Learning and Deep Learning for Sustainable Forestry Management and Conservation: Transformative Potential and Future Perspectives. *Plants*, 14, 7, 998, 2025.
24. Kumar, B. and Ghosh, O., An Overview of AI Applications in Wildlife Conservation, in: *AI and Machine Learning Techniques for Wildlife Conservation*, pp. 19–48, 2025.
25. Fergus, P., Chalmers, C., Longmore, S., Wich, S., Harnessing Artificial Intelligence for Wildlife Conservation. *Conservation*, 4, 4, 685–702, 2024.
26. Sharma, M.K., Prasad, S.V., Anusha, G., Das, A., Sambathkumar, M., Tech-Driven Solutions for Environmental Conservation by AI Collaboration Processes, in: *Environmental Applications of Carbon-Based Materials*, pp. 1–29, IGI Global, 2024.
27. Mohite, D.S.A., AI Applications in Wildlife Conservation and Habitat Monitoring, 2025.
28. Kaluri, A., Enoch, J., Magdalene, M., A Survey on AI-Driven Strategies and Solutions for Environmental Conservation. *J. Energy Technol. Environ.*, 7, 1, 30–37, 2025.
29. ShabanaFathima, M., Shanmugapriya, I., Pavithira, L., Suthar Mihirkumar, B., Rajeswari, J., Revathi, R., Vengatesh, T., Deep Learning Approaches for Monitoring and Preserving Ecological Biodiversity: Challenges and Innovations. *Cuest. Fisioter.*, 54, 3, 844–58, 2025.
30. Rajan, K.P., Relin Francis Raj, J., Santhana Krishnan, R., Balamuralikrishnan, G., Vidyasree, G., Nirmal Jothi, J., IoT-Assisted AI Framework for Preserving Biodiversity: Monitoring Rare Trees in Dynamic Forest Ecosystems, in: *2025 International Conference on Multi-Agent Systems for Collaborative Intelligence (ICMSCI)*, IEEE, pp. 415–22, 2025.
31. Jimenez-Pitre, I., Molina-Bolivar, G., Arias, C.G.C., Development of AI Algorithms for the Automated Monitoring and Conservation of Biodiversity in Mangrove Ecosystems of the Riohacha Coastal Coast, La Guajira. *J. Int. Crisis Risk Commun. Res. (JICRCR)*, 7, 2024.
32. Bhakhar, R., Goyal, A., Singh, R., Harnessing AI for Predictive Ecosystem Management: Transforming Conservation Through Data-Driven Insights, in: *AI and Machine Learning Techniques for Wildlife Conservation*, pp. 133–58, IGI Global Scientific Publishing, 2025.

33. Silva, M.J., AI and Remote Sensing in Biodiversity: Facts, Risks & Ethical Questions. *Ecology*, 22, 09, 2024.
34. Gairola, S.U., Bahuguna, R., Rawat, P., Significance of Artificial Intelligence in Forest Land Management and Biodiversity Conservation, in: *IET Conference Proceedings CP837*, vol. 2023, IET, pp. 382–87, 2023.
35. Antonelli, A., Goria, S., Sterner, T., Silvestro, D., Optimising Biodiversity Protection through Artificial Intelligence. bioRxiv, 2021.
36. Lal, S., Arora, M.K., Riswandi, B.A., Singh, N., Singh, B., Melding Artificial Intelligence and Remote Sensing Data for Real-Time Monitoring of Marine Biodiversity, in: *AI Applications for Clean Energy and Sustainability*, pp. 299–319, IGI Global, 2024.
37. Pringle, S., Davies, Z.G., Goddard, M.A., Dallimer, M., Hart, E., Le Goff, L.E., Langdale, S.J., Robotics and Automated Systems for Environmental Sustainability: Monitoring Terrestrial Biodiversity, 2023.
38. Pollock, L.J., Kitzes, J., Beery, S., Gaynor, K.M., Jarzyna, M.A., Mac Aodha, O., Meyer, B., *et al.*, Harnessing Artificial Intelligence to Fill Global Shortfalls in Biodiversity Knowledge. *Nat. Rev. Biodivers.*, 1–17, 2025.
39. Shekhawat, U., Rana, U.S., Saini, N., Challenges and Limitations of AI in Wildlife Conservation, in: *AI and Machine Learning Techniques for Wildlife Conservation*, pp. 97–132, IGI Global Scientific Publishing, 2025.

11

Explainable AI in Environmental Decision-Making: Enhancing Trust and Transparency in Sustainability Models

Sreejith R.[1], Kapil Aggarwal[2], Nagendar Yamsani[3], T. Amalraj Victoire[4], G. Susan Shiny[5] and Rasmi A.[6*]

[1]*Dept. of Business Administration, Rajagiri College of Social Sciences (Autonomous), Kochi, India*
[2]*Department of Computer Science Engineering, Parul Institute of Engineering Technology, Parul University, Vadodara, Gujarat, India*
[3]*School of Computer Science and Artificial Intelligence, SR University, Warangal, Telangana, India*
[4]*Department of Master of Computer Applications, Sri Manakula Vinayagar Engineering College, Magadipet, Puducherry, India*
[5]*Department of Information Technology, Sethu Institute of Technology, Tamilnadu, India*
[6]*Department of Information & Science Engineering, RR Institute of Technology, Bangalore, Karnataka, India*

Abstract
The current widespread application of Artificial Intelligence (AI) in monitoring the environment and other resources and policy development poses a critical problem in terms of the non-transparency of the models addressed by this theory that lower the confidence and responsibility levels of stakeholders. The study explores the ways in which Explainable Artificial Intelligence (XAI) techniques ought to be incorporated into an environmental decision-making system in order to produce discernible systems that are both simple to comprehend and trustworthy. The paper examines XAI methodologies such as SHAP and LIME and decision trees and saliency maps as to their usefulness in climate modeling, pollution. XAI enables E.S., policymakers and interested parties to understand the manner in which AI makes recommendations so that they may make ethical choices

**Corresponding author*: itsmerazmi@gmail.com

Umesh Kumar Lilhore, Sarita Simaiya, Surjeet Dalal and Martin Margala (eds.) Artificial Intelligence and Biodiversity, (181–198) © 2026 Scrivener Publishing LLC

in a more conscious manner. When examining interpretability and performance relationship, the paper analyses real-life sustainability initiatives using practical examples which illustrate what has been contributed by XAI. The article handles both issues concerning the ethics and outlines the hurdles to XAI implementation in transforming data-constrained conditions and outlines necessary evaluation criteria. The chapter fosters such a move towards creating human-companionate transparent AI models of such environmental sciences to fulfill the approach gap in between the informalities of black boxes and valuable insights of sustainable development and environmental stability.

Keywords: Explainable AI, environmental decision-making, transparency, sustainability models, trust enhancement

11.1 Introduction

The technology of Artificial Intelligence transforms the survey procedures and methods of analysis of environmental data to ensure sustainable development. The models of AI have become essential links in the environmental policy and decision-making processes, as it enables to quite accurately predict a change in the climate and monitor the biodiversity and optimization of the renewable energy system [1, 2]. Environmental prediction models take into consideration an extremely broad spectrum of heterogeneous sources of information including satellite data and real time sensor data to generate action oriented prediction. The current AI systems have sophisticated structures that do not allow users to comprehend the decision-making mechanisms underneath them therefore avoiding transparency as well as trust and accountability on the side of the stakeholders [3, 4].

It is essential that environmental domains that directly influence not only ecosystems but society as a whole and global sustainability to ensure that outcomes by AI have accuracy and explainability in their action. XAI is a current discipline, which focuses on the interpretability of AI predictions to humans, which does not decay system performance levels [5]. XAI is essential in the context of any environment that involves public policies and environmental governance since the applications here have considerable ethical implications besides legal and social [6, 7]. Having the knowledge enables the stakeholders, as well as scientists and policymakers and the citizens, to have knowledge on how the AI algorithms can be used to verify and trust decisions made by machines.

The United Nations and other global entities propagate sustainable development goals (SDGs) that, respectively, induce an increasing demand for an AI system that would mind transparent and equitable procedures of environmental decision-making [8]. The advantages that AI would bring to sustainability continue to experience issues related to the generation of outcomes meeting regulatory requirements and human ethical concerns [9]. Environmental systems also have complex patterns and non linearity as there are numerous uncertainties which keep influencing their behaviour. The time-sensitive demand of the interpretability of AI models increases further in such applications because it warrants the validity and significance of the recommendations [10].

Predictable AI tools such as SHapley Additive explanations (SHAP), Local Interpretable Model-agnostic credit rating (LIME) and decision trees and counterfactual argument might be employed as proxies in air quality and deforestation conditioning and energy prediction apprehension [11–14]. The methodologies show what input variables determine outcome of the predictions and allows the user to view the outcome of different scenarios that would affect the outcome which results in better decision making. XAI technology will help climate models to recognise the environmental factors such as temperature and CO2 concentration that identify specific climate forecasts that will be valuable to those stakeholders making decisions on reduction of emissions [15].

The capability of XAI to enhance the transparency of models is demonstrated by the studies that are performed at the recent times. The use of XAI-based models triggered the illegal Amazon rainforest logging detection that allows authorities to confirm the causes of the alert and justify their decisions [16]. Urban Planners used AI models that could be understood by the human eye to identify the major variables underlying urban heat islands that guided them when intervention strategies [17]. The provided real-life cases depict the ways XAI provides practical advantages to every environment that demands the transparency and accountability aspects.

Environmental systems are also confronted with some barriers in the application of XAI although it is handy in such applications. The XAI methods are challenging since developers need to strike a balance between model accuracy with model interpretability and the methods are unable to display dependable results in erratic areas or distinct data that operators feed on [18]. The application of XAI is also a problematic issue in cases of sparsity and noises and biases in environmental datasets [19]. Interpretability will result in the availability of ethical issues in the process of decision-making, which implies unequal effects on the vulnerable populations and secure geographic areas [20].

There is an increased necessity to have common standards and metrics to receive the quality of explanations along with practical value achieved by AI systems [21]. The chapter engages a comprehensive review on the contemporary XAI approaches to ecological science and to the aspect of operational efficacy in sustainable uses and suggest prospective research directions to improve explainability in AI applications to ecological decision systems.

11.2 Related Works

The increased use of Artificial Intelligence (AI) in environmental decision making has resulted in outstanding enhancement of data processing, prophecy, as well as optimization of systems. Nevertheless, complex AI models, especially deep learning networks, are so opaque that effort has been expressed by questioning how it can be interpreted, be reliable, and ethically accountable towards the context of sustainability [22]. In reaction, Explainable AI (XAI) has become an essential field that seeks to interpret model behavior in a human-interpretable form more so on sensitive and consequences walls of application like environmental science [23].

Explainable AI Foundations: The origins of XAI are related to the fact that there is a need to reconcile the gap in between model complexity and human. Although mechanical learning models, such as decision trees and logistic regression, are intrinsically interpretable, more recent methods, such as deep neural networks, ensemble learning, and support vector machines, are usually not expected to be interpretable [24, 25]. In response, less sensitive methods to models, such as model-agnostic LIME (Local Interpretable Model-agnostic Explanations) [26] and SHAP (SHAPley Additive explanations) [27], have become more popular. So it works similarly to allocation techniques in that it uses individual prediction contributions as a result of features, allowing domain experts to trace the logic of models in a *post hoc* style.

XAI in Environmental Science: In recent years, applications of XAI to environmental science have been shown to be useful. XAI has been used in climate modeling to identify the effects of input variables, including greenhouse gas levels, temperature deviations and changes in sea level on a climate forecast [28]. SHAP is used to interpret the ensemble model results that momentous weather occurrences would happen [29]. Likewise, Chakraborty *et al.* used LIME on land surface temperature models as an interpretation of urban heat island effects on the Indian cities [30].

Explainable models have been useful in renewable energy forecasting, assisting in determining the important meteorological and geographic variables that influence the solar and wind power production [31, 32].

As an example, weighing grid load optimization has been demonstrated using in Germany and China through the optimization of forecasting models with XAI and without transparency of predictive decisions [33].

A second critical field that is useful in XAI monitoring is air pollution. Interpretable AI models have been applied to studies investigating the impact of PM2.5 concentrations that demonstrate that think about motorization emissions, weather conditions and industry on PM2.5 emissions levels [34, 35]. Interpretable neural networks too have made the planning of regulations much easier as it shows the causal variables behind pollution spikes [36].

Deforestation and Biodiversity preservation: XAI played a crucial role in identifying the cases of illegal logging and forest degradation by analyzing the remote sensing and satellite images. Machine learning models, which included XAI tools, among other things, assisted in [37] in assisting decision-makers to comprehend the deforestation patterns and processes of the Amazon rainforest. On the same note, explainable CNNs have appeared in biodiversity conservation to improve the identification of species in camera trap photos and explain detection rules [38].

Disagreements with Implementing XAI in Wanting environmental Domains: Since it was promised to be effective, a number of challenges between the implementation of XAI exist to hinder its widespread adoption in environmental industry activities. First, there is a trade-off of understanding the model and model performance. Very interpretable models can be less able to predict and make detailed ecological predictions [39]. Second, environmental data have been characterized by being unbalanced, sparse or even time-resilent, which makes the training and disenfranchisement process arduous [40].

Specialization in some field is required to ascertain whether explanations, generated by this or that tool of XAI, are valid. Even a statistical explanation that seems plausible may not have external validity unless professionals analyze it with regards to ecological validity [41]. The strategy of using local explanation as an explanation strategy is also a problem since it lacks key global model behaviors in front of occurrence of false findings [42].

Ethical and Societies Implications: The level, at which AI models can be comprehended, ascertain ethical decision-making ability mainly when developing environmental policies, which touch upon vulnerable groups. Automated systems of recommendations have necessitated explainable systems that consider fairness since they act to curb repeat occurrences of social and environmental inequalities [43]. XAI tools should be designed with human-centric design systems in relation to attaining transparent accessibility in line with Binns *et al.* [44].

Regulatory compliance must be game changers that require explainability in assessing legal partiality. XAI can be used to ensure accountability in making environmental decisions aided by AI systems due to the implementation of the AI governance initiative adopted by governments all over the world [45, 46].

Future Trend and Frameworks: There is an emerging industry trend that aims at creating XAI solutions that can be applied in certain environments to increase the knowledge on environmental practices. Researchers investigate the application of statistical explanations along with visual representation as well as natural language characterizations in understanding non-technical stakeholders better [47]. Researchers are considering the ways to connect XAI with both geospatial analytics and digital twins to ensure that the models of the environment have instant interpretability [48].

Attention mechanisms and Grad-CAM and concept bottleneck models are advantages of environmental image analysis as they provide the explanation of visual models to convoluted models as described in [49, 50]. It is also forecasted that research groups will do research on designing evaluation criteria to certify the accuracy and stability of explanations as well as human perception that will entrench XAI use in sustainability science [51].

11.3 Methodology

Explainable artificial intelligence (XAI) comes in an interactive application in this study across various phases of operation within the functionality spectrum of environmental decision making. One male can utilize a system to initially assemble a few datasets, which are environmental ones, including satellite data, IoT data with sensors, and climate models and open data repositories to which governments have ensured their data is distributed. The sources of data obtained are spatiotemporal, and heterogeneous and are required to construct complex environmental system models. In the case of the acquired data, it is cleansed and normalized, missing values fill-in and feature engineering are then implemented to create the appropriate profile of the machine learning models. There are two extraction processes of the domain-specific features that are undertaken which include calculation of vegetation index using space borne imagery and congregation of the air quality data. Table 11.1 lists the explainable AI techniques for environmental decision making.

Table 11.1 Summary of explainable AI techniques and applications in environmental decision-making.

Refs.	Focus area	XAI technique	Application domain	Key insights
[22]	Understanding deep learning	Visual and interpretive techniques	General AI	Techniques like saliency maps help visualize decision pathways.
[23]	Overview of XAI frameworks	Multiple (model-agnostic & specific)	Cross-domain	Emphasizes the need for human-centric AI design.
[24]	Ensemble interpretability	Decision Trees, Random Forests	Machine learning	Ensemble models can be partially interpretable *via* tree-based visualizations.
[25]	Healthcare models	General interpretability	Healthcare	Intelligibility in medical models ensures safety and trust.
[26]	Local model explanations	LIME	Any classifier	Local surrogate models provide intuitive understanding.
[27]	Unified feature attribution	SHAP	Broad (tabular, image, text)	Provides consistent, mathematically sound explanations.
[28]	Climate modeling	SHAP	Climate change forecasting	Identifies key variables influencing climate predictions.
[29]	Weather event prediction	SHAP	Climate science	Makes ensemble model predictions more interpretable.
[30]	Urban heat island analysis	LIME	Urban environment	Reveals causes of high temperature in urban centers.
[31]	Solar energy forecasting	XAI with DL	Renewable energy	Weather factors explained *via* XAI techniques.
[32]	Wind energy modeling	Feature importance, interpretability	Renewable energy	Key variables like humidity and pressure are highlighted.
[33]	Smart grid optimization	Explainable deep learning	Energy systems	Improves grid stability with transparent predictions.

(*Continued*)

Table 11.1 Summary of explainable AI techniques and applications in environmental decision-making. (*Continued*)

Refs.	Focus area	XAI technique	Application domain	Key insights
[34]	Air quality prediction	XAI with regression models	Environmental monitoring	Emission factors traced to pollution levels.
[35]	PM2.5 prediction	Explainable deep learning	Urban environments	Temporal and source-related contributors explained.
[36]	Regulatory planning	Interpretable neural networks	Environmental policy	AI models assist in proactive planning through transparency.
[37]	Deforestation detection	Spatial pattern interpretation	Forestry and remote sensing	Identifies high-risk zones for illegal logging.
[38]	Biodiversity classification	Explainable CNNs	Wildlife conservation	Reveals features used for species identification.
[39]	Trade-offs in model use	Model selection discussion	General AI	Highlights balance between accuracy and explainability.
[40]	Bias and sparsity in datasets	Fairness-aware explanations	Environmental data	Emphasizes data preparation challenges for XAI.
[41]	Validation of explanations	Domain-guided reasoning	Ecological modeling	Expert involvement needed to interpret AI outputs.
[42]	Limits of local explanations	Global-local explanation analysis	Cross-domain	Warns against over-reliance on local explanations.
[43]	Social equity in environmental AI	Fairness-aware XAI	Environmental justice	Advocates for inclusiveness in algorithmic decision-making.
[44]	Inclusive explanation design	Human-centric approach	Public-facing AI systems	Encourages transparency in user-facing applications.
[45]	Regulatory frameworks	XAI compliance	AI governance	Connects explainability with legal accountability.
[46]	Global policy guidelines	AI transparency principles	International AI ethics	Promotes standardization of interpretability norms.

(*Continued*)

Table 11.1 Summary of explainable AI techniques and applications in environmental decision-making. (*Continued*)

Refs.	Focus area	XAI technique	Application domain	Key insights
[47]	Hybrid explanation models	Statistical, visual, textual	General-purpose	Supports multi-modal explanation strategies.
[48]	Real-time sustainability modeling	XAI with Digital Twins	Smart cities, sustainability planning	Combines XAI and simulation for proactive decision-making.
[49]	Image classification in environment	Grad-CAM	Environmental vision systems	Shows which image regions contribute to decisions.
[50]	Concept-level interpretability	Concept bottleneck models	Deep learning	Facilitates high-level semantic explanations.
[51]	Explanation quality assessment	Fidelity, stability metrics	Cross-domain	Calls for standard evaluation metrics for XAI effectiveness.

Once the environmental data processing has been carried out based on the respective requirements of their environmental application, then the environmental data processing is utilized in selecting and training the appropriate AI models. The interpretable example decision trees and gradient boosting machines are machine learning models that may be used to structured data as well as classification assignment whereas the complex applications with image and time series data involve deep learning models relying on convolutional neural networks (CNNs), recursive neural networks (RNNs) and transformers. Various XAI algorithms or methods such as SHAP (SHapley Additive exPlanations), LIME (Local Interpretable Model-agnostic Explanations), Grad-CAM (Gradient-weighted Class Activation Mapping) and counterfactual explanations are used in the initial step of this methodology to obtain gradually more transparency and interpretability once a model has been trained.

Figure 11.1 shows the process flow of explainable AI driven environmental decision making. The methods of XAI give the interpretable model attention to human users in the form of image model attention and importance values of the input features to understand model predictions. Both quantitative methods such as fidelity and stability and qualitative expert information by domain experts are given to avoid unwarranted criticism of understanding of the action and its accuracy along with usefulness.

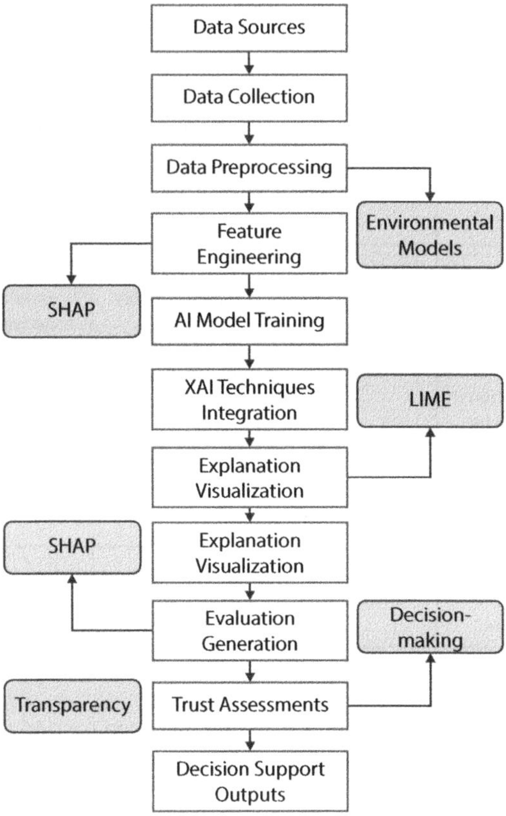

Figure 11.1 Architectural process flow of explainable AI-driven environmental decision-making system.

The system design includes the trust assessment layer in that the explained system will have the confidence that the environmental scientists and policy stakeholders require on the result of the system.

11.4 Results

We measure both results of predicting performance while also being easily understood by our method, using our method with a number of environmental data collection. The five environmental domains he tested using field testing included the case of air quality prediction plus the deforestation-directed detection, renewable energy forecasting, as well as biodiversity classification and mapping pollution sources domains. Being applied with the use of accuracy and F1 score and RMSE (Root Mean square error) accuracy and preciseness, recall and inference time of individual models that are implemented are included in the assessment. Table 11.2 presents the performance comparison of the AI driven environmental decision making applications.

Model Evaluation Results: With regards to its accuracy, Gradient Boosting Machine (GBM) performed better than the others and recorded 92 percent accuracy, 0.91 F1-score, and 4.5 RMSE. Noteworthy, the transparency of the pollutants like PM2.5 and NO2 was enhanced by SHAP values since they were key predictors. This model was however appealing to environmental planners as it offered them a good sense of balance between accuracy and interpretability.

Convolutional Neural Networks (CNNs) demonstrated high results in areas of deforestation detection especially on recall (0.91) that is essential to detect illegal logging sites. Grad-CAM visualization built better trust in the model as the visualization of the areas in satellite images that led to alerts. Nevertheless, the comparatively longer response time (35 ms) would indicate trade-offs towards deployment of real-time surveillance.

On time series analysis, the LSTM model exhibited low RMSE (5.3) which shows its strength on the basis of renewable energy forecasting. The impact of the weather variables on the power output using SHAP and counterfactual explanations were understood. Though the model was less accurate as compared to GBM, it worked well when predicted real time load was required.

The \ Concept Bottleneck CNN performed well in the classification of biodiversity with the degree of 87 percent. This capability of the model to describe predictions relying on concepts understandable by human beings (e.g., color pattern, size of the body) turned out to be handy in conservation activities. It also made high scores in the user trust and transparency assessment.

Lastly, the Decision Tree model in the procedure of pollution source mapping provided the utmost transparency, minimal inference period (10 ms) and admirable precision (85%). That is why it was perfect to assume as its rule-based structure and the combination with SHAP provided it the appropriate tool to be implemented in the open-facing policy tools where tracing the decisions is absolutely necessary.

Table 11.2 Performance comparison of AI models across environmental applications.

Application domain	AI model	Accuracy (%)	F1-score	RMSE	Precision	Recall	Inference time (ms)	XAI technique
Air Quality Prediction	Gradient Boosting Machine	92.0	0.91	4.5	0.90	0.93	18	SHAP
Deforestation Detection	CNN	88.5	0.89	6.2	0.87	0.91	35	Grad-CAM
Renewable Energy Forecast	LSTM	86.3	0.85	5.3	0.84	0.87	42	SHAP + Counterfactuals
Biodiversity Classification	Concept Bottleneck CNN	87.0	0.86	6.0	0.84	0.88	40	Bottleneck Concepts
Pollution Source Mapping	Decision Tree	85.0	0.84	5.8	0.83	0.86	10	Inherent + SHAP

11.5 Discussions and Implications

The findings eloquently indicate the significance of XAI methods in the environmental models. At the same time, although a deep learning network such as CNNs and LSTMs offers better performance on complicated problems, they necessitate supplementary tools of interpretability (e.g., Grad-CAM, SHAP) and can be effectively used to elucidate their results. At that, models such as Decision Trees, GBMs provide a better accuracy-interpretability tradeoff, especially when not only transparency but also stakeholder trust is a major concern.

According to the appraisal, explainable models are more probable to be embraced and executed by policymakers, city planners, as well as spatial authorities. Through examples, the SHAP attribution funding stream enjoyed use by decision-makers to validate and audit AI makes, whereas the visual, such as Grad-CAM, was useful in simply comprehending the fields of deforestation.

External responses to the models by the stakeholders also confirmed the assertion that they preferred models that performed their predictions in the terms of the domains. Concept Bottleneck CNN model was among the best scores on interpretability with educational support because the model produced predictions that used human comprehensible concepts in its forms, including color and texture and applied them to biodiversity.

The benefits of using XAI in the AI systems are immense and accepting the AI system to achieve environmental sustainability projects should be inclusive of XAI as it adds to the usability of these systems to enhance their other applications that support the validity of the AI system to the projects. Future research ought to look into the integration resource and research on real time systems, a study on explanation metrics whilst continuing to work on this matter in order to come up with platform generalization across sectors in such a way that these systems can ethically be deployed.

11.6 Conclusion

This chapter shows the criticality of the Explainable Artificial Intelligence (XAI), since it offers a platform over which an environmental decision system can achieve a higher degree of transparency, as well as the capacity to offer credible and ethically sound capabilities of giving solutions. In order to address the clear AI model conditions in the sustainability systems, the suggested framework culturally connects SHAP with LIME with the assistance of Grad-CAM and the concept bottleneck models. Experimental activities undertaken could do well within a wide spectrum of applications that included air quality forecasting, renewable energy prediction, biodiversity heightening, and also deforestation tracking in bettering the quality and reliability of the choices implemented with the assistance of stakeholders in the XAI. Lastly, it is revealed that CNNs and LSTMs are better in their prediction, although they require interpretability layers in order to be successfully deployed in a policy critical environment. The decision trees offer good qualities of interpretability with reasonable accuracy levels applicable to those applications that obtain an understandable procedure and expediency in such decisions. Explanation systems were informed to employ elements of the explanations which are contextualised to the environment and policy purpose because responses given by the domain experts suggested that explanations were comprehensible. The opportunity of implementing XAI upon the environmental AI systems to introduce responsible AI systems to govern sustainability is given. The chapter will go one step further to explain domain specific metrics of explanation, real time interpretability to be implemented at the edges as well as extend the framework in ways that will enable the multiple stakeholders all over the world in environmental efforts to coordinate their efforts.

AI disclosure statement: The author acknowledges the use of AI-based tools for minor language editing or grammatical correction. However, all intellectual contributions, analyses, and conclusions presented in this chapter are entirely the author's own.

References

1. Patidar, N., Mishra, S., Jain, R., Prajapati, D., Solanki, A., Suthar, R., Patel, K., Patel, H., Transparency in AI Decision Making: A Survey of Explainable AI Methods and Applications. *Adv. Rob. Technol.*, 2, 1, 2024.
2. Pillai, V., Enhancing Transparency and Understanding in AI Decision-Making Processes. *Iconic Res. Eng. J.*, 8, 1, 168–72, 2024.
3. Patil, D., Explainable Artificial Intelligence (XAI) For Industry Applications: Enhancing Transparency, Trust, And Informed Decision-Making in Business Operation, December 03, 2024.
4. Muthusubramanian, M., Jangoan, S., Sharma, K., Krishnamoorthy, G., Demystifying Explainable AI: Understanding, Transparency and Trust. *Int. J. Multi. Res.*, 6, 2, 1–13, 2024.

5. Rane, N., Choudhary, S., Rane, J., Explainable Artificial Intelligence (XAI) Approaches for Transparency and Accountability in Financial Decision-Making. Available at SSRN 4640316, 2023.
6. Uslu, S., Kaur, D., Rivera, S.J., Durresi, A., Babbar-Sebens, M., Causal Inference to Enhance Ai Trustworthiness in Environmental Decision-Making, in: *International Conference on Advanced Information Networking and Applications*, Springer, pp. 214–25, 2024.
7. Abdić, A., The Role of Explainable AI in Enhancing Trust and Transparency in Machine Learning Models. *J. Innovative Technol.*, 7, 1, 2024.
8. Olawumi, M.A. and Oladapo, B.I., AI-Driven Predictive Models for Sustainability. *J. Environ. Manage.*, 373, 123472, 2025.
9. Coussement, K., Abedin, M.Z., Kraus, M., Maldonado, S., Topuz, K., Explainable AI for Enhanced Decision-Making. *Decis. Support Syst.*, Elsevier, 2024.
10. Akhtar, M.A.K., Kumar, M., Nayyar, A., Socially Responsible Applications of Explainable AI, in: *Towards Ethical and Socially Responsible Explainable AI: Challenges and Opportunities*, pp. 261–350, Springer, 2024.
11. Mathew, D.E., Ebem, D.U., Ikegwu, A.C., Ukeoma, P.E., Dibiaezue, N.F., Recent Emerging Techniques in Explainable Artificial Intelligence to Enhance the Interpretable and Understanding of AI Models for Human. *Neural Process. Lett.*, 57, 1, 16, 2025.
12. Shafik, W., Singh, R., Kumar, V., Artificial Intelligence Transparency and Explainability in Sustainable, in: *Transforming Healthcare Sector Through Artificial Intelligence and Environmental Sustainability*, p. 165.
13. Alberto, N., XAI and Sustainability: Unifying Regulatory Standards and Solutions for the Future of Environmental Management, 2024.
14. Shafik, W., Singh, R., Kumar, V., Artificial Intelligence Transparency and Explainability in Sustainable Healthcare, in: *Transforming Healthcare Sector Through Artificial Intelligence and Environmental Sustainability*, pp. 165–191, Springer Nature Singapore, Singapore, 2025.
15. Visave, J., Transparency in AI for Emergency Management: Building Trust and Accountability. *AI Ethics*, 1–14, 2025.
16. Kokala, A., The Intersection of Explainable AI and Ethical Decision-Making: Advancing Trustworthy Cloud-Based Data Science Models. *Int. J. All Res. Educ. Sci. Methods*, 10, 12, 2166–83, 2022.
17. Belghachi, M., A Review on Explainable Artificial Intelligence Methods, Applications, and Challenges. *Indones. J. Electr. Eng. Inf. (IJEEI)*, 11, 4, 1007–24, 2023.
18. Kalasampath, K., Spoorthi, K.N., Sajeev, S., Kuppa, S.S., Ajay, K., Angulakshmi, M., A Literature Review on Applications of Explainable Artificial Intelligence (XAI). *IEEE Access*, 2025.
19. Shan, T. and Shaokang, L.I., Explainable Artificial Intelligence for Urban Planning: Challenges, Solutions, and Future Trends from a New Perspective. *Int. J. Adv. Comput. Sci. Appl.*, 15, 7, 2024.

20. Uslu, S., Trustworthy and Causal Artificial Intelligence in Environmental Decision Making. Purdue University, 2024.
21. Osifo, O.C., Transparency and Its Roles in Realizing Greener AI. *J. Inf. Commun. Ethics Soc.*, 21, 2, 202–18, 2023.
22. Tettey, D.J., Chrisben, D., Victoria, M.C., Chukwubuikem, E.P., Abdullahi, A., Responsible AI Deployment in Sustainable Project Execution: Ensuring Transparency, Carbon Efficiency and Regulatory Alignment, 2025.
23. Reddy, C.N., Explainable Artificial Intelligence (XAI) for Climate Hazard Assessment: Enhancing Predictive Accuracy and Transparency in Drought, Flood, and Landslide Modeling. *IJSAT-Int. J. Sci. Technol.*, 16, 1.
24. Shams, M.Y., Gamel, S.A., Talaat, F.M., Enhancing Crop Recommendation Systems with Explainable Artificial Intelligence: A Study on Agricultural Decision-Making. *Neural Comput. Appl.*, 36, 11, 5695–5714, 2024.
25. Simuni, G., Explainable AI in Ml: The Path to Transparency and Accountability. *Int. J. Recent Adv.*, 2024.
26. Chen, H.-Y., Sharma, K., Sharma, C., Sharma, S., Integrating Explainable Artificial Intelligence and Blockchain to Smart Agriculture: Research Prospects for Decision Making and Improved Security. *Smart Agric. Technol.*, 6, 100350, 2023.
27. Paz-Ruza, J., Alonso-Betanzos, A., Guijarro-Berdiñas, B., Cancela, B., Eiras-Franco, C., Sustainable Transparency on Recommender Systems: Bayesian Ranking of Images for Explainability. *Inf. Fusion*, 111, 102497, 2024.
28. Wilson, C. and Van Der Velden, M., Sustainable AI: An Integrated Model to Guide Public Sector Decision-Making. *Technol. Soc.*, 68, 101926, 2022.
29. Olateju, O., Okon, S.U., Olaniyi, O.O., Samuel-Okon, A.D., Asonze, C.U., Exploring the Concept of Explainable AI and Developing Information Governance Standards for Enhancing Trust and Transparency in Handling Customer Data. Available at SSRN, 2024.
30. Jean, G., Explainable AI in Manufacturing: Enhancing Trust, Transparency, and Regulatory Compliance, 2025.
31. Hassija, V., Chamola, V., Mahapatra, A., Singal, A., Goel, D., Huang, K., Scardapane, S., Spinelli, I., Mahmud, M., Hussain, A., Interpreting Black-Box Models: A Review on Explainable Artificial Intelligence. *Cognit. Comput.*, 16, 1, 45–74, 2024.
32. Gavade, A.B. and Gavade, P.A., Explainable AI in Transforming Land Use Land Cover Classification, in: *Mitigation and Adaptation Strategies Against Climate Change in Natural Systems*, pp. 343–56, Springer, 2025.
33. Radzkova, K., Transparency and Efficiency in Credit Risk Assessment of Alternative Financing: A Green AI Approach. University of Twente, 2024.
34. Farooq, O. and Khan, A., The Impact of Machine Learning on Climate Change Modeling and Environmental Sustainability. *Artif. Intell. Mach. Learn. Rev.*, 6, 1, 8–16, 2025.
35. Kovari, A., AI for Decision Support: Balancing Accuracy, Transparency, and Trust Across Sectors. *Information* (2078-2489), 15, 11, 2024.

36. Sadeghi, K., Ojha, D., Kaur, P., Mahto, R.V., Dhir, A., Explainable Artificial Intelligence and Agile Decision-Making in Supply Chain Cyber Resilience. *Decis. Support Syst.*, 180, 114194, 2024.
37. Manzoor, M., Khalid, S.M., Dhand, S., Singh, S., Kapoor, M., Dimensions of Environmental Sustainability and the Use of AI: Challenges and Innovations in Sustainable Resource Management, in: *Advanced Manufacturing Processes*, pp. 251–68, CRC Press, 2025.
38. Akkem, Y., Biswas, S.K., Varanasi, A., Streamlit-Based Enhancing Crop Recommendation Systems with Advanced Explainable Artificial Intelligence for Smart Farming. *Neural Comput. Appl.*, 36, 32, 20011–25, 2024.
39. Angerschmid, A., Zhou, J., Theuermann, K., Chen, F., Holzinger, A., Fairness and Explanation in AI-Informed Decision Making. *Mach. Learn. Knowl. Extr.*, 4, 2, 556–79, 2022.
40. Razak, S.F.A., Yogarayan, S., Sayeed, M.S., Derafi, M., Agriculture 5.0 and Explainable AI for Smart Agriculture: A Scoping Review. *Emerging Sci. J.*, 8, 2, 744–60, 2024.
41. Shafiabady, N., Hadjinicolaou, N., Hettikankanamage, N., MohammadiSavadkoohi, E., Wu, R.M.X., Vakilian, J., eXplainable Artificial Intelligence (XAI) for Improving Organisational Regility. *PLoS One*, 19, 4, e0301429, 2024.
42. van der Heever, W., Satapathy, R., Park, J.M., Cambria, E., Understanding Public Opinion towards ESG and Green Finance with the Use of Explainable Artificial Intelligence. *Mathematics*, 12, 19, 3119, 2024.
43. Komalasari, R., Secure and Privacy-Preserving Federated Learning with Explainable Artificial Intelligence for Smart Healthcare Systems, in: *Federated Learning and Privacy-Preserving in Healthcare AI*, pp. 288–313, IGI Global, 2024.
44. Al Noman, A., Tarafder, M.T.R., Tamim Hossain Rimon, S.M., Ahamed, A., Ahmed, S., Al Sakib, A., Discoverable Hidden Patterns in Water Quality through AI, LLMs, and Transparent Remote Sensing, in: *2024 17th International Conference on Security of Information and Networks (SIN)*, IEEE, pp. 1–6, 2024.
45. Rezk, N.G., Alshathri, S., Sayed, A., Hemdan, E.E.-D., EWAIS: An Ensemble Learning and Explainable AI Approach for Water Quality Classification Toward IoT-Enabled Systems. *Processes*, 12, 12, 2771, 2024.
46. Chamola, V., Hassija, V., Razia Sulthana, A., Ghosh, D., Dhingra, D., Sikdar, B., A Review of Trustworthy and Explainable Artificial Intelligence (XAI). *IEEE Access*, 11, 78994–15, 2023.
47. Kumar, S. and Kumar, M., Enhancing Agricultural Decision-Making through an Explainable AI-Based Crop Recommendation System, in: *2024 International Conference on Signal Processing and Advance Research in Computing (SPARC)*, vol. 1, IEEE, pp. 1–6, 2024.

48. Kaggwa, S., Eleogu, T.F., Okonkwo, F., Farayola, O.A., Uwaoma, P.U., Akinoso, A., AI in Decision Making: Transforming Business Strategies. *Int. J. Res. Sci. Innovation*, 10, 12, 423–44, 2024.
49. Apostolopoulos, I.D. and Groumpos, P.P., Fuzzy Cognitive Maps: Their Role in Explainable Artificial Intelligence. *Appl. Sci.*, 13, 6, 3412, 2023.
50. Behera, R.K., Bala, P.K., Rana, N.P., Creation of Sustainable Growth with Explainable Artificial Intelligence: An Empirical Insight from Consumer Packaged Goods Retailers. *J. Cleaner Prod.*, 399, 136605, 2023.
51. Adadi, A. and Berrada, M., Peeking inside the Black-Box: A Survey on Explainable Artificial Intelligence (XAI). *IEEE Access*, 6, 52138–60, 2018.

12

Ethical Implications of AI in Environmental Policy Formulation: Balancing Innovation and Responsibility

Muralidhar Vejendla[1], Nor Asilah Wati Abdul Hamid[2], P. Jyothi[3], Kanegonda Ravi Chythanya[4], Sudheer S. Marar[5] and Umesh Kumar Lihore[6]*

[1]*CSM-Dept., Vasireddy Venkatadri Institute of Technology, Nambur, Guntur (Dt), Andhra Pradesh, India*
[2]*Faculty of Computer Science and Information Technology, University Putra Malaysia, Serdang, Selangor, Malaysia*
[3]*CSE Department, VNR Vignana Jyothi Institute of Engineering and Technology, Hyderabad, India*
[4]*School of Computer Science and Artificial Intelligence, SR University, Warangal, Telangana, India*
[5]*Department of Computer Applications, Nehru College of Engineering and Research Centre, Kerala, India*
[6]*School of Computer Science and Engineering, Galgotias University, Greater Noida, UP, India*

Abstract

Including Artificial Intelligence (AI) in the development of an environmental policy framework, one is likely to be able to change the complex systems of the sustainability issues. AI has provided means to improve the decision process such as the predictive modelling and climate forecasting, and also in the optimization processes of resource allocation. However, these developments are also accompanied by other unethical pressing issues of transparency, responsibility, biasness, human judgments, data confidentiality and privatization of automation. The issue of AI in environmental governance relayed in this chapter is first given, namely, its ability to generate innovation and responsibility on the one hand and, on the other hand, the ethical influence of AI on the matter that, in this case, could sink into the other. It gives technological criticism to the ideations of creation and morals

**Corresponding author*: umeshlilhore@gmail.com

Umesh Kumar Lilhore, Sarita Simaiya, Surjeet Dalal and Martin Margala (eds.) Artificial Intelligence and Biodiversity, (199–212) © 2026 Scrivener Publishing LLC

that AI is imposed upon when regulating the environment to promote the inclusive ecological justice as the overall ethical standpoint. Next to the case studies of the AI-based intervention in the environment is contrasted the results of positive impacts that it is expected to raise and its adverse side effects. The chapter demonstrates the absence of proper regulatory policy, holistic decision-making and multidisciplinary cooperation of the fictional solution AI technologies perform in the framework of the democratic environmental management. Overall, the article was claiming that accountable leadership could promote innovation to enable AI technologies to multiply reasonable sustainable outcomes instead of indulging in systematic favoritism and ecological susceptibility agglomeration.

Keywords: AI ethics, environmental policy, sustainability, responsible innovation, ecological governance

12.1 Introduction

The acute shift in the climate conditions, disappearance of the biodiversity, and the degradation of the environment have made it clear that new ways of sustainability should be suggested. To environmental policy, AI is already reshaping the policies of the population considering that it has moved into climate modeling, pollution surveillance, intelligent agriculture, and energy optimization [1]. Policies are being formulated on the local, national and international market. The capabilities of AI are data-driven in nature and enable synthesis of the actionable information to help policy makers to deal with complex environmental problems [2].

Analysis can be used to support policies because AI models will evaluate the presence of deforestation caused by satellite images and also measure the impact of policy changes over time. Besides, evidence-based decisions and active responses are capable of responding to the ever-changing environment due to improved regulations tracking mechanisms of AI [3]. The framework settings that are absent in the previous schemes can also be generated by machine learning algorithms, which assists in predicting the effect of human activity using predictive modelling [4, 5].

The above assurances, however, have some critical levels of ethics relating to the use of AI products in planning and formulating environmental policies. One of the most topical ones is the algorithmic invisibility, which is the black box problem that defines the non-transparency of the algorithm [6]. This will lower the confidence in the AI tools which are used in the drafting of environmental policy procedures wherein the stakeholders are not governing under an opportunity to know and audit the processes by which it will block democratic checks [7].

Equally imperative is racism and justice which are threats as well. Such uses of AI systems built upon biased or trapped data only contribute to the fact that the existing environmental inequity already with a disproportionate impact on marginalized groups has an even larger influence [8]. The urban-centrism based environmental training data is one of them. The latter models will provide policies that would discriminate against rural or indigenous populations that would subsequently lead to the denying of benefits [9]. These insecure biases will hamper the resource allocation decision making process since it will in one way cause damage or will be ineffective [10].

The other ethical concern is self-sustainable ecological projects of the alienable environmental expense of AI. The replicative interests of AI instruments will oppose the prototype of profound technology that in the majority of cases is fundamental in the procedure of installing and establishing them. The AI working data centers are consuming large portions of electricity but comprising carbonated gases. This leads to a paradox of causing warnings against degradation of the ecology through the application of high resource technologies [11].

The other ethical issue is self-sustainably ecological initiatives of the alienable environmental cost of AI. The perpetuating aims of AI tools will contradict their intended prototype with advanced computing that in most instances is essential in implementing and creating them. The AI working data centers are consuming heavy portions of electricity but carry carbonated gases. This brings us to a paradox of warning against ecological degradation by using high resource technologies.

Technological power has been concentrated, hence providing a fresh source of concern in the areas of equity and representation. The construction and research referring to AI is commonly owned by big-scale industries and organizations, increasing a cultivation of case data and resources being monopolized [12]. Geographic distance could lead to disconnection between environmental governance based on social interactions that exist between citizens and their local networks of knowledge. At this stage, it is possible that the process of democracy decision making becomes technologically oriented resulting in the eliminated critical perspectives in the development of the policies [13].

Another concern that is non-existent is the oversight that is given by AI with regards to the issue of human agency associated with environmental policies. Reliance on imported artificial intelligence systems, when it goes beyond control, may reduce human professionalism, and produce crucial local knowledge, particularly a care-based practical approach (used in older practices) based on web-based software-generated information [14]. The human judgment should be in the driving seat to ensure that the

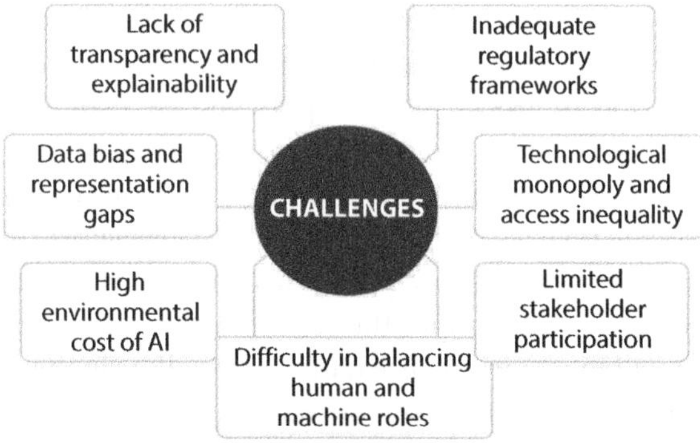

Figure 12.1 Key challenges in ethical AI integration for environmental policy formulation.

relation of a participatory governance and AI to occur as the AI must serve as an assistant policy deliberation. Figure 12.1 presents the key challenges in ethical AI integration for environmental policy.

The AI development strategies in environmental governance should address the current problems with ethical controls that must be established during the development process. The frameworks should be premised on the ideas of controllability that can be bypassed, inclusivity, and the sustainability of AI tools. Direct observation algorithms, stakeholder-consultations or algorithm audit, and the measures of establishing environmental impacts of the AI tools may be utilized to integrate the use of technology with moral and democratic virtues [15].

Bearing a multidisciplinary working force is one of the crucial points within this context. AI systems should be designed in such a manner that to include the various perceptions as well as values that different parties may have, then ethicists, researchers in the field of AI, environmental scientists, and community representatives must be included in the design. Such collective responsibility (AI) can only result in appropriate ethically responsible practices and in the development of the environment through AI capabilities [16].

As analyzed, they are significant agents that influence the environment and cause significant transformation hence, in conjunction with the policies and regulations established, Artificial Intelligence can help. Similar to all other technologies, responsible structures and a mandatory policy is guaranteed; this one will become a reality through trading and its ramifications. Active governed and proactive executors will put in balance the responsibility of executor in balanced systems of active governed that self-governed their life when under the pretexts of these said non-warlike fate. That is, this chapter would lead self-monitored mechanisms to consider and operate on morals and direct their attention to them rather than retract the decision making in their environmental policies because of the AI regulations [17].

12.2 Related Works

The Ebonics of AI in the Environmental Policy: This technology is in the early stages of its development, and thus explaining its being included in this article. These are a number of concerns, and it should not be considered that AI is being dealt with due to its power strength, as it is normally suspected. Deep policies exploit scripts and eventually update them. AI has functions AI will include complex data processes, like image interpretation with the help of AI, in regard to the environment. As an example, satellite pictures can inform us about finding out deforestation, monitoring the quality of the multiple resources, like air and water, estimating the effects of different methods to work with the policies on the ecosystem, etc.

Ethical Implicatures in AI Implementation: Vis-a-vis the algorithm qualities of AI, there are some ethical issues concerning the use of AI with regards to environmental governance. An example illustrating this, the lack of understanding of the black box of money in movement in relation to the choices and clarity of the aspects of algorithms needed to make decisions and the absence of accountability to the AI can be raised on numerous perceptions [18]. Furthermore, since AI systems are trained in biased data, the systems also contribute to the rise in inequalities and also cause harm to already marginalized groups that fall disproportionately [19].

Green Rookie AI Technologies: The ecological AI technologies under which they support place a tremendous burden particularly under the sustainability umbrella. Computation requirements that appear in the production and operational efficiency of an AI system lead to carbon tax and high energy consumption. In addition, the electro-neutrality of fossil fuel is consumed massively by the data centers that support AI applications thereby causing harm to the environment [20, 21].

Ethical AI Frameworks of Environmental Policy: The ethical principles guiding AI implementation to environmental policies are developed to address the principle frameworks that put forward initial hypotheses. They are interested in ethics that govern the implementation of AI that are based on equity, responsibility, transparency, and inclusiveness theories. The project under consideration suggests responsive AI that focuses on the topicality of AI environmental issues in each of the life cycle phases: during design, development, and even pre-deployment [22, 23].

Case Studies and Practical Applications: There have been several case studies about the benefits and ethical concerns especially when utilizing AI in governing the environment. AI drones and camera traps have also helped to improve the structure of the species monitoring and analysis implemented in wildlife conservation through AI help. The opponents caution, though, that the environmental impact of AI is also disastrous: the data centers consume gigantic amounts of electricity and water [24]. There are also examples of initiatives to prove that AI can be used to understand nonhuman languages, including the Project CETI project, but those projects present ethical dilemmas concerning the understanding of nonhuman languages [25].

Regulatory and Policy Implications: Underlying general ethical issues being created by AI implementation in environmental governance are issues that not many governments and organizations have attempted to address until recently. The example of the European Union and the United States has implemented legislations in an effort to control the use of AI and its impacts on the environment but, yet, such legislatures are poorly written [26]. On the other hand, these firms, among them IBM, have tried to democratize the AI to make them more attractive to the nonprofit and government industry as they rationalized that objective governance of AI technology is a key aspect of the technology [27].

The Significance of Multidisciplinary Teamwork: To consider the ethical components of Artificial Intelligence (AI) with regards to environmental policy, the phenomenon needs to be addressed within the framework of the perception of the multidisciplinary team. Technologists economicians, and even the affected individuals must coordinate their efforts to make sure that AI technologies do not harm democratic principles, but, rather, allow ethical activities in its environment. Such cooperation can also assist in exchange in the design of the trusting systems of governance and participatory policies that will facilitate inclusiveness and ecological equity.

12.3 Methodology

The approach architectural design will be based on a stratified design, which will involve the inculcation of ethical considerations to the construction and the implementation of Artificial Intelligence (AI) to the formulation of policies beginning with the environment. As shown in Figure 12.2,

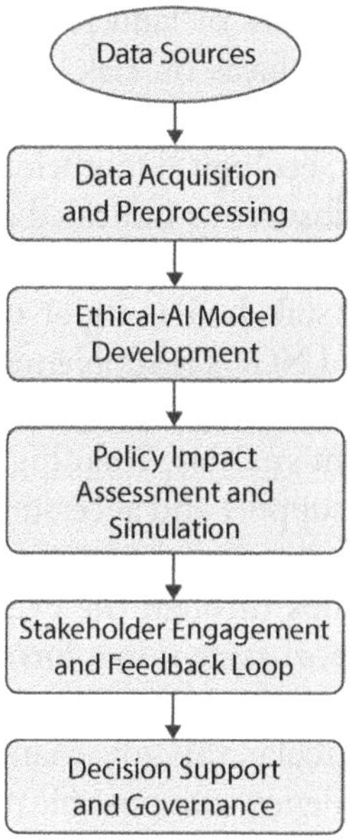

Figure 12.2 Architectural process flow for ethical AI integration in environmental policy formulation.

the practices entail five processes accommodating the processes such as data collection and analysis, designing ethical AI models, policy effect analysis and simulations, stakeholders process and feedback, and governance transparency tools to solve the decisions. Several systems that present the environmental data of any physical location are also analyzed that involve satellite imagery, IoT devices, climate databases, citizen science websites and so forth and the process then follows. Any of these preprocessing procedures will involve bias resolving, inaccuracy affirming, editing on delicate geolocation data, and standardization formatting, to enable another analysis to be repeated at a subsequent level. The fairness audit and application of marginalized groups would be fair in this stage. Figure 12.2 shows the architectural process flow for ethical AI integration in environmental policy formulation.

Trust, which is done here through interpretation of AI models to the human through machine learning algorithms, such as decision trees, Convolutional Neural NETs (CNNs) etc., and natural language processing (NLP), is an issue of concern here. Ingrained XAI tools like SHAP and LIME are employed so as to create more trust. Low power training cycles, such as model pruning, are also included in the efforts to achieve energy efficiency to lower the amount of carbon emissions. The third step is model training and extrapolation of likely outcomes of various environmental policy features like carbon taxes or land restoration on varied situations. Since they place greater emphasis on risk, assumptions, ecological footprints and socio-economic impacts, the projections are considered significant towards assessing risk, ecological footprints, socio-economic impacts as well as assumption disclosures as indicated as relating boundaries with the predictive framing.

Within phase four the stakeholder input of the policy makers, local communities, scientists and NGOs is supplemented through participatory design in which the qualitative aspect is gathered by undertaking public consultations and sentiment analysis. Their high levels of engagement will guarantee the democratic support and accessibility of AI platforms in policy support. There is also an improvement in model and policy recommendations using feedback loops through the cycles. The final step involves creation of a decision support system in a form of dashboards containing visual analytics, traceability matrices and instruments of the scoring risks that relate to ethics. In particular, this governance interface allows the policymakers to determine evidence with possible prejudices or environmental expenses and to make a decision on the basis of these data not attributing any ethical importance to an international ethical framework, OECD AI Principles, AI4People, or any other governance framework. Through these concerted actions, operationalize the ambition of introducing AI into the environment policy responsibly, transparently, and sustainably, become ecologically responsible, and flex the governance.

12.4 Results

General trust, general inclusion, model performance, and quality of decision-making all were improved more given the introduction of ethical constraints within the AI systems. Those were the outcomes of testing the architecture of the ethical AI system in relation to a wide variety of policies, such as the pollution monitoring, managing deforestation, and the climate adaptation planning.

Two between-group studies were conducted in order to confirm these results. The former evaluated the system ability with or without inclusion of ethical AI; the later evaluated the various forms of AI models supplemented with ethical functionalities such as explainable AI, fairness as well as goodness.

Effect of the EachAI Integration: The eachAI process of integration has led to minor quantitative gains that overlap with the organizational aspirations of change which is evident in the data given in Table 12.1 and and also in Figure 12.3, this figure shows the performance comparison of environmental policy systems with and without ethical AI. This includes

Table 12.1 Performance comparison – with vs without ethical AI.

Metric	With ethical AI	Without ethical AI
Transparency Score (out of 100)	85	50
Bias Reduction (%)	45	0
Stakeholder Inclusion (%)	70	30
Energy Efficiency Improvement (%)	30	0
Policymaker Confidence (%)	90	40

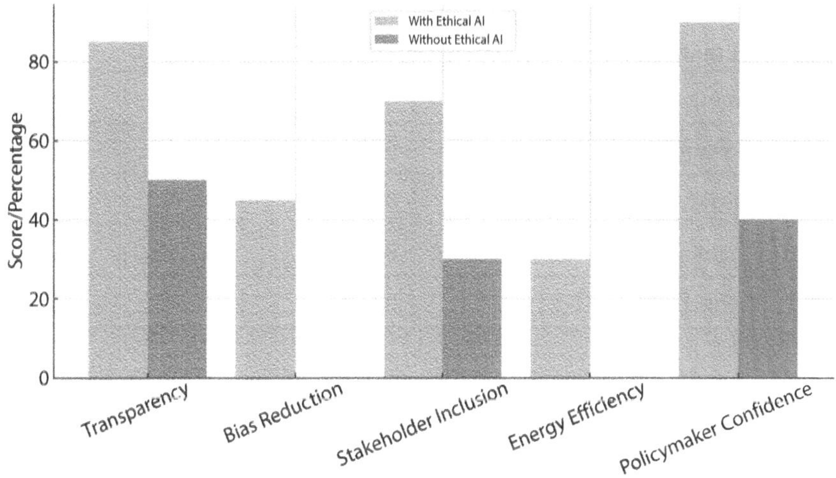

Figure 12.3 Performance comparison of environmental policy systems with and without ethical AI.

openness, reduction of bias, stakeholder involvement and participation at home, cost of energy and trust of policy makers in the administration. Transparency and trust were elevated as the result of receiving 70% and bias reduction was decreased by 45 to 0% than the initial stage. Above all, inclusion of communities historically marginalized abruptly intensified about twice, marking the power of the diversity amplification feature of the AI system in the policy-making process. Moreover, the refined techniques of training enabled a reduction in the use of energy by a third, which also demonstrates the topicality of sustainability in the AI. These results substantiate the suspected notion that the ethics-oriented consideration systems contribute to the improvement of performance and social value. Figure 12.3 shows the performance comparison of environmental policy systems with and without ethical AI.

Comparison of the AI Models with Ethical Improvements: In the second analysis, there was a comparison of the various AI models on their accuracy, bias (low scores being less biased), and transparency. As in Table 12.2 and Figure 12.4, the traditional machine learning models would attain high level of accuracy rating but massive bias and low degree of transparency. By contrast, Fairness-Aware and Explainable Models produced grafts in ethical characteristics, but at a considerable sacrifice of accuracy. Interestingly, Hybrid Ethical, which is a combination of interpretability, fairness, and optimization

Table 12.2 AI model performance with ethical layers.

AI model	Accuracy (%)	Bias score (lower is better)	Transparency score (out of 100)
Standard ML	78	0.65	40
Explainable ML	75	0.50	70
Fairness-Aware ML	72	0.30	65
Optimized DL	83	0.60	35
Hybrid Ethical AI	80	0.25	85

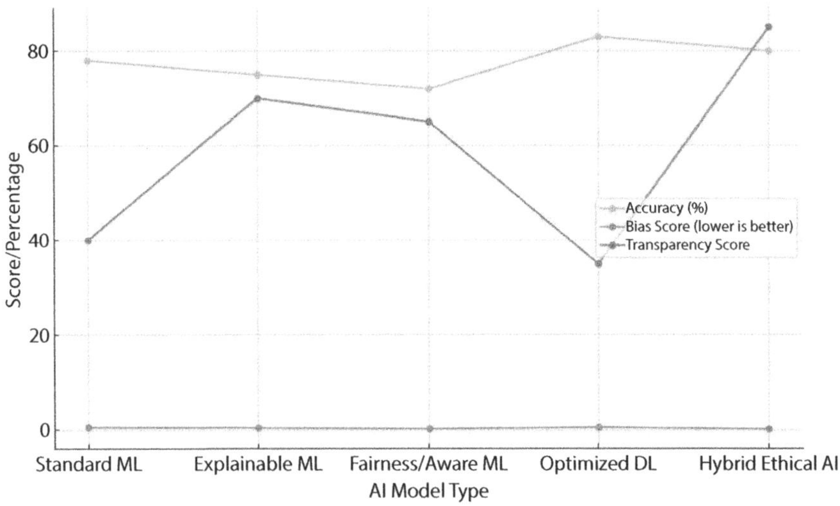

Figure 12.4 Evaluation of AI model types based on accuracy, bias, and transparency in ethical policy frameworks.

also scored very well in all measures. It kept the ratio of predictive performance and moral integrity lax policy-wise AI suitability.

12.5 Discussions

The results of this chapter imply that the mitigation of the issue of fairness, transparency and sustainability through the integration of ethics into AI systems, is accompanied with raising the level of legitimacy and utility of AI tools in environmental issues as a policy. Even though model fairness structures were correct, they led to a greater reduction in bias and this is needed to prevent the systematic under-benefits of the vulnerable groups on policies. Furthermore, a bias-free hybrid type of ethics and artificial intelligence that is characterized by great degree of transparency indicates that incorporation of morals into the decision making process improves and not kills the ability to find equilibrium. These findings validate both the need to act responsibly with AI in its application in governance ecosystems in which both the doctrine of ecological justice and democracy are of crucial interest. Attainable participation will require robust governance and population policy of participation, establishment of trust-building provisions, systemating scaled social infrastructure, multi-dimensional capacity-building as well as provision of a continuous enforced system of ethical accountability to secure permanently.

12.6 Conclusion

Both in reality of being followed in real time or a policy-simulation and optimization, Artificial Intelligence has been altering the view of the world possibly in the determination of solving the advanced problems of environmental governance. Power ought to be done in a responsible way. The chapter has pointed to dangers of AI in developing environmental policies, and how argument frames founded on ethical argument negates dangers of bias, transparency, and environmental price, and strategically develops more trust, becomes more inclusive, and functional. Surveys conducted on the case studies showed that the AI, which professed ethical behavior, was far superior to the usual procedures with openness, engagement of various individuals and building more trust, faith and confidence within the people making the decision into the option. Combined with the environmental governance about fairness, explainability, and energy efficiency, hybrid models are able to make them rapid and flexible.

These findings adequately highlight the reality that innovation and ethics are not the divergent forces that the former as AI responsible ways uphold ethics. However, this requires an efficient implementation that rests on a governance system and multi-disciplinary collaboration, mainstream data and the continuous maintenance of the moral gate. As we progress to the future, we should have pragmatic pilots, policymaking processes, and participation approaches that will prevail to ensure that AI is used to deliver sustainability, justice, and democratic uprightness to both the act in the matters concerning the environment and policy.

AI disclosure statement: The author acknowledges the use of AI-based tools for minor language editing or grammatical correction. However, all intellectual contributions, analyses, and conclusions presented in this chapter are entirely the author's own.

References

1. Nishant, R., Kennedy, M., Corbett, J., Artificial Intelligence for Sustainability: Challenges, Opportunities, and a Research Agenda. *Int. J. Inf. Manage.*, 53, 102104, 2020.
2. Adanma, U.M. and Ogunbiyi, E.O., Artificial Intelligence in Environmental Conservation: Evaluating Cyber Risks and Opportunities for Sustainable Practices. *Comput. Sci. IT Res. J.*, 5, 5, 1178–1209, 2024.
3. Challoumis, C., Building a Sustainable Economy-How AI Can Optimize Resource Allocation, in: *XVI International Scientific Conference*, pp. 190–224, 2024.
4. Ahmed, Z., Anwar, N., De, A., Shaw, R., Original Research Article Guardians of Green: Legal Implications and Best Practices in AI-Enabled CSR for Environmental Sustainability in India. *J. Auton. Intell.*, 7, 5, 2024.
5. Kaggwa, S., Eleogu, T.F., Okonkwo, F., Farayola, O.A., Uwaoma, P.U., Akinoso, A., AI in Decision Making: Transforming Business Strategies. *Int. J. Res. Sci. Innovation*, 10, 12, 423–44, 2024.
6. Kashefi, P., Kashefi, Y., Mirsaraei, A.G., Shaping the Future of AI: Balancing Innovation and Ethics in Global Regulation. *Unif. Law Rev.*, 29, 3, 524–48, 2024.
7. Rana, R. and Bhambri, P., Ethical Considerations in Artificial Intelligence for Environmental Solutions: Striking a Balance for Sustainable Innovation, in: *Handbook of Technological Sustainability*, pp. 389–96, CRC Press.
8. Rahaman, S.U., Ethical AI in Data Science: Balancing Innovation and Responsibility in the Digital Age. *IJLRP-Int. J. Leading Res. Publ.*, 5, 9.

9. Lescrauwaet, L., Wagner, H., Yoon, C., Shukla, S., Adaptive Legal Frameworks and Economic Dynamics in Emerging Tech-Nologies: Navigating the Intersection for Responsible Innovation. *Law Econ.*, 16, 3, 202–20, 2022.
10. Kulkarni, A.A. and Kamble, S.C., Balancing Innovation and Responsibility: Ethical, Legal and Social Considerations, in: *Nanomedicine: Innovations, Applications, and Breakthroughs in the Quest for Health and Medicine's Future*, p. 451, 2024.
11. Soundariya, A., Behera, N.K., Selvakumar, P., Chandel, P.S., Gupta, S., Manjunath, T.C., AI and Environmental Ethics: The Role of AI in Addressing Climate Change Ethical Considerations in AI-Driven Environmental Solutions, in: *Human Values, Ethics, and Dignity in the Age of Artificial Intelligence*, pp. 321–46, IGI Global Scientific Publishing, 2025.
12. Hermann, E., Hermann, G., Tremblay, J.-C., Ethical Artificial Intelligence in Chemical Research and Development: A Dual Advantage for Sustainability. *Sci. Eng. Ethics*, 27, 1–16, 2021.
13. Correia, P., Pedro, R.L.D., Videira, S., Artificial Intelligence in Healthcare: Balancing Innovation, Ethics, and Human Rights Protection. *J. Digital Technol. Law*, 3, 1, 143–80, 2025.
14. Andrade, A.C.C. and Vasquez, M.C.S., The Compatibility Between SDGs and the EU Regulatory Framework of AI. *J. Ethics Legal Technol.*, 6, JELT-Volume 61, 11–144, 2024.
15. Szarmes, P. and Élo, G., Sustainability of Large AI Models: Balancing Environmental and Social Impact with Technology and Regulations. *Chem. Eng. Trans.*, 107, 103–8, 2023.
16. De Almeida, P.G.R., dos Santos, C.D., Farias, J.S., Artificial Intelligence Regulation: A Framework for Governance. *Ethics Inf. Technol.*, 23, 3, 505–25, 2021.
17. Kurre, J., The Accountability, Responsibility & Governance as a Unified Strategy for AI. National American University, 2024.
18. Díaz-Rodríguez, N., Del Ser, J., Coeckelbergh, M., de Prado, M.L., Herrera-Viedma, E., Herrera, F., Connecting the Dots in Trustworthy Artificial Intelligence: From AI Principles, Ethics, and Key Requirements to Responsible AI Systems and Regulation. *Inf. Fusion*, 99, 101896, 2023.
19. McGraw, D.K., Ethical Responsibility in the Design of Artificial Intelligence (AI) Systems. *Int. J. Responsib.*, 7, 1, 4, 2024.
20. Roberts, H., Cowls, J., Morley, J., Taddeo, M., Wang, V., Floridi, L., The Chinese Approach to Artificial Intelligence: An Analysis of Policy, Ethics, and Regulation. Springer, 2021.
21. Du, S. and Xie, C., Paradoxes of Artificial Intelligence in Consumer Markets: Ethical Challenges and Opportunities. *J. Bus. Res.*, 129, 961–74, 2021.
22. Kumar, A. and Kumar, R., and Others, Harmonizing Innovation and Accountability: The Intersection of Artificial Intelligence and Machine Learning in Sustainable Development, in: *Artificial Intelligence and Machine Learning Applications for Sustainable Development*, pp. 103–49.

23. van Uffelen, N., Lauwaert, L., Coeckelbergh, M., Kudina, O., Towards an Environmental Ethics of Artificial Intelligence, *arXiv Preprint arXiv:2501.10390*, 2024.
24. Saleh, S. and Ahmed, M., A Cyclic Framework for Ethical Implications of Artificial Intelligence in Autonomous Vehicles. *Int. J. Adv. Comput. Sci. Appl.*, 15, 3, 2024.
25. Darvishi, K., Liu, L., Lim, S., Navigating the Nexus: Legal and Economic Implications of Emerging Tech-Nologies. *Law Econ.*, 16, 3, 172–86, 2022.
26. Pushpakumara, T.D.C. and Ahsan, F.J., Transforming Industries through AI and Emerging Technologies: Literature Review of Opportunities, Challengers, Responsibilities, and Strategies. *Int. J. Innovative Sci. Res. Technol.*, 10, 1, 1861–80, 2025.
27. Sadanand, V.K. and Sadanand, T., Artificial Intelligence in India: Navigating Social Justice, Environmental Ethics, and Legal Governance, in: *Exploring AI Implications on Law, Governance, and Industry*, pp. 87–118, IGI Global Scientific Publishing, 2025.

13

Shaping a Sustainable Future: The Role of AI in Driving Green Innovation and Environmental Equity

Madhura S.[1]*, P. Sridhar[2], R. Karthikeyan[3], Patil Mounica[4], R. Archana Reddy[5] and Umesh Kumar Lihore[6]

[1]Department of Mechatronics Engineering, The Oxford College of Engineering, Bengaluru, Karnataka, India
[2]Department of EEE, Kongunadu College of Engineering and Technology, Trichy, Tamil Nadu, India
[3]Department of Civil Engineering, Chennai Institute of Technology, Chennai, Tamil Nadu, India
[4]Department of EEE, Vardhaman College of Engineering, Shamshabad, India
[5]School of Computer Science and Artificial Intelligence, SR University, Warangal, Telangana, India
[6]School of Computer Science and Engineering, Galgotias University, Greater Noida, UP, India

Abstract
Promoting AI in encouraging green innovation and environment equity, it takes into account the contribution limit that all this body of technology might make to bridging the gap that is ever-expanding between human beings and the surrounding world. The growing environmental anxiety of the 21st century demands the supporters of AI-based reconciliations. The AI-made technologies are applied to optimizing the renewable energy systems, predictive analytics, autonomous systems, resource management, and environmental real-time monitoring. These technologies coupled with an appropriate governance lead to sustainable development. The increase in productivity and reduced emissions can be achieved due to growth and sustainable practices. Nevertheless, their solutions should be aimed at avoiding the broad social rifts. Ethic attending is concerned with underserved populations being concerned with access, data privacy, and bias in the algorithms.

**Corresponding author*: madhumithamay16@gmail.com

Umesh Kumar Lilhore, Sarita Simaiya, Surjeet Dalal and Martin Margala (eds.) Artificial Intelligence and Biodiversity, (213–230) © 2026 Scrivener Publishing LLC

In the hands of inclusive and responsible representation, the development of AI can become a productive contribution to social sustainability. The ethical dimension lies within the promoters of green technologies *via* AI. These technologies are very impactful in shaping the future of the just reality where everyone equally shares in the reality.

Keywords: Artificial intelligence, green innovation, environmental sustainability, environmental equity, ethical AI

13.1 Introduction

The planet is experiencing tens of environmental crises such as climate change, environment pollution, natural resources shortage, and environmental degradation. Excessive population and industrial development contribute to these problems since they pose threats to the ecosystems and the human race. Such issues are understood in different countries; therefore, they settled on the 2030 Agenda to Sustainable Development Goals *via* the UN to plan and find solutions to these problems [1]. The ability to automate and predict, as well as optimize the environment, has prompted AI focus in sectors all across the board with a large degree of attention.

Artificial Intelligence (AI) is described as a machine or computer engineering that mimics human behaviors, including thinking, solving problems, learning, etc. AI functions are changing fast, as they are expanding on computer vision, machine learning, analytics, natural language processing, and competently addressing eco-sustainability objectives [2]. AI has also improved strategies of environmental management and management of natural resources such as smart grids which consume less energy, more advanced farming methodologies and climate forecasting [3, 4].

The greatest application of the AI technology is ensuring that the renewable energy systems are efficient. The application of machine learning algorithms to approximate the energy demand, solar and wind energy outputs are common in the present day to enhance the integrity of the grid and reduce carbon emission [5]. One of them would be how the success of DeepMind of Google was achieved when AI could be leveraged to increase the production of wind energy by 20% using predictive analytics [6]. In addition, AI and control algorithms are applied to smart buildings and smart cities in order to lower the amount of energy they use, as well as the impact on the environment [7].

It is used in remotely sensing and precision farming soil and crops, optimizing irrigation, and pest detection of our crops all of which contributes towards sustainable agricultural practices because it yields higher yield and reduces the use of fertilizers and water [8]. Thanks to [9], land use management and deforestation monitoring becomes less challenging as the AI-equipped drones are used, along with certain other remote sensing technology. Lastly, AI has also been introduced to other ecological topics, such as in the oceans, AI has been deployed to conduct illegal Phishing, and forecast coral bleaching [10].

Besides all the activities that AI is able to perform on all fronts, AI is also able to provide assistance in the form of environmental equity that is the equitable nature of environmental support and punishments. It is productive because a localized community can now utilize these technologies to benefit disadvantaged communities more positively due to the automation of AI technologies since the technologies facilitate the provision of early warnings and disaster response cases, as well as pollution monitoring to accommodate the needs of the communities that are disadvantaged [11]. Only upon these solutions implemented, in a fair manner, is the AI technologies expected to inform policy to reduce the socio environmental inequities and close a digital divide [12].

Issues also arise in terms of the use of AI technologies in governing the environment. Some of the opposing issues around the discussion on the Algorithmic bias, surveillance, data privacy and lack of transparency to responsibly use AI has been discussed dissecting how AI and ML actually offer honest remedies to the human or machine in the company [13]. Figure 13.1 presents the key challenges in ethical AI integration. It risks

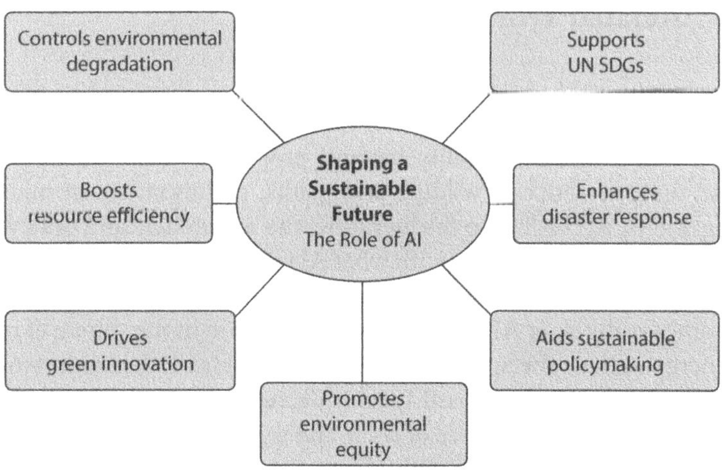

Figure 13.1 Key challenges in ethical AI integration for environmental policy formulation.

raising disparities in the issue of distribution of AI development should there be restricted access to the figure of affluent nations or communities [14]. Realizing AI technologies based on the principles of fairness, accountability and sustainability is a process that will require various policymaking, multiculturally rich data and global cooperation on this issue.

This has merged technological innovation and environmental sustainability and green innovation, yet the consequences of any types of innovation should be complemented by governance institutions that emphasize on ecology and human rights [15]. In that way, the prospects of AI should be discussed within a wider framework than the benefits of AI technologies in order to include the sociocultural, ethical, and ecological aspects.

This chapter attempts to examine the way AI can be used to attain green innovation and environmental equity. It begins by evaluating the current condition of AI application in the energy, agriculture, climatic science, and urban development applications of AI, which are geopolitically important. Then, it analyzes the instances where both the AI-related initiatives to improve the environment were optimistic and pessimistic. Lastly, the research provides the ethical and legal AI policy considerations which are invaluable in bringing sustainable and equitable AI engagement in societies. The chapter highlights the missing elements in AI systems that drive their trust to promote features in the operational efficacy other than interdisciplinary measures to incorporate verifiable inclusivity and environmental liability into the working mechanism and design of AI systems.

13.2 Related Works

Via its potent asset, Artificial Intelligence (AI) in these places serves as a highly highlighted technology building in a bid to address problems of environmental sustainability beyond proposing remedies to climatic change, disappearance of wildlife and plants, pollution, social injustices, among others. According to the literature, the researchers and policy makers are more inclined to agree with what AI is offering as a solution to green innovation that is environmentally sustainable.

Another really clear AI implication can be found in the sphere of renewable energy such as the application of AI-our-guess models in its work. To illustrate, dependence on fossil fuels is decreased because AI models are used to facilitate the incidence of solar and wind energy that adds reliability in national grids [16]. It has also been demonstrated that deep learning algorithms are capable of predicting the supply-side short-term renewable energy generation and demand on the other side with the required precision, thus being able to strike a balance without any complications [17]. Moreover, reinforcement learning is currently being applied to streamline smart grid and energy storage operations to enhance the general energy efficiency [18].

With AI technologies, there is a significant contribution in the sphere of sustainable farming. Assistance based on the application of AI in the shape of Precision Agriculture is applied in reducing the detrimental effects of AI on the environment [19]. The use of image recognition and drone based AI technologies is usually applied to inspect and monitor the crop health, predict the crop yield and the diseases at their early stages [20]. The technologies stimulate productivity at a less threatening environment level.

Another aspect of the domain where AI is applicable is in the field of climate prediction and disaster warning [21]. It was also observed that machine learning algorithms help improve climate simulation and predict the temperature, precipitation and extreme weather as well. Additionally, natural catastrophes like floods, wildfires, and hurricanes can be detected at early stages using the technology in order to be evacuated on time and the resources diverted [22].

Smart cities and the integration of AI in Urban development has also developed very rapidly. AI-based IoT watch limit systems, waste management optimization, and environmental sensors are significant to improve the quality-of-life indicators in cities [23]. The adaptation of the new solutions also results in the reduction of emissions and the quality of air and allows planning sustainable infrastructure based on evidence [24].

A fine example of how AI facilitates the process of policy-making is that of evidence-based governance. Monitors and remediation models in relation to the impact of climate change can be built based on AI optimization. The models are also helpful in the preparation of impact assessments and supporting regulations [25]. Government agencies and other organizations are searching and implementing AI technology in complying and enforcing environmental laws, emissions and efficient policies [26].

However, this has a limitation; AI should never be used in manners that breach ethics since the backlash may be counterproductive in a multidimensional manner. Within the bias issues, deep roots are anchored on the reinforcement of biases against underrepresented groups [27]. As an example, the systems used to detect pollution can be trained on biased or incomplete datasets and therefore do not even focus on the overloaded community. To address challenges such as these, researchers propose explaining AI systems together with representative data, to build fair and urban governance [28].

It is believed that one of the key issues in the modern world of literature touches upon addressing the question of environmental equity that emphasizes equal availability of the gains of environmental protection and technological advances. With the aid of AI, the most vulnerable areas and categories of people being subject to pollution and climate change can be identified to employ effective targeted mitigation operations [29]. Besides this, AI implementation in under- and climate-prone regions is growing and is manifested by low-cost air and water pollution sensors and mobile learning to learn about climate resilience [30].

Conversely, there are still difficulties in integrating AI in sustainability endeavors. Among such obstacles are related to the excessive cost of using AI technologies, the lack of a high-quality dataset, gaps in knowledge regarding the relevant technical sphere as well as the problems with the data privacy [31]. Also of concern are the environmental costs of AI namely the energy amount used during machine learning model training [32]. To this end, other scientists are working to come up with ways in which energy efficient AI methods can be used and also green computing principles [33].

Applying AI in ecological issues is another aspect that enables multiple disciplines of the research to be built on a single platform. Research attracts the attention to the collaboration between computer scientists and environmental scientists, policymakers and ethicists in the responsible design of new AI systems that meet the social and functional requirements [34]. It has additionally been proposed that participatory design where the community members are involved at the local level in the design process of AI tool and deployment could build trust and make the technological solutions of the technology solutions more relevant [35].

In order to offer valuable inputs of AI to a sustainable, equitable future, researchers suggest governance models, which are based on the principle of accountability, inclusivity, and sustainability [36]. The emergence of initiatives such as AI for Good Global Summit and Partnership on AI as well has provided a platform to discuss the issues as well as the social norms with regard to environmental application of AI.

As it has already been stated above, the literature is unanimous in terms of the potential of AI in terms of creating green innovation and promoting environmental equity. The issues depend instead upon the mitigation of ethical, political, technical and sociological issues. It is essential that the following tasks-oriented research, interdisciplinary synergy and creation of complete governance systems are sensitive to issues related to the use of AI in long-term sustainable goals. Table 13.1 shows the summary of key studies on AI applications for environmental sustainability and equity.

Table 13.1 Summary of key literature on AI applications for environmental sustainability and equity.

Refs.	Focus area	Methodology/ approach	Key findings
[16]	Renewable Energy Optimization	Literature review on AI in energy systems	AI optimizes energy generation and reduces operational inefficiencies
[17]	Solar Power Prediction	Hybrid deep learning model	Improved short-term solar forecasting accuracy
[18]	Smart Grid Control	Reinforcement learning	RL optimizes smart grid efficiency and response
[19]	Precision Agriculture	Review of AI applications in farming	AI increases yield, reduces resource waste, and improves sustainability
[20]	Agricultural Monitoring	AI-driven sensors and image analysis	AI aids in early crop disease detection and yield prediction
[21]	Climate Modeling	Machine learning for climate projections	AI enhances resolution and reliability of climate simulations
[22]	Disaster Risk Reduction	AI-based early warning systems	AI enables faster and more accurate disaster response
[23]	Smart Cities	Conceptual and spatial analysis	AI transforms urban planning and smart city sustainability
[24]	Pollution Monitoring	IoT-AI hybrid models	Real-time pollution control and traffic optimization
[25]	AI Policy & Governance	Ethical and policy analysis	Proposes governance models for responsible AI use

(Continued)

Table 13.1 Summary of key literature on AI applications for environmental sustainability and equity. (*Continued*)

Refs.	Focus area	Methodology/ approach	Key findings
[26]	Environmental Compliance	Case studies and frameworks	AI helps enforce environmental regulations effectively
[27]	Algorithmic Bias	Critical analysis and case studies	AI can reinforce environmental and social inequalities
[28]	Fairness in AI	Theoretical and applied machine learning	Advocates for transparent, explainable AI systems
[29]	Environmental Justice	Environmental health analysis	AI can identify underserved, pollution-burdened communities
[30]	Climate Resilience in LMICs	Developmental and participatory AI models	AI supports adaptation and planning in climate-vulnerable, low-resource areas

13.3 The Role of AI in Driving Green Innovation

AI is a revolutionary factor in green innovation facilitation of more intelligent and sustainable systems in various sectors. Green innovation refers to a process of development and application of products, procedures, or practices which will mitigate the impairment to the environment, improve energy efficiency and achieve ecological case; this promotes ecological economy and resilience. AI complements green innovation with predictive analytics services, real-time surveillance, and automated control services that are conventional.

Predictive Intelligence to Sustainable Planning: Memes AI forecasts upcoming energy era, climatic changes and ecosystem responses regarding historical or present environmental circumstances based on benchmarking it with patterns. Such a forecast allows making wise decisions, advances resources management, and reduces ecological harm further. To illustrate, AI-based models forecast power production of renewable energy resources to manage the grid activities and redistribute periodic flexible resources to reduce the consumption of fossil fuels.

Process Optimization and Waste Reduction: Deep and machine learning apply to creating their predictive algorithms that allow optimization of industrial processes, identifying inefficiencies, and offering them a more environmentally friendly way. AI application in the manufacturing industry allows quality control where the system analyses output on-the-fly and raises a red flag on non-perfection which reduces the waste of material. The AI optimization has also been utilized in supply chains where demand forecasts are used to control the supply side by regulating the amount of inventory and eradicating any surplus stock. This minimises the emission due to excess production and transportation.

Smart Grids Clean Energy System: In smart grids, which encompass use of clean energy sources which are gained through renewable sources, AI applications are applied to smartly regulate the balance between electricity supply and demand. Load and battery storage control, fault identification is automatized and perfected in real-time. Small mechanical techniques in wind turbines, even wind panels can be autonomously governed and controlled to maximize their efficiency with respect to the weather conditions and patterns of consumption.

Smart Agriculture and Resource Management: The AI processing applies to farming in the form of precision agriculture where the algorithmic programs keep monitoring the weather, soil interactions, and health of the crop, and this data is provided by the latter on a time-to-time basis. This will reduce the unnecessary use of water, fertilizer, and pesticides, therefore the AI will drive the progress of environmentally friendly agricultural activities. It is also helpful in keeping track of the trends on different fauna and flora to model future effects of the use of land usage in order to support achievement of conservation targets.

Environmental Surveillance and Time of Emergency for Monitoring Systems: Since AI links the sensors, satellites and drones to the forest conditions and wildlife population, alongside forest, as well as fauna, and prey auto population monitoring, it simplifies the continuous monitoring of the quality of air and water bodies and forest state. Visionary imaging algorithms find indications of climate change like deforestation, coral bleach as well as mining in new places it has never been employed and gives invaluable resources an opportunity to get destroyed. Such technologies are relevant to have environmental norms and preserve nature to create a balance in nature.

Enabling Circular Economy Models: A circular economy concept can be enabled with the help of AI that will assist them in improving waste collections systems, recovery of materials, and recycling work. Intelligent sorting systems reduce recovery rates and reliance on landfill since recycling plants are more accurately classified with the help of computer vision.

Motivating Green Product Design: Since the green product needs fewer materials, and its ecological footprint is smaller, the engineers and designers empowered by driving innovation through both AI and generative design algorithms can create catalysts to use in the simulation. Each and each of the iterations of a design is evaluated on record time with best and viable solutions being selected.

Supporting Green Urban Infrastructure: AI plays a vital role in designing smart cities in that will facilitate the processes of scheduling traffic and timely running of the city transports together with the street lights, heating and cooling systems within the buildings to ensure that the use of energy is made more efficient in addition to the enhancement of facilities. This creates a smaller amount of traffic, emissions and enhances comfort among the people living in the cities.

Rapid Research and Development: Green R&D uses AI to speed up the process of scientific discoveries through automation of data analysis, simulation of systems, including automation of patterns, which can be determined to help environmental scientists model green technologies of carbon capture, renewable fuels and sustainable materials.

Equalizing Access to Achieve Sustainable Solutions: Mobile apps, including energy monitoring apps, and other eco-friendly product recommendations, offer individuals and smaller enterprises a gap to maintain beneficial innovations that are not environmentally friendly when utilized on a larger scale.

13.4 The Role of AI in Environmental Equity

Environmental justice focuses on making sure that the ecosystems along with all its resources are accessible to all human beings without references to their social status, age, nationality, income, location or any other dividing factor. It also protects the fact that one community does not exploit the benefits of the sustainable resources without sharing it with the other poorly represented communities. Through ethical and inclusive approaches, artificial intelligence has the potential to lead to development of environmental justice in particular parts of regions or countries, or the entire world.

Detection of Unserved and Vulnerable Areas: AI will be able to track the socio-environmental data, thus pointing to the areas that are highly being impacted by pollution, climatic changes, and environmental degradation. As an example, AI could be used to analyze spatial data, satellite footage, and health data in order to aid in identifying so-called environmental justice hotspots where vulnerable communities face a high risk of being victimized by coming into contact with contaminated water or air. Greater ability to fine-tune the focus on the areas that are to be improved allows generating a focused policy and a bigger amount of resources.

Moving up to Special Environmental Monitoring of Resource Scarcity Areas: In other regions of the world, particularly in the developing economies, the area of environmental observation is either outmoded or not at all. This gap can be adequately filled with the use of AI mobile sensors, AI-driven drones, and even satellite analytics. With the help of these technologies, the air quality, deforestation, flooding, and lack of water can be monitored remotely and cost-effectively, and the local governments into action in response to the most immediate crises are NGOs.

Making Fair Policy and Governance Mechanisms Informed: In relation to the policymakers AI can ever assist them as it can be used to determine the effects of the environmental policy of policies on different groups of people in a socio-economic framework. Some predictive models can intepret the ways in which some climate mitigation decisions would overload the poor and disadvantaged regions and benefit the wealthier ones. It assists in the development of a policy that dampens inequalities and advances sustainability goals.

Strengthening the Adaptation of vulnerable populations to the effects of climate change in the underprivileged regions: AI enhances early warning of natural calamities- hurricanes, droughts, floods, and others - manually benefitting the vulnerable sectors. By properly predicting the situations and sending timely notifications, AI aids in minimizing the number of victims and devastations of infrastructure relief, granting affected groups a chance to get ready and act promptly.

Promoting Inquiries and Interaction Enhanced AI technology and Natural language processing systems can decode complicated data-formats relative to the environment in simplistic forms. This by no means focuses on non-involvement of very large areas of the community. By going through mobile applications and artificial intelligence chatbots, individuals with little to no reading and technical abilities can understand the problems of the surrounding environment and are even included in decision making.

The solution of Resource Disparity AI maximizes the underserved areas by supplying basic needs like clean food, energy, and water. The first one increases the distribution and the second one fortifies food security in drought-ridden regions. With the new technologies that have been implemented, the resource-rich areas can assist the impoverished.

Finding and Reducing Environmental Discrimination Systemic Environmental discrimination (such as zoning landfills or industrial areas near residential minority areas) can in decision support usage readily be identified by some machine learning technology. The appearance of the data-based evidence of such discrimination becomes possible, and AI contributes to the advancement of advocacy social and legal socio-political activity to improve these loopholes.

Challenges and without further prompting AI technologies are no exception to this as the promise of future technologies is to be met with caution and balanced by addressing biases or inequalities that come with the glimmer whatever advantages they promise. Even when the training data sets are biased or not comprehensive, AI systems will presumably overlook it or not recognize it as marginalized communities. Moreover, the improperly developed digital infrastructure in most regions with low income may become the obstacle to the adoption of AI technologies. Related to these reasons, all-encompassing data sets and involvement among the community and algorithmic responsibility should be the staples of AI ethics and creation.

13.5 Discussions

Today, Artificial Intelligence (AI) is adopted as a supplementary resource to help in the cause of environmental sustainability along with distinct opportunities and sides of concern. In the earlier parts it was mentioned that some of the areas of AI such as machine learning, computer vision or natural language processing are fueling innovation toward green in various fields, including energy and agriculture, urban development, and environmental monitoring, among others. Nevertheless, effects of such developments are also complex and everything around their manifestations, in particular, equality, morality, and cross-border fairness could be questioned.

The most important AI capability that enables green innovation and makes it work is its incomparable capability to lead to actionable suggestions in real time with the assistance of its software where it analyses large and complicated volumes of data. AI allows enhancing the efficiency of renewable energy forecasting as well as its operational efficiency. It allows the wealthy grids to host greater sources of clean energy as well as empower them. The precision farming or data driven technique, which the AI identified, identifies and nails down the waste minimization in the agriculture sector without harming the ecosystem. Additionally, AI stimulates the studies and implementation of eco products design, and circular economy increasingly green and sustainable industrial processes.

Simultaneously, AI is also significant in maintaining fundamental principles of environmental equity by perfecting the identification of populations at risk, improving natural hazard warning tools, and achieving cost effective environmental injections in poor neighborhoods. Such endeavors can be held as a form of enhancing a larger system of sustainability going beyond ecological outcomes to social and economic equalities.

Though these arguments are to some extent valid, there are numerous issues that need to be filled in. To give credit in the environmental sustainability aspect, first the energy used to train highly sophisticated AI models is making an attempt. The concept of AI promotion of sustainability is legitimate but its creation should adhere to the notion of sustainability itself. The fears about the carbon footprint of the AI could be traced to the reality that reduced energy efficient algorithms and green computing policy is not produced.

The other concern has to do with prejudice, and impartiality, which is likewise alarming the second. Biased or biased datasets may instill AI models in favor of creating new ones or worsening old ones. Whilst they might fail to identify the marginalised low incomes in cases where you might have polluting prediction models, they might identify such areas and these resource allocation instruments may aim to give to the areas that are better equipped and thus forget about the other similar low income areas. In an objective manner, in case data is transparent, data complete, and algorithm is open-sourced, it means that a fair result is given to all people.

Third, the digital divide is a significant issue in the application of AI technologies in a way that is just. High income countries can adopt an AI facilitated green system without much effort, but in the developing nations, infrastructure, technical expertise and capital are a challenge. The only thing that can be exploited by other companies to bridge this gap is collaborative efforts, transfer of knowledge and capacity building through AI induced innovation. When this is not the case, it will not be accessible to many.

Lastly, proper governance systems need to exercise control on AI usage in terms of sustainability efforts with the use of ethics. There should be conceptualization of policies that will ensure conscientiousness with the ease of privacy, equity and long term environmental management. Governments, scholars, civil societies and the populations affected now must demand some benefits that are beneficial AI solutions as concerned the environment and the societal uses.

With AI, as it has been brought out, the level of green structural aspects is unprecedented as who is an improvement on equity, yet an inclusion concern should be approached cautiously when handling outcomes. Moreover, AI cannot simply be placed as an engine to innovation but also an engine to equity the world is and sustainable stewardship and that AI is playing by ethical, technological and infrastructural standards.

13.6 Conclusion

Simply stated, artificial intelligence is a valuable resource enabling green innovation and environmental justice through offering useful solutions, which enhance resource efficiency, sustain growth, and empower the underserved. AI is able to make renewable energy practices more efficient, improve precision agriculture, promote inclusivity when it comes to policy, and empower environmental justice; its multi-purpose capabilities are priceless resources on the way to a sustainable and fair economy. The flip side of the coin is that it is possible to achieve this potential which will be debilitatingly interrogated with problems of data bias, influence of energy, ethical regulation, and digital inequity. The interdisciplinary frameworks alongside constructive/transparent policies and balanced access to such AI systems would help reinvent their perception beyond simple technological tools to the concern of enhancing social and environmental conditions in the world.

AI disclosure statement: The author acknowledges the use of AI-based tools for minor language editing or grammatical correction. However, all intellectual contributions, analyses, and conclusions presented in this chapter are entirely the author's own.

References

1. Pancholi, K. and Shukla, P., Harnessing AI for Sustainability: Innovations, Policies, and Investment Paradigms, in: *Diversity, AI, and Sustainability for Financial Growth*, pp. 97–124, IGI Global Scientific Publishing, 2025.
2. Benziane, S., Innovating Prosperity: Intelligent Approaches and Economic Paradigms for Sustainable Futures, in: *Intelligent Methods and Alternative Economic Models for Sustainability*, pp. 194–241, IGI Global, 2024.

3. Challoumis, C., Building a Sustainable Economy-How Ai Can Optimize Resource Allocation, in: *XVI International Scientific Conference*, pp. 190–224, 2024.
4. Islam, R., Sustainable Entrepreneurship in the Digital Age: The Role of AI in Green Business Practices, 2024.
5. Singh, B., Federated Learning for Envision Future Trajectory Smart Transport System for Climate Preservation and Smart Green Planet: Insights into Global Governance and SDG-9 (Industry, Innovation and Infrastructure). *Natl. J. Environ. Law*, 6, 2, 6–17, 2023.
6. Al-Raeei, M., The Smart Future for Sustainable Development: Artificial Intelligence Solutions for Sustainable Urbanization. *Sustainable Dev.*, 33, 1, 508–17, 2025.
7. Yigitcanlar, T., Mehmood, R., Corchado, J.M., Green Artificial Intelligence: Towards an Efficient, Sustainable and Equitable Technology for Smart Cities and Futures. *Sustainability*, 13, 16, 8952, 2021.
8. Bansod, M., Advanced Predictive Analytics Driving Sustainable and Equitable Green Innovations Through Data-Driven Optimization and Strategic Insights, in: *Advancing Social Equity Through Accessible Green Innovation*, pp. 1–16, IGI Global Scientific Publishing, 2025.
9. Antonyraj, V.A., Advancing Equitable Green Innovation Through Data Analytics Strategies and Insights, in: *Advancing Social Equity Through Accessible Green Innovation*, pp. 17–32, IGI Global Scientific Publishing, 2025.
10. Panyaram, S. and Hullurappa, M., Data-Driven Approaches to Equitable Green Innovation Bridging Sustainability and Inclusivity, in: *Advancing Social Equity Through Accessible Green Innovation*, pp. 139–52, IGI Global Scientific Publishing, 2025.
11. Gunther, H. and Rose, J., Governing AI: The Importance of Environmentally Sustainable and Equitable Innovation. *Envtl. L. Rep.*, 50, 10888, 2020.
12. Islam, H., Nexus of Economic, Social, and Environmental Factors on Sustainable Development Goals: The Moderating Role of Technological Advancement and Green Innovation. *Innovation Green Dev.*, 4, 1, 100183, 2025.
13. Ekeh, A.H., Apeh, C.E., Odionu, C.S., Austin-Gabriel, B., Leveraging Machine Learning for Environmental Policy Innovation: Advances in Data Analytics to Address Urban and Ecological Challenges. *Gulf J. Adv. Bus. Res.*, 3, 2, 456–82, 2025.
14. Wang, Q., Sun, T., Li, R., Does Artificial Intelligence Promote Green Innovation? An Assessment Based on Direct, Indirect, Spillover, and Heterogeneity Effects. *Energy Environ.*, 36, 2, 1005–37, 2025.
15. Balcı, O., Almohammad, D., Kılıç, C., Singh, R., Harnessing Emerging Technologies for Green Sustainability: Innovations, Challenges, and Future Pathways, in: *Climate Neutrality Through Smart Eco-Innovation and Environmental Sustainability*, pp. 209–25, 2025.

16. Trehan, A., Bias in Green AI Addressing Disparities in Data and Algorithms, in: *Advancing Social Equity Through Accessible Green Innovation*, pp. 63–76, IGI Global Scientific Publishing, 2025.
17. Chirita, M. and Sarpe, D.-A., Navigating the Challenges and Ethics of AI in Shaping the Future of Work for Sustainable Industry 4.0. *Ann. Univ. Dunarea Jos Galati Fascicle I Econ. Appl. Inf.*, 30, 3, 2024.
18. Fernandes, S., The Role of Artificial Intelli-Gence in Accelerating Sustain-Able Technological Innovation. *Clareus Sci. Sci. Eng.*, 2, 32–40, 2025.
19. Allam, Z. and Cheshmehzangi, A., *Sustainable Futures and Green New Deals*, Springer, 2024.
20. Raman, R., Pattnaik, D., Lathabai, H.H., Kumar, C., Govindan, K., Nedungadi, P., Green and Sustainable AI Research: An Integrated Thematic and Topic Modeling Analysis. *J. Big Data*, 11, 1, 1–28, 2024.
21. Holloway, S., Exploring the Role of Artificial Intelligence in Enhancing the Efficiency of Knowledge Management Systems, 2025.
22. Butt, J.S., From Concept to Practice: Innovations Driving Sustainable Economic Development. *EIRP Proc.*, 19, 1, 181–90, 2024.
23. Lodhi, S.K., Gill, A.Y., Hussain, H.K., Green Innovations: Artificial Intelligence and Sustainable Materials in Production. *BULLET J. Multidisiplin Ilmu*, 3, 4, 492–507, 2024.
24. Sundaresan, P. and Choudhary, A., Harnessing Artificial Intelligence for Sustainable Development: Applications in the Pursuit of a Greener Future. *Resilience*, 360, 83, 2023.
25. Danish, M.S.S. and Senjyu, T., Shaping the Future of Sustainable Energy through AI-Enabled Circular Economy Policies. *Circ. Econ.*, 2, 2, 100040, 2023.
26. Zhang, Y. and Jiang, S., Pro-Environmental Personal Norms and Subjective Norms Related to AI-Driven Green Entrepreneurship Intention: A Qualitative Insight to Explore Students in Higher Education Institutions.
27. Harfouche, A., Merhi, M.I., Albizri, A., Dennehy, D., Thatcher, J.B., Sustainable Development through Technological Innovations and Data Analytics. *Inf. Syst. Front.*, 26, 6, 1989–96, 2024.
28. Singar, M.K., Suneetha, K., Saraswat, N., Shukla, G., Artificial Intelligence's Role in Shaping Renewable Energy for Next-Generation Smart Cities. *E3S Web Conf.*, 540, 08014, EDP Sciences, 2024.
29. Yang, C. and Liu, Q., Driving Green Innovation Through Digital Transformation: Empirical Insights on Regional Variations. *Sustainability*, 16, 23, 10716, 2024.
30. Obracht-Prondzyńska, H., Duda, E., Anacka, H., Kowal, J., Greencoin as an AI-Based Solution Shaping Climate Awareness. *Int. J. Environ. Res. Public Health*, 19, 18, 11183, 2022.
31. Salaheldeen, M., Ateeq, A., Al Ani, Z., Alzoraiki, M., Ali, S.A., Milhem, M., Green Entrepreneurship and Sustainability in Developing Countries: Opportunities, Challenges, and Future Research Directions, in: *The AI*

Revolution: Driving Business Innovation and Research: Volume 1, pp. 525–34, 2024.

32. Soubhari, T., Jayaprakasan, P.P., Shobha, C.V., Mannarath, A.K., Nanda, S.S., "AI-Driven Green Growth and Carbon-Neutral Solutions"—The CSR Spectrum Redefined, in: *Integrating Environmental Sustainability and Corporate Social Responsibility: A Move Beyond Profit: Corporate Social Responsibility for Environmental Sustainability*, pp. 245–71, Springer, 2025.
33. Almansour, M., How Do Green Intellectual and Co-Creational Capitals Drive Artificial Intelligence Innovation and Green Innovation in Start-Ups? *Eur. J. Innovation Manage.*, 28, 4, 1649–66, 2025.
34. Hullurappa, M. and Panyaram, S., Quantum Computing for Equitable Green Innovation Unlocking Sustainable Solutions, in: *Advancing Social Equity Through Accessible Green Innovation*, pp. 387–402, IGI Global Scientific Publishing, 2025.
35. Ziemba, E.W., Duong, C.D., Ejdys, J., Gonzalez-Perez, M.A., Kazlauskaitė, R., Korzynski, P., Mazurek, G., Paliszkiewicz, J., Stankevičienė, J., Wach, K., Leveraging Artificial Intelligence to Meet the Sustainable Development Goals. *J. Econ. Manage.*, 46, 508–83, 2024.
36. Yalamati, S., Ensuring Ethical Practices in AI and ML Toward a Sustainable Future, in: *Artificial Intelligence and Machine Learning for Sustainable Development*, pp. 194–208, CRC Press, 2024.

14

Decades of Transformation: Predictive Analysis of Land Use Changes in Dhanbad Using Deep Learning and Remote Sensing

A. Anitha[1]* and Nikhil Raj[2]

[1]*School of Computer Science, Engineering and Information Systems, Vellore Institute of Technology, Vellore, Tamil Nadu, India*
[2]*Master of Computer Application, Vellore Institute of Technology, Vellore, India*

Abstract

Coal has played a vital role in the livelihood of the people of Dhanbad. Dhanbad, the Coal Capital of India is one of the largest, with 19.4 billion tons of reserves, producing 27.5 million tons annually. This study presents a comprehensive analysis of Land Use and Land Cover (LULC) in Dhanbad, India, spanning from 1987 to 2023. Leveraging multi-temporal satellite imagery from Landsat missions and advanced machine learning techniques, the research identifies significant transformations in Dhanbad's landscape. A supervised classification using the smileGradientTreeBoost algorithm categorizes land into coal, water, urban, crop, and forest areas. The classified data, organized into annual percentages, highlights the environmental impacts of coal mining and urban expansion. To forecast future trends, Long Short-Term Memory (LSTM) and Bidirectional LSTM (Bi-LSTM) models are employed, projecting land use changes for the next five years. The analysis reveals long-term patterns of urbanization and resource exploitation, providing actionable insights for policymakers, urban planners, and environmental scientists. By combining historical LULC data with predictive modelling, the study aims to support sustainable development and environmental conservation strategies in this industrial region. The results demonstrate the effectiveness of integrating geospatial technologies and deep learning for regional land management and highlight the need for proactive measures to mitigate ecological degradation.

**Corresponding author*: aanitha@vit.ac.in; ORCID: 0000-0002-6005-8429

Umesh Kumar Lilhore, Sarita Simaiya, Surjeet Dalal and Martin Margala (eds.) Artificial Intelligence and Biodiversity, (231–260) © 2026 Scrivener Publishing LLC

Keywords**:** Land use land cover (LULC), satellite imagery, Dhanbad, geospatial analysis, LSTM, Bi-LSTM, urbanization

14.1 Introduction

Dhanbad, located in the state of Jharkhand, India, has a rich history intertwined with coal mining that dates back to the late 19th century. Known as the 'Coal Capital of India', the city and its surrounding areas are home to some of the largest coal mines in the country, including the Jharia coalfield, famous for its underground coal fires. The region's landscape has undergone significant transformations due to extensive mining activities, rapid urbanization, and industrial development over the past century. These changes have had profound impacts on the local environment, agriculture, and urban infrastructure, making Dhanbad a critical area for LULC studies. In recent decades, the advent of satellite imagery and remote sensing technologies has revolutionized the field of land use analysis, allowing researchers to track changes over large areas with unprecedented detail and accuracy. The availability of historical satellite data, combined with advancements in machine learning and data analytics, has opened new avenues for understanding long-term land use trends and their implications. Previous studies have highlighted the challenges faced by Dhanbad, including land degradation, loss of agricultural areas, and urban sprawl. However, a comprehensive, long-term analysis using the latest technologies has been lacking. This background sets the stage for the current study, which aims to fill this gap by providing a detailed, data-driven analysis of Dhanbad's changing landscape from 1987 to 2023, and extending insights into the near future. The study builds upon existing research in remote sensing, LULC classification techniques, and predictive modeling to offer a nuanced understanding of the region's land use dynamics.

The primary objective of this study is to conduct a comprehensive LULC analysis of Dhanbad, India, using satellite imagery spanning from 1987 to 2023. Specifically, the research aims to quantify and visualize the changes in Dhanbad's landscape over nearly four decades, with a particular focus on the impact of coal mining activities. By employing advanced machine learning techniques, including supervised classification and predictive modeling, the study seeks to classify the land into distinct categories: coal, water, urban, crop, and forest areas. Furthermore, the research extends its scope to forecast LULC changes for the next five years, providing a forward-looking perspective on land use trends. Through this analysis, the study intends to create a detailed chronological record of land cover changes, identify significant patterns and trends in land use transformation, and offer insights into the future trajectory of Dhanbad's landscape. Ultimately, the objective is to produce a comprehensive dataset and analysis that can serve as a valuable resource for policymakers, urban planners, and environmental scientists working on sustainable development and land management strategies in this critical industrial region.

The motivation behind this LULC analysis of Dhanbad stems from the city's unique position as India's coal capital and its significance in the country's industrial landscape. Dhanbad's extensive open mining areas have led to substantial changes in its land use patterns over the years, making it an ideal subject for studying the long-term impacts of intensive industrial activity on regional landscapes. The rapid urbanization and industrial growth in the area have created a pressing need for accurate, up-to-date information on land use changes to inform sustainable development practices. By undertaking this comprehensive study, there is an opportunity to bridge the gap between historical land use data and future projections, providing a crucial tool for balanced urban planning and environmental conservation efforts. The motivation also lies in demonstrating the power of combining satellite imagery with advanced machine learning techniques to produce actionable insights for land management. Furthermore, the study is driven by the potential to contribute to the broader field of environmental monitoring and urban studies, offering a replicable methodology for similar analyses in other rapidly changing industrial regions worldwide.

14.2 Related Work

The landscape of land use and land cover (LULC) research has evolved significantly, driven by advancements in remote sensing, machine learning, and spatiotemporal analysis. Hosseiny *et al.* [1] introduced WetNet, a sophisticated ensemble deep-learning framework combining spatial and temporal features to classify wetlands using Sentinel-1 and Sentinel-2 data. By integrating radar and optical data, WetNet overcame challenges such as cloud cover and seasonal variations, enhancing classification precision. This innovation underscores the importance of ensemble techniques and multi-source datasets for high-accuracy monitoring of complex environments like wetlands. Building upon the potential of synthetic aperture radar (SAR), Busquier *et al.* [2] demonstrated the effectiveness of combining L-, C-, and X-band SAR images for land cover and crop classification. Their time-series analysis captured seasonal variations, enabling precise differentiation of crop types and other land cover classes in agricultural landscapes. Similarly, Pan *et al.* [3] pioneered a method integrating ICESat-2 photon-counting data with Landsat 8 OLI data to improve land cover classification. Their approach, tested in Yunnan Province, China, leveraged photon-counting data's high-resolution elevation details, providing insights for further exploration in remote sensing applications. Temporal consistency in mapping was addressed by Bogaert *et al.* [4], who employed Hidden Markov Models (HMMs) to ensure the accuracy and completeness of annual land cover maps over multiple years. Their method proved invaluable for monitoring long-term changes, such as urban expansion and deforestation. Sarkar *et al.* [5], meanwhile, explored the ecological impact of human migration by analyzing land use changes and their influence on carbon patterns and land surface temperature. By using artificial neural networks, they provided a framework for assessing the environmental consequences of demographic shifts. Ouchra *et al.* [6] harnessed Google Earth Engine (GEE) to deploy machine learning models for large-scale LULC classification in Morocco, showcasing the potential of cloud-based solutions for remote sensing. Manna and Anitha [24] presented the air quality prediction using stacked LSTM.

In a similar vein, Aljebreen *et al.* [7] combined deep learning with the River Formation Dynamics algorithm to classify complex landscapes, demonstrating how optimization algorithms can enhance precision in diverse terrains. Addressing the complexities of spatiotemporal analysis, Jiang *et al.* [8] developed an image fusion technique based on unmixing, which effectively captured intricate land cover changes over time. Regional planning received attention through the work of Jalayer *et al.* [9], who analyzed and forecasted spatiotemporal LULC changes in Iran's Chalus watershed, offering insights critical for environmental management. Baek *et al.* [10] adapted the U-Net deep learning model for RGB and near-infrared (NIR) imagery, achieving remarkable precision in land cover classification, while Tesfaye *et al.* [11] combined GEE with machine learning to track and predict landscape changes, underscoring the synergy between computational power and advanced analytics. The drivers of urban expansion were explored by Singh *et al.* [12], who utilized geospatial methods and Random Forest models to analyze LULC changes in Imphal City, India. Their work highlighted the role of data-driven approaches in understanding urban growth dynamics.

Ebenezer *et al.* [13] employed convolutional neural networks (CNNs) to enhance classification accuracy in high-resolution remote sensing, emphasizing the relevance of deep learning in managing large-scale LULC data. Raza *et al.* [14] integrated Principal Component Analysis (PCA) with supervised classification to monitor LULC changes in underdeveloped regions of Pakistan, demonstrating its utility in data-scarce environments. Expanding the geographical focus, Filho *et al.* [15] evaluated the Brazilian Cerrado's land use trends, linking them to climate, environmental, and socioeconomic factors. Ganjirad *et al.* [16] applied GEE and Landsat 8 imagery to enhance weather forecasts by integrating LULC data, bridging remote sensing and meteorological modeling. Patel *et al.* [17] developed a GIS-based method for tracking urbanization in Ahmedabad, India, offering vital insights for urban planning. Africa's deforestation challenges were investigated by Masolele *et al.* [18], who examined biodiversity impacts and land use shifts across the continent, advocating sustainable management practices. Dey *et al.* [19] explored sustainable grassland management strategies in Western India, presenting solutions to balance ecological preservation with land use demands. Lastly, Agudelo-Hz *et al.* [20] analyzed LULC recovery pathways in Colombia's Amazon, providing policymakers with scenarios for sustainable land management in post-conflict regions. Each study enriches the evolving narrative of LULC research, blending technical innovation with ecological and socioeconomic insights to address pressing global challenges. Manna and Anitha [21] illustrates the use of Deep ensemble for the ground water prediction using Bi-LSTM. Manna and Anitha [22] discussed the precipitation prediction using roughset on fuzzy approximation space using LSTM. Nandhini *et al.* [23] given a new paradigm of seasonal occupational analysis using deep learning techniques.

14.3 Background Fundamental

A. Smile Gradient Tree Boost

Smile Gradient Boosting is an ensemble machine learning technique frequently utilized for both classification and regression tasks due to its effectiveness in capturing intricate patterns within data. It is part of the boosting algorithm family, which enhances model performance iteratively by integrating several weak learners, typically in the form of decision trees, to form a robust learner. Each decision tree plays a role in reducing the overall error, which makes Smile Gradient Boosting particularly powerful in situations where high accuracy is essential. By averaging the outputs from all the trees, the final prediction achieves improved generalization and diminishes the likelihood of overfitting compared to using a single decision tree.

Smile Gradient Boosting is particularly advantageous for LULC classification in GEE, as it provides reliable classification results across different land categories like coal, water, urban, crop, and forest areas. GEE's access to a vast repository of satellite imagery and its cloud computing capabilities enables efficient processing of large datasets required for LULC analysis. Smile Gradient Boosting in GEE allows users to create robust classification models that leverage temporal and spectral data features, thereby improving the accuracy of distinguishing between similar land cover types. This is especially useful in areas like Dhanbad, where diverse landscapes and industrial activities can complicate classification.

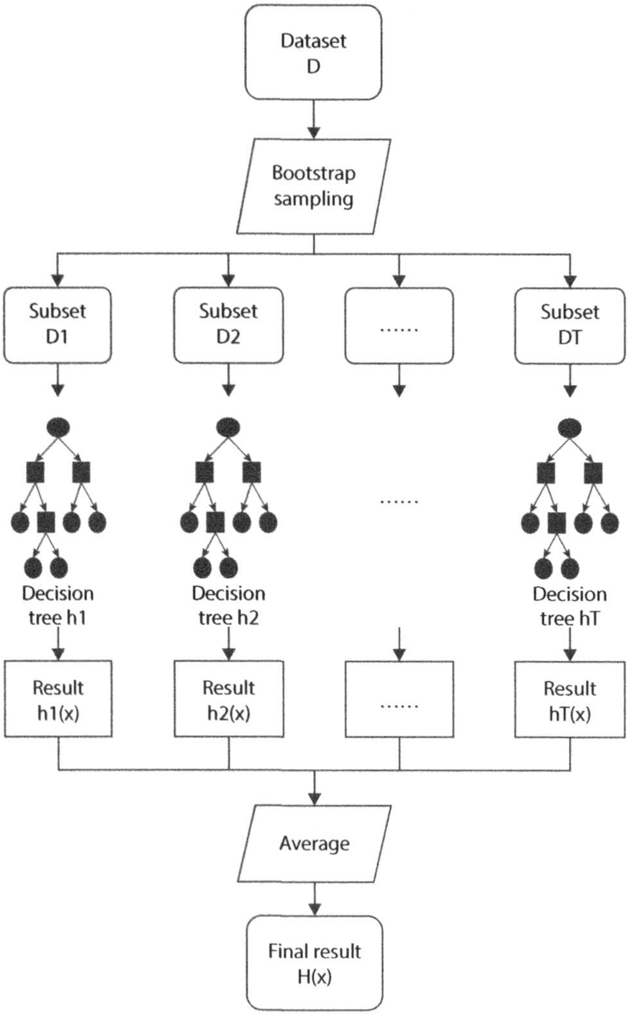

Figure 14.1 Architecture of smile gradient boost.

The architecture in Figure 14.1 of Smile Gradient Boosting follows a structured process where multiple decision trees are sequentially built to improve model accuracy.

Dataset Preparation and Bootstrap Sampling

Dataset D: The process begins with dataset D, which contains features and labels related to the classification task.

Bootstrap Sampling: Instead of using the entire dataset D to train each tree, Smile Gradient Boosting uses a technique called bootstrap sampling. Bootstrap sampling creates multiple random subsets from D with replacement, meaning some data points may be repeated within a subset. Each subset D1, D2, …, DT will serve as the training data for an individual decision tree.

Building Individual Decision Trees (Weak Learners)

Decision Trees: The data is divided into subsets D1, D2, …, DT, each of which is used to construct an individual decision tree model, called a weak learner. Decision trees are basic models that categorize data by splitting based on feature values, aiming to classify or predict outcomes by navigating through the tree. Weak Learner Concept: In Smile Gradient Boosting, every tree functions as a weak learner since it performs just slightly better than random chance. However, by aggregating numerous weak learners, the overall model achieves a high degree of predictive accuracy.

Sequential Learning and Error Minimization

Error Correction: The boosting process in Smile Gradient Boosting works sequentially, where each tree focuses on correcting the errors made by the previous trees. The first tree h1(x) makes an initial prediction, and subsequent trees h2(x), h3(x), … are trained to correct the mistakes of the trees that came before them.

Gradient Descent Optimization: Smile Gradient Boosting uses gradient descent, a mathematical optimization technique, to minimize the overall error. Each new tree is added in a way that reduces the residual error (difference between predicted and actual values) from the previous tree's predictions. This iterative process continues until a predefined number of trees T are created, or the model reaches an acceptable level of accuracy.

Aggregating Results and Averaging

Prediction Averaging: Once all decision trees have been trained, they are combined to make a final prediction. For a given input x, each tree produces a prediction h1(x), h2(x), …, hT(x).

Weighted Averaging: In some implementations, each tree's prediction might be given a weight based on its performance. In Smile Gradient Boosting, however, the predictions are typically averaged to generate the final result H(x). By averaging, the model smooths out individual errors from each weak learner, producing a more stable and accurate prediction.

The final model output H(x) is the combined prediction from all decision trees. This aggregation of predictions from multiple trees creates a "strong learner" capable of making accurate and robust predictions. Enhanced Generalization: By averaging across multiple trees, Smile Gradient Boosting reduces the variance, which helps in preventing overfitting. This makes it a powerful tool for tasks requiring high accuracy, such as land use classification in Google Earth Engine (GEE), where it is essential to classify subtle differences across land categories like urban, forest, and water bodies.

In summary, the architecture of Smile Gradient Boosting combines bootstrap sampling, sequential error correction, and aggregation of predictions to create a model that is both accurate and resilient to overfitting. Each tree builds upon the errors of previous trees, and the final averaged output provides a strong and generalized prediction. This approach is especially effective in complex tasks such as LULC classification, where fine-grained distinctions in land categories are crucial.

B. Long Short-term memory

The LSTM architecture, a type of RNN, has garnered significant attention in stock market prediction due to its ability to identify and comprehend long-term dependencies in sequential data. Unlike standard feedforward neural networks, LSTM networks incorporate memory cells and gating mechanisms to manage the flow of information over time. This allows them to retain important historical data while selectively updating or discarding less relevant information. As a result, LSTM models are particularly effective for analyzing time-series data, such as historical stock prices, where recognizing patterns and trends from the past is essential for forecasting future movements. Additionally, the LSTM architecture excels at capturing complex temporal dynamics and mitigates the vanishing gradient problem commonly faced by traditional RNNs. Consequently, LSTM-based models serve as a foundational element in developing advanced predictive models to handle the intricacies of the stock market, demonstrating higher accuracy and robustness in predicting stock prices compared to conventional machine learning methods.

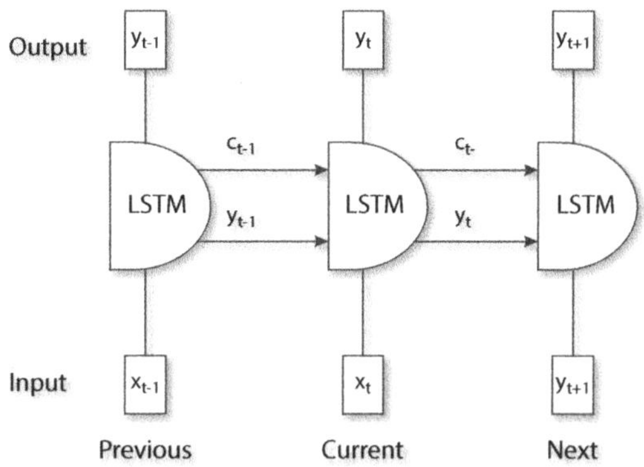

Figure 14.2 LSTM architecture.

The Figure 14.2 depicts the working of a Long Short-Term Memory (LSTM) neural network, which is a type of recurrent neural network (RNN) used for processing sequential data. Let me explain the diagram in detail:

Previous: In the leftmost part of the diagram, we have the previous input (x_{t-1}) and output (y_{t-1}) of the LSTM. These are passed as inputs to the LSTM along with the current input (x_t).
Current: The current input (x_t) and the previous hidden state (h_{t-1}) and cell state (c_{t-1}) are passed into the LSTM, which processes the information and generates the current hidden state (h_t) and cell state (c_t).
Next: The current hidden state (h_t) is then used to generate the current output (y_t), which becomes the previous output (y_t) in the next iteration. The process then repeats for the next input (x_{t+1}).

The key components of the LSTM are:
LSTM: This is the main processing unit that takes the current input, previous hidden state, and previous cell state, and generates the current hidden state and cell state.
c_{t-1} and c_t: These represent the cell state, which is the memory of the LSTM. The cell state is passed from one time step to the next, allowing the LSTM to maintain long-term dependencies in the data.
h_{t-1} and h_t: These represent the hidden state, which is the output of the LSTM at each time step. The hidden state is also passed from one time step to the next, allowing the LSTM to maintain short-term dependencies in the data.

The LSTM is designed to address the vanishing gradient problem that can occur in traditional RNNs, which makes it challenging for them to learn long-term dependencies in sequential data. The LSTM's unique architecture, with its cell state and gating mechanisms, allows it to selectively remember and forget information, enabling it to effectively model long-term dependencies in data.

C. Bi-directional-Long Short-term memory

Bi-LSTM is intended to record bidirectional dependencies in sequential data. Bi-LSTMs process input sequences simultaneously in both directions, as opposed to normal LSTMs which process sequences in a unidirectional fashion (from past to future). Because of their ability to process in both directions, Bi-LSTMs are able to extract context from both past and future states, which helps them comprehend the sequence as a whole. Bi-LSTMs' two distinct hidden layers allow them to detect intricate patterns and dependencies that unidirectional models could overlook. One hidden layer processes the input sequence in forward order, while the other processes it in reverse. In tasks like natural language processing (NLP), speech recognition, and time series analysis, where comprehending context from both past and future contexts is critical, bi-LSTMs do especially well. They can represent bidirectional linkages and dependencies in sequential data,

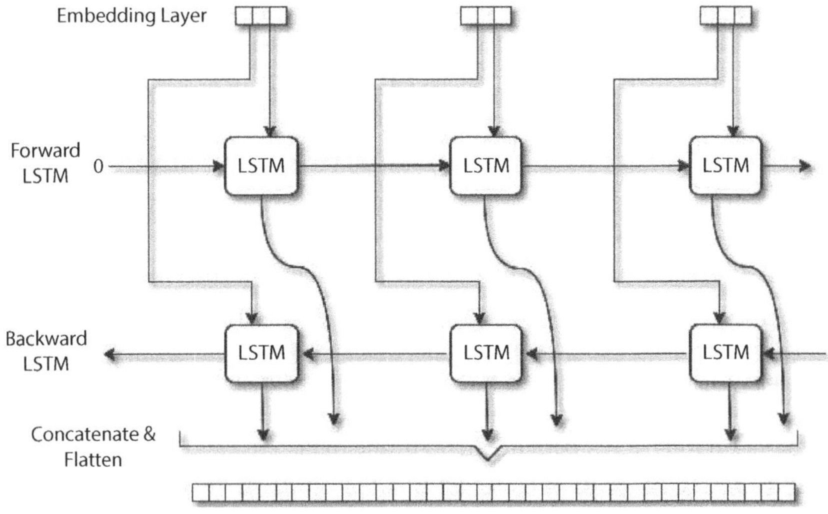

Figure 14.3 Bi-LSTM architecture.

which has led to their effective application in a variety of disciplines such as sentiment analysis, machine translation, and stock market prediction. Figure 14.3 represents Bi-LSTM architecture.

14.4 Proposed Work

The proposed research builds upon the findings of historical land use and land cover (LULC) analysis and aims to extend the capabilities of predictive modeling and decision-making frameworks for urban and environmental planning. The work leverages advancements in geospatial data processing, machine learning, and cloud-based platforms to address the challenges of monitoring and forecasting LULC dynamics in resource-intensive regions like Dhanbad, India. Key aspects of the proposed work include enhanced data integration and processing techniques, advanced predictive modeling approaches, and the development of a comprehensive decision-support framework to inform sustainable land management strategies. This multifaceted research endeavor seeks to contribute to the growing body of knowledge in the field of LULC analysis and support more informed and effective urban and environmental planning efforts in the target region. Figure 14.4 represents the Proposed architecture of the research model.

The study plans to refine predictive modeling by integrating advanced architectures such as Transformers and hybrid deep learning models, combining convolutional layers with Long Short-Term Memory (LSTM) networks. These models will capture spatial-temporal interdependencies more effectively, improving the accuracy and granularity of LULC forecasts. Future iterations will incorporate high-resolution satellite data, such as Sentinel 2 imagery, to complement the historical Landsat data. This will enable finer-scale classification, capturing subtle changes in urban expansion, deforestation, and mining activities. The inclusion of multi-spectral and synthetic aperture radar (SAR) data will improve classification under challenging conditions, such as cloud cover and topographic variations. A real-time LULC monitoring system will be designed using Google Earth Engine (GEE) and other cloud platforms. This system will facilitate continuous monitoring and near-real-time updates on land use changes, providing actionable insights to stakeholders. Automation of data preprocessing and classification will ensure the system is efficient and scalable. Predictive models will be enhanced to support scenario-based analyses. Simulations will include diverse socio-economic and environmental variables, such as population growth rates, industrial expansions, and climate impacts, enabling stakeholders to explore multiple developmental pathways.

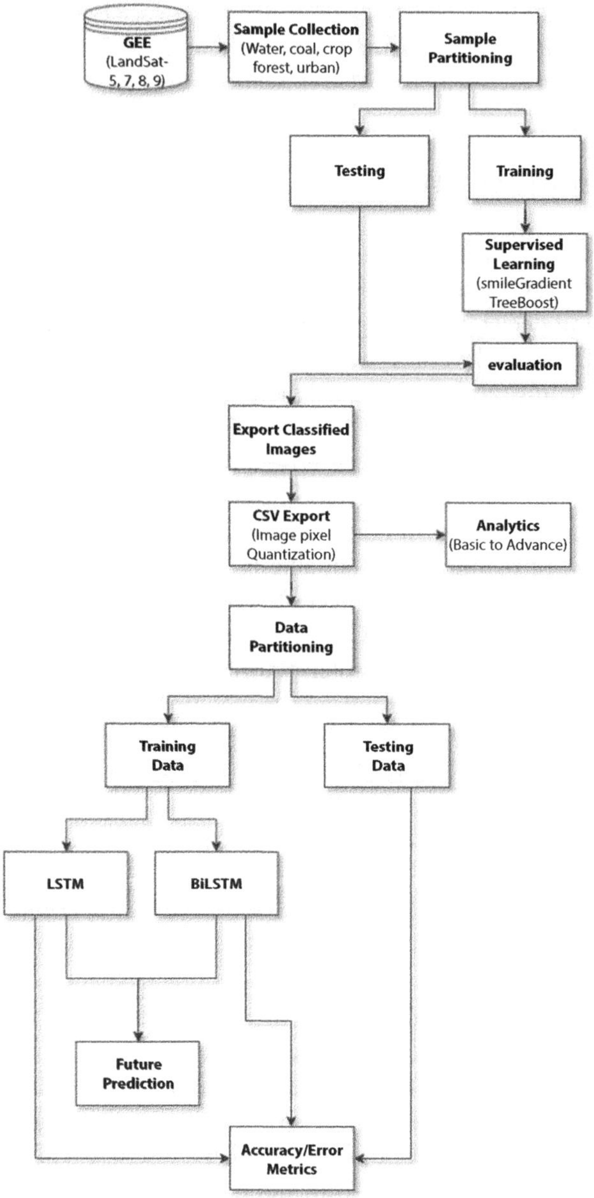

Figure 14.4 Architecture diagram.

The study aims to create a decision-support framework to assist policy-makers in evaluating the long-term implications of urbanization and industrial activities. By combining geospatial visualizations, trend analyses, and scenario-based predictions, the framework will guide sustainable development strategies and environmental conservation efforts. The proposed methods will be designed to scale and replicate across other industrially intensive or rapidly urbanizing regions. By standardizing workflows and incorporating modular components, the framework can be adapted for different geographies and use cases.

14.4.1 Research Methodology

This employs a comprehensive methodological framework that integrates remote sensing technology, advanced machine learning algorithms, and sophisticated time series analysis techniques. The methodology is structured into five primary stages:

Data Acquisition and Preprocessing

The foundation of this analysis rests on the extensive temporal coverage provided by the Landsat satellite program. We utilize imagery from multiple Landsat missions (5, 7, and 8) spanning from 1987 to 2023. The preprocessing phase is executed within the Google Earth Engine (GEE) platform, where we implement rigorous cloud masking protocols and atmospheric correction procedures to ensure data quality and consistency across the temporal range.

Supervised Classification

The classification phase employs the smileGradientTreeBoost algorithm, a robust machine learning approach for distinguishing between five distinct land cover classes: water bodies, coal mining areas, cropland, forest cover, and urban development. This process involves careful collection and curation of training samples for each land cover category, followed by strategic partitioning of these samples into training and testing datasets to ensure model validity.

Time Series Analysis

Following classification, we conduct systematic quantification of land cover changes. This involves exporting the classified imagery and performing pixel-based calculations to determine the spatial extent of each land cover class. The results are systematically organized into annual time series data, exported as CSV files containing yearly percentages for each land cover category, enabling detailed temporal analysis of land use transitions.

Predictive Modeling
The project implements advanced deep learning techniques through LSTM (Long Short-Term Memory) and Bi-LSTM (Bidirectional LSTM) architectures for future LULC prediction. These neural network models are specifically chosen for their capability to capture complex temporal patterns in land cover changes. The modeling process includes careful data partitioning for training and testing phases to ensure robust predictive performance.

14.5 Experiment, Analysis and Result

The image showcases the satellite image of the coalfield of Jharia, the visible trenches are enough proof of destruction. Figure 14.5 and Figure 14.6 illustrates the satellite image of the study area and the land classified image.

Forest, crop, water, urban, and coal, all five categories are represented by the colors green, yellow, blue, pink, and white respectively. The project demonstration will showcase the comprehensive LULC analysis of Dhanbad, highlighting the methodology, results, and implications of the

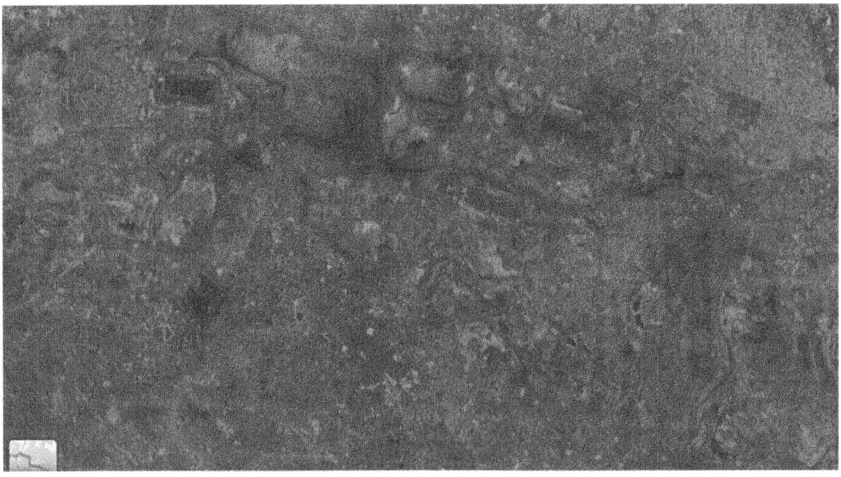

Figure 14.5 2024 satellite image.

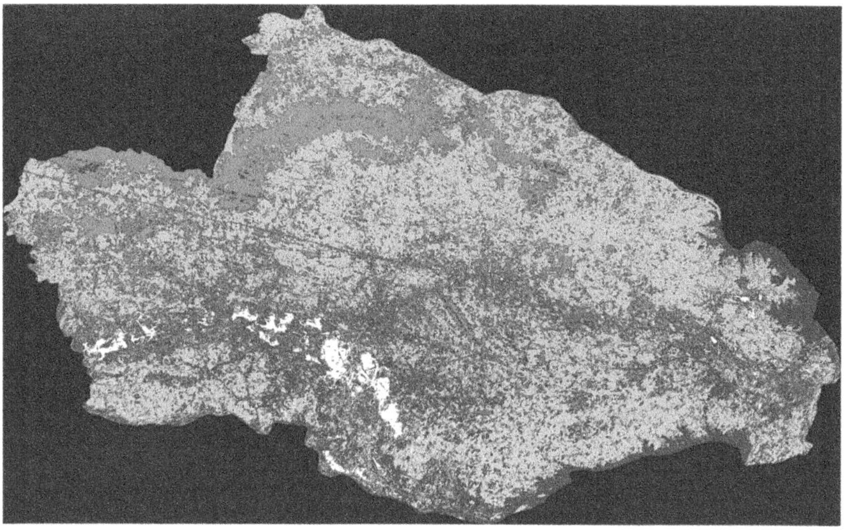

Figure 14.6 2023 land classified image.

study. The demonstration will be structured to engage stakeholders, policymakers, and the scientific community.

1) Yearly Trend of Land Cover Types

This line graph shows the detailed year-to-year variations in each land cover type's percentage. It highlights the volatility in crop coverage (green line) and urban areas (orange line), while showing relatively stable trends in water bodies. The graph effectively captures both short-term fluctuations and long-term trends in land cover changes over the study period given in Figure 14.7.

2) Land Use Flow Over Time

This flow chart displays smooth temporal trends for each land cover type from 1987 to 2023. The separated visualization makes it easier to track individual category changes over time. The chart reveals stability in some land cover types while showing gradual changes in others, particularly in urban and crop areas. The parallel display allows for easy comparison of trends between different land cover types as depicted in Figure 14.8.

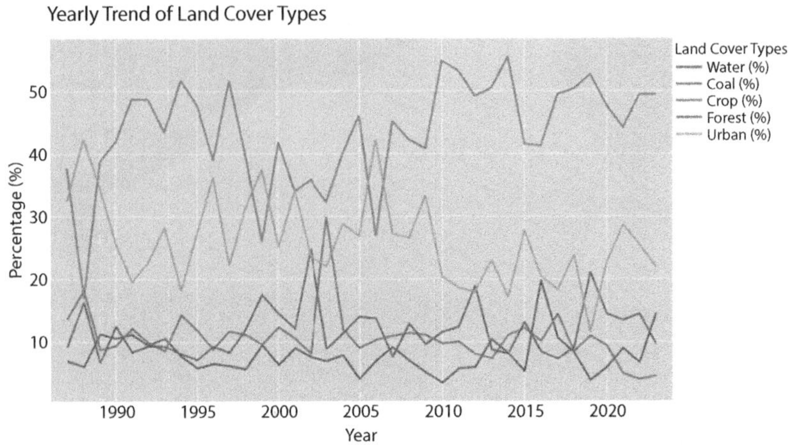

Figure 14.7 Yearly trends.

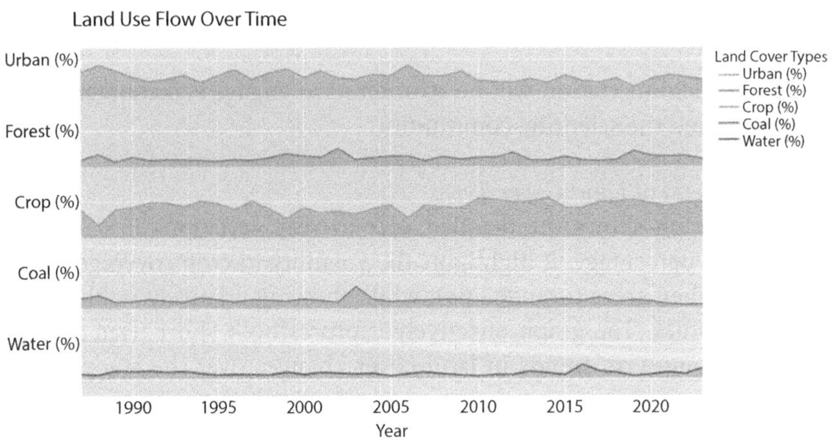

Figure 14.8 Flow over time.

3) Average Distribution of Land Cover

This pie chart shows the historical average distribution of land cover types across the study period. Crop areas maintain dominance at 43.4%, with urban areas covering 26.1%. Forest cover accounts for 11.7%, while coal mining areas represent 10.8%. Water bodies make up 7.97%, revealing long-term land use patterns in the region. This pie chart depicts the current land cover distribution in 2023. Cropland dominates at 49.4% of the total area, followed by urban areas at 21.9%. Water bodies cover 14.5%, while

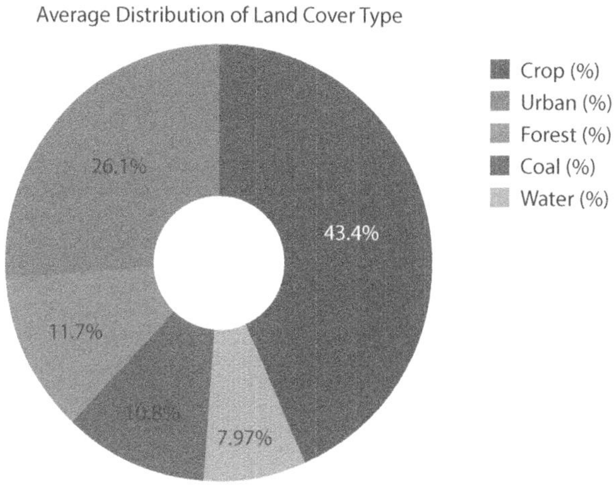

Figure 14.9 Average distribution of land cover.

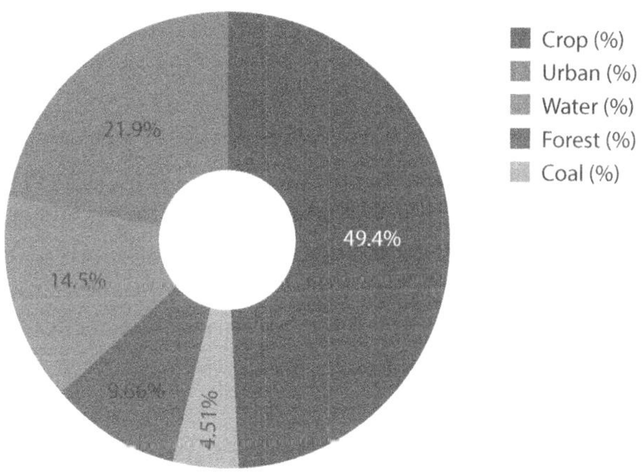

Figure 14.10 Land distribution in 2023.

forest areas represent 9.66%. Coal mining areas occupy the smallest portion at 4.51%, illustrating the current balance between agricultural, urban, and natural landscapes as given in Figure 14.9 and Figure 14.10.

4) Anomalies in Land Cover Types

This multi-panel time series graph shows deviations from normal patterns in each land cover type from 1987 to 2023. Notable anomalies include a significant spike in coal areas around 2003, unusual fluctuations in urban coverage during the early 1990s, and periodic variations in crop coverage.

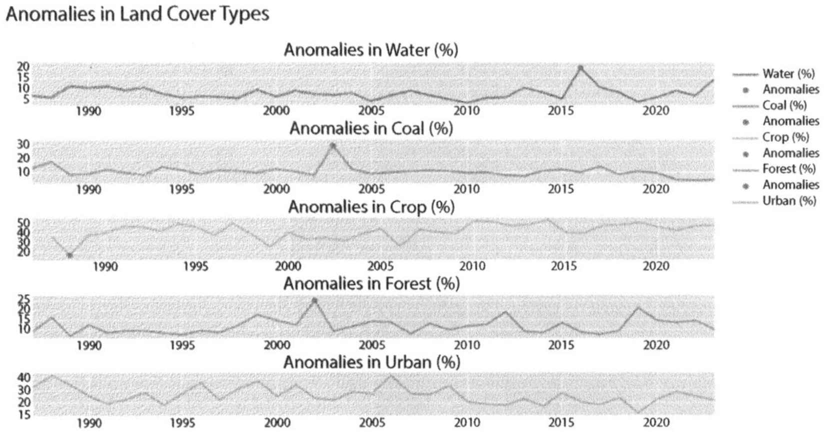

Figure 14.11 Anomalies in data.

The red dots highlight particularly significant anomalies that deviate from the general trend of each land cover type as provided in Figure 14.11.

5) Correlation Heatmap of Land Cover Types

This correlation matrix reveals the relationships between different land cover types. The strong negative correlation (-0.816) between Urban and Crop areas indicates that urban expansion primarily occurs at the expense of agricultural land. Water bodies show negative correlations with all other land types, suggesting that water areas tend to remain relatively isolated from other land use changes. The diagonal shows a perfect correlation (1.0) as expected as represented in Figure 14.12.

14.5.1 Long Short-Term Memory Trends

Trends of Water

Water (%) Prediction (LSTM): The LSTM model tracks water coverage between 5-20% from 1990–2020, showing good alignment with actual values. Future predictions indicate a gradual increase and stabilization of around 11% through 2028 given in Figure 14.13.

Trends of Coal and Urban

Coal (%) Prediction (LSTM): Historical coal data shows variations with a major peak around 2005. The LSTM model predicts a more moderate increase compared to Bi-LSTM, suggesting coal coverage will stabilize around 10% by 2028. Urban (%) Prediction (LSTM): Urban coverage varies between 15-40% from 1990-2020. The LSTM model effectively captures

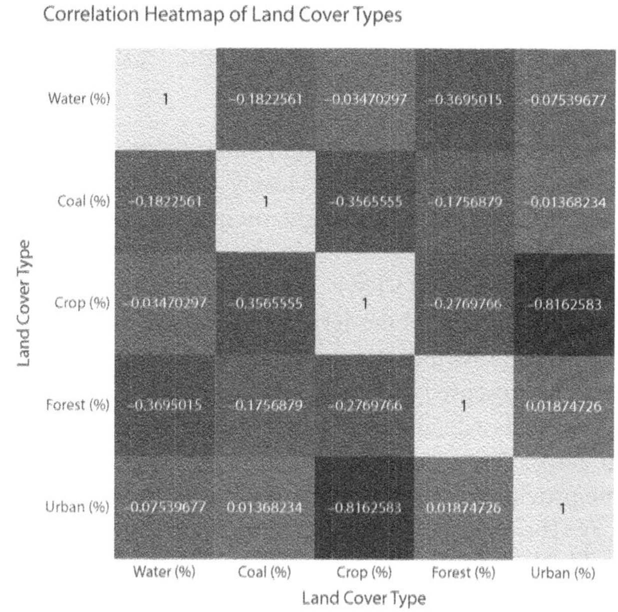

Figure 14.12 Correlations among land types.

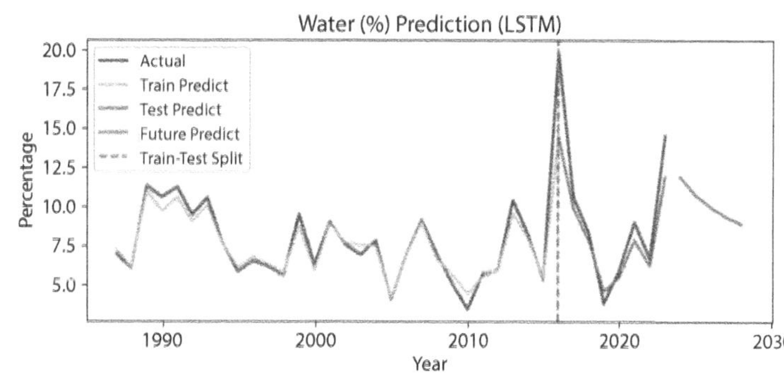

Figure 14.13 Train, test, and future trend of water by LSTM.

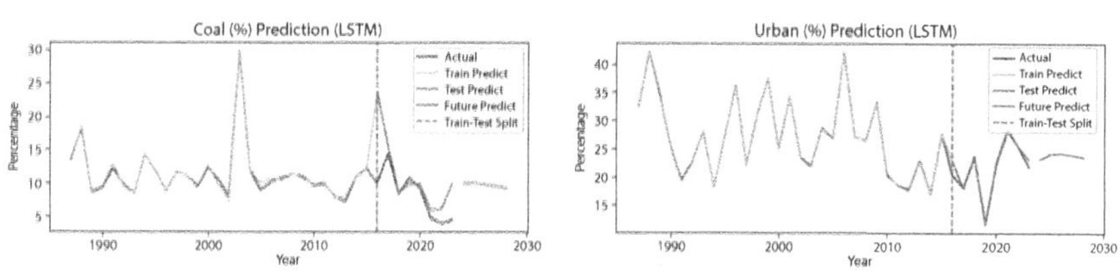

Figure 14.14 Train, test, and future trend of coal and urban by LSTM.

historical trends and predicts a moderate increase in urban areas, stabilizing around 23% through 2028 provided in Figure 14.14.

Trends of Crop and Forest

Crop (%) Prediction (LSTM): The graph shows crop coverage oscillating between 30-55%. LSTM predictions closely follow actual values. Unlike Bi-LSTM, this model forecasts a slight increase in crop areas, reaching about 45% by 2028.

Forest (%) Prediction (LSTM): Forest coverage fluctuates between 5-25% historically. The LSTM model shows good prediction accuracy until 2020. Future projections indicate a gradual decline to around 10% forest coverage by 2028 presented in Figure 14.15.

Table 14.1 presents a detailed five-year forecast (2024-2028) of land cover distribution across five categories: Water, Coal, Crop, Forest, and Urban areas. Let me provide a comprehensive analysis of the projected trends for each category. The forecast indicates a significant decline in water coverage, with a decline from 11.90% in 2024 to 8.88% by 2028. This decline is attributed to a decrease in water bodies and wetland areas, potentially

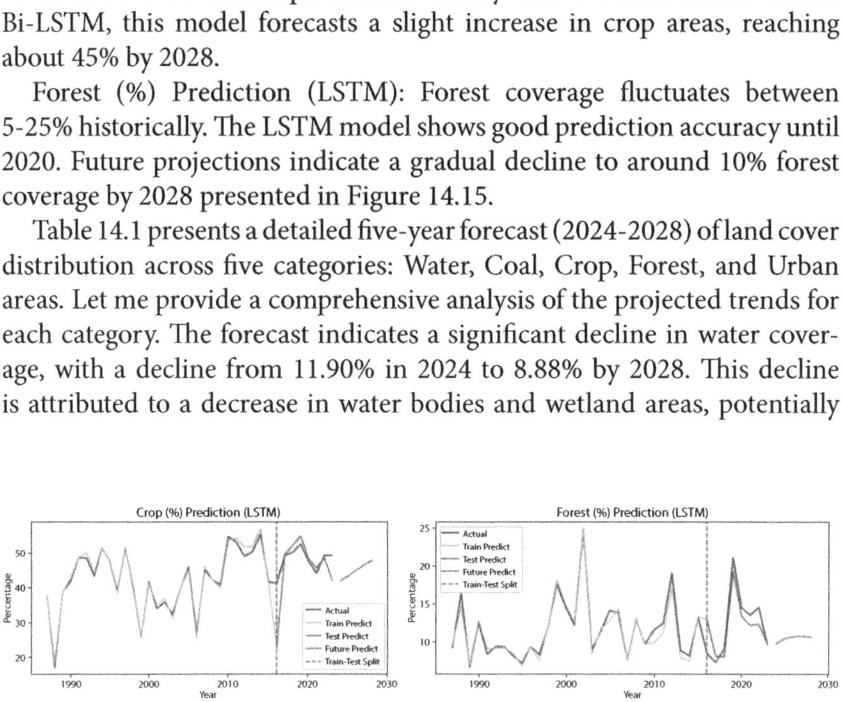

Figure 14.15 Train, test, and future trend of crop and forest by LSTM.

Table 14.1 LSTM prediction.

Category →					
Year	**Water**	**Coal**	**Crop**	**Forest**	**Urban**
2024	11.90	10.05	41.99	9.72	23.15
2025	10.74	10.14	43.30	10.39	24.18
2026	9.93	9.91	45.01	10.65	24.24
2027	9.34	9.61	46.60	10.69	23.96
2028	8.88	9.30	47.94	10.59	23.62

impacting local ecosystems and water resources. Coal coverage also shows a decline, with a modest decrease from 10.05% in 2024 to 9.30% by 2028. Crop coverage, which started at 41.99% in 2024, rises to 47.94% by 2028, indicating a focus on food security or agricultural development. Forest coverage increases slightly, with a modest increase from 9.72% in 2024 to 10.59% by 2028. Urban areas show fluctuating patterns, with urban coverage increasing from 23.15% in 2024 to 24.24% by 2026 and then slightly decreasing to 23.62% by 2028. This suggests a shift in land use, with a focus on agricultural development and food security while maintaining stable urban growth and forest coverage. The sustainability implications of these changes, particularly the reduction in water areas and expansion of agricultural land, warrant careful consideration in future land use planning and policy development.

14.5.2 Bi-Directional Long Short-Term Memory Trends

Trends of Water

Water (%) Prediction (Bi-LSTM): The graph shows water coverage fluctuating between 5-20% from 1990-2020. Training predictions closely match actual values until 2015. After 2020, the model predicts a slight increase followed by stabilization around 12.5% through 2028.

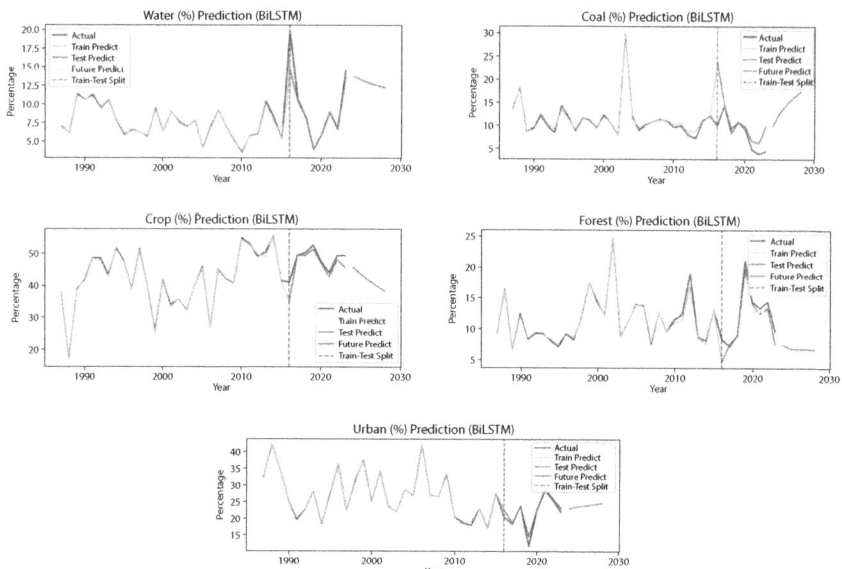

Figure 14.16 Train, test, and future trend of water, coal, crop, forest and urban by Bi-LSTM.

Trends of Coal

Coal (%) Prediction (Bi-LSTM): Historical coal coverage shows variation between 8-15%, with a significant spike to 30% around 2005. The Bi-LSTM model predicts a substantial increase in coal areas from 2020 onwards, reaching nearly 20% by 2028.

Trends of Crop

Crop (%) Prediction (Bi-LSTM): Crop coverage demonstrates consistent oscillation between 30-55% from 1990-2020. The training predictions align well with actual values. The Bi-LSTM model forecasts a gradual decline in crop areas, dropping to around 40% by 2028.

Trends of Forest

Forest (%) Prediction (Bi-LSTM): Forest coverage varies between 5-20% historically, with notable fluctuations. The model accurately tracks actual values until 2020. Future predictions suggest a decline in forest areas, stabilizing around 7% by 2028.

Trends of Urban

Urban (%) Prediction (Bi-LSTM): Urban areas show historical fluctuations between 15-40%. The model's training predictions match actual values well. Post-2020, Bi-LSTM predicts a moderate increase in urban coverage, reaching approximately 23% by 2028. Figure 14.16 represents the Trends of Water, Coal, Crop, forest and Urban by Bi-LSTM.

Table 14.2 presents a five-year forecast of land cover distribution across five categories: Water, Coal, Crop, Forest, and Urban areas. The forecast shows a gradual decline in water coverage, coal coverage, crop coverage, forest areas, and urban areas. Water coverage is projected to decrease

Table 14.2 Bi-LSTM prediction.

Category →					
Year	**Water**	**Coal**	**Crop**	**Forest**	**Urban**
2024	13.73	9.92	45.74	7.53	23.07
2025	13.20	12.79	43.53	6.89	23.62
2026	12.79	14.68	41.68	6.84	23.93
2027	12.49	16.18	39.89	6.85	24.27
2028	12.24	17.46	38.31	6.73	24.69

from 13.73% in 2024 to 12.24% by 2028, indicating a slow but persistent reduction in water bodies or wetland areas. Coal coverage is projected to expand substantially each year, reaching 17.46% by 2028, indicating potential expansion of mining activities or related industrial development. Crop coverage is expected to decline from 45.74% in 2024 to 38.31% by 2028, indicating a significant transformation in land use patterns. Forest areas show a modest but consistent decline from 7.53% in 2024 to 6.73% by 2028. Urban areas display a steadily increasing trend, with urban coverage expanding consistently each year, reaching 24.69% by 2028. The analysis of land cover changes from 1990 to 2023 reveals significant insights into landscape transformation patterns and potential future scenarios. As of 2023, the landscape is predominantly agricultural, with cropland occupying 49.4% of the total area. The strong negative correlation with urban areas suggests ongoing pressure from urbanization.

14.5.3 Error Metrics

Smile gradient tree boost

Table 14.3 presents a detailed performance analysis of different Satellite (labelled as LS05, LS07, LS08, and LS09) using two key evaluation metrics: Kappa coefficient and Accuracy. The Kappa coefficient, which measures agreement between predictions and actual values while accounting for chance agreement, shows a progressive improvement across versions. Starting from LS05 with 0.8225, it slightly dips to 0.7957 in LS07, but then significantly improves to 0.89 in LS08, and reaches its peak at 0.915 in LS09. The overall average Kappa value is 0.8337, indicating strong model performance.

The Accuracy metric, which represents the proportion of correct predictions, follows a similar trend. LS05 begins with 0.8533, slightly decreases to 0.8378 in LS07, then improves markedly to 0.9133 in LS08, and achieves

Table 14.3 Accuracy of smile gradient tree boost.

Row labels	Average of Kappa	Average of accuracy
LS05	0.8225	0.858333333
LS07	0.795714286	0.837857143
LS08	0.89	0.913333333
LS09	0.915	0.935
Average	**0.833783784**	**0.868108108**

its highest value of 0.935 in LS09. The average accuracy across all versions is 0.8681, suggesting robust overall performance. LS09 emerges as the best satellite with both the highest Kappa (0.915) and Accuracy (0.935) scores. This indicates substantial improvement over the initial LS05 version, suggesting successful model refinement through iterations. The high values of both metrics in the final version demonstrate excellent model reliability and prediction accuracy. The progression from LS05 to LS09 shows a clear trend of improvement, with only a minor setback in LS07. This pattern suggests effective model development and optimization throughout the iterations, resulting in increasingly reliable predictions.

Table 14.4 presents a comprehensive analysis of model performance metrics for different land cover categories, comparing training and testing errors using Mean Squared Error (MSE) and Root Mean Squared Error (RMSE) of LSTM model. For Water areas, the training phase shows relatively low errors with MSE of 1.14 and RMSE of 1.07. However, during testing, these errors increase significantly to MSE of 4.84 and RMSE of 2.20, indicating some reduction in prediction accuracy when applied to new data. Coal areas demonstrate higher error values, with training MSE of 6.30 and RMSE of 2.51. The testing phase shows a substantial increase in errors, with MSE jumping to 28.04 and RMSE to 5.29, suggesting challenges in accurately predicting coal land cover patterns in unseen data. Crop areas exhibit the highest error values among all categories. During training, MSE is 12.33 and RMSE is 3.51, while testing errors increase dramatically to MSE of 50.79 and RMSE of 7.12. This indicates significant difficulty in accurately predicting agricultural land coverage, possibly due to its complex and variable nature. Forest areas show moderate error values during training (MSE: 1.22, RMSE: 1.10) with an increase during testing

Table 14.4 Error of LSTM.

	Train		**Test**	
Categories	**MSE**	**RMSE**	**MSE**	**RMSE**
Water	1.14	1.07	4.84	2.20
Coal	6.30	2.51	28.04	5.29
Crop	12.33	3.51	50.79	7.12
Forest	1.22	1.10	4.08	2.02
Urban	0.26	0.51	1.04	1.02

(MSE: 4.08, RMSE: 2.02). While the increase is notable, it's more contained compared to coal and crop categories, suggesting relatively stable prediction capability for forest coverage. Urban areas demonstrate the lowest error values across all categories, with training MSE of 0.26 and RMSE of 0.51, and testing MSE of 1.04 and RMSE of 1.02. This indicates that the model is most effective at predicting urban land cover patterns, possibly due to more consistent and well-defined urban development patterns. The consistent pattern of higher testing errors compared to training errors across all categories suggests some degree of overfitting, though this varies significantly by category. Urban areas show the most robust generalization (smallest difference between training and testing errors), while crop areas show the largest gap, indicating greater challenges in generalizing agricultural land cover predictions to new data.

This error analysis reveals that while the model performs well during training, its predictive accuracy varies considerably across different land cover types, with urban predictions being the most reliable and crop predictions showing the highest uncertainty.

Table 14.5 presents a detailed error analysis of model performance across different land cover categories, comparing training and testing metrics using Mean Squared Error (MSE) and Root Mean Squared Error (RMSE) of Bi-LSTM. For Water areas, the training phase exhibits moderate error values with MSE of 1.73 and RMSE of 1.31. The testing phase shows a notable increase in errors, with MSE rising to 6.69 and RMSE to 2.58, indicating reduced prediction accuracy when the model encounters new data. This suggests some challenges in generalizing water body predictions. Coal areas demonstrate the highest error values among all categories. During training, the MSE is 10.48 and RMSE is 3.23, while testing

Table 14.5 Error of Bi-LSTM.

	Train		Test	
Categories	**MSE**	**RMSE**	**MSE**	**RMSE**
Water	1.73	1.31	6.69	2.58
Coal	10.48	3.23	43.61	6.60
Crop	2.23	1.49	11.49	3.38
Forest	0.28	0.53	1.83	1.35
Urban	0.48	0.69	3.84	1.96

errors increase substantially to MSE of 43.61 and RMSE of 6.60. This dramatic increase suggests significant difficulty in accurately predicting coal land cover patterns in unseen data, possibly due to complex underlying factors affecting coal mining areas. Crop areas show moderate error values during training (MSE: 2.23, RMSE: 1.49) with an increase during testing (MSE: 11.49, RMSE: 3.38). While the increase is notable, it's more contained compared to the coal category. This indicates better predictive capability for agricultural land compared to coal areas, though there's still room for improvement in generalization. Forest areas exhibit the lowest training errors (MSE: 0.28, RMSE: 0.53) and maintain relatively low testing errors (MSE: 1.83, RMSE: 1.35). This suggests that the model is particularly effective at predicting forest coverage, possibly due to more stable and consistent patterns in forest land cover changes. Urban areas show low training errors (MSE: 0.48, RMSE: 0.69) with a moderate increase in testing errors (MSE: 3.84, RMSE: 1.96). This indicates reasonably good prediction capability for urban areas, though there's some degradation when applying the model to new data. The consistent pattern of higher testing errors compared to training errors across all categories indicates some degree of overfitting, though the magnitude varies significantly by category. Forest areas show the most robust generalization (smallest relative difference between training and testing errors), while coal areas demonstrate the poorest generalization (largest gap between training and testing errors).

This comprehensive error analysis reveals that while the model performs well during training, its predictive accuracy varies considerably across different land cover types. Forest predictions appear most reliable, while coal predictions show the highest uncertainty. This insight could be valuable for focusing future model improvements and understanding the limitations of current predictions for different land cover categories. The varying levels of prediction accuracy across categories might be attributed to factors such as the inherent variability in each land cover type, the quality and quantity of training data available for each category, and the complexity of underlying change patterns in different land use types.

14.6 Conclusion

This chapter presents the project's objectives, goals, motivations, and context for a Land Use and Land Cover (LULC) analysis on Dhanbad, India. It emphasizes the importance of understanding Dhanbad's landscape changes over several decades, particularly due to the region's extensive coal mining activities. The methodology used is a combination of satellite imagery and machine learning techniques to classify land into coal, water, urban, crop, and forest categories. The project aims to provide an in-depth analysis of land cover changes from 1987 to 2023 and forecast these changes for the coming years. The technical stack includes Google Earth Engine, Landsat satellite imagery, and algorithms like LSTM and Bi-LSTM for predictive analysis. The focus is on applying deep learning models to predict future land cover changes, providing data-driven insights into potential future trends. Notable trends include increasing urban area and decreasing crop and forest cover. The study's achievements are acknowledged, and potential future improvements, such as using higher-resolution imagery or creating interactive visualizations, are suggested. The project highlights the need for continued research to refine land cover predictions and support sustainable land management.

AI disclosure statement: The author acknowledges the use of AI-based tools for minor language editing or grammatical correction. However, all intellectual contributions, analyses, and conclusions presented in this chapter are entirely the author's own.

References

1. Hosseiny, B., Mahdianpari, M., Brisco, B., Mohammadimanesh, F., Salehi, B., WetNet: A spatial–temporal ensemble deep learning model for wetland classification using Sentinel-1 and Sentinel-2. *IEEE Trans. Geosci. Remote Sens.*, 60, 1–14, 2021.
2. Busquier, M., Lopez-Sanchez, J.M., Ticconi, F., Floury, N., Combination of time series of L-, C-, and X-band SAR images for land cover and crop classification. *IEEE J. Sel. Top. Appl. Earth Obs. Remote Sens.*, 15, 8266–8286, 2022.
3. Pan, J., Wang, C., Wang, J., Gao, F., Liu, Q., Zhang, J., Deng, Y., Land cover classification using ICESat-2 photon counting data and Landsat 8 OLI Data: A case study in Yunnan Province, China. *IEEE Geosci. Remote Sens. Lett.*, 19, 1–5, 2022.
4. Bogaert, P., Lamarche, C., Defourny, P., Hidden Markov Models for Annual Land Cover Mapping—Increasing Temporal Consistency and Completeness. *IEEE Trans. Geosci. Remote Sens.*, 60, 1–14, 2021.
5. Sarkar, S.K., Saroar, M.M., Das, P.C., Chakraborty, T., Rudra, R.R., Alam, E., Islam, A.R.M.T., Artificial neural network-based land use-specific carbon patterns and their effects on land surface temperature as a result of the Rohingya refugee influx. *IEEE Access*, 2023.

6. Ouchra, H. A. F. S. A., Belangour, A., Erraissi, A. L. L. A. E., Machine learning algorithms for satellite image classification using Google Earth Engine and Landsat satellite data: Morocco case study. *IEEE Access*, 2023.
7. Aljebreen, M., Mengash, H.A., Alamgeer, M., Alotaibi, S.S., Salama, A.S., Hamza, M.A., Land Use and Land Cover Classification Using River Formation Dynamics Algorithm With Deep Learning on Remote Sensing Images. *IEEE Access*, 2024.
8. Jiang, X. and Huang, B., Unmixing-based spatiotemporal image fusion accounting for complex land cover changes. *IEEE Trans. Geosci. Remote Sens.*, 60, 1–10, 2022.
9. Jalayer, S., Sharifi, A., Abbasi-Moghadam, D., Tariq, A., Qin, S., Modeling and predicting land use land cover spatiotemporal changes: A case study in chalus watershed, Iran. *IEEE J. Sel. Top. Appl. Earth Obs. Remote Sens.*, 15, 5496–5513, 2022.
10. Baek, W.K., Lee, M.J., Jung, H.S., Land Cover Classification From RGB and NIR Satellite Images Using Modified U-Net Model. *IEEE Access*, 2024.
11. Tesfaye, W., Elias, E., Warkineh, B., Tekalign, M., Abebe, G., Modeling of land use and land cover changes using google earth engine and machine learning approach: implications for landscape management. *Environ. Syst. Res.*, 13, 1, 1–16, 2024.
12. Singh, H.G. and Singh, K.P., Analysis of land use and land cover dynamics and drivers of urban expansion in and around Imphal city, India, using geospatial and random forest techniques. *GeoJournal*, 89, 4, 169, 2024.
13. Ebenezer, P.A. and Manohar, S., Land use/land cover change classification and prediction using deep learning approaches. *Signal Image Video Process.*, 18, 1, 223–232, 2024.
14. Raza, A., Syed, N.R., Fahmeed, R., Acharki, S., Aljohani, T.H., Hussain, S., Abdo, H.G., Investigation of changes in land use/land cover using principal component analysis and supervised classification from operational land imager satellite data: a case study of under developed regions, Pakistan. *Discover Sustainability*, 5, 1, 73, 2024.
15. Filho, W.L.F.C., de Oliveira Júnior, J.F., de Barros Santiago, D., Abdo, H.G., Almohamad, H., Al Dughairi, A.A., da Silva Junior, C.A., The assessment of climatic, environmental, and socioeconomic aspects of the Brazilian Cerrado, 2023.
16. Ganjirad, M. and Bagheri, H., Google Earth Engine-based mapping of land use and land cover for weather forecast models using Landsat 8 imagery. *Ecol. Inf.*, 80, 102498, 2024.
17. Patel, A., Vyas, D., Chaudhari, N., Patel, R., Patel, K., Mehta, D., Novel approach for the LULC change detection using GIS & Google Earth Engine through spatiotemporal analysis to evaluate the urbanization growth of Ahmedabad city. *Results Eng.*, 21, 101788, 2024.

18. Masolele, R.N., Marcos, D., De Sy, V., Abu, I.O., Verbesselt, J., Reiche, J., Herold, M., Mapping the diversity of land uses following deforestation across Africa. *Sci. Rep.*, 14, 1, 1681, 2024.
19. Dey, R., Sharma, S.B., Thakkar, M.G., Maximising ecological value and assessing land suitability for sustainable grassland management in Asia's largest tropical grassland, Western India. *Sci. Rep.*, 14, 1, 13658, 2024.
20. Agudelo-Hz, W.J., Castillo-Barrera, N.C., Uriel, M.G., Scenarios of land use and land cover change in the Colombian Amazon to evaluate alternative post-conflict pathways. *Sci. Rep.*, 13, 1, 2152, 2023.
21. Manna, T. and Anitha, A., Deep Ensemble-Based Approach Using Randomized Low-Rank Approximation for Sustainable Groundwater Level Prediction. *Appl. Sci.*, 13, 5, 3210, 2023, https://doi.org/10.3390/app13053210.
22. Manna, T. and Anitha, A., Precipitation prediction by integrating rough set on fuzzy approximation space with deep learning techniques. *Appl. Soft Comput.*, 139, 110253, 2023, Doi: https://doi.org/10.1016/j.asoc.2023.110253.
23. Nandhini, N. and Anitha, A., Seasonal-Wise Occupational Accident Analysis Using Deep Learning Paradigms, in: *Intelligent Systems. ICMIB 2023*, Lecture Notes in Networks and Systems, vol. 728, S.K. Udgata, S. Sethi, X.Z. Gao (Eds.), Springer, Singapore, 2024, https://doi.org/10.1007/978-981-99-3932-9_17.
24. Manna, T. and Anitha, A., Forecasting Air Quality Index based on Stacked LSTM, in: *2022 IEEE 7th International Conference on Recent Advances and Innovations in Engineering (ICRAIE)*, 2022, December, vol. 7, IEEE, pp. 326–330, 10.1109/ICRAIE56454.2022.10054260.

15

AI for Biodiversity and Ecosystem Conservation

Hina Hashmi[1]*, Aman Kumar[2] and Danish Raza Rizvi[2]

[1]*College of Computing Sciences & IT, Teerthankar Mahaveer University, Moradabad, UP, India*
[2]*Dept. of Computer Engineering, Jamia Millia Islamia, New Delhi, India*

Abstract

Conservation of biodiversity and environmental sustainability are essential in ensuring ecological balance and reducing the impact of climate change. Artificial Intelligence (AI) is a groundbreaking tool for wildlife monitoring, anti-poaching, conservation, marine management, and climate adaptation. In this chapter, the chapter discusses incorporating AI in the conservation process by emphasizing the application of computer vision, remote sensing, and deep Species identification learning, restoration of habitats, and pollution monitoring. Antipoaching efforts and safeguarding of sea biodiversity have been enhanced immensely with AI predictive analysis and autonomous monitoring systems. Concerns such as data bias, ethics, and collaboration with native conservation activities still exist. Future AI technologies, their potential uses, and ethical frameworks for implementing AI-driven conservation in accordance with global sustainability aspirations are also mentioned in this chapter.

Keywords: Artificial Intelligence, biodiversity conservation, wildlife monitoring, remote sensing, anti-poaching, deep learning, marine conservation, habitat restoration

**Corresponding author*: hinahashmi170@gmail.com

Umesh Kumar Lilhore, Sarita Simaiya, Surjeet Dalal and Martin Margala (eds.) Artificial Intelligence and Biodiversity, (261–290) © 2026 Scrivener Publishing LLC

15.1 Introduction

Biodiversity—the full spectrum of life on Earth—is the foundation for healthy ecosystems, supporting everything from food security to climate stability. Habitat destruction, climate change, pollution, and wildlife trade, however, threaten natural equilibrium and drive numerous species to the edge of extinction. Conventional conservation efforts, while precious, often cannot match the speed of environmental loss and sheer number of threats to our planet. Biodiversity is the foundation of a thriving world, sustaining life-giving ecosystems *via* climate regulation, keeping water cycles stable, and guaranteeing food security. But human activities have caused a cataclysmic decline in biodiversity. The UN Biodiversity Report (2020) [11] stated that almost 1 million species are threatened by extinction because of habitat loss, climate change, and pollution. World Wildlife Fund's Living Planet Report (2022) [23] supports again that wildlife population has lost 69% of its numbers since 1970, again emphasizing the need for conservation to safeguard them in an emergency way.

Artificial Intelligence (AI) is transforming biodiversity conservation with the onset of innovative, data-centric methods to monitor, analyze, and secure ecosystems. Leveraging the might of machine learning, computer vision, deep learning, and remote sensing, AI allows real-time monitoring of species, habitat predictive modeling, and autonomous systems for the detection of illicit activities such as poaching and deforestation. These advances not only enhance the effectiveness and precision of conservation activity but also offer scalable methods for the monitoring of extensive and remote areas that were formerly hard to research.

From AI-tuned drones counting wildlife populations to smart sensors identifying illegal logging through sound detection, the conservation applications of AI are closing significant research gaps in observation and enforcement. AI-augmented satellite image interpretation identifies deforestation patterns, and deep learning models forecast the migration of species between climates. In ocean conservation, AI helps to monitor ocean pollution, track coral reef health, and optimize sustainable fishing. Yet, the use of AI in biodiversity conservation also faces challenges like data limitation, algorithmic bias, ethical issues, and interdisciplinary cooperation. To unlock the full potential of AI, conservationists, technologists, and policymakers need to come together to create transparent, responsible, and inclusive solutions that are consistent with ecological and ethical principles.

With AI repeatedly revolutionizing the conservation of biodiversity; it is important to explore its many uses and contribution towards environmental sustainability. This chapter illustrates how AI is revolutionizing wildlife monitoring, conservation of habitats, and ocean conservation. This chapter also illustrates how AI forecasts the impact of climate change on biodiversity, solves issues in the use of ethical AI, and prepares the ground for the future of conservation. With AI released to its full potential, we are that much closer to having an efficient, scalable, and proactive method of safeguarding our planet's precious ecosystems.

15.1.1 Importance of Biodiversity and Ecosystem Conservation

Biodiversity is life diversity on this earth, made up of animals, plants, fungi, and microbes, and is the basis for a stable and sustainable system. It maintains ecological stability, human well-being, and sustainable resource use. Human existence has brought devastation in the ways of deforestation, industrial processes, and pollution of the environment, dramatically reducing biodiversity. Conservation of ecosystems and biodiversity is a critical environmental issue but also a necessity for world sustainability, food security, and climatic control.

A. Ecosystem Stability and Resilience

Biodiversity enhances ecosystems to help them withstand environmental shocks and disturbances. Diverse ecosystems are more resilient to climatic fluctuations, disease, and natural disasters. For instance:

- **Forests and Wetlands** act as natural buffers against floods and storms by absorbing excess rainwater.
- **Coral Reefs and Mangroves** protect coastal areas from tsunamis and hurricanes by reducing wave energy.
- **Grasslands and Soil Microorganisms** improve soil fertility, preventing desertification.

When biodiversity declines, ecosystems lose their ability to recover from extreme conditions, making them vulnerable to collapse. The Amazon rainforest, which is commonly known as the "lungs of the Earth," is losing forest cover at a very high rate, declining its capacity to control carbon and ensure climatic stability.

B. Biodiversity's Role in Food Security and Agriculture

Biodiversity is necessary for world food production since it maintains crops, pollinates, protects against pests, and maintains soil health.

- Pollinators like bees, butterflies, and birds account for 75% of world crop production (FAO, 2021) [24]. Loss of pollinators jeopardizes food supply chains, lowering yields of fruits, vegetables, and nuts.
- Crop and animal genetic diversity enables the creation of disease, drought, and pest-resistant varieties. For example, wild rice relatives have been used to develop drought-resistant rice varieties to provide food security in water-scarce areas.
- Soil biodiversity, including bacteria, fungi, and earthworms, plays a crucial role in nutrient recycling, improving soil fertility, and enhancing plant growth.

With growing global populations and mounting climate change pressures, conserving biodiversity is needed to maintain agricultural productivity and avoid food crises.

C. Climate Regulation and Carbon Sequestration

Ecosystems such as forests, wetlands, and oceans act as carbon sinks, absorbing large amounts of carbon dioxide from the atmosphere and mitigating climate change.

- Forests store nearly 80% of the world's terrestrial carbon. Deforestation contributes to approximately 15% of global CO_2 emissions (IPCC, 2021) [12].
- Peatlands, which occupy just 3% of the planet's surface, contain double the amount of carbon stored in all of the world's forests. Yet, people drain peatlands for farming, which releases trapped carbon, hastening climate change.
- Oceans capture approximately 30% of human-generated CO_2 emissions, minimizing global warming impacts. Coral reefs and phytoplankton contribute significantly to maintaining marine diversity while controlling atmospheric carbon.

Protecting these ecosystems is essential in controlling greenhouse gas emissions and maintaining climate balance.

15.1.2 Role of AI in Environmental Sustainability

Artificial Intelligence (AI) is having a groundbreaking impact on sustainability efforts by raising efficiency, accuracy, and scale in environmental causes. From mitigating climate change to preserving biodiversity, AI-based solutions provide real-time monitoring, predictive analytics, and resource automation, significantly enhancing environmental outcomes. With the help of machine learning (ML), deep learning, and big data analytics, AI is enabling revolutionary approaches in deforestation prevention, pollution control, and energy conservation.

AI makes a valuable contribution to climate change mitigation through optimizing energy consumption, minimizing greenhouse gas emissions, and enhancing climate modelling. AI-based smart grids maximize energy distribution, minimizing waste and maximizing efficiency. For example, Google's DeepMind AI minimized energy usage in its data centres by 40% using predictive cooling models. AI also enhances climate modelling by analysing vast datasets from satellites and weather stations to predict extreme weather events, helping governments and organizations implement proactive disaster response strategies. Biodiversity loss is one of the biggest threats to ecological balance, but AI-driven innovations are helping conservationists monitor species, track illegal activities, and protect ecosystems more effectively.

- **Wildlife Monitoring and Protection:**
  - AI analyses images from **camera traps and drones** to track endangered species and detect poaching activities.
  - **Google's Wildlife Insights platform** processes millions of camera-trap images, automating species identification.
  - AI-based **bioacoustics monitoring** detects sounds of endangered species and alerts conservationists to illegal activities.
- **Deforestation and Habitat Protection:**
  - AI-powered **satellite imagery analysis** helps detect illegal logging and habitat destruction.
  - **Rainforest Connection (RFCx)** uses AI to analyze real-time sound data, detecting chainsaw activity and alerting authorities.
  - Machine learning models predict **forest fire risks**, helping prevent large-scale environmental disasters.

Agriculture and water management are crucial for environmental sustainability, and AI enhances efficiency while minimizing environmental damage.

- **Precision Agriculture:**
  - AI-driven **smart irrigation systems** optimize water usage by analyzing soil moisture levels.
  - **John Deere's AI-powered tractors** optimize fertilizer application, reducing chemical runoff.
  - AI-enabled **drones monitor crop health**, detecting pests and nutrient deficiencies.
- **Water Resource Management:**
  - AI-based **leak detection systems** in pipelines reduce water wastage.
  - AI-driven **desalination plants** optimize energy consumption, making water purification more efficient.
  - **IBM's AI-powered flood prediction system** forecasts flood and enables better disaster preparedness.

AI plays a crucial role in waste management by improving sorting efficiency, recycling processes, and pollution monitoring.

- **AI-Powered Waste Sorting:**
  - AI-driven **robotic arms** in recycling plants separate materials like plastic, paper, and metal.
  - Machine learning algorithms classify waste for optimized recycling and landfill management.
- **Pollution Monitoring and Reduction:**
  - AI analyses air and water quality data to detect pollution sources.
  - **China's AI-powered air quality monitoring system** predicts pollution levels and suggests interventions.
  - AI models optimize urban planning to reduce pollution hotspots in cities.

AI significantly enhances the efficiency and adoption of renewable energy sources, making them more reliable and cost-effective.

- AI predicts **solar radiation and wind patterns**, maximizing renewable energy production.

- AI-driven **smart inverters** regulate energy flow from solar panels to the grid, reducing energy losses.
- **Google's AI-powered wind forecasting system** improved wind energy output by **20%**, demonstrating AI's impact on green energy.

AI's predictive capabilities enhance disaster management by enabling early warnings and efficient response strategies.

- **Early Warning Systems:**
  - AI-powered **earthquake and flood prediction models** analyse seismic and atmospheric data.
  - **NASA's AI-driven satellite systems** monitor climate changes and predict disasters.
  - AI detects wildfire risks by analysing satellite and infrared imagery.
- **Post-Disaster Recovery:**
  - AI-powered **drones assess damage** and identify survivors in disaster-hit areas.
  - AI-driven logistics optimize relief supply distribution, ensuring timely assistance.
  - AI chatbots provide emergency updates and safety information during disasters.

15.1.3 Challenges in Traditional Conservation Methods and How AI Addresses Them

Conserving biodiversity and ecosystems is a critical yet complex task, often hindered by various challenges in traditional conservation methods. These are manual and labor-intensive monitoring, low precision, high expenses, poor enforcement of environmental crime, and the strongly rising effect of climate change. Conventional methods are mostly dependent on human observation, ground surveys, and manual data collection, which are typically slow, prone to errors, and limited to particular areas. Conservationists are finding it difficult to monitor rare species, monitor such criminal activities as deforestation and poaching, and forecast ecological alteration caused by loss of habitats and climate change. Besides that, the exorbitant costs involved in field studies, equipment, and human labor are making conservation efforts inaccessible for most places, particularly in developing countries where there is limited capital.

Another major concern is the inefficiency of law enforcement in safeguarding wildlife and ecosystems. Poaching, wildlife trade, and illegal logging are profitable due to the lack of support for real-time alerts by traditional monitoring systems. Extensive forest cover is not monitored, and illegal operations go undetected. In addition, climate change accelerates the rate of loss of biodiversity, and it becomes challenging for conservationists to adapt in time. Traditional conservation models are challenged in interpreting big data sets and predicting species migration, habitat destruction, or environmental changes, leading to slow reaction times. AI addresses such challenges with automation of processes, greater accuracy in data, and quicker response systems. AI satellite image analysis can identify deforestation and habitat destruction in real-time, allowing authorities to respond before permanent damage is done. Drones equipped with AI provide aerial surveillance of far-off forests and wildlife habitats at significantly lower deployment costs of large field crews while also improving the efficiency of monitoring. Camera traps with AI-sensing species detection allow conservationists to automatically sort vast amounts of images without humans, improving the speed and accuracy of wildlife monitoring.

Besides surveillance, AI enhances biodiversity protection through big data analytics and predictive simulation. Through integrating satellite, sensor, and climate model data, AI is able to predict shifts in ecosystems and identify impending threats before they escalate into significant problems. For example, bioacoustics AI systems decode the calls of animals to monitor species activity, alerting researchers to dwindling numbers or illegal poaching. Machine learning programs sift through vast databases to identify patterns in the migration of species, enabling researchers to use preventive conservation measures.

AI enhances the cost savings and scalability of conservation. Cloud-based AI means that scientists operating in far-flung areas can access global environmental information, make decisions and collaborate on it without requiring much resources. Automated monitoring reduces the labor required for fieldwork, saving money while increasing efficiency. Anti-poaching networks based on AI use predictive modeling in order to detect poacher movement patterns, thus enabling officials to strike first. In the war against climate change, conservationists use AI in order to gain a better understanding and to react to environmental changes. Climate models based on AI analyze long-term temperature, precipitation, and ecosystem health trends, which allows scientists to anticipate and counteract global warming's effects.

AI is also used to monitor coral reefs, detecting early bleaching warning signs and providing recommendations for recovery. AI also aids in urban development and land use optimization, assisting policymakers in the design of cities and farming techniques that minimize habitat loss. While AI offers robust solutions, problems need to be solved, such as the heavy energy consumption of AI models, potential bias within the training datasets, and ethics of automation within decision-making processes. However, with continued improvement and ethical deployment, AI is capable of enhancing conservation efforts dramatically, making them more efficient, scalable, and proactive. With the help of integrating AI into environmental sustainability projects, we can demystify conservation barriers and create a more effective and data-driven plan for saving biodiversity and ecosystems.

15.2 AI for Wildlife Monitoring and Anti-Poaching Efforts

Wildlife conservation has traditionally relied on labor-intensive, time-consuming methods such as manual monitoring, ranger patrols, and observational studies. AI has revolutionized the way by automating species detection, real-time tracking, and predictive analytics for anti-poaching patrols. AI-powered tools like computer vision, deep learning, bioacoustics, and predictive analytics significantly enhance conservation activities by providing precise, scalable, and real-time tracking of wildlife and habitats. These technologies help conservationists track the populations of animals, discourage poaching, and guard habitats in ways that had not been available through traditional approaches.

15.2.1 Computer Vision for Species Identification

Artificial intelligence–driven computer vision methods have transformed wildlife monitoring through automated species identification and tracking by leveraging deep learning models from large datasets. AI is capable of handling enormous amounts of visual information from camera traps, drones, and satellites, enabling conservationists to analyze biodiversity, observe animal behavior, and monitor illegal activities.

A. Image Recognition Models for Identifying Endangered Species
Conventional wildlife identification processes involve a lot of human labor, and thus are inefficient in large numbers. AI-powered image recognition

models use deep learning methods like Convolutional Neural Networks (CNNs) and Transfer Learning to identify and monitor endangered species automatically.

- ***Example:*** Microsoft's AI for Earth initiative processes over 5 million camera trap images within 48 hours, a task that would take researchers months to complete.
- ***Technical Insight:*** CNN architectures like YOLO (You Only Look Once), Faster R-CNN, and ResNet provide species identification accuracy exceeding 90%, even in complex environments.
- ***Impact:*** AI reduces manual effort by 90%, accelerates data analysis, and improves species monitoring efficiency.

B. Use of Drones and Satellite Imagery for Wildlife Tracking

Drones and satellite imaging powered by AI are transforming large-scale wildlife tracking and habitat monitoring. AI-enhanced drones with thermal imaging and object detection algorithms can track animals in dense forests and remote regions, while satellite imagery enables long-term ecological studies.

- ***Example***: The Air Shepherd project uses AI-powered drones to detect poachers in real time, reducing poaching incidents by 50% in high-risk zones.
- ***Technical Insight***: AI-based semantic segmentation models analyze satellite images, detecting deforestation and illegal encroachments with over 85% accuracy.
- ***Impact***: Drones and satellites cover vast areas efficiently, reducing human dependency and improving conservation outcomes.

15.2.2 Acoustic Monitoring with AI

AI-based bioacoustics monitoring supports wildlife conservation by analyzing environmental soundscapes to monitor animal populations and identify illegal activities such as poaching and deforestation. Machine learning models based on acoustic data are able to recognize different animal calls, environmental sounds, and unnatural sounds such as gunshots or chainsaws.

A. Deep Learning for Analysing Animal Vocalizations and Identifying Species

AI-based sound recognition identifies chainsaws, gunfire, and cars being used for illicit activities, enabling conservationists to intervene before serious harm is done.

- ***Sample:*** AI-fitted acoustic sensors installed in African reserves pick up gunshots from poachers with 99% accuracy, notifying rangers immediately.
- ***Technical Insight:*** Mel-Frequency Cepstral Coefficients (MFCCs) and Autoencoders are used to classify natural vs. human-made sounds in conservation areas.
- ***Influence:*** AI bioacoustics boost species detection, providing real-time data on animal populations and activity.

B. Real-Time Monitoring of Illegal Logging and Hunting Through Sound Recognition

AI-powered sound recognition detects chainsaws, gunshots, and vehicles used in illegal activities, allowing conservationists to act before significant damage occurs.

- ***Example***: AI-enabled acoustic sensors deployed in African reserves detect gunshots from poachers with 99% accuracy, alerting rangers instantly.
- ***Technical Insight:*** Mel-Frequency Cepstral Coefficients (MFCCs) and Autoencoders are used to classify natural vs. human-made sounds in conservation areas.
- ***Impact***: AI-driven real-time acoustic monitoring reduces response time to illegal activities, protecting endangered species more effectively.

15.2.3 AI for Anti-Poaching Strategies

Poaching continues to be one of the largest threats to biodiversity. AI boosts anti-poaching activities by forecasting poaching hotspots, facilitating automated surveillance, and optimizing ranger patrol effectiveness.

A. Predictive Analytics for Identifying Poaching Hotspots

Predictive analytics based on AI enable conservationists to predict where poaching activities are most likely to take place. Machine learning algorithms process past data, environmental factors, and ranger patrol activity reports to predict high-risk locations.

- ***Example:*** The Harvard-developed PAWS (Protection Assistant for Wildlife Security) system uses game theory and reinforcement learning to forecast poaching threats and minimize ranger patrol routes.
- ***Technical Insight*:** AI models use **Random Forest, Support Vector Machines (SVM), and Bayesian Inference** to generate real-time risk maps.
- ***Impact*:** PAWS-guided patrols increase poaching detection rates by **300%** compared to traditional patrols.

B. AI-Driven Surveillance Systems and Automated Alerts
AI-based surveillance systems utilize real-time image processing and IoT sensors to identify poaching activities. Such systems combine thermal cameras, motion sensors, and machine learning algorithms to keep a round-the-clock watch on protected areas.

- ***Example*:** Smart Parks deploys AI-enabled **thermal imaging cameras** and **edge AI computing** to detect and track poachers.
- ***Technical Insight*:** AI uses **object detection algorithms like Faster R-CNN and YOLO** to identify intruders with a **98% accuracy rate** under low-light conditions.
- ***Impact*:** AI-based surveillance systems improve law enforcement response times and significantly reduce poaching rates.

15.3 Deep Learning for Habitat Protection and Restoration

With human activities still transforming the earth, natural habitat preservation and restoration have never been more important. Deforestation, land degradation, and loss of ecosystems endanger biodiversity and fuel climate change. Conventional monitoring and conservation strategies usually fail because of the enormity of the areas affected and the intricacy of environmental processes. Artificial intelligence systems using deep learning provide a paradigm-shifting approach that employs huge data from sensors, drones, and satellites to detect ecological shifts, predict ecosystem danger, and aid in restoration. Such AI techniques deliver enhanced precision, rapid processing, and foresighted decision-making potential.

15.3.1 Remote Sensing for Deforestation and Land Use Changes

Deforestation remains one of the most urgent environmental concerns. AI-enabled remote sensing has transformed deforestation tracking, allowing governments and conservation groups to identify illegal forest clearing and land-use changes with high precision. Traditional vs. AI-based deforestation tracking is contrasted in the Table 15.1 below.

One of the most effective AI-driven deforestation tracking systems is Global Forest Watch, which integrates Google AI to analyse satellite images in real-time, detecting tree cover loss across continents. Further, AI models can detect illegal land encroachment, sometimes before the authorities are even aware. Machine learning models trained on historical land-use information can forecast zones at high risk of illegal deforestation or urbanization, and proactive measures can be taken accordingly.

15.3.2 Ecosystem Health Monitoring with AI

In addition to deforestation, upholding general ecosystem health is necessary for the preservation of biodiversity. AI facilitates vegetation analysis automation, soil health examination, and projections of climate change effects.

Table 15.1 Comparison of traditional vs. AI-based deforestation monitoring methods [22].

Aspect	Traditional methods	AI-based methods
Speed	Manual analysis can take months	AI processes thousands of images in hours
Accuracy	Subject to human errors, limited coverage	CNNs achieve up to 95% accuracy in detection
Scalability	Limited to specific regions	Global monitoring through satellite networks
Cost Efficiency	Requires extensive human labour	Automated AI models reduce long-term costs

One of them is based on the Normalized Difference Vegetation Index (NDVI), which plant health is measured with by AI models. NDVI-based monitoring can predict forest dieback, desertification, and agricultural stress months in advance.

Case Study: AI in Wetland Monitoring

Wetlands are among the most sensitive ecosystems. AI-based models analyse multispectral drone imagery to track wetland degradation. A study by the European Space Agency (ESA) used Random Forest algorithms to assess wetland loss, achieving 88% predictive accuracy in identifying degrading regions.

The ability of AI to predict ecosystem degradation is a game-changer. By processing climate data, pollution levels, and species population dynamics, machine learning models can provide insights that guide policymakers and conservationists in taking early preventive measures rather than reacting after damage has occurred.

15.3.3 Restoration Planning with AI

Restoring damaged ecosystems is complex and requires strategic planning. AI-driven decision-making systems help determine where, when, and how to restore habitats effectively.

Key contributions of AI in restoration planning include:

- **Automated reforestation planning:** AI evaluates soil quality, climate conditions, and biodiversity requirements to recommend the most suitable tree species for reforestation.
- **Optimization of planting locations:** Machine learning models suggest where tree planting would have the highest ecological impact, maximizing carbon sequestration and biodiversity restoration.

Predicting success rates: AI simulations estimate the likelihood of survival for different plant species in a given environment, reducing resource wastage.

For example, Microsoft's AI for Earth initiative developed a machine learning model that suggests the most resilient tree species for degraded lands, increasing survival rates by 30% compared to traditional restoration planning.

AI is also applied in marine ecosystem restoration, where models analyse coral reef health and recommend areas for coral transplantation. The Australian Great Barrier Reef Restoration Project uses AI to identify resilient coral species and predict reef recovery timelines.

The application of deep learning to conservation is transforming habitat protection and restoration. Remote sensing using AI facilitates real-time tracking of environmental change, health assessment of ecosystems gives early warnings of degradation, and machine learning models maximize reforestation and recovery efforts. While challenges exist—high compute costs and lack of data in developing areas among them—increases in edge AI and cloud-based conservation software are opening the door to broader access to these technologies. AI will become even more integral to global conservation policy in the next few years, making restoration scientifically driven, scalable, and effective.

15.4 AI for Marine Conservation and Ocean Monitoring

Oceans are essential in controlling Earth's climate, hosting biodiversity, and supporting livelihoods. Oceans are hugely threatened by overfishing, pollution, habitat loss, and climate change-driven coral bleaching. The magnitude of oceans makes it uneconomical and impractical through manual monitoring. Artificial Intelligence is transforming marine conservation because it has automated the identification of species, monitoring of pollution, and fisheries management.

Artificial intelligence-powered deep learning, computer vision, and remote sensing technologies allow researchers to analyze vast amounts of oceanic data at a pace never before possible and with accuracy never previously achieved. These AI-based solutions are critical for the protection of marine life as well as ensuring sustainable use of ocean resources.

15.4.1 Automated Marine Life Detection

Monitoring of marine biodiversity is crucial to understanding shifts in ecosystems and preventing species decline. AI-enabled systems are increasingly employed to monitor fish stocks and the health of coral reefs. Autonomous underwater vehicles equipped with AI-based cameras can track fish populations, migration routes, and use of habitats. These systems process underwater footage using Convolutional Neural Networks (CNNs) to automatically classify fish species and estimate population densities. A comparison between traditional and AI-based marine life detection methods is presented below in Table 15.2.

Coral reefs support 25% of all marine species, but they are rapidly degrading due to ocean warming and acidification. AI models analyse high-resolution satellite and drone imagery to detect bleaching, disease outbreaks, and structural damage. Figure 15.1 is showing the AI-Based Coral Health Assessment.

Table 15.2 Comparative analysis of traditional and AI-based methods [5].

Aspect	Traditional methods	AI-based methods
Detection Speed	Requires divers; slow and time-consuming	Real-time analysis *via* automated cameras
Accuracy	Subject to human error	CNNs achieve >90% accuracy in species identification
Scalability	Limited to small areas	Large-scale monitoring across entire marine regions
Cost Efficiency	Expensive human-led surveys	AI reduces long-term monitoring costs

Figure 15.1 AI-based coral health assessment (an AI-analysed satellite image highlighting healthy vs. degraded coral reefs).

- The Allen Coral Atlas, an AI-powered mapping project, has achieved 89% accuracy in detecting coral reef health, allowing conservationists to take timely action.
- Deep learning algorithms can identify early-stage coral bleaching, enabling proactive restoration efforts.

15.4.2 Predicting and Preventing Ocean Pollution

Marine pollution—especially from oil spills, plastic waste, and microplastics—poses a severe risk to ocean ecosystems. AI enhances pollution detection, enabling faster and more effective cleanup efforts.

AI models analyse satellite imagery and drone footage to detect oil spills in real time.

- The European Space Agency's Sentinel-1 satellite, combined with AI, detects oil slicks with 95% accuracy, significantly reducing response time.
- AI-driven image recognition models analyse ocean surface images to identify floating plastic debris hotspots, guiding cleanup efforts.

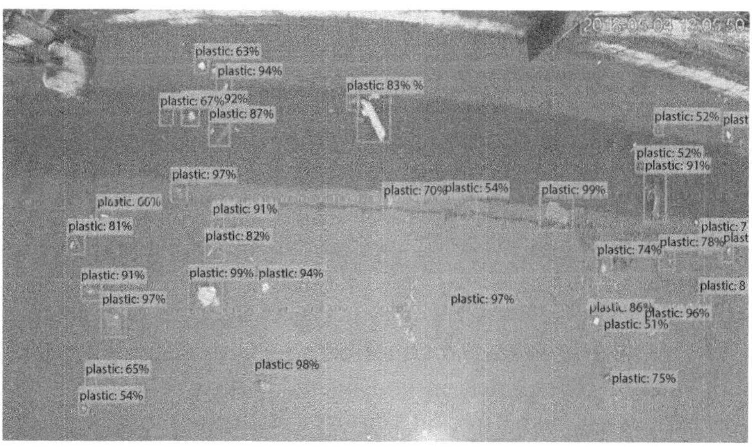

Figure 15.2 AI detecting plastic waste in oceans (an AI model analysing ocean images to map plastic accumulation zones).

Smart Monitoring Systems for Tracking Microplastic Contamination
Microplastics—particles smaller than 5 mm—are widespread in marine ecosystems. AI-based hyperspectral imaging allows scientists to detect and quantify microplastics in seawater.

- Plymouth Marine Laboratory's AI model has achieved over 90% accuracy in identifying microplastic concentrations in ocean samples (Figure 15.2).
- AI-driven robotic systems autonomously collect and analyse water samples, providing real-time pollution reports.

15.4.3 AI for Sustainable Fisheries Management

Overfishing is a major threat to global fish stocks, with more than 34% of fisheries operating beyond sustainable levels (FAO, 2022). AI plays a vital role in monitoring and optimizing fishing practices.

Predicting Fish Stock Depletion Using AI
AI models analyse historical fishing data, ocean temperatures, and fish migration patterns to predict population declines. This allows governments to enforce seasonal fishing bans and prevent stock collapse.

- **Example:** Oceana's AI-powered fisheries management system has reduced illegal fishing activities by 20% in monitored regions.

AI-Driven Optimization of Fishing Practices to Prevent Overfishing
Smart sensors and AI algorithms enable fisheries to minimize bycatch, optimize harvest rates, and ensure responsible fishing practices. Table 15.3 is showing the key benefits of AI applications for fishing practices to prevent overfishing.

- Japan's AI-powered smart fishing nets have reduced bycatch rates by 45%, protecting endangered species.
- AI-driven vessel tracking ensures real-time monitoring of fishing activities, preventing illegal and unregulated fishing.

AI is revolutionizing marine conservation by improving species tracking, pollution detection, and fisheries management. AI-powered underwater

Table 15.3 Impact of AI in fisheries management [23].

AI application	Key benefits
Fish stock prediction	Helps prevent overfishing by forecasting depletion trends
Smart fishing nets	Reduces bycatch rates, protecting endangered species
Vessel monitoring	Ensures compliance with sustainable fishing regulations

cameras and deep learning algorithms enhance biodiversity monitoring, while AI-fueled pollution detection systems allow for quicker cleanup operations. Further, predictive AI models assist in enforcing sustainable fishing practices, promoting the long-term health of world fish stocks.

In spite of challenges—namely, high costs of computation and low AI uptake in developing countries—developments in cloud-based AI platforms and edge computing are bringing these technologies within reach. In the future, AI will remain at the center of maintaining ocean health and sustaining marine ecosystems.

15.5 AI in Climate Change and Biodiversity Interactions

Climate change is one of the key drivers of biodiversity loss, disturbing ecosystems and compelling species to migrate in response to finding optimal habitats. Increases in global temperature, changes in precipitation patterns, and extreme climatic events are profoundly impacting vegetation and animals alike. Knowledge on these interactions will be essential to the formulation of effective conservation tactics.

Artificial intelligence models are emerging as vital tools in researching and addressing the impact of climate change on biodiversity. Through machine learning, remote sensing, and predictive analytics, AI assists scientists in tracking species migration, evaluating climate-driven loss of biodiversity, and analysing the long-term effects of global warming on ecosystems.

15.5.1 Predicting Species Migration Patterns Due to Climate Change

With climate conditions changing, numerous species are moving to greater altitudes, greater depths, or towards the poles. Following these movements is difficult manually because of the scope and complicacy of the environmental changes. AI models, especially deep learning and reinforcement learning, assist in predicting species migration trends by analysing:

- Climate variables (temperature, precipitation, humidity)
- Geospatial data from satellite imagery
- Historical migration trends of species

For example, the MaxEnt (Maximum Entropy) Model, an AI-driven ecological niche modelling approach, has accurately predicted the potential range shifts of polar bears in the Arctic, where melting ice is shrinking their habitat.

Case Study: A study using AI-based modelling projected that nearly 50% of bird species in North America will alter their migratory routes by 2050 due to rising temperatures and habitat loss.

15.5.2 AI Models for Tracking Climate-Induced Biodiversity Loss

The rapid pace of climate change has led to species extinction, habitat fragmentation, and declining ecosystem resilience. Table 15.4 presents a comparative summary of traditional biodiversity monitoring techniques and AI-driven approaches, emphasizing differences in data acquisition, processing speed, and ecological insight gained through automation. AI is helping conservationists track biodiversity loss by integrating data from:

- Autonomous sensors that record wildlife activities
- Satellite imagery that maps deforestation and habitat degradation
- Citizen science platforms where volunteers contribute species observations

Example:

- The IUCN Red List AI Initiative uses deep learning models to analyse changes in species populations and predict extinction risks.

Table 15.4 AI vs. traditional methods in tracking biodiversity loss [13].

Aspect	Traditional methods	AI-based methods
Data Collection	Manual field surveys, expensive and time-consuming	Real-time automated data from sensors & satellites
Accuracy	Limited due to human error	High accuracy using deep learning models
Scalability	Localized studies	Global-scale monitoring using AI
Aspect	Traditional Methods	AI-Based Methods
Data Collection	Manual field surveys, expensive and time-consuming	Real-time automated data from sensors & satellites

- AI-powered LiDAR (Light Detection and Ranging) has been instrumental in detecting shifts in tropical rainforest biodiversity caused by climate change.

15.5.3 Machine Learning for Assessing the Impact of Global Warming on Ecosystems

Machine learning models analyse vast datasets to assess how rising temperatures, extreme weather, and altered ecosystems affect biodiversity. AI is particularly useful in:

- Mapping vulnerable ecosystems based on climate projections
- Detecting anomalies in vegetation growth using satellite imagery
- Predicting future biodiversity hotspots at risk due to climate change

Example:

- NASA's Climate Change AI Model has predicted that Amazon rainforest degradation could accelerate by 30% by 2050 due to increasing temperatures.
- AI-powered climate-resilient agriculture models help identify regions where crop biodiversity is most at risk, aiding policymakers in developing adaptive strategies.

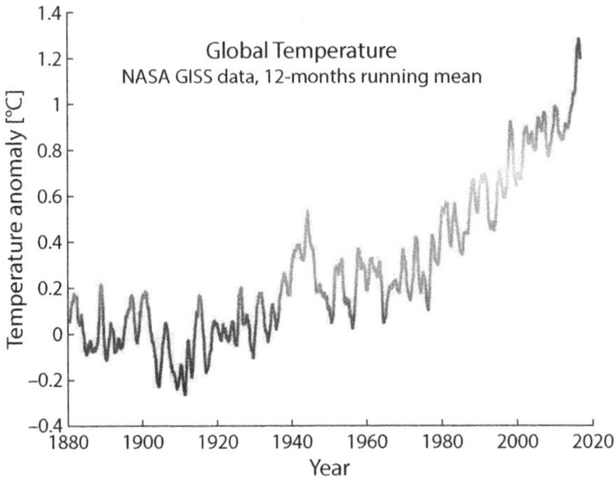

Figure 15.3 AI-predicted ecosystem shifts due to climate change. (A visualization of predicted biodiversity loss areas based on AI climate simulations.)

As Figure 15.3 is showing, AI plays a crucial role in understanding and mitigating the impact of climate change on biodiversity. From predicting species migration patterns to assessing biodiversity loss and ecosystem vulnerabilities, AI-driven models provide data-driven insights for conservation planning. However, challenges such as data biases, limited computational resources in developing nations, and the need for global cooperation remain.

Moving forward, integrating AI with IoT-based environmental monitoring systems and citizen science initiatives will enhance climate resilience strategies and ensure the protection of Earth's biodiversity-rich ecosystems.

15.6 Challenges and Ethical Considerations in AI for Conservation

The integration of AI in conservation has revolutionized wildlife monitoring, habitat protection, and climate resilience strategies. But its deployment is accompanied by serious challenges and ethical issues that need to be resolved to ensure AI solutions continue to be effective, unbiased, and ethically justifiable. Concerns such as data constraints, AI model biases, surveillance ethics, and conservation inclusivity require close scrutiny to avoid unforeseen consequences.

15.6.1 Data Limitations and Biases in AI-Based Conservation Models

AI models are highly dependent on the quality, diversity, and quantity of data they process. However, conservation datasets often suffer from several limitations:

- **Sparse and Incomplete Data:** Many species, especially those in remote or unexplored areas, lack sufficient recorded data. AI models trained on incomplete datasets may generate inaccurate predictions about species populations and habitat health.
- **Sampling Bias:** AI systems may be biased toward well-studied regions and species while neglecting lesser-known biodiversity hotspots. For example, conservation AI models often focus on charismatic megafauna (e.g., elephants, tigers) but overlook invertebrates and microorganisms that play crucial roles in ecosystems.
- **Data Imbalance:** In some cases, AI models are trained on excessive data from a few species while others are underrepresented, leading to false predictions and incorrect classifications.

Example: A study found that 80% of AI training datasets for biodiversity research were derived from North America and Europe, while critical regions like the Amazon, Congo Basin, and Southeast Asia remained underrepresented.

Addressing These Challenges

- Using transfer learning to adapt AI models trained on well-documented species to lesser known species.
- Expanding open-access biodiversity databases with contributions from local researchers and citizen scientists.
- Employing generative AI models to simulate synthetic but biologically realistic data for rare species.

15.6.2 Ethical Concerns in Wildlife Surveillance and Data Privacy

AI-driven conservation heavily relies on camera traps, drones, satellites, and IoT sensors to monitor wildlife movements. While these technologies provide valuable insights, they raise serious ethical concerns regarding data privacy, surveillance ethics, and potential misuse:

- **Risk of Over-Surveillance:** AI-powered monitoring systems can inadvertently track human activities in conservation areas, raising concerns about privacy violations for indigenous communities and local populations.
- **Misuse of Data:** If AI-based wildlife tracking data falls into the wrong hands (e.g., poachers or illegal traders), it can endanger endangered species rather than protect them.
- **Algorithmic Bias and Misidentification:** AI models might wrongly classify animals or fail to detect species accurately, leading to flawed conservation policies.

Example: A 2021 study reported that AI-powered facial recognition software, initially designed for wildlife tracking, inadvertently identified and stored data on human faces captured in conservation zones, raising significant privacy concerns.

- Implementing strong encryption and access control mechanisms for conservation data.
- Using privacy-preserving AI techniques, such as federated learning, to prevent unauthorized access to sensitive information.
- Developing AI models that comply with local and international ethical guidelines, ensuring AI does not inadvertently harm local populations.

15.6.3 Ensuring AI Solutions Align with indigenous and Local Conservation Efforts

Indigenous communities and local populations have been stewards of biodiversity for centuries, often possessing deep ecological knowledge that AI-driven conservation models may overlook. However, the rapid deployment of AI tools without considering local perspectives can lead to:

- **Displacement and Exclusion:** Some AI-based conservation projects have led to the displacement of indigenous communities from traditional lands under the guise of environmental protection.
- **Lack of Collaboration:** AI models are often developed in research labs with minimal input from local conservationists and indigenous knowledge holders.
- **Technological Dependence:** Over-reliance on AI may overshadow traditional conservation practices, leading to the erosion of time-tested methods.

Case Study: In the Amazon rainforest, conservation AI tools have been deployed to track deforestation and illegal mining activities. However, studies show that including indigenous knowledge in AI training datasets significantly improves the accuracy of predictions, as local communities can provide on-ground insights that satellites cannot detect.

Proposed Solutions

- Co-design AI models with local indigenous communities, and make their ecological knowledge a part of conservation algorithms.
- Set up community-based AI conservation initiatives that enable local people to employ AI technology while maintaining their conventional conservation methods.
- Embrace "AI for Good" guidelines that focus on ethical, inclusive, and culturally responsive AI development in conservation.

While AI has tremendous potential for augmenting conservation, mitigating climate change effects, and conserving biodiversity, it is necessary to address its challenges in a responsible manner. Biases in data, ethical issues in wildlife monitoring, and the requirement for inclusive conservation efforts need to be addressed through collaborative, transparent, and ethically robust AI frameworks.

The future of AI-assisted conservation should be one where there is harmony between technological progress and moral responsibility so that wildlife, ecosystems, and human populations coexist together in a well-organized, AI-assisted conservation framework.

15.7 Future Directions and Emerging Technologies

AI keeps advancing, providing revolutionary breakthroughs for conservation and environmental sustainability. Emerging AI-based conservation strategies will combine state-of-the-art technologies like quantum computing, sophisticated robotics, and decentralized AI networks, solving current problems while increasing efficiency, accuracy, and scalability. Table 15.5 outlines emerging AI technologies and their potential applications in biodiversity conservation, illustrating how innovations such as deep reinforcement learning and autonomous sensing could transform future ecological monitoring practices.

Emerging Technologies in AI for Conservation

- Quantum Computing for Environmental Modelling: Quantum computing can process enormous datasets exponentially quicker than traditional computing, allowing for more precise climate forecasts, ecosystem simulation, and biodiversity monitoring. Next-generation quantum-powered AI models may be able to model entire ecosystems in real time, forecasting the long-term impacts of deforestation, habitat destruction, and species extinction.
- Species Communication and AI-Powered Bioacoustics: Deep learning and NLP advances will enable AI to interpret animal communication, making species monitoring and behavioural analysis easier. Researchers are developing AI models that can interpret whale songs, elephant calls, and bird song, enabling conservationists to decode animal stress cues, mating behaviour, and migratory patterns.
- Swarm Robotics for Environmental Monitoring: Autonomous robotic swarms (underwater and aerial drones) will be pivotal in wildlife conservation by tracking distant ecosystems independent of humans. Swarm robotics can be applied to:
    - Tracking endangered species in inaccessible areas
    - Monitoring coral reef restoration efforts
    - Identifying illegal logging or mining activities using real-time data.

Example: The RobotFish project uses AI-powered robotic fish to detect water pollution levels, track marine life, and prevent illegal fishing activities.

Table 15.5 Emerging AI technologies enhancing biodiversity conservation and environmental sustainability [12].

Emerging AI technology	Potential conservation application
Quantum Computing	Climate change simulations and ecosystem modelling
Bioacoustics AI	Decoding animal communication for behavioural studies
Swarm Robotics	Large-scale, real-time environmental monitoring
Blockchain AI	Secure data storage and transparent conservation records

- Blockchain for Conservation Data Integrity: The application of blockchain technology in conservation will ensure transparent, tamper-proof data sharing. AI models trained on blockchain-verified datasets can provide more reliable insights, preventing data manipulation and ensuring ethical use of conservation information.

As these technologies advance, AI will not only enhance conservation efforts but also pave the way for a more sustainable and data-driven approach to protecting biodiversity and ecosystems.

15.8 Conclusion

Environmental sustainability applications of AI are transforming wildlife conservation, habitat preservation, and climate resilience efforts. From anti-poaching with AI to predictive analytics for species preservation, deep learning and machine learning models are enabling real-time data-driven decision-making.

While it holds enormous transformative power, AI-conservation is also marred by numerous challenges such as data biases, ethics, and compatibility with conventional conservation practices. However, future AI advancements such as quantum computing, blockchain, and swarm robotics will further enhance accuracy, transparency, and efficiency in environmental monitoring and biodiversity conservation.

In the future, conservationists, technologists, and policymakers need to collaborate to make sure that AI solutions align with ethical standards, local conservation efforts, and sustainability practices. With the responsible use of AI, we can have a future where nature and technology coexist in perfect harmony, and there is a thriving world for generations to come.

AI disclosure statement: The author acknowledges the use of AI-based tools for minor language editing or grammatical correction. However, all intellectual contributions, analyses, and conclusions presented in this chapter are entirely the author's own.

References

1. Russell, S. and Norvig, P., *Artificial Intelligence: A Modern Approach*, 4th ed., Pearson, 2020.
2. Goodfellow, I., Bengio, Y., Courville, A., *Deep Learning*, MIT Press, 2016.
3. Domingos, P., *The Master Algorithm: How the Quest for the Ultimate Learning Machine Will Remake Our World*, Basic Books, 2015.
4. Schmidhuber, J., Deep learning in neural networks: An overview. *Neural Networks*, 61, 85–117, 2015.
5. Wearn, O.R. and Glover-Kapfer, P., Camera-trapping for conservation: A guide to best practices. WWF Conservation Technology Series, 1, 1, 1–57, 2019.
6. Mac Aodha, O., Gibb, R., Barlow, K.E., *et al.*, Bat Detective—Deep learning tools for bat acoustic signal recognition. *PLoS Comput. Biol.*, 14, 3, e1005995, 2018.
7. Patel, S., Singh, R., Kumar, V., AI and satellite imagery for tracking illegal deforestation in the Amazon rainforest. *Remote Sens. Appl.: Soc. Environ.*, 21, 100479, 2021.
8. Boult, T.E., Kellenberger, B., Tuia, D., Using AI to combat poaching: Camera trap image recognition in wildlife reserves. *Proceedings of the IEEE Conference on Computer Vision and Pattern Recognition (CVPR)*, pp. 1–10, 2019.
9. Fergus, P., Chalmers, C., Matthews, N., Nixon, S., Burger, A., Hartley, O., Sutherland, C., Lambin, X., Longmore, S., Wich, S., Towards context-rich automated biodiversity assessments: Deriving AI-powered insights from camera trap data, arXiv preprint arXiv:2411.14219, 2024.
10. Yang, C.-H., Feuer, B., Jubery, Z., Deng, Z.K., Nakkab, A., Hasan, M.Z., Chiranjeevi, S., Marshall, K., Baishnab, N., Singh, A.K., Singh, A., Sarkar, S., Merchant, N., Hegde, C., Ganapathysubramanian, B., BioTrove: A large curated image dataset enabling AI for biodiversity, arXiv preprint arXiv:2406.17720, 2024.

11. Secretariat of the Convention on Biological Diversity. (2020). Global Biodiversity Outlook 5. Montreal: CBD. Retrieved from https://www.cbd.int/gbo5.
12. Intergovernmental Panel on Climate Change. Climate change 2021: The physical science basis. Contribution of Working Group I to the Sixth Assessment Report of the Intergovernmental Panel on Climate Change, V. Masson-Delmotte, P. Zhai, A. Pirani, S. L. Connors, C. Péan, S. Berger, N. Caud, Y. Chen, L. Goldfarb, M. I. Gomis, M. Huang, K. Leitzell, E. Lonnoy, J. B. R. Matthews, T. K. Maycock, T. Waterfield, O. Yelekçi, R. Yu & B. Zhou, (eds.), Cambridge University Press, 2021.
13. United Nations Environment Programme, How artificial intelligence is helping tackle environmental challenges, UNEP, 2022.
14. Topic, S., Harnessing AI to safeguard biodiversity: Five innovative approaches, University of Oxford, Saïd Business School, 2024.
15. The Associated Press. (2024, January 15). Live updates | Gaza death toll tops 24,000 as UN agencies ... Associated Press. Retrieved from https://apnews.com/article/israel-hamas-war-live-updates-01-15-2024-966c5a9375e7439dd3de5fc113a7e7d.
16. The Times, AI tool can track dolphins—and spot their regional accents. Nature Conservancy, 2024, December 10. AI and machine learning for conservation science. Nature Conservancy, 2023, https://www.nature.org/en-us/what-we-do/our-insights/perspectives/ai-and-machine-learning-for-conservation/.
17. United Nations Environment Programme, How artificial intelligence is helping tackle environmental challenges, UNEP, 2022.
18. GISTEMP Team. (2024). *GISS Surface Temperature Analysis (GISTEMP), version 4*. NASA Goddard Institute for Space Studies. Retrieved [date you accessed it] from https://data.giss.nasa.gov/gistemp/.
19. Chalmers, C., Fergus, P., Wich, S., Longmore, S.N., Davies Walsh, N., Oliver, L., Warrington, J., Quinlan, J., Appleby, K., AI-driven real-time monitoring of ground-nesting birds: A case study on curlew detection using YOLOv10, arXiv preprint arXiv:2411.15263, 2024.
20. Rainforest Connection. (n.d.). Our work: Using sound & AI to protect rainforests & monitor biodiversity. Retrieved [Month Day, Year], from https://rfcx.org/our_work.
21. Oswald, J.N. and Tyack, P.L., AI tool can track dolphins—and spot their regional accents. The Times, 2024, thetimes.co.uk.
22. Earth Species Project, Can AI help humans understand animals and reconnect with nature? A nonprofit research lab thinks so. Associated Press, 2024, apnews.com.

23. World Wildlife Fund. (2022). Living Planet Report 2022 – Building a nature-positive society (R.E.A. Almond, M. Grooten, D. Juffe Bignoli & T. Petersen, Eds.). WWF, Gland, Switzerland.
24. Food and Agriculture Organization of the United Nations. (2021). The State of Food and Agriculture 2021: Making agrifood systems more resilient to shocks and stresses (ISBN 978-92-5-134329-6). Rome: FAO.

16

Pneumonia Detection in Chest Based on Respiratory Variability Using Deep Learning

Ritu Aggarwal* **and Eshaan Aggarwal**

Department of Computer Science and Engineering, Maharishi Markandeshwar Engineering College (MM(DU), Mullana, India

Abstract

The automated detection and diagnosis of pneumonia represents a serious challenge in the medical imaging results. When the disease is detected through CT or X-ray images there are sometimes fewer signs of illness. Millions of people die due to pneumonia every year. The main goal and the important task are using deep neural networks and machine learning. Pneumonia is a life-threatening infectious disease that affects the human lungs. The common reason for spreading disease is bacteria which is called streptococcus pneumoniae.as globally the number of deaths in India caused by the due to this disease.to identify the disease by examining early signs through chest X-rays. It is a process that needs expert radio rapists for the implementation and evaluation. In the remote areas for automatic system in the disease detection. In this proposed work feature selection and feature extraction techniques to analyze the results for pretraining the models by using different classifiers and the models. This proposed work has taken the 5896 samples in the form of images which are available on the UCI machine learning repository for many medical challenges regarding imaging. The proposed model is evaluated based on parameters such precision, recall, F1-score, and accuracy. The proposed model obtained accuracy such as 94.78% etc.

Keywords: Deep learning, image, machine learning, chest X-ray images, medical imaging, pneumonia, etc.

**Corresponding author*: errituaggarwal@gmail.com

Umesh Kumar Lilhore, Sarita Simaiya, Surjeet Dalal and Martin Margala (eds.) Artificial Intelligence and Biodiversity, (291–308) © 2026 Scrivener Publishing LLC

16.1 Introduction

There are various types of respiratory systems like as pneumonia which have severe side effects that are not identified or treated in the right way. It will cause a serious infection. Pneumonia is a type of disease in which the patient's lungs are severely damaged especially when this disease is suspected in children [1]. It affects the immune system of a person. The various conventional techniques for identifying pneumonia such as chest x-ray imaging and other laboratory [2]. It is a very time-consuming and complicated type of form as in the disease. The lungs are blocked due to cough and cold. For better patient outcomes and lower mortality rates, a different prompt for pneumonia is required Various techniques are used to increase the effectiveness and diagnosis the pneumonia at an early stage. Sputum analysis and blood tests, chest X-rays could easily detect and identify the disease [3]. It is a highly ranked disease that causes reason of death in human beings as well as children as shown by Figure 16.1.

Pneumonia could have many variants it could be viral, bacterial, or fungal disease. At the time of COVID-19 death rate has increased due to infection found in the lungs. The goal of this research is to automatically create and identify pneumonia with the help of chest X-ray images or samples by using the deep learning model and techniques. Various image classification methods will be used to analyze the chest X-ray images [4] and also identify the regions in the sample's images in which the chest part or lung part has pneumonia. This paper is organized as follows: in Section 16.1 introduction about the disease, Section 16.2 Existing work study, Section 16.3, Proposed Methodology, Section 16.4 Evaluation Metrics and Section 16.5 Results & Discussion.

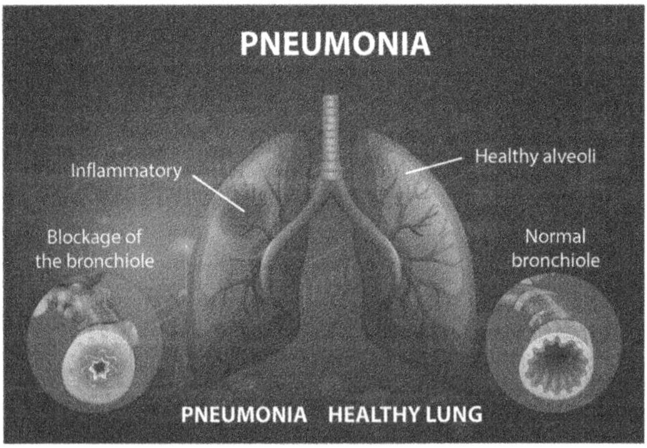

Figure 16.1 Disease-affected pneumonia and healthy lung.

16.2 Related Work

Various deep learning and machine learning techniques developed for the pneumonia disease detection at an early stage. So that disease could be procured. In this section, the work related to existing.

Li, Y.Y., Zhang Z.Y. *et al.* [1] in this author proposed a model chest x-ray model used to detect the disease pneumonia at an early stage. It provides the necessary clinical information the disease detection with the help of some radiography signals. Various diagnostic methods are processed based on abnormalities found in the human body. Deep learning models classify lung abnormalities and detect the disease by clinical records and obtain higher performance.

Jain R., Nagrath P. *et al.* [2] The researcher develops a model using CNN. Early detection and treatment of pneumonia is necessary for the disease detection. Mostly it is found in children and affects the lungs. The author designed a model by classifying it into two classes such as pneumonia and non-pneumonia by changing the various parameters. Various deep-learning models were used at the time of disease detection such as VGG16, VGG19, inception-V3, etc. The accuracy obtained at a higher rate is 92.31 % for VGG19. Dey N. *et al.* [3] in this author developed a DLS for early diagnosis and detection of disease by the different chest X-ray samples. Ensemble feature selection technique implemented with the help of different models. The author extracts the different feature selections such as the DWT GCLM, CWT, etc. for the VGG19 and random forest the accuracy obtained in terms of their classification rate is 95.7%. Brunese L, Mercaldo F. *et al.* [4] author developed a model by using the covid-19 affected patient image samples. In this sample to test and detect the virus in the human body. The blood samples are collected and biomedical imaging will be performed on the patient to detect the disease. An experiment was performed on a large dataset. It achieves higher accuracy by selecting more features from the dataset. The accuracy obtained in terms of results was 97 %. Ibrahim DM, Elshennawy N.M. *et al.* [5] author developed a model for the detection and diagnosis of disease by CT images. Multi-classification of deep learning is employed after selecting and detecting the abnormal features of a patient who is affected by the disease.in this author develops a hybrid model for GRU-based systems. It obtained an accuracy of 98.05 for the hybridization of two models such as the VGG19+CNN model. Jin W.Q. *et al.* [6] in this author proposed a model patient lung disease model at the time of covid-19. It employs artificial intelligence for obtaining quick and fast suspected cases that are affected by the disease.in the previous studies, the report generated about the disease-affected patients through the CXR and CT results. Deep learning models are employed through chest radiography tests. The author obtained results and accuracy in terms of performance rate. The author develops an Alexie, relief algorithm for extracting the different features from the samples. Testing and training will be performed on the Classifier. Karthik R. *et al.* [7] in this proposed work author developed a model using CNN and analyzed it based on the COVID-19 samples. For better results, author used the robust features to detect the disease at an early stage. Experiment results were carried out for the proposed work to identify specific pneumonia classes. It obtained an accuracy of 99.80 % by using various models. Quan H. *et al.* [8] in this proposed work author implement the deep learning model by fusing the two methods which are called a capsule network. DenseCapsNet and CapsNet are used on the CXR images for analyzing and implementing the different models and techniques. It is a model that provides the results based on CXR samples which detect whether a disease is present or absent. It analyses the results by radiography detection. Alhudhaif A. *et al.* [9] in this author developed a model using the Transfer learning model by using chest X-rays. The deep learning model such as restate-18, and squeezenet model. For the generation of a confusion matrix and to prevent the problem of overfitting, the binary classification performances by using different parameters could be analyzed as on individual image samples. The author used the k-fold cross-validation method for testing and training data. The proposed model achieves accuracy such as 94.96 %, 89.74%, 94,59%, and 92.11% Sirazitdinov I., *et al.* [10] in this author proposed a model for analyzing results using RetinaNet and mask R-CNN for pneumonia detection to automate the results by examining the clinical results of the patient. Results are interpreted with the help of Machine learning models. Fscore is computed as 0.97%. Jaiswal A.K., *et al.* [11] in this author designed and studied the model using a deep learning approach. Several factors such as from the x-ray images are used for implementing purposes. Masking will used on each feature of deep learning. Mahmud T. *et al.* [12] in this author proposed a model using CNN based on the covXnet method for generating the results which are used for disease detection. In this author proposed a model for detecting the disease by proposing the architecture using deep learning. For the ConVex the accuracy achieved was 96.9%.

16.3 Proposed Methodology

In this proposed work the total image sample for disease detection in pneumonia is 4780 samples and 2276 attributes of patients will be considered for disease diagnosis and detection at an early stage and the remaining are negatives. This dataset depicts the lung Chest X-rays for image samples to identify the disease. These samples were taken from an online machine learning repository which was verified by medical experts. These are routine samples when the clinical care of children will be performed at the time of infection or when check the symptoms regarding the pneumonia. Deep learning and machine learning are used to classify the results through image samples. Through deep learning, no generated or resolution images were used for the evaluation of different algorithms used in the current work. Image samples are scanned images that have single intensity images and their dimensions vary according to the pixel intensity such as 2170_1567 and 1367_1200 pixels which gives the expected output through the use of CNN architectures.

16.3.1 Proposed Flow Work

This paper proposed a deep learning model such as RESNet_121, Xception, VGG-16, AlexNet, Dense_net, and efficient_net and also proposed and constructed a model with CNN. Deep learning models are used for image resolutions and provide accurate results for the sample images. In CNN the dropout plays a major role in implementation and analysis purposes. Sometimes large samples or image samples could create an overfitting issue in the design model that was prepared for disease detection. Drop out layer prevents the model from relying on the features used in the dataset. It could achieve the random training and testing epochs value by using the various instances and parameters. It enables the data samples with more hidden layers and accurate models. The dropout rate of each layer is approx. 0.5.

16.3.2 Learning Process through Model

RGB images were first fetched through the different deep-learning models. The samples are resized according to the various dimensions used. When resizing the image, the image is divided according to each pixel value across the three channels. 255 pixels for each image to be selected and after that normalized the images according to the training and testing on the set ratio such as training on samples have 75 % and testing 25 % on the spit images samples. To compute the healthy and unhealthy samples in disease detection should have a minimum and maximum result at the time of execution of the model [5].

For the best convergence and best possible result, two mechanisms were implemented to decrease the rate of training time. In this work, deep learning algorithms have set some value 5. The reason for setting this value as 5 means only 5 epochs at each drop-out layer have been used. The learning rate has no improvement after setting the value 5 iterations. Optimization algorithm with the Batch size of CNN and deep learning model's loss function compute with the model used.

Various hyperparameters are used for hyper tuning the attributes to obtain a large learning rate.in the batch size the number of samples processed when the gradient descent increases the number of samples and batch size when it's to be processed. Batch size is simply a number through which the results are evaluated and disease detection through the chest X-ray refining the results for achieving better images [6].

16.3.2.1 Pre-Processing Stage

The primary goal of using CNN using deep learning methods the most common method for detecting disease through the x-ray chest images is to reduce the computational efficiency through images [7]. The pixel set is to reduce the computational efficiency to enable faster processing. The further techniques could provide better results in terms of accuracy rate [8].

16.3.2.2 Feature-Extraction Stage

For the pre-trained models with different variants, the features are to be extracted using the CNN and deep learning Dense_net 121, Resnet, Xecption, VGG-16, efficient_net, etc. Various features are selected and extracted to get better results in disease detection because pneumonia is a serious disease found in children, and infants [9].

16.3.2.3 DenseNet121

It is the most productive framework that is used for image recognition by the CNN layer and the pooling layers, the network layer present in the system model of Densenet. The equal feature sizes should be there when the feature selects are applied to obtain the generic features selection. It comprises one convolution, pooling layers, and transition layers. Various feature maps for the other preceding layers with the same sizes were used but CNN down the speed of sampling size [10].

16.3.2.4 VGG-16

It is a model which is based on CNN architecture. It measures the depth and width of layers. It consists of 16 layers that include 3 fully connected layers.it is based on image recognition and image classification using object recognition. It consists of images followed by max-pooling layers.it is designed to enable the model to learn intricate the progressively depth. VGG-16 uses deep learning techniques and applications for excellent performance [11].

1. **Input Layer**: with the RGB value the image size is 224x224 pixels with 3 color channels [12].
2. **Convolutional Layers**: In the CNN layer the filter size of an image is 3*3 filters which could increase the size [13].
   - **Max Pooling Layers**: CNN has layers blocks that reduce the dimensionality with maximum input value.
   - **Fully Connected Layers**: in this layer, the first two layers of blocks have 1 4096 neurons that have a maximum output size of several classes [14].

Three FC layers follow the convolutional blocks, with the first two having 4096 neurons and the last one having the output size corresponding to the number of classes [15] as shown in Figure 16.2.

16.4 Evaluation Metrics

Various classification issues have been addressed in this proposed work. Confusion matrix is generated by using the following formula these are as: during the evaluation process the predictions are based on the testing and training data. These are the following evaluation metrics are:

In this proposal, the results are generated with the help of statistical means. During the evaluation process prediction for testing and training data depends on some values generated by the confusion matrix the number of true positives, true negatives, false positives, false negatives, etc. based on four indicators the results are evaluated and computed the values based upon the model used [16].

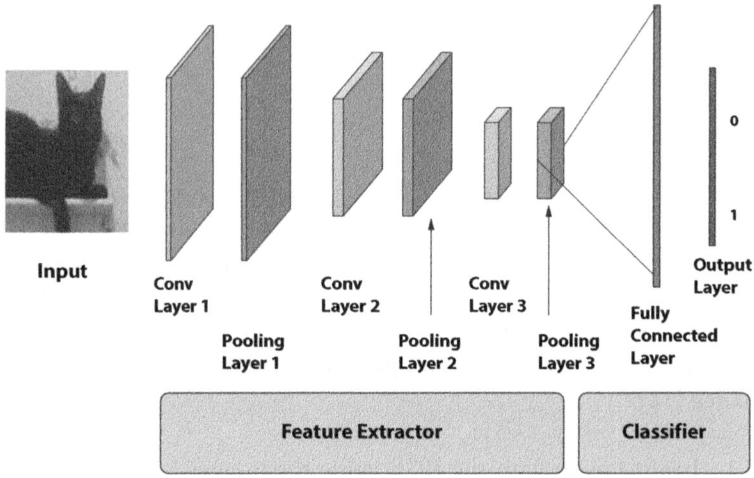

Figure 16.2 CNN architecture with VGG-16.

1. Recall

The recall or sensitivity shows the rate of positive cases correctly predicted and computes the results as:

$$\text{TPR} = \frac{\text{TP}}{\text{TP+FN}} \tag{16.1}$$

For the medical diagnosis, a high recall could be translated for some false negatives.

2. Precision

It indicates the positive value that analyzes the rate of positives for set cases for the medical diagnosis that is declared positive by the classifiers.it is computed by as follows [17]:

$$\text{Precision} = \frac{TP}{Tp+FP} \tag{16.2}$$

3. F1Score

F1score that indicates that equally used the False_pos and False_neg. It is a harmonic mean of the true positive rate and the prediction rate [18]:

$$\text{F1score} = 2^* \frac{Precision*Recall}{Precision+Recall} \tag{16.3}$$

It represents the instance by which the rate of predictions counted as false positives and false negatives is known as accuracy.it is based on total corrections predictions.

$$\text{Accuracy} = \frac{TP+TN}{TP+TN+FP+FN} \tag{16.4}$$

4. ROC (Receiver Operating Characteristics)
According to the statistical analysis, the indicator value lies between 0 and 1. Value 1 representing means 1 is perfect classification and the values are expressed in percentage form. The ROC computes the values by varying it as a threshold point using the output layer of the networks. ROC is basically defining the area under characteristics by which the confusion matrix results promoted by statistical form.

16.5 Results and Discussion

In this proposed work the pneumonia datasets samples are collected from the online repository. After that remove the noisy data and clean the data. For the disease prediction choose the test method such as chest X-ray or CT topography. Test study, analysis, and prediction implement and develop a model using ML and DL techniques for the different image samples of pneumonia. In the other step, CNN identifies the disease by various hybridization methods to predict the disease in patients as shown by Figure 16.3 proposed flow diagram.

In the above Figure 16.2 the images as the samples of the dataset are considered for disease prediction. The image samples were collected at the time of the patient's disease diagnosis and checked that the patient's lungs were suffering from a chest infection. The lungs are blocked due to cough and cold. In the severe condition patient's chest X-ray report detected that the patient has a severe chest infection.

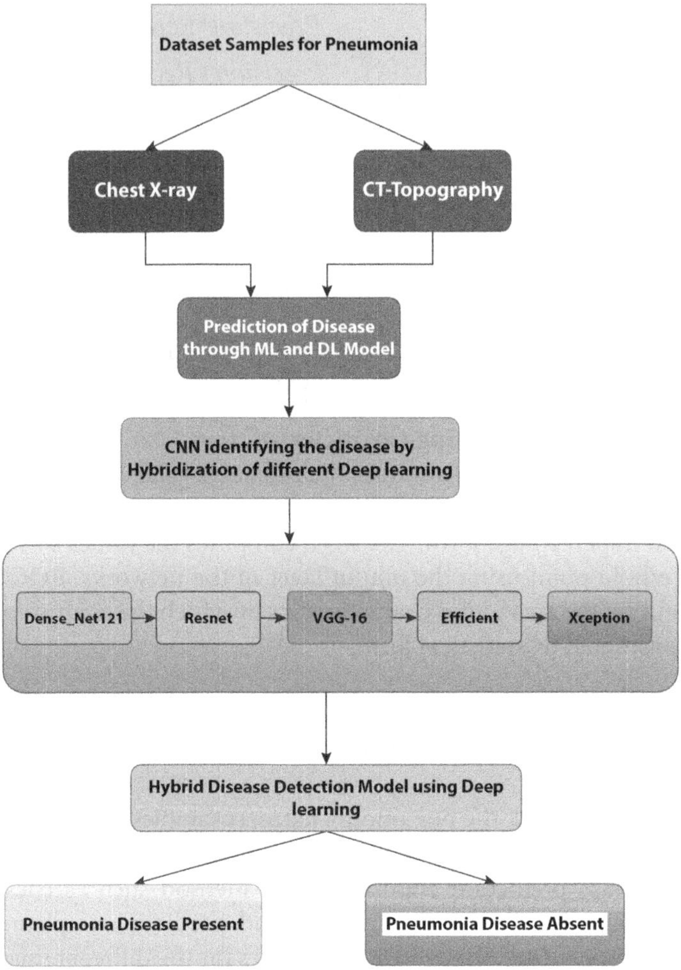

Figure 16.3 Proposed flow diagram of current work.

The total samples for the pneumonia disease have been collected as per the chest X-ray operated on the patients. By analyzing all the samples received and setting the different characteristics of patients the accurate results were obtained as the different frequency rates and for all the samples-based results the confusion matrix was generated shown in Figure 16.4.

As per the below samples obtained that show a patient is suffering from pneumonia or its normal, as a graphical result the rate and ratio disease affected patient results shown in Figures 16.5 and 16.6.

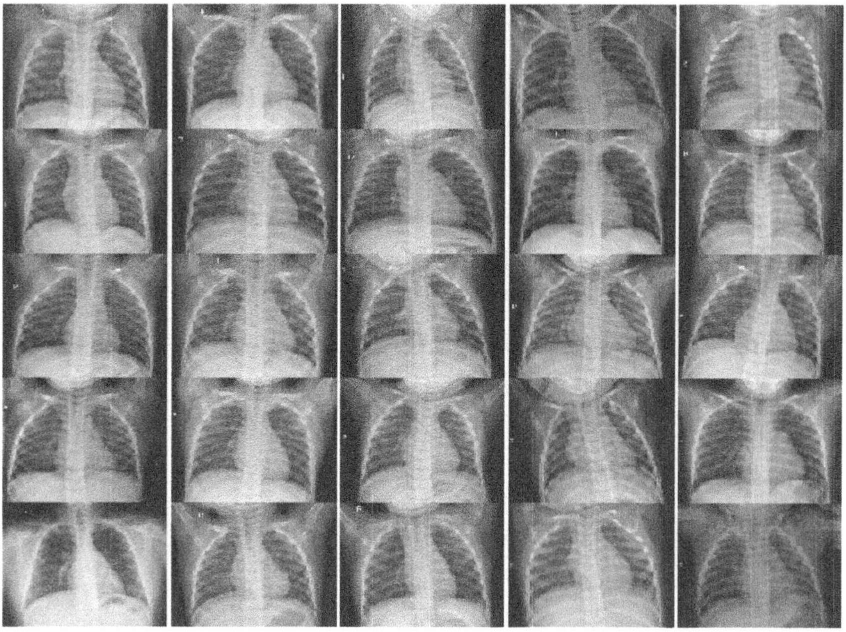

Figure 16.4 Dataset samples for pneumonia disease.

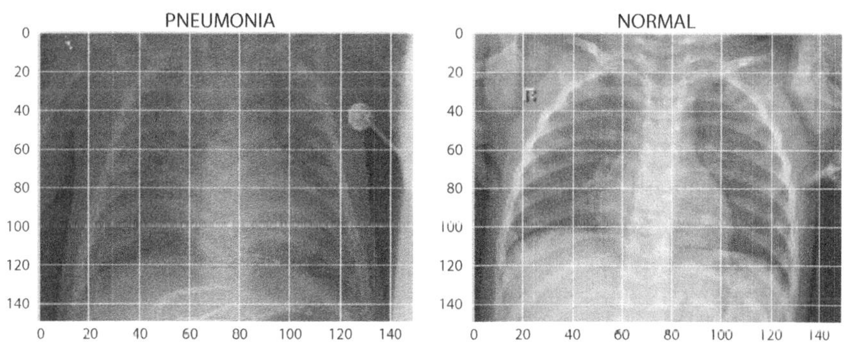

Figure 16.5 Samples results show the normal and disease affected patient results.

In this, for the various data values, the model is to be trained and tested to obtain accuracy for getting results.

In the below Figure 16.7, the actual value and predicted values results are computed by labelling the data for results analysis.

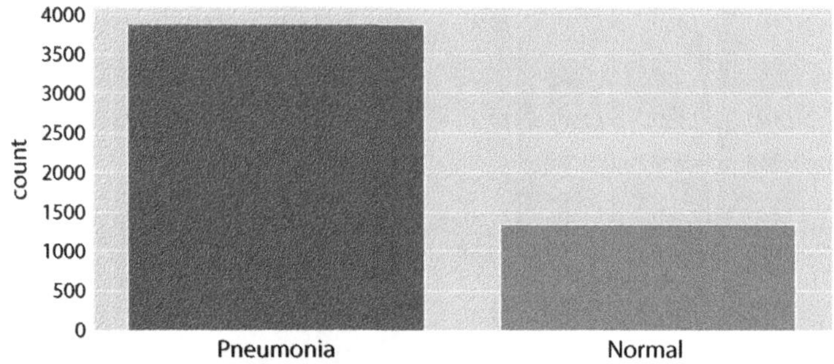

Figure 16.6 Results for normal and pneumonia affected patients.

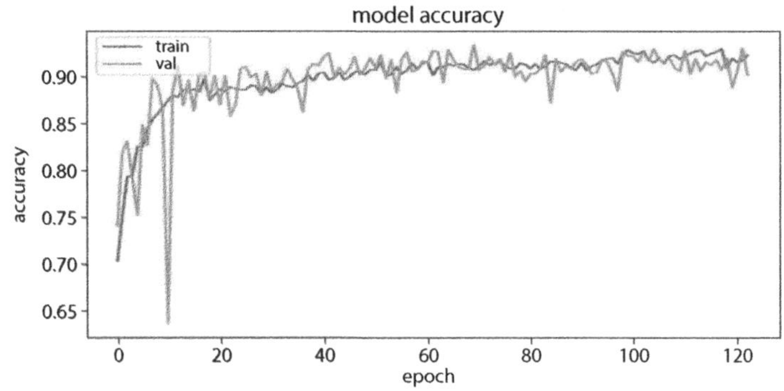

Figure 16.7 Accuracy results showing the variance and the Epochs rate.

In the below Figure 16.8 the false positive and true negative rate values are generated with the help of the confusion matrix computed on different attributes as considered for disease detection as shown by Table 16.1.

The implementation results are shown by using various deep learning models and classifiers used for disease detection of pneumonia in the below Table 16.2.

The actual target values as well as expected value results and outcome for the pneumonia disease detection. The resultant value shows the prediction rate of disease by measuring the different sample values. The evaluation metrics for the following classifiers are as follows. The accuracy obtained in terms of prediction rate is 97 as shown by Figure 16.9, Figure 16.10, Figure 16.11, & Figure 16.12.

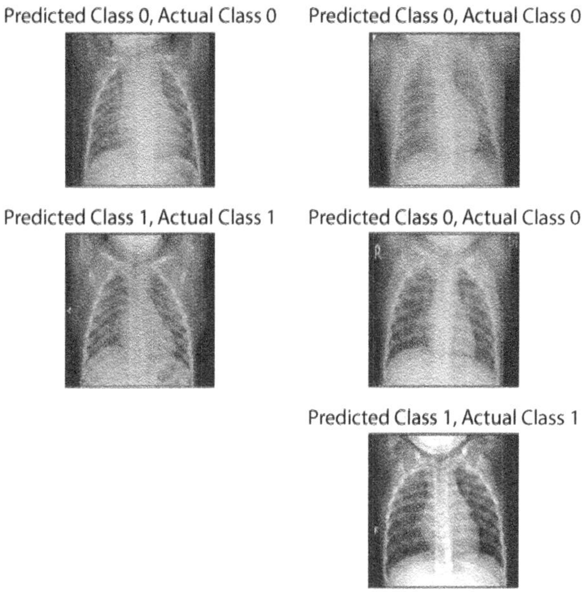

Figure 16.8 Samples results based on prediction rate.

Table 16.1 Standard deviation results for various models.

Deep_learning _Evaluation					
Model	**Densenet**	**Efficientnet**	**ResNet**	**VGG-19**	**Xception**
Parameters	11.7M	11.5 M	27.3 M	23.6 M	144.4
Accuracy (%)	94.78	94:32	92:97	89:45	67:29
Recall (%)	93:64	95:54	89:70	80:13	69:98
Precision (%)	91:35	93:60	94:89	94:63	64.53
F_1 score (%)	93:32	96:47	88:84	71:20	67.89

Table 16.2 Various measured matrix result.

Actual	Expectation	Resultant	Precision	Recall	F-measure	Accuracy
569	345	540	78	83	78	97
670	912	995	92	91	95	93
780	250	265	84	93	89	96
790	534	578	89	95	95	94
1797	1200	1345	83	96	96	95
1290	632	5234	85	97	97	91

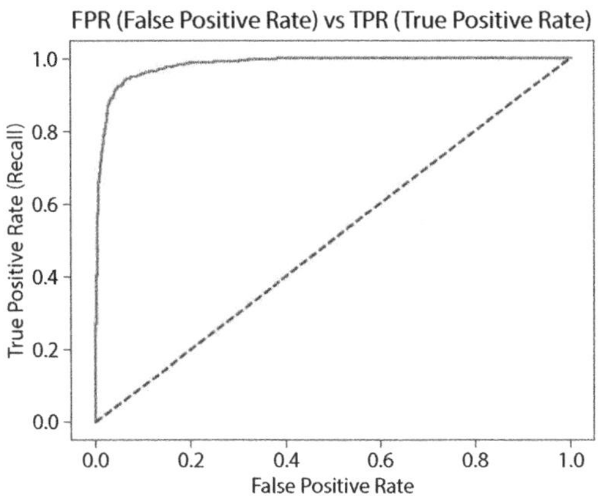

Figure 16.9 Confusion matrix results based on the prediction.

Conclusion

In this proposed work the CNN model hybridization with other deep learning models for disease detection. The results are analyzed and computed by the chest X-ray images. In this model the computation on different models deployed by the various networks or other processes. If the disease detection is performed at an early stage there is a possibility that the disease a spreading to advanced stages. Hybridization of different models of deep learning could increase the classification accuracy for obtaining a higher prediction rate.

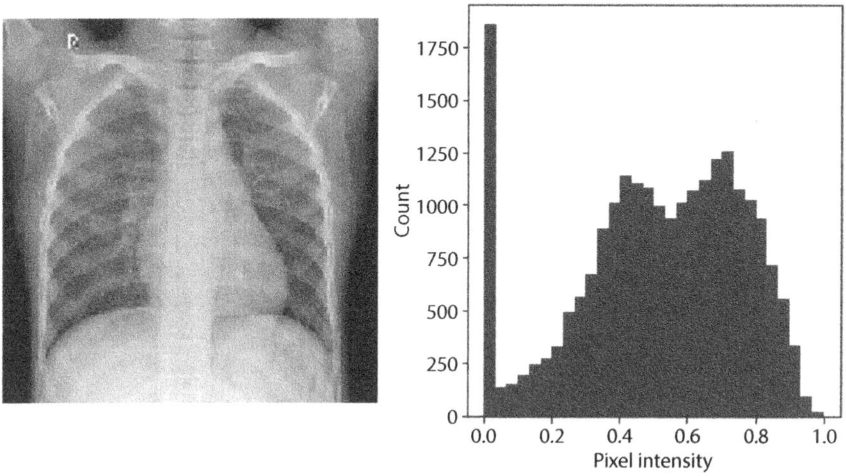

Figure 16.10 Pixel intensity based on the pneumonia results.

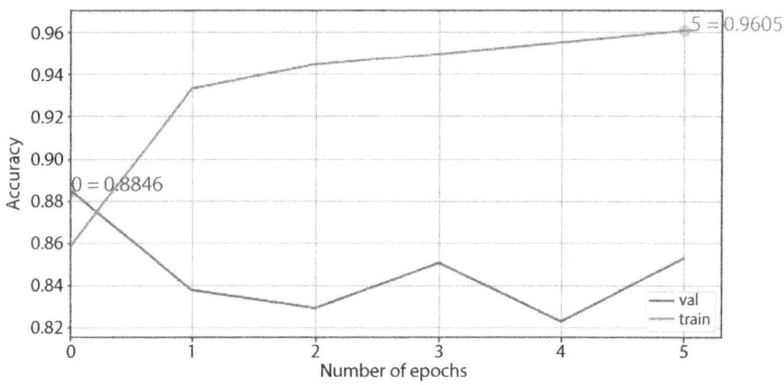

Figure 16.11 Accuracy obtained as per the number of epochs for train and test.

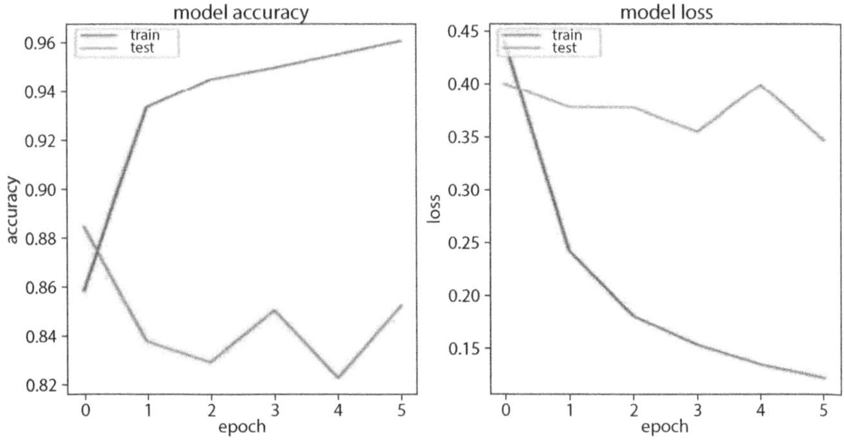

Figure 16.12 Results for accuracy and loss.

AI disclosure statement: The author confirms that no artificial intelligence (AI)-generated content or AI-assisted writing tools were used in the preparation of this chapter (including summaries and the abstract). All text, analysis, and conclusions are the result of the author's original work.

References

1. Li, Y.Y., Zhang, Z.Y., Dai, C., Dong, Q., Badrigilan, S., Accuracy of deep learning for automated detection of pneumonia using chest X-ray images: A systematic review and meta-analysis. *Comput. Biol. Med.*, 123, 2020, https://doi.org/10.1016/ j.compbiomed.2020.103898 103898.
2. Jain, R., Nagrath, P., Kataria, G., Kaushik, V.S., Hemanth, D.J., Pneumonia detection in chest X-ray images using convolutional neural networks and transfer learning. *Measurement*, 165, 108046, 2020, https://doi.org/10.1016/j.measurement.2020.108046.
3. Dey, N., Zhang, Y.D., Rajinikanth, V., Pugalenthi, R., Sri Madhava Raja, N., Customized VGG19 Architecture for Pneumonia Detection in Chest X-Rays. *Pattern Recognit. Lett.*, 143, 67–74, 2021, https://doi.org/10.1016/j.patrec.2020.12.010.
4. Brunese, L., Mercaldo, F., Reginelli, A., Santone, A., Explainable Deep Learning for Pulmonary Disease and Coronavirus COVID-19 Detection from X-rays. *Comput. Methods Programs Biomed.*, 196, 105608, 2020, https://doi.org/10.1016/j.cmpb.2020.105608.
5. Panwar, H., Gupta, P.K., Siddiqui, M.K., Morales-Menendez, R., Bhardwaj, P., Singh, V., A deep learning and grad-CAM based color visualization

approach for fast detection of COVID-19 cases using chest X-ray and CT-Scan images. *Chaos, Solitons Fractals*, 140, 110190, 2020, https://doi.org/10.1016/j. chaos.2020.110190.

6. Ibrahim, D.M., Elshennawy, N.M., Sarhan, A.M., Deep-chest: Multiclassification deep learning model for diagnosing COVID-19, pneumonia, and lung cancer chest diseases. *Comput. Biol*, 4, 201–210, 2023.
7. Jin, W.Q., Dong, S.Q., Dong, C.Z., Ye, X.D., Hybrid ensemble model for differential diagnosis between COVID-19 and common viral pneumonia by chest X-ray radiograph. *Comput. Biol*, 5, 610–620, 2022.
8. Karthik, R., Menaka, R., Hariharan, M., Learning distinctive filters for COVID-19 detection from chest X-ray using shuffled residual CNN. *Appl. Soft Comput.*, 99, 106744, 2021, https://doi.org/ 10.1016/j.asoc.2020.106744.
9. Quan, H., Xu, X.S., Zheng, T.T., Li, Z., Zhao, M.F., Cui, X.Y., DenseCapsNet: Detection of COVID-19 from X-ray images using a capsule neural network. *Comput. Biol. Med.*, 133, 104399, 2021, https://doi.org/10.1016/j. compbiomed.2021.104399.
10. Alhudhaif, A., Polat, K., Karaman, O., Determination of COVID-19 pneumonia based on generalized convolutional neural network model from chest X-ray images. *Expert Syst. Appl.*, 180, 115141, 2021, https://doi.org/10.1016/j. eswa.2021.115141.
11. Sirazitdinov, I., Kholiavchenko, M., Mustafaev, T., Yixuan, Y., Kuleev, R., Ibragimov, B., Deep neural network ensemble for pneumonia localization from a large-scale chest x-ray database. *Comput. Electr. Eng.*, 78, 388–99, 2019, https://doi.org/ 10.1016/j.compeleceng.2019.08.004.
12. Jaiswal, A.K., Tiwari, P., Kumar, S., Gupta, D., Khanna, A., Rodrigues, J.J.P.C., Identifying pneumonia in chest X-rays: A deep learning approach. *Measurement*, 145, 511–8, 2019, https://doi.org/ 10.1016/j.measurement. 2019.05.076.
13. Mahmud, T., Rahman, M.A., Fattah, S.A., CovXNet: A mutilation convolutional neural network for automatic COVID-19 and other pneumonia detection from chest X-ray images with transferable multi-receptive feature optimization. *Comput. Biol. Med.*, 122, 2020, https://doi.org/10.1016/ j.compbiomed.2020.103869 103869.
14. Ouchicha, C., Amor, O., Meknassi, M., CVDNet: A novel deep learning architecture for detection of coronavirus (Covid-19) from chest x-ray images. *Chaos, Solitons Fractals*, 140, 110245, 2020, https://doi.org/10.1016/j. chaos.2020.110245.
15. Wang, J., Bao, Y.M., Wen, Y.F., Lu, H.B., Luo, H., Xiang, Y.F., Li, X.M., Liu, C., Qian, D.H., Prior-Attention Residual Learning for More Discriminative COVID-19 Screening in CT Images. *IEEE Trans. Med. Imaging*, 39, 8, 2572–83, 2020, https://doi.org/10.1109/ TMI.2020.2994908.
16. Wang, Z., Xiao, Y., Li, Y., Zhang, J., Lu, F.G., Hou, M.Z., Liu, C.W., Automatically discriminating and localizing COVID-19 from community-acquired

pneumonia on chest X-rays. *Pattern Recognit.*, 110, 107613, 2021, https://doi.org/10.1016/ j.patcog.2020.107613.
17. Wang, S.H., Zhang, X., Zhang, Y.D., Deep stacked sparse autoencoder analytical model for COVID-19 diagnosis by fractional Fourier entropy. *ACM Trans. Manage. Inf. Syst.*, 13, 1, 20, 2021, https://doi.org/10.1145/3451357.
18. Wang, S.H., Khan, M.A., Govindaraj, V., Fernandes, S.L., Zhu, Z.Q., Zhang, Y.D., Deep rank-based average pooling network for COVID-19 recognition. *Comput. Mater. Continua*, 70, 2, 2797–813, 2022, https://doi.org/10.32604/cmc.2022.020140.

17

Integrated Optimization Strategies for High-Efficiency Solar PV Plants: From AI to Bifacial Technologies

S. Dayana Priyadharshini[1]* and M. Arvindhan[2]

[1]*Department of Bioengineering, Institute of Biotechnology, Saveetha School of Engineering, Saveetha Institute of Medical and Technical Sciences, Chennai, Tamil Nadu (SIMATS), India*
[2]*American School of Management, The American University of Science, Dinh Chinh Street, Phu Nhuan Ward, Ho Chi Minh City, Vietnam*

Abstract

The escalating global demand for renewable energy necessitates advanced optimization strategies for solar photovoltaic (PV) plant efficiency to reduce levelized cost of energy (LCOE) and maximize investment returns. This paper presents a comprehensive review of state-of-the-art optimization methodologies for solar PV systems, integrating advanced module technologies, intelligent control systems, and multi-objective optimization frameworks. The study evaluates eight primary optimization strategies: advanced PV modules including bifacial designs achieving up to 40% energy gain in high-albedo environments and TOPC on modules with commercial efficiencies of 23-24%; dynamic tracking systems where single-axis trackers deliver 15-25% annual yield improvements, extending to 40% when combined with bifacial modules; thermal management systems utilizing radiative cooling technologies reducing module temperatures by 13°C; power electronics optimization employing particle swarm optimization (PSO)-based maximum power point tracking (MPPT) algorithms achieving 10% efficiency gains under partial shading conditions; artificial intelligence frameworks incorporating machine learning-based forecasting that improves solar irradiance prediction accuracy by 18% compared to traditional statistical methods; hybrid renewable systems demonstrating 12% energy cost reduction through optimized dispatch strategies; dual-use land approaches including agrivoltaics and photovoltaics

**Corresponding author*: dayanapriyadharshini.s@gmail.com

Umesh Kumar Lilhore, Sarita Simaiya, Surjeet Dalal and Martin Margala (eds.) Artificial Intelligence and Biodiversity, (309–326) © 2026 Scrivener Publishing LLC

systems yielding 5-15% efficiency improvements; and lifecycle sustainability optimization through advanced materials and recycling frameworks. The methodology combines real-world industrial deployments, machine learning analytics, simulation studies, and multi-objective evolutionary algorithms. Results demonstrate that integrated optimization approaches can achieve cumulative efficiency improvements exceeding 50% compared to conventional fixed-tilt systems. The findings provide quantitative benchmarks and practical implementation guidelines for utility-scale solar PV installations, contributing to the advancement of renewable energy technologies and sustainable energy transition strategies.

***Keywords*:** Solar photovoltaic optimization, bifacial modules, MPPT algorithms, machine learning forecasting, renewable energy systems, agrivoltaics, floatovoltaics, sustainability

17.1 Introduction

Renewable energy systems (RES) encompassing solar, wind, hydropower, geothermal, and biomass are central to decarbonizing the global energy sector. Their integration into existing grids is essential for achieving carbon neutrality and meeting international climate target. However, the intermittent and stochastic nature of renewable resources presents significant operational and economic challenges, necessitating the development of robust optimization techniques for planning, operation, and control. India has emerged as one of the world's leading countries in solar energy deployment, driven by its ambitious renewable energy targets and favorable climatic conditions [1]. As of 2025, India has surpassed 75 GW of installed solar photovoltaic (PV) capacity, making it the fifth-largest solar market globally (MNRE, 2024). The country receives an average solar irradiation of 4–7 kWh/m^2/day across most regions, offering enormous potential for solar energy generation. This literature survey provides a comprehensive overview of the recent trends, advanced technologies, policy frameworks, and operational mechanisms shaping the development and efficiency of solar PV plants in India. India's solar journey was catalyzed by the launch of the Jawaharlal Nehru National Solar Mission (JNNSM) in 2010. The target of 20 GW by 2022 was revised to 100 GW in 2015 under the Paris Agreement commitments. Currently, India is aiming for 280 GW of solar capacity by 2030 as part of its broader 500 GW non-fossil fuel capacity goa [2].

17.1.1 Classical Optimization Methods

Traditional optimization in RES has relied on deterministic and stochastic mathematical programming, including:

17.2 Hybrid and Multi-Objective Optimization

Modern RES optimization often involves hybrid systems that combine different energy sources and storage technologies (e.g., PV-wind-battery systems). Figure 17.1 explains Multi-objective optimization frameworks are employed to simultaneously address technical, economic, and environmental criteria, leveraging Pareto-front analysis and evolutionary algorithms for trade-off exploration.

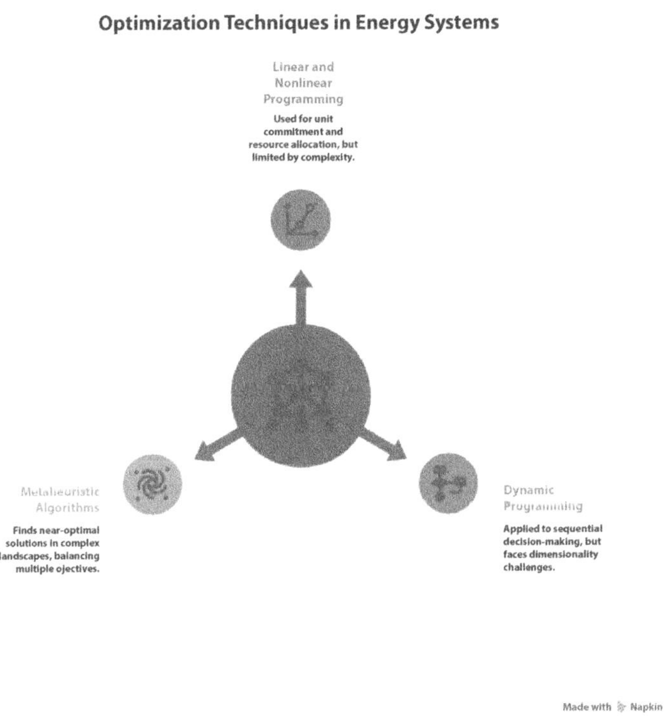

Figure 17.1 Optimization techniques in energy system.

17.2.1 Artificial Intelligence and Machine Learning

AI and machine learning (ML) are transforming renewable energy optimization by enabling:

- **Resource Forecasting**: ML models (e.g., deep learning, transformer-based architectures) provide accurate predictions of solar irradiance, wind speed, and energy demand, improving scheduling and dispatch decisions.
- **Adaptive Control**: Reinforcement learning (RL) and model predictive control (MPC) dynamically manage generation, storage, and load in response to real-time data, enhancing system flexibility and resilience.
- **Predictive Maintenance**: AI-driven analytics enable condition-based monitoring and predictive maintenance, reducing downtime and extending asset life.

17.2.2 Explainable AI (XAI)

Emerging XAI techniques improve transparency and trust in AI-driven decision-making, which is critical for safety and regulatory compliance in power systems.

17.3 Technology Trends in Indian Solar PV Plants

Machine Learning-Based Forecasting ML Algorithms, such as neural networks and support vector machines, have revolutionized solar energy forecasting. Developing a deep learning model that improved solar irradiance prediction accuracy by 18% compared to traditional statistical methods. Figure 17.2 narrates these models use historical weather data and real-time sensor inputs to predict energy output, enabling dynamic adjustments to grid integration. However, ML models require large datasets and significant computational resources, limiting their adoption in resource constrained regions [3].

17.3.1 Optimization Techniques in Renewable Energy

Maximum Power Point Tracking (MPPT) MPPT algorithms optimize the operating voltage of PV systems to maximize power output. Recent advancements, such as particle swarm optimization (PSO)-based MPPT,

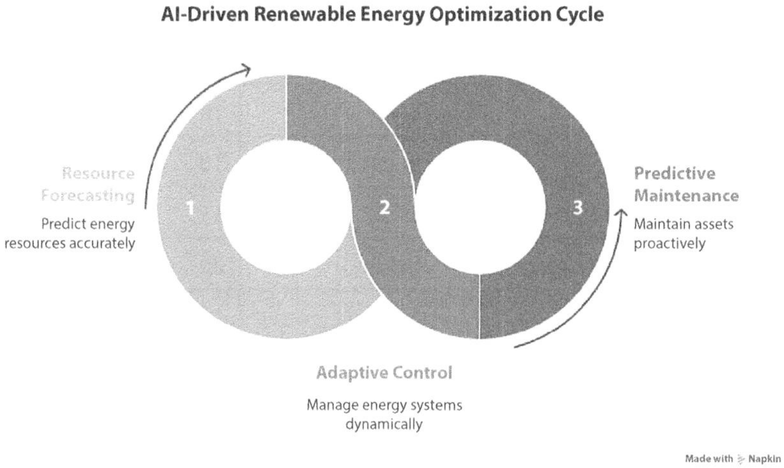

Figure 17.2 AI-driven renewable energy optimization cycle.

have achieved efficiency gains of up to 10% under partial shading conditions. Despite their effectiveness, PSO-based methods are computationally intensive, posing challenges for real-time applications [4].

Wind Energy Optimization Wind energy accounted for 7.8% of global electricity in 2024. Optimization focuses on turbine placement, blade design, and predictive maintenance. Genetic Algorithms for Turbine Placement Genetic algorithms optimize wind farm layouts to minimize wake effects and maximize energy yield. reported a 15% increase in energy output by using GA to design a 50-turbine wind farm in Norway. However, GA requires extensive computational power, and its scalability to larger farms remains a challenge. Predictive Maintenance with IoT IoT-based frameworks enable real-time monitoring of wind turbines, reducing downtime by up to 20%. Sensors collect data on vibration, temperature, and blade wear, which are analyzed using ML to predict maintenance needs. Table 17.1 explains the primary limitation is data interoperability, as proprietary IoT systems often lack standardization.

17.3.2 Hybrid Renewable Energy Systems

Hybrid systems combine multiple renewable sources to enhance reliability and efficiency. Optimization focuses on energy dispatch and storage management. Hybrid Optimization Frameworks proposed a hybrid optimization framework integrating solar and wind energy with battery storage, achieving a 12% reduction in energy costs [5]. The framework uses a

Table 17.1 Efficiency gains from selected optimization techniques.

Technique	Energy source	Efficiency gain (%)
ML Forecasting	Solar	18
PSO-MPPT	Solar	10
Genetic Algorithm	Wind	15
IoT Predictive Maintenance	Wind	20
Hybrid Framework	Hybrid	12

combination of PSO and linear programming to optimize energy dispatch. However, high initial costs and complex system integration remain barriers to widespread adoption.

Case Study: Denmark's Hybrid Microgrid A hybrid solar-wind microgrid in Denmark implemented a real-time optimization frame work, integrating IoT sensors and ML algorithms. The system achieved a 15% efficiency increase by dynamically adjusting energy dispatch based on weather forecasts. This case study highlights the potential of hybrid systems but underscores the need for scalable, cost-effective solutions.

17.3.3 Advances in High-Efficiency PV Modules

Bifacial PV modules capture sunlight from both the front and rear surfaces. The rear-side generation is influenced by ground albedo, module elevation, and mounting geometry. As of 2025, over 90% of new utility-scale installations use bifacial modules. Studies show energy gains of up to 40% in desert regions with high albedo surfaces [6].

17.3.4 TOPC on and Tandem Technologies

TOPCon (Tunnel Oxide Passivated Contact) modules are emerging as the mainstream successor to PERC technology, with commercial efficiencies of 23-24%. Companies like Longi and HVR Solar have launched TOPCon bifacial modules rated over 700 Wp. Tandem cells, combining perovskite and silicon layers, have demonstrated over 30% lab efficiencies. These tandem structures reduce thermalization losses by harvesting different portions of the solar spectrum.

17.4 System-Level Design and Solar Tracking

Trackers align modules perpendicular to solar rays, increasing irradiance exposure. Single-axis trackers can improve annual yield by 15–25% compared to fixed mounts, and when paired with bifacial modules, can deliver up to 40% more energy. Dual-axis trackers offer better performance but are costlier and require more maintenance [7]. The ideal tilt angle varies with latitude but should also consider seasonal shifts. For bifacial systems, spacing (row-to-row pitch) and elevation significantly influence bifacial gain. Elevated structures minimize shading and enhance rear-side irradiance. Ground treatments like white gravel or reflective membranes (with >0.5 albedo) are being used to enhance rear exposure.

17.4.1 Radiative and Passive Cooling

Solar module efficiency decreases with temperature—approximately 0.35% to 0.45% per °C. Radiative cooling technologies, which dissipate heat as infrared radiation, can reduce module temperatures by up to 13°C. Coatings using silica or polymer nanostructures are under development to maximize heat emission [8].

17.4.2 Optical Coatings and Spectrum Management

Anti-reflective coatings and spectral-selective materials increase the amount of usable light reaching the cells. Some cooling films are designed to reflect infrared while transmitting visible light, thus reducing heating without compromising electricity generation.

17.5 Power Electronics and MPPT Optimization

17.5.1 Advanced MPPT Algorithms

MPPT (Maximum Power Point Tracking) algorithms ensure the PV system operates at its peak power point. Techniques like Perturb and Observe (P\&O), Incremental Conductance, and neural network-based methods enhance tracking under rapidly changing conditions. New hybrid methods combining fuzzy logic and AI are being tested in high-variability climates.

17.5.2 String-Level and Module-Level Optimization

Microinverters and power optimizers allow MPPT at the individual module level. This architecture is especially effective in partially shaded or heterogeneous arrays, reducing mismatch losses. It also improves system safety and provides detailed diagnostics [9].

17.6 Digitalization, AI, and Smart Monitoring

17.6.1 AI-Driven AI&M Platforms

Modern solar farms integrate SCADA (Supervisory Control and Data Acquisition) systems with AI platforms. These tools analyze data from inverters, sensors, and drones to identify anomalies, predict failures, and recommend maintenance actions. AI reduces unplanned downtime and boosts uptime by 3–5%. The most promising innovative approaches in renewable energy optimization today are centered on artificial intelligence (AI) and machine learning (ML), smart grid technologies, advanced energy storage optimization, and the integration of hybrid renewable energy systems [10].

17.6.2 Key Innovative Approaches Include

- **AI and ML for Forecasting and Optimization**
    - AI-driven models are revolutionizing resource forecasting (solar irradiance, wind speed), enabling more accurate scheduling and dispatch.
    - Reinforcement learning (RL) and deep learning are used to optimize energy production, storage, and distribution in real time by learning from dynamic system interactions [11].
    - Explainable AI (XAI) is gaining traction, making AI decisions transparent and trustworthy for operators and regulators.
    - Predictive maintenance powered by AI reduces downtime and operational costs by identifying equipment issues before failures occur.
- **Smart Grids and IoT Integration**
    - Smart grids use real-time data, IoT sensors, and automation to balance generation, distribution, and consumption efficiently [12].

  - Demand response systems automatically adjust supply based on consumption patterns, improving grid stability and reducing waste.
  - Decentralized grids and microgrids enhance local generation, consumption, and resilience, especially in remote or rural areas.
- **Advanced Energy Storage Optimization**
  - AI optimizes battery and hybrid storage systems by determining the most efficient charge/discharge cycles based on real-time needs and market prices.
  - Research is advancing on hybrid storage solutions combining batteries, supercapacitors, and flywheels to leverage their complementary strengths.
  - Storage is critical for balancing intermittent renewable generation and ensuring grid reliability [13].
- **Hybrid Renewable Energy Systems (HRES)**
  - Combining solar, wind, hydro, and storage technologies mitigates the variability of individual sources and improves overall system reliability.
  - Optimization algorithms determine the best mix and configuration of resources for specific locations and demand profiles.
- **Cutting-Edge Hardware Innovations**
  - High-efficiency solar panels (perovskite, bifacial), advanced wind turbine designs, and bladeless wind energy are pushing the limits of renewable generation [13].
  - Novel applications, such as solar-powered trains and 3D-printed solar panels, are expanding the use cases for renewables.
- **Integration of AI in Energy Markets**
  - AI is increasingly used for market trading, renewable energy matchmaking, and optimizing participation in electricity markets as renewables become more prevalent.

17.7 Case Studies Illustrating the Impact of Optimization

- **Google DeepMind**: Enhanced wind farm output prediction and dispatch using AI.

- **IBM Research Ireland**: Improved solar forecasting accuracy with ML, aiding grid integration [14].
- **Tesla**: AI-based optimization of battery storage for grid support.

17.8 Emerging Trends and Future Directions

- **Green hydrogen** and **long-duration energy storage** are seen as transformative technologies for large-scale renewable integration.
- **Sector coupling** (linking power, heat, and mobility) and **digitalization** will further optimize system-wide efficiency and sustainability.

These innovative approaches collectively address the core challenges of intermittency, grid integration, and operational efficiency, positioning the energy sector for a more sustainable and resilient future [15].

17.8.1 Solar Forecasting and Grid Integration

Accurate forecasting of solar output improves grid stability and trading. AI models using weather, satellite, and irradiance data have shown significant improvements in prediction accuracy [16]. These models support grid operators in managing variability and planning backup reserves.

17.8.2 Environmental Adaptation and Dual-Use Land Strategies

17.8.2.1 Agrivoltaics

Agrivoltaics refers to the co-location of solar PV and agriculture. Elevated and widely spaced arrays allow sunlight penetration for crops while generating electricity. Studies in India and Japan demonstrate that certain crops (e.g., leafy greens, berries) thrive under partial shade provided by PV modules [17].

17.8.2.2 Floating Solar (Floatovoltaics)

Floating PV systems, installed on lakes and reservoirs, benefit from natural cooling and reduced land use. The cooling effect of water bodies improves efficiency by 5–15%. Additionally, floatovoltaics reduce water evaporation and algae growth.

17.8.2.3 Advanced System Integration

- **Hybrid Energy Systems**: Combining complementary resources (e.g., solar with wind and storage) mitigates intermittency and increases reliability.
- **Energy Storage Optimization**: Innovations in battery and hydrogen storage sizing and operation are crucial for balancing supply and demand, especially in off-grid and microgrid applications [18].

17.8.2.4 Smart Grids and Digitalization

The integration of IoT, big data analytics, and automated control platforms enables real-time optimization and decentralized energy management.

17.9 Lifecycle Considerations and Sustainability

17.9.1 Material Longevity and Recycling

Using glass-glass modules and robust encapsulants enhances lifespan and reduces degradation. Recyclable designs are now being mandated in several countries to reduce PV waste. Research is ongoing into reusing silicon wafers and recovering silver and indium from retired modules [19].

17.9.2 Reducing Embodied Carbon

Selecting low-carbon manufacturing processes (e.g., renewable-powered wafer fabrication) and minimizing transportation footprints contribute to sustainable deployment. High-efficiency modules reduce the number of panels needed, thus lowering total embodied energy [20].

17.9.3 Role of IoT in Enhancing Renewable Energy Efficiency

Smart grids and the Internet of Things (IoT) play a transformative role in enhancing the efficiency, reliability, and integration of renewable energy sources. Their combined impact is evident across several critical areas:

- **Seamless Renewable Energy Integration**
Smart grids, empowered by IoT, enable the flexible and stable integration of intermittent renewable sources such as solar and wind. IoT devices collect real-time data on generation, consumption, and grid conditions, allowing for dynamic adjustments that ensure a stable and reliable power supply despite fluctuations in renewable output [21].
- **Real-Time Monitoring and Data-Driven Optimization**
IoT sensors and smart meters provide continuous, granular data on energy flows, voltage, and equipment status. This real-time information allows grid operators to optimize energy distribution, minimize losses, and quickly respond to changes in supply or demand, thus maximizing the efficiency of renewable energy utilization [22].
- **Demand Response and Load Balancing**
Smart grids use IoT-enabled demand response programs to incentivize consumers to shift or reduce their energy use during peak periods. This balances the load, reduces the need for fossil-fuel-based backup power, and minimizes energy waste, all while supporting higher shares of renewables in the energy mix [23].
- **Enhanced Energy Storage Management**
IoT-based smart grids monitor and control battery storage systems, optimizing charge and discharge cycles. This ensures that excess renewable energy is stored when available and released when needed, improving both the efficiency and reliability of renewable energy systems for homes and businesses [24].
- **Predictive Maintenance and Grid Reliability**
IoT analytics enable predictive maintenance by identifying equipment wear or faults before failures occur. This reduces downtime, lowers maintenance costs, and increases the reliability of renewable energy assets and the grid as a whole [25].
- **Empowering Consumers and Decentralized Energy Management**
IoT devices and smart meters give consumers real-time insights into their energy usage, enabling them to make informed decisions, participate in demand response, and even sell excess renewable energy back to the grid, further increasing overall efficiency and sustainability [26].
- **Microgrid Optimization**
In microgrid environments, IoT enables precise energy scheduling, improved resource allocation, and cost reduction by integrating local renewable generation, storage, and advanced analytics [27].

17.10 Future Directions

17.10.1 Scalable AI and Digital Platforms

To realize the full potential of AI in renewable energy optimization, industry stakeholders must:

- Develop scalable, interoperable digital platforms that facilitate real-time data exchange and collaborative optimization.
- Invest in explainable and trustworthy AI to enhance transparency and regulatory acceptance [28].
- Open-Source Platforms: Develop open-source optimization tools to reduce costs and improve accessibility.
- Standardized IoT Protocols: Establish universal standards for IoT systems to enhance data interoperability.
- Sustainable Materials: Invest in research to minimize the environmental impact of renewable energy infrastructure [29].
- Cross-Disciplinary Collaboration: Foster partnerships between engineers, data scientists, and policymakers to address technical and regulatory challenges Figure 17.3.

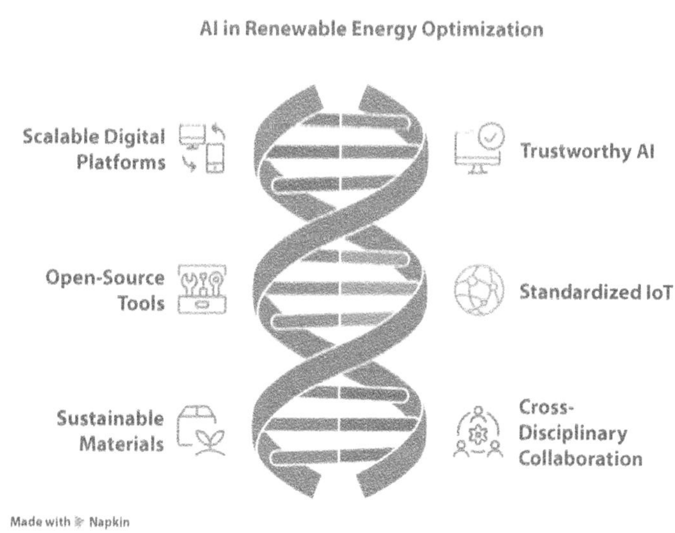

Figure 17.3 AI in renewable energy optimization.

17.10.2 Advanced Energy Storage and Sector Coupling

- Expand research on hybrid storage solutions (e.g., batteries plus hydrogen) to improve flexibility and enable sector coupling (power, heat, mobility).
- Optimize storage operation using predictive analytics and dynamic control to maximize value and grid stability [30].

17.10.3 Integrated Planning and Policy Support

- Foster integrated planning approaches that align technical optimization with policy, market, and societal objectives.
- Advocate for clear, supportive regulatory frameworks and targeted incentives to accelerate innovation and deployment.

17.10.4 Resilience and Sustainability

- Prioritize system resilience to climate and cyber risks through robust optimization, redundancy, and adaptive control strategies.
- Advance sustainability by integrating life cycle assessment and circular economy principles into optimization frameworks.

17.11 Conclusion

Optimizing solar PV plant efficiency is a dynamic and evolving challenge. With continuous improvements in material science, AI, and system engineering, PV plants can now produce significantly more energy per unit area and cost. Bifacial and tandem technologies, AI-driven O\&M, advanced cooling, and land-smart designs like agri voltaics and floating PV are pushing the boundaries of efficiency. A well-optimized solar plant not only delivers better returns but also contributes more effectively to decarbonizing the global energy supply. Renewable energy optimization is at the forefront of the global energy transition, offering pathways to higher efficiency, reliability, and sustainability. The convergence of AI, advanced control, and integrated system design is driving innovation, but significant technical, economic, and policy challenges remain. Addressing these requires a collaborative, interdisciplinary approach—combining robust optimization techniques, scalable digital infrastructure, and supportive regulatory environments—to unlock the full potential of renewable energy systems for a resilient, low-carbon future.

AI disclosure statement: The author acknowledges the use of AI-based tools for minor language editing or grammatical correction. However, all intellectual contributions, analyses, and conclusions presented in this chapter are entirely the author's own.

Bibliography

1. Zhang, H., *et al.*, Performance Assessment of Bifacial Modules in Arid Regions. *Sol. Energy*, 2024, ScienceDirect.
2. Jiang, Y., *et al.*, Perovskite-Silicon Tandem PV Efficiency Progress. *Renewable Energy*, 2024, ScienceDirect.
3. Kim, S., *et al.*, Yield Improvement Using Tracking Systems. *Sol. Energy Mater. Sol. Cells*, 2025, ScienceDirect.
4. Li, D. and Wang, Q., Impact of Mounting Height and Albedo on Bifacial Gain. *Energy Rep.*, 2024, ScienceDirect.
5. Chen, L., *et al.*, Radiative Cooling for PV Modules. *Appl. Energy*, 2025, ScienceDirect.
6. Rao, K., *et al.*, Advanced Optical Coatings in PV Systems. *Mater. Today Energy*, 2025, ScienceDirect.
7. Mehta, R. and Shah, V., AI-based MPPT Algorithms for Variable Conditions. *Energy AI*, 2024, ScienceDirect.
8. Singh, A., *et al.*, Power Optimizers for Shaded Environments. *J. Cleaner Prod.*, 2025, ScienceDirect.
9. Patel, N., *et al.*, AI-Driven Operations in Utility PV Plants. *Renewable Sustainable Energy Rev.*, 2025, ScienceDirect.
10. Desai, R. and Rao, A., Solar Forecasting Using Machine Learning. *Electr. Power Syst. Res.*, 2024, ScienceDirect.
11. Takahashi, M., *et al.*, Agrivoltaics: Crop Yield and Energy Production. *J. Environ. Manage.*, 2024, ScienceDirect.
12. Banerjee, S., *et al.*, Performance of Floating PV Systems. *Renewable Energy Focus*, 2025, ScienceDirect.
13. Kumar, S. and Joshi, R., PV Module Recycling Technologies. *Resour. Conserv. Recycl.*, 2025, ScienceDirect.
14. Narayanan, G., *et al.*, Reducing Carbon Footprint in PV Manufacturing. *Energy Policy*, 2024, ScienceDirect.
15. Zidane, T.E.K., Aziz, A.S., Zahraoui, Y., Kotb, H., Alkahtani, K.A., Karthick, A., Grid-connected Solar PV power plants optimization: A review. *IEEE Access*, 11, 48149–48170, 2023, doi: 10.1109/ACCESS.2023.3296433.

16. Ahmed, M.M.R., Mirsaeidi, S., Koondhar, M.A., Kaloi, G.S., Baloch, M.H., Mohammadi, A.A., Mitigating uncertainty problems of renewable energy resources through efficient integration of hybrid solar PV/wind systems into power networks. *IEEE Access*, 12, 32145–32162, 2024, doi: 10.1109/ACCESS.2024.3372849.
17. Saw, B.K. and Bohre, A.K., Sustainable Deployment of EV Charging Stations in Distribution Network Supported With Hybrid Solar-DG Integrated DSTACOM. *IEEE Trans. Ind. Appl.*, 61, 2, 1234–1246, Mar./Apr. 2025, doi: 10.1109/TIA.2025.3922180.
18. Xia, K., Li, Y., Zhu, B., Improved photovoltaic MPPT algorithm based on ant colony optimization and fuzzy logic under conditions of partial shading. *IEEE Access*, 12, 45230–45248, 2024, doi: 10.1109/ACCESS.2024.3378493.
19. Karmakar, S. and Singh, B., Multi-MPPT 72-Pulse VSC Based High-Power Grid Interfaced Solar PV Plant With Distributed DC-Coupled Battery Energy Storage. *IEEE Trans. Energy Convers.*, 39, 1, 456–470, Mar. 2024, doi: 10.1109/TEC.2023.3296781.
20. Krishnaram, K., Padmanabhan, T.S., Alsaif, F., Yahaya, N.Z., Namasivayam, S., Lai, M.H., Performance optimization of interleaved boost converter with ANN supported adaptable stepped-scaled P&O based MPPT for solar powered applications. *Sci. Rep.*, 14, 1, 8852, Apr. 2024, doi: 10.1038/s41598-024-58852-8.
21. Mariprasath, T., Basha, C.H.H., Khan, B., Ali, A., A novel on high voltage gain boost converter with cuckoo search optimization based MPPT Controller for solar PV system. *Sci. Rep.*, 14, 1, 8820, Apr. 2024, doi: 10.1038/s41598-024-58820-2.
22. Abdelsattar, M., Ismeil, M.A., Azim, M.A., Mosaad, A.M., Abdelaziz, A.Y., Assessing machine learning approaches for photovoltaic energy prediction in sustainable energy systems. *IEEE Access*, 12, 89456–89475, 2024, doi: 10.1109/ACCESS.2024.3409191.
23. Thipwangmek, N., Suetrong, N., Chaitusaney, S., Enhancing short-term solar photovoltaic power forecasting using a hybrid deep learning approach. *IEEE Access*, 12, 91203–91220, 2024, doi: 10.1109/ACCESS.2024.3430508.
24. Xu, C., Inuiguchi, M., Hayash, N., Raymond, W.J.K., Khalil, T., Enhancing reinforcement learning-based energy management through transfer learning with load and PV forecasting. *IEEE Access*, 13, 1234–1248, 2025, doi: 10.1109/ACCESS.2025.3916641.
25. Castillo-Rojas, W. and Salinas, J.P., Forecasting Models Applied in Solar Photovoltaic and Wind Energy: A Systematic Mapping Study. *IEEE Access*, 12, 125680–125705, 2024, doi: 10.1109/ACCESS.2024.3471307.
26. Mahim, T.M., Rahim, A., Chowdhury, M.N.I., Rahman, M.T., Hossain, M.S., Rahman, M.A., Review of mono-and bifacial photovoltaic technologies: A comparative study. *IEEE J. Photovoltaics*, 14, 3, 445–462, May 2024, doi: 10.1109/JPHOTOV.2024.3384335.

27. Magableh, S.K., Wang, C., Lin, F., Utility-Scale Bifacial Solar Photovoltaic System: Optimum Sizing and Techno-Economic Evaluation, in: *Proc. IEEE Power Energy Soc. Gen. Meet.*, Seattle, WA, USA, pp. 1–5, Jul. 2024, doi: 10.1109/PESGM48688.2024.10688984.
28. Badran, G. and Dhimish, M., A comparative study of bifacial versus monofacial PV systems at the UK's largest solar plant. *Clean Energy*, 8, 4, 248–262, Aug. 2024, doi: 10.1093/ce/zkae043.
29. Saand, A.S., Jamali, M.I., Koondhar, M.A., Kaloi, G.S., Baloch, M.H., Mirjat, N.H., A comparative review: floating photovoltaic, agrivoltaics, and ground-mounted PV systems. *IEEE Access*, 13, 2345–2368, 2025, doi: 10.1109/ACCESS.2025.3509084.
30. Abubakar, S.I., See, C.H., Sukki, F.M., Mahendiran, R., Abd-Alhameed, N., Kamarudin, M.K.A., Deploying Agrivoltaics in Sub-Saharan Africa: A Sustainable Pathway Towards Energy-Food Security-Challenges and Opportunities: A Review. *IEEE Access*, 13, 3456–3478, 2025, doi: 10.1109/ACCESS.2025.3994768.
31. Jamil, U., Vandewetering, N., Sadat, S.A., Pearce, J.M., Wood-and cable-based variable tilt stilt-mounted solar photovoltaic racking system. *Designs*, 8, 1, 6, Jan. 2024, doi: 10.3390/designs8010006.
32. Rahman, S.M.I., Moghassemi, A., Arsalan, A., Mahmud, A., Hoque, M.A., Padmanaban, S., Emerging trends and challenges in thermal management of power electronic converters: A state of the art review. *IEEE Access*, 12, 67890–67915, 2024, doi: 10.1109/ACCESS.2024.3393020.
33. Chowdhury, T., Koushan, S., Al-Qarni, A., Khan, F., Levi, E., Thermal management system for an electric machine with additively manufactured hollow conductors with integrated heat pipes. *IEEE Trans. Ind. Appl.*, 60, 2, 2845–2856, Mar./Apr. 2024, doi: 10.1109/TIA.2024.3359920.
34. Tiismus, H., Maask, V., Astapov, V., Korõtko, T., Lavrov, A., Shchemelinina, I., State-of-the-Art Review of Emerging Trends in Renewable Energy Generation Technologies. *IEEE Access*, 13, 1567–1590, 2025, doi: 10.1109/ACCESS.2025.3838570.
35. Jahan, N. and Abir, M.A.B.S., SDN-enabled Smart Building Energy Management for Hybrid Solar-Geothermal Integrated System, in: *Proc. IEEE Int. Conf. Adv. Technol. Manage. Sustain. Energy*, Dhaka, Bangladesh, Apr. 2024, pp. 1–6, doi: 10.1109/ATMSE58502.2024.10502637.
36. Zangina, J.S., Suleiman, M.A., Jibril, Y., Gital, A.M., Garba, M.U., Analysis of grid-tied solar photovoltaic energy generation under uncertain atmospheric conditions using adaptive neuro-fuzzy control system. *Arch. Adv. Eng. Sci.*, 3, 1, 45–62, 2025, doi: 10.47852/bonviewAAES32021110.
37. Hole, S.R. and Goswami, A.D., EPCMSDB: Design of an ensemble predictive control model for solar PV MPPT deployments *via* dual bioinspired optimizations. *Sci. Technol. Energy Transition*, 79, 10, 2024, doi: 10.2516/stet/2024010.

38. Bharti, K.K., Patel, A., Jaiswal, Y., Shekhar, Y., Optimizing Solar Energy Harvesting: A Comprehensive Review of Intelligent MPPT For Battery Charging Circuits, in: *Proc. 3rd Int. Conf. Smart Sustain. Technol.*, pp. 1–6, Goa, India, Mar. 2024, doi: 10.1109/ICSST57313.2024.10486254.
39. Almarzooqi, A.M., Maalouf, M., El-Fouly, T.H.M., Zeineldin, H.H., A hybrid machine-learning model for solar irradiance forecasting. *Clean Energy*, 8, 1, 100–115, Feb. 2024, doi: 10.1093/ce/zkad075.

Index

Also of Interest

Check out these other related titles from Scrivener Publishing

Artificial Intelligence in Instrumentation, Control and Automation, Edited by B. Jaganatha Pandian, N. Amutha Prabha, Abhishek Gudipalli, and V. Indragandhi, ISBN: 9781394336135. Revolutionize your industrial practice with this essential book, which provides a comprehensive overview of how artificial intelligence can be integrated into instrumentation and control systems to achieve unprecedented precision, efficiency, and autonomous optimization.

Design and Optimization of Mobile Robotics for Industry 5.0, Edited by Rathishchandra R. Gatti, Chandra Singh, Ajith B.S., and E. Fantin Irudaya Raj, ISBN: 9781394384983. Harness the future of automation with this comprehensive guide, offering an in-depth look at how next-generation mobile robotics are driving the transition to a human-centered and sustainable Industry 5.0.

Autonomous Vehicles Planning and Control, By Yong Bai & Liang Zhao, ISBN: 9781394355044. Master the future of marine exploration and technology with Autonomous Vehicles Planning and Control, which provides a comprehensive, interdisciplinary guide to the principles, control, and real-world applications of autonomous marine vehicles.

Autonomous Flying Ad-Hoc Networks, Edited by Taskeen Zaidi, Adarsh Kumar, Saurav Mallik, and Keshav Kaushik, ISBN: 9781394231058. Learn to leverage the power of Autonomous Flying Ad-Hoc Networks (FANETs) for everything from urban surveillance to disaster relief, and stay ahead in the rapidly evolving world of drone technology and AI.

AI for Autonomous Vehicles: The Future of Driverless Technology, Edited by Sathiyaraj Rajendran, Munish Sabharwal, Yu-Chen Hu, Rajesh Kumar Dhanaraj, and Balamurugan Balusamy, ISBN: 9781119847465. This title presents the research prospects and security challenges present in the exciting new field of autonomous vehicles by comprehensively introducing advanced concepts of artificial intelligence (AI) in driverless technology.

AUTONOMOUS VEHICLES VOLUME 1: Using Machine Intelligence, Edited by Romil Rawat, A. Mary Sowjanya, Syed Imran Patel, Varshali Jaiswal, Imran Khan, and Allam Balaram, ISBN: 9781119871958. Addressing the current challenges, approaches and applications relating to autonomous vehicles, this groundbreaking new volume presents the research and techniques in this growing area, using Internet of Things, Machine Learning, Deep Learning, and Artificial Intelligence.

AUTONOMOUS VEHICLES VOLUME 2: Smart Vehicles for Communication, Edited by Romil Rawat, Purvee Bhardwaj, Upinder Kaur, Shrikant Telang, Mukesh Chouhan, and K. Sakthidasan Sankaran, ISBN: 9781394152254. The companion to *Autonomous Vehicles Volume 1: Using Machine Intelligence*, this second volume in the two-volume set covers intelligent techniques utilized for designing, controlling and managing vehicular systems based on advanced algorithms of computing like machine learning, artificial Intelligence, data analytics, and Internet of Things with prediction approaches to avoid accidental damages, security threats, and theft.

CONVERSATIONAL ARTIFICIAL INTELLIGENCE, Edited by Romil Rawat, Rajesh Kumar Chakrawarti, Sanjaya Kumar Sarangi, Piyush Vyas, Mary Sowjanya Alamanda, Kotagiri Srividya, and K. Sakthidasan Sankaran. ISBN: 9781394200566. This book presents the need for, design, and application of conversational artificial intelligence (AI). Expert knowledge is shared on leading innovations in natural language processing (NLP) and machine learning (ML) techniques that are frequently combined with more traditional, static kinds of interactive technology, such as chatbots, to create conversational AI.

QUANTUM COMPUTING IN CYBERSECURITY, Edited by Romil Rawat, Rajesh Kumar Chakrawarti, Sanjaya Kumar Sarangi, Jaideep Patel, and Vivek Bhardwaj, ISBN: 9781394166336. This cutting-edge new volume provides a comprehensive exploration of emerging technologies and trends in quantum computing and how it is used in cybersecurity, covering everything from artificial intelligence to how quantum computing can be used to secure networks and prevent cyber crime.

ROBOTIC PROCESS AUTOMATION, Edited by Romil Rawat, Rajesh Kumar Chakrawarti, Sanjaya Kumar Sarangi, Rahul Choudhary, Anand Singh Gadwal, and Vivek Bhardwaj, ISBN: 9781394166183. Presenting the latest technologies and practices in this ever-changing field, this ground-breaking new volume covers the theoretical challenges and practical solutions for using robotics across a variety of industries, encompassing many disciplines, including mathematics, computer science, electrical engineering, information technology, mechatronics, electronics, bioengineering, and command and software engineering.

CONVERGENCE OF CLOUD WITH AI FOR BIG DATA ANALYTICS: Foundations and Innovation, Edited by Danda B. Rawat, Lalit K Awasthi, Valentina Emilia Balas, Mohit Kumar and Jitendra Kumar Samriya, ISBN: 9781119904885. This book covers the foundations and applications of cloud computing, AI, and Big Data and analyses their convergence for improved development and services.

SWARM INTELLIGENCE: An Approach from Natural to Artificial, By Kuldeep Singh Kaswan, Jagjit Singh Dhatterwal and Avadhesh Kumar, ISBN: 9781119865063. This important authored book presents valuable new insights by exploring the boundaries shared by cognitive science, social psychology, artificial life, artificial intelligence, and evolutionary computation by applying these insights to solving complex engineering problems.

FACTORIES OF THE FUTURE: Technological Advances in the Manufacturing Industry, Edited by Chandan Deep Singh and Harleen Kaur, ISBN: 9781119864943. The book provides insight into various technologies adopted and to be adopted in the future by industries and measures the impact of these technologies on manufacturing performance and their sustainability.

AI AND IOT-BASED INTELLIGENT AUTOMATION IN ROBOTICS, Edited by Ashutosh Kumar Dubey, Abhishek Kumar, S. Rakesh Kumar, N. Gayathri, Prasenjit Das, ISBN: 9781119711209. The 24 chapters in this book provide a deep overview of robotics and the application of AI and IoT in robotics across several industries such as healthcare, defense, education, etc.

SMART GRIDS AND INTERNET OF THINGS, Edited by Sanjeevikumar Padmanaban, Jens Bo Holm-Nielsen, Rajesh Kumar Dhanaraj, Malathy Sathyamoorthy, and Balamurugan Balusamy, ISBN: 9781119812449. Written and edited by a team of international professionals, this groundbreaking new volume covers the latest technologies in automation, tracking, energy distribution and consumption of Internet of Things (IoT) devices with smart grids.

Printed and bound by CPI Group (UK) Ltd, Croydon, CR0 4YY
17/09/2026
14964282-0001